s Symposium was sponsored by
Swiss National Research Fund

PSYCHOTHERAPY
OF SCHIZOPHRENIA

Th
the

PSYCHOTHERAPY OF SCHIZOPHRENIA

PROCEEDINGS OF THE 6th INTERNATIONAL SYMPOSIUM ON
PSYCHOTHERAPY OF SCHIZOPHRENIA

LAUSANNE, SEPTEMBER 28-30, 1978

Edited by:
CHRISTIAN MÜLLER, M.D.
Professor of Psychiatry, Lausanne, Switzerland

 1979
EXCERPTA MEDICA, AMSTERDAM-OXFORD

International Congress Series No. 464

ISBN Excerpta Medica 90 219 0389 X
ISBN Elsevier/North-Holland 0-444-90076-4

Library of Congress Cataloging in Publication Data

International Symposium on Psychotherapy of
Schizophrenia, 6th, Lausanne, 1978.
    Psychotherapy of schizophrenia.

    (International congress series ; no 464)
    Includes bibliographical references and index.
    1. Schizophrenia--Congresses.   2. Psychotherapy--
Congresses.   I. Müller, Christian, 1921-   II. Title.
III. Series. [DNLM: 1. Psychotherapy--Congresses.
2. Schizophrenia--Therapy--Congresses.   W3 EX89
no. 464 1978 / WM203.3 1616 1978p]
RC514.153 1978   616.8'982'06   79-13531
ISBN 0-444-90076-4 (Elsevier North-Holland)

Publisher:
Excerpta Medica
305 Keizersgracht
1000 BC Amsterdam
P.O. Box 1126

Sole Distributors for the USA and Canada:
Elsevier North-Holland Inc.
52 Vanderbilt Avenue
New York, N.Y. 10017

Printed in The Netherlands by Groen, IJmuiden

LIST OF AUTHORS

DR G. ABRAHAM
Clinique Psychiatrique
Universitaire de Bel-Air
1225 Chêne-Bourg
Genève
Switzerland

PROF Y.O. ALANEN
Department of Psychiatry
University of Turku
Kurjenmäentie 4
20700 Turku, 70
Finland

DR A. ANDREOLI
Centre Psycho-Social Universitaire
Bd. St-Georges 16-18
1211 Genève 6
Switzerland

PROF G. BENEDETTI
Psychiatrische
Universitätspoliklinik
Petersgraben 4
4051 Bâle
Switzerland

PROF. A.R. BODENHEIMER
Letzistrasse 5
8006 Zurich
Switzerland

DR P.H. BOVIER
Clinique Psychiatrique
Universitaire de Bel-Air
1225 Chêne-Bourg
Genève
Switzerland

WILLIAM T. CARPENTER JR,
M.D.
Maryland Psychiatric Research
Center
P.O. Box 3235
Baltimore, MD 212228
U.S.A.

J.P. DOCHERTY, M.D.
Yale Psychiatric Institute
P.O. Box 12A
Yale Station
New Haven, CT 06520
U.S.A.

T.W. DOWNEY, M.D.
Yale Psychiatric Institute
P.O. Box 12A
Yale Station
New Haven, CT 06520
U.S.A.

DR J. DUBUIS
Clinique Psychiatrique
Universitaire de Bel-Air
1225 Chêne-Bourg
Genève
Switzerland

DAVID B. FEINSILVER, M.D.
2800 McKinley Place, N.W.
Washington, D.C. 20015
U.S.A.

E. FIVAZ
Hôpital de Cery
1008 Prilly/Lausanne
Switzerland

R. FIVAZ
Prof. E.P.F.L.
1000 Lausanne
Switzerland

DR THOMAS FREEMAN
Royal Dundee Liff Hospital
Dundee DD2 5NF
U.K.

DR P. GIACOBINO
Centre Psycho-Social Universitaire
Bd. St-Georges 16-18
1211 Genève 6
Switzerland

DR E. GILLIERON
Policlinique Psychiatrique
Universitaire
Caroline 11 bis
1003 Lausanne
Switzerland

JOHN G. GUNDERSON, M.D.
McLean Hospital
Belmont, MS 02178
U.S.A.

DR S. HAUGSGJERD
Trøndelag Psykiatriske Sykehus
Avd. Rotvoll
7050 Charlottenlung
Norway

DR TORSTEN HERNER
Kungsholmstorg 13A
S-112 21 Stockholm
Sweden

JOHN S. KAFKA, M.D.
5323 Connecticut Avenue, N.W.
Washington, D.C. 20015
U.S.A.

PROF L. KAUFMANN
Hôpital de Cery
1008 Prilly/Lausanne
Switzerland

DR J. LAAKSO
Department of Psychiatry
University of Turku
Kurjenmäentie 4
20700 Turku, 70
Finland

DR I. LAHTI
Oulun Yliopisto
Clinic of Psychiatry
90210 Oulu 21
Finland

DR H. LANG
Psychiatrische Klinik der
Universität Heidelberg
Voss-Strasse 4
6900 Heidelberg
Federal Republic of Germany

DR P. LEHTINEN
Department of Psychiatry
University of Turku
Kurjenmäentie 4
20700 Turku, 70
Finland

DR DANIEL MASSON
Av. Riant-Mont 11
1004 Lausanne
Switzerland

DR ODETTE MASSON
Av. Riant-Mont 11
1004 Lausanne
Switzerland

PROF PAUL MATUSSEK
Max-Planck-Gesellschaft
Montsalvatstr. 19
8 München 40
Federal Republic of Germany

PROF CHRISTIAN MÜLLER
Clinique Psychiatrique
Universitaire de Lausanne
Hôpital de Cery
CH-1008 Prilly/Lausanne
Switzerland

DR M. NAARALA
Oulun Yliopisto
Clinic of Psychiatry
90210 Oulu 21
Finland

DR V. RÄKKÖLÄINEN
Department of Psychiatry
University of Turku
Kurjenmäentie 4
20700 Turku, 70
Finland

DR R. RASIMUS
Department of Psychiatry
University of Turku
Kurjenmäentie 4
20700 Turku, 70
Finland

DAVID RUBINSTEIN, M.D.
Eastern Pennsylvania Psychiatric
Institute
Henry Avenue and Abbottsford
Rd.
Philadelphia, PA 19129
U.S.A.

DR H. SALMINEN
Elsankuja 2 F 58
02230 Espoo 23
Finland

DR R. SALOKANGAS
Department of Psychiatry
University of Turku
Kurjenmäentie 4
20700 Turku, 70
Finland

DR RAOUL SCHINDLER
Bennogasse 8
1080 Wien
Austria

CLARENCE G. SCHULZ, M.D.
P.O. Box 6815
Baltimore (Towson), MD 21204
U.S.A.

DANIEL P. SCHWARTZ, M.D.
Austen Riggs Center, Inc.
Stockbridge, MA 01262
U.S.A.

HAROLD F. SEARLES, M.D.,
P.A.
Suite 623 W, Bethesda Air Rights
Building
7314 Wisconsin Avenue
Washington, D.C. 20014
U.S.A.

W.H. SLEDGE, M.D.
Yale Psychiatric Institute
P.O. Box 12A
Yale Station
New Haven, CT 06520
U.S.A.

A. SORRI, M.D.
Oulun Yliopisto
Clinic of Psychiatry
90210 Oulu 21
Finland

PROF HELM STIERLIN
Klinikum der Universität
Heidelberg
Mönchhofstr. 15a
6900 Heidelberg 1
Federal Republic of Germany

S. STIERLIN
Psychiatrische Klinik der
Universität Heidelberg
Voss-Strasse 4
6900 Heidelberg
Federal Republic of Germany

JOHN S. STRAUSS, M.D.
Yale Psychiatric Institute
P.O. Box 12A
Yale Station
New Haven, CT 06520
U.S.A.

PEKKA TIENARI, M.D.
Oulun Yliopisto
Clinic of Psychiatry
90210 Oulu 21
Finland

DR E. VÄISÄNEN
Oulun Yliopisto
Clinic of Psychiatry
90210 Oulu 21
Finland

DR ENDRE UGELSTAD
Trøndelag Psykiatriske Sykehus
Avd. Rotvoll
7050 Charlottenlung
Norway

CONTENTS

Dear Colleagues,

It falls to me to make an introduction to this symposium and it is
with the greatest pleasure that I welcome you all here. As this is
the 6th. time that we meet to speak of psychotherapy with schizophrenics, these meetings already have a whole history. I hope you
will forgive me if I cannot help speaking briefly of this history.
It was in 1956 that for the first time Dedo Benedetti and myself
organised a meeting of the psychoanalysts involved in the work
with schizophrenics. It gathered in this hospital. What a distance
we have since covered ! Psychiatry and its institutions have deeply
changed ; there has been a conceptual change, but also a profound
change as far as the structures of the institutions are concerned.
We have but to look aroud us. In 1956 we met here in a hospital
which was rather like an asylum where hundreds of patients were
indeed shut up in overcrowded wards, whereas today we have a
spacious, confortable and modern equipment at our disposal. Twenty
two years ago, in 1956, we were, Dedo Benedetti and I, young
psychoanalysts in the making, strongly influenced by our common
teacher Manfred Bleuler, as well as by our psychoanalysis teachers,
Bally, Blum, de Saussure, Gressot and others. We were no longer
happy with the classical theory of schizophrenia and we were
mainly in the search of new directions in treatment. Mrs. Séchehaye
brought us her experiences. Dedo Benedetti had just returned from
the United States where American psychoanalysts had contributed
to his training. We were optimistic and enthusiastic and the
possibility of a psychotherapeutic access to the world of
schizophrenics appeared to us like the dawn of the new era. We
wanted to learn, we wanted to exchange our points of view with
others, speak ou our experiences and stimulate one another. It
was in this frame of mind that we organised that first meeting
and we were lucky to have the support of various eminent persons
of the time. If I look at the list of the 1956 participants, I
find among them names such as Gustav Bally, Alfred Storch, Ludwig
Binswanger, Anne-Marie Séchehaye, Michel Gressot, all dead now,
but the remembrance of whom shall remain vivid in our minds.

That first meeting, 22 years ago, was important to us. It gave us
the courage to continue in our direction, it enriched us, and
personal ties were then created. We were not many of course, not
more than forty. I am particulary pleased to greet among you the
veterans of the two first meetings 22 and 19 years ago who will
continue, during these next days, to enrich us with their contributions. I am speaking, besides D. Benedetti, of Mr. Bister, Mr
Helm Stierlin and his wife, Mr. Matussek, Mr. Racamier, Mrs.
Selvini, Mr. Siirala, Mr. Elrod, Mr. Bach, Mr. Beese, Mr. Schindler,

Mr. Bodenheimer and Mr. Herner. In quoting these names to you, I also think naturally about the destiny each one of them has known. All of you, my dear friends, have met with success ; some have distinguished themselves in the academic career, others have become well known by their works. But we all necessarily belong to what the young may call the establishment. Have we also become a little sclerosed ? Must it be feared that this coming back to Cery, 22 years later, indicates a spirit of conservatism ? Must it be feared that what the young part of our audience will hear these next two days will be no more than useless repetitions ? I do not think so. One has but to look at the program to notice that around the central theme of schizophrenia and its psychotherapeutic treatment new dimensions are open, the perspectives have changed and without meaning to underestimate what was said 22 years ago, our position today is very different. The heroical duel with the schizophrenic, sometimes in a total psychological isolation, has given way to a very flexible understanding and to strategies of approach in which it is no longer a question of the exclusive couple patient-therapist but in which the whole family is included. I have said it on other occasions and I repeat it : family dynamics has been for me, these past years, a mode of approach of the utmost interest and I am particulary happy to think that in Lausanne a very competent team has been created to work in this direction. In this hospital we have adopted the view that the main approach to the schizophrenic should have a psychotherapeutic nature and although the number of schizophrenic patients undergoing long-term treatment has perhaps not increased, the general atmos- phere in the hospital has certainly benefited from our unwearing desire to see in the schizophrenic something other than a patient with hypothetical metabolic problems. We have also tried to deepen our knowledge by means of follow-up studies. These studies seemed, at first, to be very far from our psychotherapeutics preoccupations and interests. But on second thoughts one becomes quickly aware of the fact that it is only by following a patient throughout his life that one can gain a better understanding of certain aspects of his identity problems. It is only through these studies that we can have a better perception of the interactions and interferen- ces between the patient and his environment of the profoundly intricate interrelations between the so-called symptomatology and the circumstances of life. But it is not my purpose here and today to talk at length about the research conducted during the last ten years. I would simply like to remind you that after having made these studies we find ourselves still farther than before from a simple concept, from a simple idea of causality or from an unidi- mensional therapy. Each schizophrenic represents an unique destiny, hardly comparable to others. The struggle he undertakes, his attemps to adapt, to solve his problems, to abandon and resign, exclude all generalisation. Therefore, this catamnestic research, far from discouraging us in the sphere of psychotherapy, show us that nothing in the schizophrenic's life is determined in a

2

definite way, that all remains open, that the forces may die down, as they may also revive, so that a hope is always permitted. We have two very busy days before us. Let us try to use to the full the time that is granted to us. I hope you will also find some moments of relaxation and above all the occasion to discuss, outside the sessions, with the colleagues you will be interested in. We are over two hundred today in this auditorium, which may be too many. In recalling the atmosphere that prevailed when we were no more then thirty or fourty, we have tried to do all that was possible in order not to become a congress like any other. Unfortunately we have only partially succeded. The applications for participation flew towards us. mainly these last few weeks, I would say nearly like an avalanche that almost overwhelmed us. We no longer knew what to do and we had to write several letters everyday to people wanting to participate in our meeting, explainning to them that this was not possible anylonger, that the maximum number had already been attained and even exceeded. I hope that all those to whom we were forced to refuse the access to our meeting will forgive us. But I would be reassured if I could think that the veterans of our symposiums will not be too shocked by the great number of participants.

And now, in agreement with the organising committee, I would like to propose the nomination of an honorary president for this symposium. Naturally, the choice is very wide as you are numerous, but nevertheless, it seems to me that one name springs to mind straight away. It is that of a pioneer in our domaine - I am talking about Prof. T. Lidz. If you agree, please show by applauding, that you hold him in as much esteem as I do.

Concerning the general organisation I must ask you to be lenient : we are not a professional congress organisation and we have certainly forgotten or badly organised a number of things. Psychoanalysts and psychotherapists are not always the best organisers ! We have nevertheless tried to do our best with the means at our disposal, and I should like to thank very warmly those who have helped me for several months, namely Mrs. Anne Marin, Miss Christiane Wolf, Mrs Francesca Battaglia and Mrs. Jacqueline Bourquin. Our administration has shown much understanding and I should also like th thank it. I also address my thanks to the organisations which provided us with a financial help. First of all the National Fund for Scientific Research which granted us an important subsidy. We also had a subsidy from a local scientific university fund. But of course all that would not have sufficed if we had not received the material contributions from our audience that I should also like to thank.

I declare the symposium open and I give the floor to my friend Ugelstad, the president of this meeting.

NON-DIFFERENTIATION OF EGO-FUNCTIONING IN THE BORDERLINE INDIVIDUAL, AND ITS EFFECT UPON HIS SENSE OF PERSONAL IDENTITY

Harold F. Searles

Supervising and Training Analyst, Washington Psychoanalytic Institute, Washington, D. C., U. S. A.

In earlier papers I (4) have discussed some of the impairments of ego-integration and -differentiation which are manifested by schizophrenic patients in the course of their psychoanalytic therapy. Here I shall explore some aspects of ego-non-differentiation which I have encountered in working with borderline individuals. For brevity's sake, I shall not attempt to discuss these patients' comparable difficulties with ego-integration.

The ways in which the borderline patient manifests his difficulties with ego-differentiation are fascinatingly subtle, by contrast to the relatively manifest struggles, in this regard, of schizophrenic patients. Typically, it is only after several to many months of therapy that we begin to see how pervasively unable he is to differentiate, at a more than superficial level, between nocturnal dreams or daytime fantasies on the one hand, and perceptions of outer reality on the other hand; between memories of the past and perceptions of the present; between emotions and physical sensations; between thoughts (and/or feelings) and behavioral actions; between symbolic and concrete levels of meaning in communications; between himself and the other person; between himself and the whole outer world; between human and nonhuman, animate and inanimate, ingredients of the outer world; and so on. We become accustomed to hearing him say, as one woman reported several years along in her therapy, "I woke up this morning with a feeling that I couldn't remember whether it was a dream, fantasy, or real. I'm referring to my daughter's telling me, 'Grandpa called this morning, and said that he and Grandma are coming for a visit.' I think I dreamt it or imagined it, but I wish it were true."

It usually requires years of therapy for the borderline patient to achieve a durable, internalized image of himself and of the therapist. Prior to the achievement of this degree of differentiation in his ego-functioning, he experiences the therapist's physical absence in outer reality as abolition of the therapist's total existence, from within the patient at the level of mental imagery as well as from outer reality. Also, as I (9) have described in an earlier paper, when the patient has become involved with a newly-developed, deeply cherished, internalized mental image of the therapist, the actual therapist in the patient's outer reality may come to feel pitted, paradoxically, in jealous odds with that very mental image of him, with "whom" the patient has become so enthralled.

A man who had been in psychoanalytic therapy with me for several years said something which helped me to understand why borderline patients tend to be so audience-oriented during their treatment

sessions - why, that is, instead of their being oriented toward dis-
covering what thoughts, or other internal experiences, occur to them
during the course of the session, and verbally reporting these insofar as possible to the therapist, they are concerned instead with
the therapist as an ever-present audience whose needs (to be kept
interested, or entertained, or what-not) must be kept constantly in
the forefront of the patient's attention. This man said, "The only
way I know a person is there - that a person exists - is, I have to
keep a person in mind, or the person dies, the person disappears."
He then referred, by way of example, to a session a week previously
during which, for the first time in his therapy, "I completely for-
got about you, and when I thought of you again I had no way of
knowing that you were alive ... unless I could see you again and
know you were there and get you back in my mind. That's the only
way you exist, is in my mind."

It was evident that, at this stage of his treatment, he had not
yet established a durable internalized image of me, an image differentiated as such from his perceptions of me in outer reality.
Thus, the recurrent loss of his tenuous internalized image of me -
a loss occasioned by lack of perceptual reinforcement of that image,
while he was lying on the couch and I was sitting silently behind
him - tended to have, for him, the impact that I had actually died.

Another man said, at the beginning of a session following my
having been out of town for a day, "I really missed you," and went
on to say that he never had missed me before at times when I had been
away. He explained that previously, at such times, "Everything felt
unreal, and I felt unreal; but I didn't connect it with your being
away. This time, I missed you, but everything didn't feel unreal
this time." Hearing this, I made a note to myself (without inter-
preting to him) that "It is evident that I am no longer everything
to him; I am a separate person to him. He is just growing out of a
phase in which I am [i.e., have been] the whole world - all of
reality, including the reality of himself, such that the loss of me
causes [i.e., has caused] him to experience a feeling of unreality
about 'everything' as well as about his 'I'."

In a monograph in 1960 entitled, The Nonhuman Environment in
Normal Development and in Schizophrenia, I (2) described human maturation as involving the individual's struggling to achieve and maintain a sense of identity as being human and as being differentiated,
thus, from the nonhuman realm of his environment. I described the
schizophrenic individual as having failed in this struggle and as
having a fundamental need, therefore, for the therapist to help him
to achieve this in the long and oftentimes stormy course of psychoanalytic therapy. In a paper in 1972 entitled, "Unconscious
Processes in Relation to the Environmental Crisis", I (6) commented
that

" ... Over recent decades we have come from dwelling
in an outer world in which the living works of nature
either predominated or were near at hand, to dwelling in
an environment dominated by a technology which is wondrous-
ly powerful and yet nonetheless dead, inanimate. I suggest
that in the process we have come from being subjectively
differentiated from, and in meaningful kinship with, the

6

outer world, to finding this technology-dominated world
so alien, so complex, so awesome, and so overwhelming
that we have been able to cope with it only by regress-
ing, in our unconscious experience of it, largely to a
degraded state of nondifferentiation from it. I suggest,
that is, that this 'outer' reality is psychologically
as much a part of us as its poisonous waste products
are part of our physical selves."

In my therapy of borderline patients, I find that these persons'
subtle and largely unconscious, but pervasively important, incomplete
differentiation between their human self and their nonhuman environment gives rise to as frequent and varied distortions, in their own
sense of identity and in their transference-perceptions of the therapist, as was so profusely evident in my work with frankly schizophrenic patients at Chestnut Lodge between 1949 and 1964. To give
but one example here, a borderline internist commented, concerning
a medical colleague with whom he was working in a clinic, "That's
a despicable situation, that Powell [entirely as though the person,
Powell, were a situation and not at all a human individual] ...
Probably I'm unfit to be a physician. I realize a physician of all
things should not feel so much contempt." His tone, as well as his
words, in saying, "a physician of all things" clearly referred to
a physician as a thing. Further, I could glimpse here an unconscious
identity-aspect of himself as being a physician to, or for, all
things everywhere.

The borderline individual has so much difficulty in integrating
feelings concerning change and loss that we find in him, although
relatively subtly manifested, the kind of confusion as regards
geographic location which is comparatively conspicuous in the
chronically schizophrenic person. In a paper concerning my nearly
seven years of intensive psychoanalytic therapy with a chronically
schizophrenic woman, I (7) reported that

"I came to see, within the first year..., that
Mrs. Hendricks, rather than missing any one or any
experience from her past, instead re-experienced
the past in such vivid detail that she tended to
become lost in it - immersed in the past. It became
evident that her walking about on the hospital grounds
followed a very complex pattern indeed; there were
many areas of the grounds which she avoided because
they tended to remind her of grief-laden areas of her
past. I came to see that it was not simply that
entering into those areas would cause her to experience
grief, but that she had to avoid becoming actually lost
in those areas of the past."

A woman whose long-chronic schizophrenia had subsided, after
much therapy, to a borderline level of severity said at the beginning
of a session, getting toward summer, "It is so hot on Wisconsin
Avenue, and then when you turn off it and walk down Oliver Street,
there's such a cool breeze, it's like you're in a different city!"
She said this in such a tone as clearly to indicate that it was hard
for her to be sure that she was not actually in a different city.
That is, she tended to feel really confused, disoriented in place,

by encountering the cool breeze. I am reminded, here, of the experiences which Proust (1) chronicled in Remembrance of Things Past. This woman's life was lived, for a long time as she gradually moved more and more fully outside of and away from the sanitarium, in such a way that each of three places became central to her sense of identity: the sanitarium, her apartment in the city, and my office where she had therapy-sessions several times a week. It became evident to me that she had often to struggle, behind a relatively self-possessed demeanor, to keep clear whether at any one moment she were in my office, or rather in the sanitarium or her apartment. There were undoubtedly many times when she was in all three, simultaneously, at a largely but not entirely unconscious level.

I find fascinatingly subtle the borderline individual's manifestations of his unconscious conviction that his thinking possesses an omnipotent power. This subjective omnipotence of thinking is based in an incomplete differentiation between inner and outer reality. In my paper in 1962 entitled, "Scorn, Disillusionment and Adoration in the Psychotherapy of Schizophrenia", I (3) noted that

> "The child's too early, too great 'disillusionment' -
> a repressed and incomplete process, rather than a completed
> one - with the mother, occurring before differentiation
> between inner and outer reality has solidly occurred,
> leaves him with the unconscious conviction that the emotion
> of disillusionment, if one permits oneself to feel it,
> destroys the other person."

That is, such an individual would feel not merely that his formerly idealized image of the mother has been destroyed but that the flesh-and-blood mother in outer reality has been destroyed in the same process - for he cannot differentiate between the internalized image and the corresponding person in outer reality.

In a paper in 1969 entitled, "A Case of Borderline Thought Disorder", I (5) reported that among various determinants of this disorder was a subjective omnipotence of thinking, on the following basis:

> "This man's thought disorder, at perhaps its deepest
> level, included a lack of qualitative differentiation
> between inner and outer reality - between mental images
> and verbal thoughts, on the one hand, and the correspond-
> ing objects in outer reality. This reification of his
> thoughts greatly complicated his ability to think freely,
> for he feared the tangible power of thoughts to do harm
> either to him or ... to others."

One man was saying, " ... - I was thinking in my head of all sorts of different things - ...", said fully as though he does some of his thinking elsewhere. My impression, based upon long work with him by then, was that he unconsciously regarded changes in the outer world as equivalent to, or as caused by, his thinking. Another man whose treatment I supervised for many months mentioned, similarly, to his therapist, "... I've been thinking in my mind that ..."

A woman said, in reference to her long-depressed mother, who had died several years before, "The more I think about my mother, the more it seems that she was depressed." I had had enough experience with her, by now several years along in her therapy, to hear in this superficially unremarkable comment a subtle hint of her unconscious conviction that her own thinking possessed the power to have caused her mother to become increasingly depressed, and even dead. Significantly, it was extraordinarily difficult, for years, for me to help her to resolve her resistance to allowing her thinking really free rein in the free-associational process.

A man made a comment, during one of his sessions, very similar in nature to the one I have quoted from the just-mentioned woman. He said, while reminiscing about his mother and maternal grandmother, " ... - Probably if I looked at pictures of Mom and Grandma, they would be quite similar - ..." This sounded to have an unconscious meaning that he could cause the two actual persons to come to appear quite similar to one another, by looking at pictures of them.

A woman commented, thoughtfully, "The things of the past - the physical things of the past - are no more as I think of them - ..." This statement, again superficially unremarkable, seemingly expressive of a growing realization that various things of the past were now irretrievably gone, was said in such a tone as to convey her unconscious conviction that her very thinking of the things of the past had destroyed them.

The previously-mentioned woman who had been chronically schizophrenic, and was now borderline, was expressing disillusionment with doctors; she spoke, for example, of a news item about doctors' politically agitating, in a convention in Atlantic City, for some selfish goals. She went on to express disillusionment with people in general for being so untidy; she described in detail, for example, how littered with papers and other refuse was the area about her apartment building. She said, with intense feeling, "It's awful to think that people would be so untidy! - ..." I had become, by now, long used to knowing what violence such a kind of thinking, on her own part, wrought upon her most cherished, idealized images of herself, and clearly heard an unconscious meaning, here, of "It's awful of me to think that people would be so untidy!" It was becoming increasingly evident, in other words, that a long-maintained, unconscious denial on her part, a denial of large sectors of outer reality (including the reality of most of what had gone on in her parental home during her formative years), had had to be sustained for the major reason that the sheer perceiving of any "outer" ugliness, and the sheer thinking in acknowledgment of that, brought with it a comparable denigration of her own formerly idealized image(s) of herself - a self still so incompletely differentiated from that "outer" reality.

Some two years later, this same woman, commenting upon the recent blackout - general failure of electricity - in New York City, said, "It's awful to think that anything like that would happen - ..." She was sitting (rather than lying) on the couch, as she often did, and as she said this I could see on her face a look of horror. Her facial expression, coupled with those words, conveyed the unconscious meaning, as many times before, "It's awful of me to think that anything like that would happen."

A few months later, in the closing minutes of a session during which she had spoken, as usual, of many things, she said, "I got some very sad news." She went on to describe that a saleslady who had often waited upon her, in a fashion shop, and whom she had found very helpful over the years, had been robbed and beaten so severely, by some teenagers, as to have been hospitalized. She said, "I'm very worried about it; it's terrible to think _[my emphasis]_ that anything like that would happen." I immediately felt that this linked up with her having given evidence, earlier in the session, of dissociated rage toward her social worker, a lady whom she ordinarily found helpful to her but who had had to cancel her most recent weekly appointment with the patient. It appeared that rather than her becoming aware of a rageful fantasy of beating her social worker, she instead felt intensely self-condemnatory for even think-ing of the other lady's (upon whom her unconscious rage was dis-placed) having been severely beaten. Very characteristic of her had been her describing the cancelled appointment in such a way that, while conspicuously free from any manifested outrage herself, she had put me under intense pressure to become outraged at the social worker on her behalf. Specifically, although remaining silent, I had felt under intense pressure to feel and say, "You mean she didn't even let you know? - Why, that's outrageous!"

I have been trying here to show that, in borderline ego-func-tioning, sometimes the disillusionment may be experienced as destroying predominantly the person in outer reality, whereas on other occasions it has a predominant impact, through the individual's introjection of that disillusioning other person, of a real diminu-tion of the patient's own self. Thus, just as one individual could speak of a time when he had become disillusioned with his father's athletic prowess by saying, "When my father's athletic ability vanished," so can another individual say, of a person whom she has come to despise, "Just seeing her makes me feel diminished."

One woman was clearly in a general state of disillusionment and was expressing this in regard to, for example, the quality of our public schools, and of those in Maryland more specifically. "This whole state, I guess, is bullshit when ya think about it," she said, in such a tone as to convey the unconscious meaning that one's thinking about Maryland causes the whole state to become, literally, bullshit.

A man speaking, very similarly, of his mother whom he had visited recently and with whom he was feeling, currently, deeply disillusioned, said, "I think of my mother being a stupid whore - in my mind _[his emphasis; all this said with startling concreteness, as though his mother in his mind were a flesh-and-blood, stupid whore there]_ - ... a mess of garbage, that's what I feel like - ..." It was clear that he was so largely undifferentiated from his mother that disillusionment with her brought with it disillusionment with himself, and vice versa; and, further, that each side of this dis-illusionment served, momentarily, as a defense against his exper-iencing the fullness of the other side of it.

One woman while free associating spoke, by parapraxis, of her eldest brother, Ben, while intending to speak of her eldest son, Bill; she said, " ... - Ben - Bill - Why do I mix them up? - ... I know from the way I confuse people _[this emphasis mine]_ that I have no appreciation of people in their own right - ... I just don't differentiate between people at all - they just don't exist as separate people - ..." The way she said, "I confuse people" here conveyed the unconscious meaning that she confuses not only her mental images of people, but also people in outer reality. That is, as with disillusionment, so with confusion, the borderline individual unconsciously experiences his own confusion as causing this same confusion in the outer world. The just-mentioned woman persisted, through several years of therapy, in experiencing herself as endowed with witchlike powers, including the power to sow confusion in the world around her, and was variously delighted with and terrified of these subjectively suprahuman powers.

A major reason for the borderline patient's persistent difficulty in becoming able to differentiate between an internal, mental transference-image of the therapist on the one hand, and the therapist himself on the other hand, consists in the fact that his transference-reactions and -attitudes are so powerful in their effect, over the long course of the therapy, as to mold the therapist's actual feelings and behavior, during the sessions, into conformity with those transference-images. This basically delusional-transference impact is so effective that the therapist himself comes to have great difficulty in perceiving the element of the transference, differentiated as such from the reality of his usual sense of his own identity.

In this connection, the treatment of the borderline individual presents difficulties only somewhat more moderate in degree than those I (4) have described as true of the work with the frankly and chronically schizophrenic individual.

When I left the staff of Chestnut Lodge, about 15 years ago, I had been working for several years with six chronically schizophrenic individuals, four hours per week in each instance. It was only some few years later that I came to realize, in retrospect, how important in my collective work with all these patients had been his or her transference, from the outset of the treatment in each instance, to me as being a basically ineffectual mother. I had felt realistically ineffectual, with each of them and all of them collectively, to such a very high degree that it was only now, after the interim of these years, years during which my self-esteem had been finding greater support from various sources, that I could achieve a better-differentiated perspective upon that Chestnut Lodge experience. I now discerned clearly, in retrospect, that I had been unable fully to differentiate, and maintain as differentiated, these patients' transference-based, unquestioned assumptions that I was an ineffectual mother, as distinct from my own then-current-experience-based perceptions of my own effectiveness or ineffectiveness in the actual work of the therapy, day after day and year after year.

It is generally agreed that denial is one of the major unconscious defense-mechanisms in borderline ego-functioning. The main point I wish to make in this paper is that unconscious denial of all sorts of aspects of "outer" reality has, as one of its major determinants, the unconscious inability to differentiate clearly between the self - including the sense of personal identity - and the outside world. The woman who had conveyed unconsciously the conviction that it was terrible of her to think of the recent blackout in New York City was threatened with an unconscious image of herself as _being_ the frightening blackout with its looting and other chaotic aspects. Linked with this dissociated image of herself as omnipotently malevolent was a contrasting image of herself as limitlessly vulnerable, totally impotent, in face of an invading outside world which had the power thus to mold her sense of identity, dependent only upon the changing conditions in the "outside" world. Whereas at one extreme she unconsciously believed her own thinking (and fantasying) to control omnipotently the outer reality, at the other extreme she experienced her internal world, including her sense of personal identity, to be totally controlled by that outer reality.

During the past two or three years I have come to see more clearly why such a patient needs so desperately to maintain, perhaps for many years in therapy, her denial. It is not merely that she is failing to perceive and take full account of some important _aspect_ of _outer_ reality. Far beyond that, she is struggling to preserve her familiar sense of personal identity, which otherwise would be replaced by that denial-encysted sector of "outer" reality. She is threatened unconsciously lest her familiar sense of identity as a human being be replaced by, for example, a sense of identity as nonhuman and omnipotently malevolent.

In a paper in 1975 entitled, "The Patient as Therapist to His Analyst", I (8) included a clinical vignette which is relevant here. The patient, here called Miss J., is the previously mentioned woman who, formerly chronically schizophrenic, has been functioning for some years now at a predominantly borderline level. An important part of this woman's history consisted in her having come to occupy the parental-family role of caretaker to her emotionally disturbed mother.

"The last room-mate she had, for about a year before moving to an apartment of her own in Washington, was a highly psychotic woman whose verbal and physical behavior was often highly disorganized. Miss J. would describe it that Edna was being, once again, 'in a whirl'. In one of her analytic sessions with me during that year, she asked me whether it would be all right with me for her to go to New York City on the following Sunday, to visit her female cousin there, and to miss her Monday hour. I said that it was all right with me; for reasons I shall not detail here, I did not respond in an analytic-investigative manner, as I would do in working with a neurotic patient. She then said something about not being sure she could do it - i.e., make the trip to New York City alone. 'I feel so little in New York. ... I guess I always think of New York as a big city in a whirl. ...'

"The idea which struck me, upon hearing this, is that she projected onto New York City her own still-largely-repressed confusion, and tended to feel responsible - a responsibility overwhelmingly awesome to me as I sensed it - for the whole gigantic, perceivedly confused city. Her psychosis had first become overt, many years before, shortly following a visit to this cousin in New York City, and I felt that here I was being given a brief glimpse into the nature of her psychotic experience then. Later on, in looking over my notes on this session, I realized that New York City was unconsciously equivalent, for her, to her overwhelmingly confused mother, for whom the patient felt so totally responsible.

"About two years later, in a relatively recent session, she was describing to me her weekly visit to her current social worker at Chestnut Lodge, a woman toward whom Miss J. has a mother-transference which involves, amidst clearly ambivalent feelings, a great deal of admiration, fondness of a sisterly sort, and a maternal caring for the social worker. She said, 'Recently she's been so busy, her office looks like a whirl!', making an illustrative whirling gesture with her arm as she said this."

This same woman, in a session about two months later, manifested some of the psychodynamics of her confusion which are relevant here. Although continuing to maintain herself in her apartment in Washington, she had not become able to drive a car, but had to rely upon buses to get to her therapy-sessions with me four hours per week, and to attend unit meetings on her former sanitarium-ward once or twice a week.

She began the session by speaking of her "confusion" in "going from one place to another." She was detailing, by way of example, her bus-trip to Rockville (the suburb where the sanitarium is located) yesterday, and the ward-unit meeting she attended, all of which evidently had proved confusing to her. The confusion of which she spoke was manifest in her demeanor, and it was evident to me that her having come, even, from my waiting room into my office, a few moments before, had contributed to her confusion. It became apparent within the first few minutes that this confusion resulted from an unconscious need on her part to dissociate both (a) her fury at the change (a new insight to me in this connection) and, as I had known for many years to be true of her, (b) her feelings of loss evoked by the change. Both these kinds of dissociated feelings were evident in her facial expressions as she sat on the couch and talked.

She had said about a week previously that "I suppose if I were driving a car I could be many places in a day." This statement conveyed to me an unconscious meaning that she would be in many places simultaneously in one day. I realized, more clearly than before, that she felt threatened, unconsciously, lest she would become confused by driving a car - would come confusedly to experience herself as being in many places at once.

In a subsequent session she complained that "The bus I got on was so shaky, I almost fell over. ..." She then added, "It made me very nervous, to be such a shaky bus." Although it was clear that she consciously meant something to the effect that "Because the bus proved to be such a shaky one, I became very nervous," her statement clearly conveyed an additional, unconscious meaning to the effect that "It made me very nervous to become such a shaky bus." Incidentally, my (2) monograph concerning the nonhuman environment contains many comparable examples of patients' unconsciously feeling at one with various nonhuman ingredients of their surroundings.

Another woman struggled, for years, with a conflict as to
whether to continue living in the Washington area or to return to
Chicago, where she had spent the first twenty-five years of her
life. She projected this conflict, and with it much of her unconscious sense of her personal identity, upon these two cities to a
striking degree. On occasion she spoke in a tone as though the
two huge cities were at war with one another. In one session when
she said, "I think I mentioned to you, when I was talking about
the New York-Chicago conflict _[my emphasis_]...", this was said
in such a tone as to conjure up, in my mind, an even vaster conflict, one of interplanetary dimensions, à la H. G. Wells.

The woman I have mentioned several times was planning, at one
point relatively early in her out-patient living, upon a rare visit
to her cousin in New York City. One concern of hers was that the
smog in both cities was, as attested by the news-reports, very bad.
As the time for her trip drew near, she said that, because the smog
in New York was worse now than that in Washington (confirmed by the
newscasts), she didn't know whether she would be making the trip
after all, and she indicated that her cousin had become exasperated
with her for being so indecisive. "I can't guarantee anything,"
she said protestingly. I had been saying nothing; yet she seemed
unsure whether I expected some guarantee from her. "Betty _[her
cousin_] is very annoyed and angry _[said in such a context, and so
ambiguously, that I was not sure whether she meant that Betty was
angry at her, or at the smog in New York_] ... I told her _[during
one of their many telephone calls_] I can't help it; it'll depend
on whether the smog gets less - I can't help it that the smog is
so bad - ..."

Parenthetically, I had encountered an abundance of data from
her, over the years, to indicate that her parental-family members
did indeed tend to hold her responsible for innumerable events and
situations which were far beyond the realistic control of any human
individual. Surely she had been given to feel, from very early
childhood on, an uneasy sense of total responsibility for the unpleasant, obscure, vaguely threatening emotional climate, so to
speak, of the family home. Throughout many years of my work with
her, she clearly tended variously to feel responsible for the
weather, or to project upon me such a responsibility.

Later in the session which I have been detailing, she said,
"Well, maybe things will clear up," consciously referring to the
smog in New York, but unconsciously conveying the additional meaning, "Well, maybe things will clear up between Betty and me."

It turned out that she did make the trip in question, and
upon her return felt that she had done relatively well during it.
She commented that the weather had been good, " - So that went
pretty well," she said, in a tone implying that this had been one
of her own more successful accomplishments during the visit.

In a later session she commented, "...I was glad to stay in
my apartment yesterday. ... - I noticed the air wasn't good yesterday - I didn't know if it was me or the air _[my emphasis_], but
they _[i.e., the T. V._] did say it was very polluted - ..."

The sense of personal identity, in some of these patients, is
projected upon the outer world to a very striking degree. One

14

woman, for instance, spoke of a

> " ... - Feeling that everything outside of myself has
> more value, is more me, than I am - ... my surroundings;
> so I try to control all of it, because if something's
> happening to my surroundings, it's happening to me - not
> as though it's happening to me, but it is happening to
> me - ... I'm the shell, but the content of me is all
> outside of myself: ... You're part of it and this room
> is part of it, and a lot of other people are part of it -
> Ed ⌐her husband⌐, of course, and my children, and my
> house. ... I'm just a lifeless shell that walks around
> among these things, that imagines it's alive. But it
> isn't; I'm really not - being in a coffin, as mother
> was - ..."

In the instance of one woman whom I treated for several years,
I came to see with considerable clarity, relatively late in the
work, that she had had a powerful transference to all of outer
reality as personifying, in her unconscious experience, a dominating,
withholding mother whose power she was determined to minimize and
whose existence, in fact, she strove insofar as possible to deny.
I had never seen this particular kind of transference-attitude,
with this degree of clarity, in my work, years before, with hospitalized, chronically schizophrenic patients, and I immediately felt
that this transference-phenomenon helped, in retrospect, to account
for their so massive, and so long maintained, unconscious denial
of outer reality. Time does not allow me, here, to spell out some
of the transference-events which helped me to see this in the
instance of this woman. Suffice it to say that she, similarly to
the far more ill, long-hospitalized patients, had shown heretofore,
year after year, a maddeningly high degree of self-containment,
of imperviousness to the outer world which included myself and my
attempts at interpretation.

SUMMARY

In this paper I have emphasized that the borderline individual's
signs and symptoms of ego-non-differentiation are fascinatingly
subtle, by contrast to the frankly schizophrenic patient's relatively conspicuous difficulties in this area. His tenuous internal
image, if any, of the therapist is easily lost in the absence of
much perceptual feedback from the latter. In that event, since the
internal image is not well differentiated from the object in outer
reality (the therapist), he reacts as though not only the image but
the therapist himself has gone out of existence.

His sense of personal identity is not well differentiated from
his surroundings - not only the human but also the nonhuman environment. Geographic moves thus tend to cause him confusion and loss
of his sense of personal identity.

His incomplete ego-differentiation between inner and outer
reality causes him to react to his own thinking, and various aspects
of his affective life, as having an omnipotent power over external
reality. Experiences of disillusionment tend to make him feel that
not merely has his image of the disillusioning person now changed,

but that he has destroyed that actual person in outer reality. Similarly when he becomes confused, he reacts unconsciously in terms of his having sown confusion, omnipotently, throughout his outer world.

Denial, which is widely agreed to be among his major defenses, is one of the bulwarks of his tenuous sense of personal identity. Admission into awareness of that area of outer reality which has long been encapsulated by denial brings with it, for him, two enormous threats. First, because perceiving is unconsciously equated with omnipotently causing, he feels overwhelming guilt at perceiving such things as illness and death and damage in the world. Secondly, his incomplete differentiation between inner and outer reality tends to make him experience this newly revealed realm as being predominantly in the nature of a horrifying and strange inner world, in which his personal identity is, if not limitlessly weak and vulnerable, then malevolently omnipotent.

I have touched, also, upon some of the inherent difficulties in the therapist's working with borderline individuals, such as his becoming unable to differentiate between the patient's transference-distorted images of him, and his usual sense of his own identity as being relatively healthy and competent; and his vulnerability to becoming jealous of the patient's newly-established and enthralling internal image of him.

REFERENCES

1. Proust, M. (1927): A la Recherche du Temps Perdu, VII, Le Temps Retrouvé. Librairie Gallimard, Paris. Published in English in 1970 as Time Regained, Chatto & Windus Ltd., London, and as The Past Recaptured, Random House, Inc., New York.
2. Searles, H. F. (1960): The Nonhuman Environment in Normal Development and in Schizophrenia. International Universities Press, New York.
3. _____ (1962): Scorn, Disillusionment, and Adoration in the Psychotherapy of Schizophrenia. Psychoanalysis and the Psychoanalytic Review, 49, 39. Quote is from p. 49.
4. _____ (1965): Collected Papers on Schizophrenia and Related Subjects. Hogarth Press, London; and International Universities Press, New York. See especially papers 10, 11, 18, 19.
5. _____ (1969): A Case of Borderline Thought Disorder. International Journal of Psycho-Analysis, 50, 655. Quote is from p. 661.
6. _____ (1972): Unconscious Processes in Relation to the Environmental Crisis. Psychoanalytic Review, 59, 361. Quote is from p. 368.
7. _____ (1972): Intensive Psychotherapy of Chronic Schizophrenia. International Journal of Psychoanalytic Psychotherapy, 1, 30. Quote is from p. 41.
8. _____ (1975): The Patient as Therapist to His Analyst. On p. 95 in Tactics and Techniques in Psychoanalytic Therapy – Vol. II - Countertransference, ed. by P. L. Giovacchini. Jason Aronson, New York.

9. _____ (1976): Jealousy Involving an Internal Object. Presented at New York Conference on Borderline Disorders, New York City, November 20, 1976. To be published in Stable Instability - Modern Approaches to the Borderline Syndrome, ed. by J. LeBoit and A. Capponi. Jason Aronson, New York, 1979.

CLINICAL AND THEORETICAL CONSIDERATIONS WHICH RESULT FROM
PSYCHOTHERAPEUTIC INTERVENTION IN SCHIZOPHRENIA

Thomas Freeman

Consultant Psychiatrist, Royal Dundee Liff Hospital, Dundee,
Scotland.

Whoever decides to devote his energies to the psychotherapy of
schizophrenic psychoses soon finds himself preoccupied with problems,
some of which he has heard or read about and others which are
provoked by his own clinical experiences. Who amongst us had not
heard, even before our first therapeutic endeavours, that Freud
considered that transference did not occur in cases of schizophrenia?
In the theoretical field who was unaware of the hypothesis that
persecutory delusions had their origin in repressed homosexual
wishes?
      The literature on the psychotherapy of schizophrenia, which
now extends over not less than sixty years, attests to the fact
that the practical difficulties which have been encountered and the
theoretical ideas which have been formulated have largely depended
on the types of cases under treatment and the circumstances under
which the therapy has been conducted. Some reports are based on
experiences with patients whose psychosis has been of recent onset
while others describe therapeutic efforts with patients whose illness
has been present for many years.
      These contributions to the literature have come from state
mental hospitals, from university clinics and from private mental
hospitals. Each institution has differed in the enthusiasm shown
by the staff for the psychotherapeutic approach to the psychoses,
in the ratio of doctors and nurses to patients, in the educational
standard of the nurses and in the availability of ancillary
services. All these factors must have affected patient and
doctor so influencing the mode of expression and content of the
clinical data as well as the course of the illness. In these
latter respects the greatest impact has been made by the advent of
drug therapy. It has altered the way in which the morbid process
finds expression and as a result has affected the patient's
responses to psychotherapeutic treatment.
      The fact that greater or lesser degrees of fragmentation of
the personality can co-exist with a wide variety of delusional
ideas and differences in outcome of illness led Bleuler (1911) to
suggest that there is more than one type of schizophrenia. He
believed that the splitting or fragmentation of the personality
which occurs is a result of the morbid process while the delusions
and hallucinations are a response to the dissolution of healthy
mental life. However, as delusions, hallucinations and catatonic
signs are prominent phenomena and therefore easily identifiable,
particularly at the onset of a psychosis, they have tended to usurp

the place of the primary symptoms as being diagnostic of schizo-phrenia. This shift of emphasis in diagnostic practice has created rather than resolved problems for those concerned with the treatment of this group of psychoses.

CLINICAL CONSIDERATIONS

For many years my psychotherapeutic experience with schizo-phrenic patients was confined to those whose illness had reached a state of chronicity. For the most part these individuals had fallen ill in adolescence or shortly afterwards. They were with-drawn, neglectful of themselves, cognitively disorganised and apparently indifferent to my colleagues and myself. These first psychotherapeutic ventures were mostly undertaken in groups with the collaboration of nurses who knew the patients well (Freeman, Cameron and McGhie, 1958). The phenothiazine drugs had not yet appeared on the scene and bouts of disturbed behaviour were more frequent than they would be today with comparable patients.

It was tempting to believe that these upsets were reactions to the therapy and at times there was much evidence to favour such a hypothesis. The invaluable information obtained from the nurses confirmed the earlier reports of Sullivan, (1947), Fromm-Reichman, (1939) and others that patients suffering from chronic schizophrenia retain some form of emotional tie to others and this leads to reactions of various kinds.

A year at least passed before I realised that the patients' lack of interest in the proceedings of the group was not entirely inappropriate. The hospital ward was their home and it was the nurses and the other patients who were important to them – not the doctors in the group. Without any aim other than that of widening my knowledge of schizophrenic psychoses I abandoned the group approach in favour of work with individual patients. In this way I hoped I would be of value to them and psychotherapeutic work would become possible.

On separate occasions I worked daily with two patients, one male the other female, who were typical cases of hebephrenic-catatonic schizophrenia. Both had fallen ill about the age of 17 years and the psychoses had persisted, apart from one or two brief partial remissions for about eight years. Neither welcomed my interest. I had to search them out each day otherwise the meetings would not have taken place. The woman spoke little while the man was difficult to follow because he had a private language, parts of which only I later came to understand.

In spite of their seeming indifference they were sensitive to how I behaved and to what I had to say. Their reactions rarely had an immediate expression or they were displaced to nurses and other patients. This sensitivity reflected the egocentrism which determined the way in which they responded to their own needs, wishes and affects and to the utterances and behaviour of others. I was of interest only if it appeared that I might be able to satisfy a need or wish.

In the case of the woman the need was for cigarettes or to help her get out of the hospital. In the case of the man the wish was that I assist him in achieving a delusional ambition.

20

My failure to satisfy these wishes led to withdrawal or to anger which was expressed elsewhere. Whenever I told them that I had to be away for a few days there was always a reaction. Sometimes this consisted of withdrawal but as with other frustrations it was over-taken by rage. On one occasion when this was expressed directly against myself it enabled the man to violently criticise his mother. No therapeutic benefit followed from this.

My daily visits to these patients were not without other results. They were clear in the man but faint in the woman although in common with other observers I have encountered similar dramatic events in female patients. The episode which I will now describe occurred more than once during my contact with the male patient. It began with grandiosity and in this mood he talked freely. He was irritable if he thought I was not sufficiently respectful. "I am the time" he screamed when I dared to suggest that the dining room did not open until 12 noon.

The face was the body part selected by this young man to give expression to wishes of various kinds. "I was the perfect art gallery face", he said, meaning that his face was sufficiently fine to be portrayed in an art gallery. "I am God", he told me, "I am the Jesus face, the face of Our Lady". When he saw a woman whose face he admired he claimed he had a face like her husband. He claimed a woman's face as easily as that of a man.

In common with many male patients whose schizophrenia is in a chronic state he was preoccupied with thoughts of a girl he had once known. Through wish fulfilment he believed that they would soon marry - "Una (the girl) is very sincere, she is too beautiful to bear children, she can only marry the prepared person by God, that's me, it was a marriage made by God". As the mode of his relating at this time was predominantly on the basis of iden-tification he merged with his fantasy girlfriend. One day I could not find him for our meeting. When I saw him the next day he said "I had to protect Una from a medical examination. If I confided in the doctor she would too and I do not want that".

While in this grandiose state he gave a glimpse of his sexual (genital) conflict - "you say to me that you still nurture the wish to be a saint. If you marry you ruin your chance of being a saint. It was always Una's plan to marry. I know she has 'no winks' (not flirtatious). I had a tremendous dream last night, it was a wild dream, more wild than you can describe, I thought the penis might turn into a snake. It's such a powerful thing, of course I'm a normal boy and a normal size of penis, of course I'm 26 and not being instructed against tossing off (masturbation), that's a sin. I could not have perfected beauty without a good moral life, of course all these things are shocking and alarming to me".

Gradually the grandiosity diminished and was replaced by acute anxiety. He was restless and agitated. "I am in such a terrible condition, life is unbearable" he would say. The very body parts of which he had been so proud had become the source of great distress - "my face is a nightmare, it's shape is changing, I'm not one face but a thousand faces, everyone has a serious illness. Last night I had a break-up of the penis, I seemed to lose a lot of yellow like the picture on the ward, only it was white (seminal emission), I wish I could restore it".

These fears were accompanied by other anxieties - "it was terrifying last night" he said. "Voices on the television started baiting me. They were saying I have got you and then for a multiplier". When I asked him what a multiplier was he replied - "if you're caught and you suffer and it gets worse all the time, voices on the television, getting away with terrible things. The multiplier is a trap by devils. It was a night of terror (contrast the earlier "wild dream"). Snakes escaped from Edinburgh Zoo". His attitude towards me was beginning to change. He was no longer friendly and at times looked at me in a menacing way. Suddenly he accused me of disturbing him through the television and causing the changes in his face. I was not to come and see him again. For some weeks he was withdrawn and unresponsive.

Some years later when I had the opportunity to treat patients whose psychosis was of recent origin I had the opportunity to witness a similar sequence of events during acute psychotic attacks. The case I wouldlike to describe is that of a young man of 18 years who was brought into hospital in a state of panic resulting from his belief that he was in his words - "a homosexual".

When the anxiety subsided and the delusion receded he told me that for some months he had been in excellent spirits and full of self-confidence. He felt himself to be attractive to girls and believed that they looked at him admiringly when he walked in the street. He felt sorry for his brother, six years older than himself, whom he regarded as unmanly and effeminate. Gradually he realised that his brother envied his masculinity because he was copying his manner and his dress. They must seem identical. He was convinced that his brother was trying to steal his masculinity and make him effeminate. He was frightened and angry. He threatened to kill his brother and it was at this time he was sent to hospital. Soon after arrival he attacked a male nurse because he feared he was about to assault him sexually.

After the acute attack passed he was willing to meet for psychotherapeutic sessions. After some months he became disturbed once more. At first he was elated and self-confident. Then he accused me of being a homosexual. I was trying tomake him one also - "I can feel you pushing the word 'homosexual' into my mind and I'm using all my strength to push it out", he said. He objected to my sitting with my legs crossed. This was because a girl at school, who excited him to the point of masturbation, sat in this way. I was trying to make him masturbate instead of telling him to stop this bad habit.

Small quantities of an anti-psychotic drug reduced his anxiety and he was able to speak with less upset. He remembered trying to enact coitus with other boys. He recalled putting his penis against the family dog's anus. He was frightened by this act and wondered if he was a homosexual. During a subsequent session he reported that he was having evil thoughts, one of which was of my backside. At this point he was upset by memories of his parents arguing and by noises which he heard in his head but could not identify. Then he had a picture in his mind of his mother's buttocks and his father pushing against her. He hearda girl's voice outside the room. He hoped this would take away any homosexual thoughts he may have. He wanted to spit because spit and nasal secretions were the

22

same as seminal fluid. If he spat the girl could become pregnant and that would mean he was not a homosexual.

This heterosexual fantasy, a counterpart to the feminine one relating to myself, had a childhood forerunner which had caused him much anxiety and distress. After puberty he was in the habit of disposing of seminal fluid by throwing it into a lavatory which was connected to a septic tank. He feared that the semen would mix with his mother's and sister's menstrual blood which he knew also ended up in the septic tank. He dreaded the periodic arrival of the men who came to empty the septic tank lest they found dead infants inside.

The two patients I have described, the one chronically ill the other recently unwell, showed many features in common when they were acutely disturbed. During these attacks they gave free expression to the delusions and hallucinations which constituted their psychotic reality. Once the acute phase passed the chronic patient slipped back into his prior withdrawn and negativistic state but the recently ill patient regained contact with reality. This return of healthy mental life made a psychotherapeutic approach possible.

During the withdrawn periods the chronically ill patient behaved as I described earlier. I was only of interest if I could supply a need. I tried to discover from nurses and others whither he might be displacing the affects and thoughts which were arising from his contact with me. I attempted to identify responses whose expression was subject to delay in the hope that I might be able to build up a picture of his inner reactions to our daily meetings. I always met with a lack of response when I presented him with the results of my researches unless some chance event evoked a hidden affect. Illustrative was an occasion when I told him we would not meet for four weeks as I was going away on holiday. At the end of the session he followed me from the consulting room into the adjoining ward where I stopped for a minute to talk to a male nurse. Suddenly he burst out in a furious rage. No-one cared about him, he said. He had not had a holiday for six years. He was ill-treated. He cursed the nurse and myself. Then he relapsed into the previous withdrawn state.

The egocentrism which determined the direction of the recently ill patient's thoughts and feelings disappeared once the acute attack passed. He could then accept personal responsibility for his unhappy feelings and for his anxieties. Such a change did not take place in the case of the chronic patient. His egocentrism continued and his mental activity was conditioned by this. I was at fault. Conceivably his reactions to me were repetitive in nature, having their origin in the distant past, but his egocentrism precluded any chance of his recognising, through a verbal communication, that what he was experiencing was a revival of childhood affect.

I worked regularly with the young man whose illness was of recent origin for about six years. During this time he was responsive and aware of the fact that he had suffered from delusional experiences. The only exception to this being those occasions when he sustained acute attacks of which there were four in number.

In the quiescent phases his attention was taken up with anxieties about his bodily health, with complaints of lack of

confidence at work, with girls and of depression of mood. He
worried about his brother, his parents and about the viability of
the family business. As long as he remained free of delusions his
attitude towards me was one of dependency, seeking reassurance and
support. This was how he had related to his mother throughout his
childhood. Only in the psychotic episodes did he relate in any
other way.

THEORETICAL CONSIDERATIONS

My reason for presenting these two cases in some detail has
been to draw attention to the fact that at the onset and during the
course of schizophrenia it is the rule for brief periods of pleasureable wish fulfilment and need satisfaction to be followed by intense
anxiety as represented in delusions and hallucinations with a
persecutory content. How are these sequences of conscious mental
events to be understood? The transformation of pleasure into
anxiety — transiently or permanently — is not peculiar to persecutory
types of psychosis. It is characteristic of the neuroses,
particularly anxiety hysteria, and it is also to be encountered in
the dreams of the mentally healthy. In these latter instances it
is possible to demonstrate that the anxiety signals a danger caused
by unacceptable mental derivatives of instinct. Does a similar
explanation hold for the psychotic patient who is in terror of being
assaulted mentally and physically?

A start can be made by examining the nature of the needs and
wishes which bring the acutely disturbed patient such pleasure.
The need may be for exhibitionism with the patient obtaining satisfaction from being looked at by others or from looking at himself.
The need may be genital with the object as often homosexual as
heterosexual. As a rule these needs are accompanied by a belief
in the reality of wishful fantasies. In the least grandiose of
these the patient considers himself to be superlatively endowed with
physical and mental attributes. He is admired by everyone. Sometimes he believes a particular woman is in love with him. This
erotomania usually gives way to a persecutory delusion with the
patient believing that the former admirer is trying to do him an
injury.

The wishful fantasies may equally well have a destructive
content with anal-sadistic and oral-sadistic wishes to the fore.
The patient obtains great satisfaction, however briefly, from the
power he wields over the objects of his violence. A young man
believed, during an acute attack, that every time he passed wind
per anum he caused a destructive storm. A young woman who believed
that she was both Christ and Cain said that she had eaten Abel.
When she saw her uncle sharpening a knife she thought he was about to
kill her and eat her for revenge. All the family were to participate in this sacrificial meal.

There are many authors who subscribe to the view that the
wishful delusions and need satisfying behaviour of the acute attack
are not in themselves primary phenomena. Instead they are regarded
as reactions to an unconscious complex or fantasy and as such
constitute a defence against the possibility of the derivatives of
these instinctual complexes gaining access to consciousness. There

24

are however a number of facts which contradict such a hypothesis.

When one is fortunate enough to treat a patient during the initial stage of a psychosis and later when the acute break with reality takes place it is possible to observe how the anxieties, guilt and inhibitions which characterise the initial phase give way to wish fulfilment and need satisfaction. For example an adolescent girl of 15 believed that she was "smelly" and feared leaving the house because others looked at her on this account. She was forever washing herself. She accused boys of watching her undress and of saying that she was sexy. She feared that her parents were planning to have her murdered.

At the onset of the acute attack she attacked her mother with a knife. She delighted in smelling herself and others. She smeared her body with faeces and attributed a magic power to these bodily products. She tore off her clothes and admired her image in the mirror. "Look at me", she would say, "I love my body" and in saying this would enjoy feeling her breasts and buttocks. She masturbated in front of other patients and made sexual advances to both men and women.

A similar sequence of events was to be observed in the case of the young man to whom I referred earlier. Before an acute attack whose onset I witnessed, he feared that some harm might befall his brother. He might be injured in an accident, fall ill or even give way to criminality or become a homosexual. During the acute attack he made to attack his brother, wished him dead and accused him of being a homosexual. In both these cases the symptoms of the initial phase of the psychosis were a response to a danger created by instinctual wishes. This danger finds expression, in the established case of schizophrenia, in a dread of sexual (genital or pregenital) excitement represented by condemnation of masturbation. This was so with the chronically ill patient except for those occasions when the sexual wishes broke through during an acute attack.

In view of these considerations it seems reasonably to assume that the wishful delusions and the need satisfying behaviour of schizophrenic patients are primary phenomena resulting from an extensive dissolution of the personality. This hypothesis is further strengthened by the fact that an acute attack, whenever it occurs during the psychosis, is always characterised by transitivistic signs and by the phenomena of appersonation indicating that psychical differentiations have been lost. Physical and mental aspects of the self are attributed to others and equally the characteristics of others are assimilated into the self.

The dissolution of the personality exposes a state not unlike that existing in the mentally healthy child of two years of age. Like the child the patient finds his body pleasureable. He enjoys exhibiting it to others, touching others and finds satisfaction in oral and anal activities. As in early childhood others are treated as if they were without feelings or sensitivities. The patient is indifferent to the welfare and safety of his body as is the infant and he relates on the basis of need satisfaction. As with the young child the adult patient's love can suddenly turn to hate. This hatred can be evoked by frustration but may equally have a spontaneous expression. The infantile egocentrism determines the way in which others are judged. Both good and bad experiences appear to have an external cause.

The pleasureable episodes are, as we know, soon replaced by anxiety which turns into panic. The self is utterly deflated and the omnipotence which was enjoyed is now attributed to known and unknown persecutors. Later in the attack the reverse process recurs with the self transiently regaining its power and the persecutors vanishing from sight. An explanation of these changes requires the use of economic concepts. Drive energy (drive cathexis) located in the self is transferred to real or imaginary object representation and vice versa. The nature of the volitional and affective phenomena demonstrate that these drive cathexes are primitive in quality and are to be regarded as another consequence of the dissolution of the personality. It is the redistribution of drive energies and their ideational representations from the self to objects which leads to the anxiety and to panic.

The phenomena which occur at or soon after the onset of a schizophrenic illness suggest that following the dissolution there is activity in what Hughlings Jackson (1894) described as "...what remains of the highest cerebral centres". This evolution, to use Jackson's word, leads to new psychical formations which fill the void created by the loss of healthy mental life.

The tendency to relate on the basis of identification, the predominance of wish fulfilment in thought and action (primary process) and the intense ambivalence are a direct result of the dissolution. While this continues the defused drive cathexes are at the patient's disposal. The reconstructive activity ("evolution going on in what remains of the highest cerebral centres", Jackson, 1894) reveals its presence with the appearance of the persecutory anxieties. The attribution of omnipotence to the persecutors results from the drive energies, albeit in a primitive condition, attempting to provide a substitute for the former normal object relationships.

What I have just described is Freud's (1911) two phase formulation of symptom formation in schizophrenia. In the first phase there is a loss of those aim inhibited drive cathexes which ensure normal object relationships and perception of the self. Dissolution of the personality occurs contemporaneously with this loss of object cathexis. No sooner has this happened than the defused drive energies strive to recathect the abandoned object representations. It is this outward movement of instinctual wishes which leads to anxiety. The closer the drive derivatives come to the "rejected piece of reality" (Freud, 1924) the more intense does the anxiety become. This drive towards the object, which aims at a remodeling of reality through projection and/or a hallucinatory mechanism, is strenuously opposed by the forces which initiated the loss of object cathexis. The course of the illness and its clinical characteristics depend on the balance which is struck between the forces promoting the decathexis of objects and the pressure exerted by the primitive instinctual wishes seeking to recathect the objects, that is between destruction and reconstruction.

Such an explanation satisfactorily accounts, at present anyway, for the sequence of events which were to be observed in the long-standing case of schizophrenia. As his sexual wishes for the girl,

26

Una, intensified, a dangerous situation developed leading to anxiety. The only defence left to the damaged ego was a withdrawal of drive energy from the fantasy object ("the rejected piece of reality") with the inevitable heightening of egocentrism. In the patient whose illness was of recent origin the dissolution of the personality was followed by the reconstruction of psychic structures. Newly formed pathological forms of defence (projection) replaced those which had existed in the healthy state prior to the dissolution.

It follows from this hypothesis that the object relationships which characterise cases of schizophrenia have different origins. First, the dissolution of the personality results in a loss of developmental achievements and leads to the reappearance of infantile modes of relating to the self and to others. Second, the reconstructive tendencies lead to the object relationships which comprise the nucleus of the psychotic reality. Third, there are the residues of normal relationships. All three forms of relating occur in the one patient and in differing proportions depending on the extent of the morbid process.

Are we justified in describing these different forms of relating when they occur in the treatment situation under the concept of transference? The infantile behaviours are repetitions which occurred in the predominantly pre-verbal period of childhood. These repetitive phenomena can be described as transferences but are they "working transferences" in the manner of those which form the core of the psychoanalytical treatment of a neurosis?

The delusional object relationships can only be regarded as repetitions in so far as the reconstructive tendencies make use of formerly repressed infantile experiences to provide perceptual and conceptual material for the psychotic reality. The delusional fears of the schizophrenic patient are only descriptively similar to the anxieties of the healthy or neurotic child. These anxieties are quickly dispelled by the parents' presence thus indicating that the child's ties with reality remain intact. The anxieties of borderline and psychotic children may be descriptively similar to the persecutory fears of the adult patient but in the child the arrest of development is clear to see. Perhaps the difference between the anxious child and the adult or adolescent schizophrenic patient lies in the fact that in these cases, where there is a known persecutor, only certain of the latter's character-istics can be traced back to infantile perceptions of the parental objects. The persecutor always represents some aspect of the patient's mental or physical self. The persecutor is a new creation and attracts the whole of what was previously the patient's object cathexis. It is the loss of this cathexis which renders him insensitive to our attempts to influence his irrational beliefs.

I would like to conclude this paper with a few comments on the part conflict plays in symptom formation in schizophrenia. All psychotherapeutic work with schizophrenic patients reveal a person-ality divided against itself. In this respect neuroses are no different from psychoses. In the former the conflict takes place between the drive derivatives and the ego acting under the influence of the superego - so called internalised conflict. Neurotic symptoms being substitutes and compromises give no sign whatever of the wishes which form one element of the conflict. In the latter both sides of the conflict are there for all to see.

Although it is dangerous to generalise from more than a handful of cases it appears to me that the conflicts characteristic of the schizophrenias are fundamentally different from those which are uncovered in the neuroses in the course of psychoanalytical treatment. Here the conflict is internalised in kind and is based on full psychical differentiation. The psychotic conflicts consist of clashes between masculinity and femininity, between activity and passivity and between love and hate. An established sexual identity is endangered or a love relationship is transformed by hatred. This oscillation between masculinity and femininity, activity and passivity and between love and hate is reminiscent of the internal conflicts which occur in early childhood when the ego has become differentiated from the id but before the establishment of the superego.

The personality of the schizophrenic patient is altered on a scale never found in the neuroses. The extensive loss of developmental achievements in the acute psychotic attack is accompanied by the emergence of mental activity comparable to that of the infant as he makes the first moves away from identification with the mother to the mother as a love object, from need satisfaction to object constancy and from the primary to the secondary process. Is it not conceivable that the conflicts which appear during the acute attack and which continue in the established case are but a further result of the loss of developmental achievements caused by the dissolution of the personality?Viewed in this way the conflicts would be a result rather than a cause of the psychotic development.

I would like to suggest, following Anna Freud (1965), that mental symptomatology in the adult, as in the child, may not always be the result of conflict. Faulty development compounded of internal and external influences can promote dysharmony within the personality aggravating and intensifying the conflicts which are an inevitable aspect of healthy mental evolution. These dysharmonies may leave the individual vulnerable when he comes to make the transition from adolescence to adulthood. This development, involving as it does changes in the direction, quality and distribution of psychical energies, may impose an intolerable strain on a personality handicapped by the effect of long-standing stresses between mental structures. Regression rather than a progression is the outcome leading to the psychotic attack.

This formulation runs counter to theories of schizophrenia which are based on the model of symptom formation in the neurosis. However it has the value of drawing attention to the possibility that some factor additional to that of conflict operates in psychoses to produce the striking differences which exist between these conditions and other mental disorders.

REFERENCES

1. Bleuler, E. (1911): Dementia Praecox or the Group of
   Schizophrenias. New York, Int. Univ. Press, 1951.
2. Freeman, T. Cameron, J.L. and McGhie, A. (1958): Chronic
   Schizophrenia. London, Tavistock.

3. Freud, A. (1965): Normality and Pathology in Childhood. New York, Int. Univ. Press.
4. Freud, S. (1911): Psychoanalytical Notes on an Autobiographical Account of a case of Paranoia. Standard Edition, 12, London, Hogarth Press.
5. Freud, S. (1924): The Loss of Reality in Neurosis and Psychosis. Standard Edition, 19.
6. Fromm-Reichmann, F. (1939): Transference Problems in Schizo-phrenics in Psychoanalysis and Psychotherapy. Chicago, University of Chicago Press, 1959.
7. Jackson, J.H. (1894): The Factors of Insanities. In Selected Writings, 2, New York, Basic Books, 1958.
8. Sullivan, H.S. (1947): Conceptions of Modern Psychiatry. Washington, William Alanson White Foundation.

THE STRUCTURE OF THE PSYCHOTHERAPEUTIC RELATIONSHIP IN THE INDIVIDUAL TREATMENT OF SCHIZOPHRENIA

Gaetano Benedetti

Psychiatric University Out-Patient Clinic, Petersgraben 4
CH-4031 Basel, Switzerland

Individual psychotherapy of the schizophrenic patients begins with the "entrance" of the psychotherapist into the actual situation and into the world of his partner. "Entrance" is something that all psychotherapists of the schizophrenic ill have experienced and described, although with different words, as something fundamental. They speak of participation (Sullivan 14), of therapeutic love (Rosen 10), of relatedeness (Arieti 1), therapeutic symbiosis (Searles 12), of intentionality (Schultz-Hencke 11), of identification (Benedetti 2b) etc.

I believe that such a relation is not only symbolic, as is transference, but also symbolising, as is reality itself. Only in this way can the relationship create a dual world of experience with goes far beyond what can be clinically grasped, and which also contributes to the "individuation" of the psychotherapist himself.

Entrance into the actual situation and into the world of the ill is experienced by the psychotherapist as a gift given to him by the patient himself and by his own unconscious, but it can also be trained and stimulated by our meditation. This situation of entrance, once it has arisen, reveals itself on different levels, which can all either coexist simultaneously or appear singly. I shall describe only two of them:

1. Therapeutic dreams arise and show us our unconscious concern with the patient, as has recently been so beautifully illustrated by Isotti (7). They lack the classical dichotomy between latent and manifest content, postulated by Freud for all dreams (6), because they serve therapeutic communication and can, therefore, be used to reinforce it. The two following examples may illustrate this:

A patient feared the eyes of his therapist. He felt that he was being hypnotized and killed by them. The following night the therapist dreamed that he saw the eyes of his patient, which were staring at him. They were enormous and terrible, as the therapist's eyes had been in the patients experience. The therapist trembled with anxiety, but could withstand the look because it seemed to him, in his dream, to be that of eternity itself. We see here a reversal of the death-experience of the patient into a fearful, but grandiose life-experience of the therapist.

Another therapist dreamed: "I found myself together with an incurable schizophrenic in a gloomy, lonely and cheerless room. Only few words were spoken. Suddenly it was as if a curtain lifted, a second level of reality appeared (the psychotherapeutic transformation of the phenomen of a splitting between a first and a second level of symbolisation). In a vision of eternity the patient appeared to me as a hero, as leader of many shining knights charging into infinity. Astonished, I looked at this picture and I suddenly knew that both levels, that of the psychotic reality and that of the transcendental vision were complementary in C.G. Jung's sense of the word."

2. Some negative feelings of the patient, which he is not aware of and cannot verbalize, are perceived by the therapist as his own. In this way he experiences the patient's unconscious by sensing it within his own being. For example, it can happen that the patient can realize his own latent aggressivity only after his therapist, who has not yet discovered it, wonders about his own aggressive mood, which seems to him to be without any cause. In one supervision I controlled a problematic counter-transference of a therapist, who felt disgusted by her patient without, however, finding any reason for it. I guessed that such a feeling could be a manifest sign of her capability to come in touch with some "disgusting" parts of the patient's unconscious. After the therapist could, with the help of my interpretation, overcome her negative transference, the patient (a girl) become conscious of a sexual problem, which disgusted her (and no longer the therapist). She (the patient) then dreamed of a loathsome man, whose features became more and more gross and repulsive, and who urinated into the glasses of the people at the table. At this point it became possible to work through the patient's sexual disturbance. But this problem only came to light through the transient therapeutic "appersonation" (germ. "appersonierung") which was no refusal of the patient's sexuality, but the sign that the therapist's unconscious had merged with that of the patient, in order to structure it.

We see also that a psychopathological phenomenon becomes, in the therapeutic "identification" with the patient, a way of "taking over" his existence. "Taking over" (Siirala) here means that the patient's unconscious is not discovered by the interpretation of verbal signals, as in the psychoanalysis of neurosis, but it must be carried

mutually by both the patient and his therapist in order
to become articulated. Whereas, in classical psychoanalysis, transference is an alteration of reality and must be
shown as such to the patient, mutual identification is
the ground for a dual reality in psychotic autism. It
sometimes seems that even the schizophrenic unconscious
is disintegrated, as Freud himself surmised when he spoke
of the loss of intrapsychic images in the psychotic unconscious. This must therefore not only become discovered,
but first be born as a structure out of the act of a primary duality which lies at the very roots of psychic life.

Without a therapeutic "receiver" the patient's sensations are so far disorganised and derealised that they
can never be transformed into structured ego experiences.
They are not simply repressed as phantasies or affects,
as in neurosis, but they disintegrate to parts of senten-
ces, to voices and abstruse meanings in the psychotic
world.

Therapeutic entrance into the actual situation is in
psychosis more important than is the reconstruction of the
past in the psychoanalysis of neurosis; it is the very
therapist's message to the patient.

I must discuss now an objection to such a personal
therapeutic approach which has been raised by many authors. Laing (9) for example speaks of the danger of an
"implosion", that is, the dissolving of the schizophrenic
ego when confronted with our emotions. Frieda Fromm-Reichmann also tells us that any offer of love or friendship
to the mentally ill should be avoided. I agree, of course,
with these authors, insofar as they warn against a superficial emotional approach to the patient, which can only
be sensed by him as a demand from us. The matter is, however, different, if "therapeutic love" means our readiness
to be with the patient in his world of death. Our messages
to the patient convey that we do not expect anything from
him expect that we want only to be with him in his dreams,
phantasies and terryfying experiences.

A therapist, for example, listens to a patient who
feels surrounded by screaming devils; he tells the patient that he, too, is there; and, by leaping into the
demonic circle, forces the patient to perceive his presence in the very core of his psychotic world.

Another patient relates a frightening hallucination
in which he is overwhelmed by a flood of water. The
therapist "sees" the deluge, "la creux de la vague" (in
French also the term for impending catastrophe), and he
braces himself to withstand this vision. In another case
the therapist relates to his suicidal patient his own
dream, in which the latter throws herself out of the
window; in an attempt to save her, the therapist runs to

the window and can hold her in the air with his eyes.

The patient said, after hearing this dream, that she was then no longer able to kill herself.

I do not deny that even this mutual dwelling in death can be rejected by the patient. But in my experience the patient longs for nothing as much as he does the object of his resistance, his therapist. Then only that death which has been taken over by the therapist can be overcome by the patient. The patient then asks fearfully whether the therapist is still alive, whether he eats and sleeps well, whether he still exists, for if the therapist exists, so, too, can he.

Ma point here is that the therapist does not first try to rationalize the symptoms of the psychotic patient, but wants to be together with him within his symptoms. The first step of the psychotherapy is this dualized psychopathology. This was well expressed by a patient of mine who, during her psychosis, had a terror of the world as if it were a train bearing down upon her. During psychotherapy she developed a "therapeutic hallucination" in which she heard the therapist tell her to lie between the rails. She asked, frightened, how she could do this. The hallucinated therapist answered that he would lie between the rails with her.

I call this mutual process "identification" and "counter-identification", and I mean that the fragmented patient's ego finds its own identity by identification with the integrated ego of the therapist.

At the end of this process, the psychopathological phenomenon of "transitivism" is transformed into an act of psychotherapeutic mutuality. This is shown by the following dream of a patient, in which an animal lay bound in a stall, dying of hunger and thirst. "What a good fortune that you have come to save me in the last minute", cried the animal to the patient, as she began to cut its ropes. In this dream the patient had assumed the role of the therapist, as it was as she herself who had cut the ropes to save herself. This identification was only possible because the therapist had often identified with the suffering of the patient and had thereby experienced himself as the bound animal.

Another fundamental point concerns the problem of psychodynamic interpretation. We can reach the core of the question by asking ourselves how we can distinguish between therpeutic interpretations in schizophrenia and in neurosis.

1) Interpretations in the psychotherapy of schizophrenia can hardly grasp the connections of an individual psychogenesis in such an exhaustive manner that they could really explain why conflicts must be carried out by the

patient in a schizophrenic way. Interpretations are, therefore, "operational" in nature in that they do not discover a specificity of psychodynamics at the roots of schizophrenia. They give rather pictures of the dynamic and existential situations between the patient and his therapist. They can be also formed by therapeutic phantasies without, therefore, being untrue, because they unfold in this way the therapeutic relationship. Interpretations translate schizophrenic processes into psychogenetic events in order to give to the patient the key to the structuring of his psychotic experiences, as they are mirrored back to him by the therapist.

2) Secondly, interpretations are concerned not only with drives and instinctual needs of the patients, as in neurosis, but also with what I would call "structural needs" of the schizophrenic ego. I mean by these the needs of the patients to distinguish between egoic and alien, to grasp the frontiers of their own egos, to structure associations in time and space, to find an intrapsychic coherence, and so on. To understand such conditions demands a new level of psychodynamics which does not exist in neurosis, and which must be reached by the psychotherapist by being with the patient in the depth of his abnormal psychology.

3) Third, the psychotherapy of psychosis is different from the psychoanalysis of neurosis because of the different emphasis put on the resistances of the patients.

Freud taught us that we can often overcome neurotic resistances by telling them to the patient. This presupposes a healthy part of the ego which can work with us and look on the sick part of itself. Only those few schizophrenics who are similar to neurotics are able to do this.

Most schizophrenics are so dependent upon their own autistic, delusional, aggressive, paranoid behaviour, that their clinging to their systems and symptoms is more than a resistance, it seems to be an attempt at survival by means of organizing a last psychotic identity in the vacuum of their "non existence."

It would be naive to assume that it could be of use to the ill to be only confronted with the psychodynamics of such phenomena, as the knowledge of them would be, for him, only a tiny reality which would not fill the terrible vacuum within himself.

We may, however, reach the patient if we convey to him, through our interpretations, the feeling that we accept and understand his resistances as necessary expressions of himself which permit us to know his world and so to relate to it. We do not merely wish to reduce his resistance to psychological mechanisms.

In this connection I remember a patient who idealized me as God himself. It was of no use to reduce this delusional transference to the loss of her beloved mother during childhood. She maintained that the origin of her feelings towards me was the actual dual reality. The patient was, however, impressed by my interpretation that I felt to be for her the mirror of a radiating metaphysical sun, which could reach her through me in order to become, later, a part of herself.

If such interpretations are aimed at putting ourselves into the psychotic world of the patient, then this psychotic world must become valuable to us as a message of a human longing for personal existence.

In summary, my work and the experiences of several authors in the field of the psychotherapy of schizophrenia have shown us that understanding the patient requires a special relationship to him which is different from that in the psychoanalysis of neurosis because it implies an intrapsychic process which can be described in the following terms.

Parts of the ill personality are introjected by the psychotherapist, and parts of his personality are adopted by the patient, as shown by the fact that the dreams and the unconscious phantasies and strivings of the therapist reflect the anxieties of the patient, and the dreams of the latter are structured by the inner movements of the former, as if there were a partially shared identity between them both. I call this phenomenon "identification". The psychotherapy of schizophrenia has shown us the fact that there are realms of existence in which understanding is not only a cognitive function of personality, but also a transformation of personality by the act of being near the patient.

LITERATUR

1. Arieti, S.: Interpretation of Schizophrenia. Brunner, New York, 1955.
2a Benedetti, G.: Ausgewählte Aufsätze zur Schizophrenielehre. Vandenhoeck & Ruprecht, Göttingen, 1975.
 b Der Geisteskranke als Mitmensch. Vandenhoeck & Ruprecht Göttingen, 1975
3. Binswanger, L.: Schizophrenie. Neske, Pfullingen, Tübingen, 1957.
4. Bleuler, E.: Dementia praecox oder Gruppe der Schizophrenien. In: B. Aschaffenburg. Handbuch der Psychia-

trie. Deuticke, Leipzig, 1911.

5. Bleuler, M.: Zur Psychotherapie der Schizophrenie.
   Dtsch. med. Wschr. 79: 841-842, 1954.
6. Freud, S.: Die Traumdeutung (1900). Internationaler
   Psychoanalytischer Verlag, Leipzig, 1925.
7. Isotti, M.: Amore mio nemico. Rizzoli, Milano, 1978.
8. Jung, C.G.: Ueber die Psychologie der Dementia praecox
   Marhold, Halle 1907.
9. Laing, R.D.: The Devided Self. Tavistock Publ. London,
   1959.
10. Rosen, J.N.: Direct Analysis. Grune and Stratton,
    New York, 1953.
11. Schultz-Hencke, H.: Das Problem der Schizophrenie.
    Thieme, Stuttgart, 1952.
12. Searles, H.F.: Phasen der Wechselbeziehung zwischen
    Patient und Therapeut bei der Psychotherapie der
    chronischen Schizophrenie. Psyche 18:494, 1964.
13. Sechehaye, M.A.: Introduction à une psychothérapie
    des schizophrènes. Presses Univ. de France, Paris,
    1954.
14. Sullivan, H.S.: Schizophrenia as a Human Process. Nor-
    ton, New York, 1962.

PSYCHOTHERAPY FOR LATE-MANIFESTING SCHIZOPHRENICS.

Raoul Schindler

7th.Department of the Psychiatric Hospital and Mental Health Service
of the City of Vienna, Austria.

Generally, psychotherapy is indicated up to the thirtieth year
of age, whereas later attempts at interfering with the development of
personality with a view to structural changes seem to have little
value. Erikson (2) and others, however, have pointed to phases of
maturing in adults: the EGO's development does not seem to come to
a complete standstill with puberty but to go on in a way. Psychoanalytical literature available contains several careful clues to this
effect. but neither the concept of "creative capacity" nor that of
"EGO integrity" are being seriously discussed. Generally speaking,
there can be no doubt, however, that a person's ability to undergo
change decreases proportionately to the degree to which expectation
and imagination are surpassed by experience actually lived through.

This is of course also true in the area of psychotherapy for
schizophrenics. Here, more than in other areas, therapeutists are
attracted by the imaginative and dramatic early phases of the disease,
but are overtaxed and repulsed by the resignative emptiness of later
phases. The approach along lines of family therapy, which has made
such great progress over the past decades, always entails the availability of the family and, consequently, such age groups as can still
be helped by the cooperation of parents. This is true of the "Bifocal
group therapy"(5,6), which I developed 1947-1952 and which we are
still practising, just so of Stierlin's analysis of delegational pro-
cesses(11,12),just so of the method of Boszormenyi-Nagy(1) or Kauf-
mann(3), or in the sense of paradoxical intervention à la Watzlawick
(13,14) and Mrs.Selvini(10).

On the other hand, the number of first treatments in the age of
over thirty is increasing and it will not satisfy to simply leave them
to pharmaco-psychiatry. Also, Also, development of the EGO seems to
be strangely arrested early in schizophrenics and to start moving again only when the disease erupts: i.e., concepts of age groups can
perhaps be used meaningsfully only in relation to the development of
the disease. Often the intensity of actual experiences lags behind
expectations and imaginations quite substantially; reality does not
leave indelible traces on the personality, but is added in a rather
passive way, falling short of the interpretation it is being assigned.

Parental groups within bifocal group therapy show the following
pattern: 27 parents (i.e.:individuals) out of 200 show schizophrenia
proven beyond doubt by past treatment, whereas 34 such individuals
show traces of a subclinical, stabilized schizophrenic prozess in
earlier phases; thus 61 out of 200 parents can be expected to show
some type of schizophrenia. In terms of genetics, this is not very

interesting because there are no parameters clearly separating the genetic effects on children from the psychological ones. But each of these parents represents a model of a succesfully mastered pattern of disease: they have mastered their psychotic crisis to the point of founding a family and integrating their problems into it. These parents are examples of a success brought by self-therapy; its success - choice of partner and the shifting of problems - could be imitated in psychotherapeutical transfers in many way. Quite a few of these parents have managed to improve their condition decisively far above the critical age of thirty.

In order to base our discussion on firm ground I have evaluated 116 cases of succesfully treated schizophrenics and have subjected them to treatment again. They had been treated psychotherapeutically within the past 30 years, the minimum interval of katamnesis being 3 years. The treatment's success is definded socially: they were all able to reintegrate socially and did not need in-patient treatment during the last three years. Methods of treatment are not uniform, although the bifocal method prevails; therapists are different and sometimes somatic treatment was used as well. As a result, the study does not permit judgment on the value of such therapies themselves.

At first I was interested in the age at which patients had undergone psychotherapy: I put them into 15-year sections, from 15 to 75. The result was 50 patients who had been treated before their thirtieth year as again 66 who had been treated after their thirtieth year; numbers decrease in higher age groups, but their are still 5 therapeutically treated cases in the age over 60. Since unsuccessful therapies and those therapies broken off altogether could not be included, an assessment of efficiency has not been possible. Numbers reflect the relationship between indication and psychtherapy in the various age groups, thus showing that efforts have paid off about the same in all age groups. Pessimism toward older age groups is not justified. (Table 1)

Differentiation according to the diseases clinical pattern at the time is struck and inclusion of its over-all development showed that psychotherapy was indicated above all for paranoid patterns. They prevail with a total of 95 cases and a frequency rate pretty much corresponding to the over-all distribution within individual age groups. On the other hand, only 8 procedural cases were treated, primarily in the age group under 30. Obviously, no indication at all was specified for older patients of this chronical pattern, whose characteristic is a marked receding of contents as opposed to the formal disorder. Also, a surprisingly low number of catatonics was treated, a total of 13, which is not in keeping with the bulk of relevant literature on the subject. This corresponds to our ideas of the generally favorable prognosis for catatonics, - a prognosis that does not justify the use of such time-consuming treatment. The rather high percentage of the age group above 60 - 3 out of 5 treatments taken over - is striking. Each was exceptionally intelligent, displayed a somewhat monomaniac personality with a touch only of age-conditioned dementia; one had gone through a catatonic phase in his puberty without relapse until shortly after retirement as head doctor of a well-run country hospital. They were all highly endangered in their psychotic crisis, and I do not know wether the therapist's engagement, i.e. his readiness to use psychotherapy, draws some of its motivation from this struggle or wether this engagement was essential for success. To me there seems to be a connection which, however, I cannot prove. I am all the more interested in the experiences of the others regarding the fate of such late catatonics, especially the experience of the Lausanne School of Christian Müller (4) with its significant insights into the senility of schizophrenics.

The release of the manifest psychotic crisis, i.e. of the disease in the clinical sense, is of primary importance. In all cases there was such a release although emphasis on it varied during psychotherapy. I have the impression that younger psychotherapists consider it to be central to their work whereas older ones tend to integrate it into the development of the total personality. One may view all these releases as failure of attemts to emancipate, - emancipation here meaning liberation from a certain identity with the aim of setting up a new one. Since we can describe identity on the subject itself only vaguely, we usually grasp it by way of the world this identity creates for itself, especially in the form of the human relationships. Emancipation becomes visible as the person leaves his reference group and enters into another frame of reference, as when he leaves his mother, or later his family, and enters into a new partnership.

Emancipation is a passing through, which may fail in different phases: 1) in the final phase if the old relationship has been discontinued but a new one is either not accepted or deteriorates; following its basic element, we want to call it failure due to "rejection." 2) It may fail in the in-between phase of "searching". This is the case when the person tried to give up the old relationship without finding anything new meeting his expectations or if all new ties turn out to be disappointing; the return into the old situation, too - back into the family framwork after an attempt to escape - is nothing but a disappointing makeshift that drags under the weight of feelings of resignation. 3) we also find failures deriving from an ambivalent refusal to take advantage of an opportunity to emancipate; the personality experiences this new opportunity like a threatening "pressure", much like an asylum inmate who suddenly finds herself by an open door and is offered the chance to leave. Classification of these 3 categories shows clearly: catatonics usually founder due to "rejection", paranoiacs during the in-between phase of "searching" and procedural psychosis because of the threats resulting from "emancipatory pressure". With increasing age, release itself shifts into the realms of "search" and "emancipatory pressure" more and more while the personality seems to become ever more sensitive and apprehensive about risk of emancipation.

If psychotic crises mark breakdowns of emancipatory onsets, then psychotherapy of such conditions can best be judged from a viewpoint of how to help along emancipation. It grants encouragement, reduces exaggerated expectations and notions of value, and tries to remove fixing needs of "family balance"(5) through other gratifications, - or at least to distract from such needs. Under such protection and stimulation patients establish new identities and find new reference groups for themselves that accept and reinforce them. Sometimes this is the founding of a family, sometimes only a rather subtile relationship within a job situation or an ideologically close-knit group;

occasionally it may also be reintegration into the original family.
If none of these succeeds, setbacks are to be expected. Thus the
psychotherapist imparts his impulse - sometimes after a certain
interval - to a reference person or reference group which the patient
has found for himself. Such newly formed relationships can be kept
track of far more easily than inner psychic processes. By registering
these relationships I have therefore tried to establish of how much
help these psychotherapies really are. This does of course not permit
any conclusions regarding the art, technique, or value of the individual psychotherapy; it does, however, permit a type of social
profit calculation from a specific viewpoint. (Table 2)

   At first, it is striking that such a high number of patients -
89 out of 116 - were able to establish new relationships for themselves; it is also striking that of these, 29 were looking after
children (some of them admittedly only step children: some patients
married into families, one couple adopted a child). This stands in
striking contrast to the usual familiar image of the lonely schizophrenic without any social contacts; such absence of all contacts
I witnessed only 4 times. Evidently psychotherapy had accomplished
a high degree of social contact readiness or made, unconsciously,
a selection in this direction, - possib/ly both. Quantitative
differences between age groups barely existed: in each there was
only one eccentric lonely case and individuals who did not maintain
their partner relationship with a concrete person but, figuratively,
with a group; one of these individuals virtually ran a communal
living arrangement that seemed to work out fine. Upon closer scrutiny
of the families, however, it becomes obvious that the new formations
tend to become more unusual with increasing age, both as to the
choice of partners and the structure of the relationship: the former
patients appear to be the healthiest within the family framework
whereas the partners display physical or psychic defects and the
children cause problems. Often marriage partners show a high degree
of dependency and must taken care of or protected in one way or
another. The type of defect appears to me to be rather non-specific,
though in many cases they limit sexual activity to the point where
it is stopped upon mutual agreement. About a third of the patients,
among them a surprising number of men, idealize this situation;
two thirds are unsatisfied, emphasize their renunciation, or blame
their partners for this situation. Here the blame is oftentimes met
by a kind of humble dependency on the part of the partner. Other
patients keep bringing up the subject with their partners, provoke
ever new attempts at sexual contacts, half-hearted from the very
start, which they ridicule immediately and cynically; their "castra-
ting dominance" comes out clearly in the crude frankness with which
they talk about their own (from their viewpoint: about their partners)
intimate problems. In 25 marriages jealousy overshadowed the
relationship: the respective partners are accused of voyeurism or
unfaithfulness for no sound reason whatever and are even forced into
admitting acts of faithlessness they never comitted. Partners usually
bear all this with amazing patience. As a rule, they suffer from
some sexual disorder themselves and unconsciously relish such bragging
imputations. In 11 marriages it turned out they had actually been
unfaithful and dominate the partner through sado-masochistic dependency. Such situations often include children who were conceived

after attempts to break out were thwarted. The drama of such a
situation does not trigger out new bouts of disease in any case, but
the birth of another child has done exactly that in 2 cases. I interpret this to mean that the sado-masochistic mock separations are
understood by both partners as such and they really lack the desire
for emancipation; conversely, the birth of a child releases genuine
desire to run off with this new partner and to emancipate from the
identity of a girl-friend to motherhood. Sometimes this may happen
when the relationship to the aggressive individual continues, who,
aware of his partner's loss of feelings for him, never fails to make
the child the pawn of an ensuing power struggle. Although the
children are well taken care of by the formerly psychotic mother,
by now suffering from masochism, it is strangely enough the father
they cling to, - even if he treats them downright callously, alter-
nately tearing them away from and pushing them toward their mother.
Boys tend to break out of family during puberty, while girls have
more problems and are exposed to psychic break-down. (Table 3)

Marital crises of the late paranoid type often carry with them
long histories of mutual accusations of jealousy. Though divorce is
discussed at great length by both partners, it is rarely carried
through without an outside impetus; although lack of faithfulness
is the perennial subject, an almost absurd degree of faithfulness
prevails in actual behavior: this is obviously based on severe
sexual insecurity, which is balanced by these phantasies of jealousy;
these phantasies are therefore indispensable. The long history of
the disease is concealed behind a wall of common intimacy. The
psychotic, and therefore also the social, crisis comes about only
through changes in the balance within the family such as through
attempts to emancipate on the part of the only child or professional-
ly conditioned changes of life-style. These cause the relationship
between the partners to undergo certain shifts while actually com-
patitive relationships trigger causes only rarely. Great sensitivity
prevails concerning the correct distance between partners. It also
determines the direction of psychotherapy; two alternatives emerge:
1) the psychotherapist makes possible the child's emancipation by
assuming the transfer relationship, but he does not liberate partners
from clutching each other. Social balance is reestablished, but the
manner of the relationship - its foundation on figments of the
imagination and on reproaches - is dragged on. 2) Rarely and
usually with younger partners, separation follows. Even if he is not
aware of it, the partner's need for security is borne by the therapist without whose help partners could not separate. The weaker part
still needs to overcome the phase of discouragement in order to be
able to enter into a new situation later on. For this phase, which
lasts at least six months, group therapy is vastly superior to individual therapy. While in a group the therapist only has to see to it
that no fixation develops in the "omega-position", he is exposed
to such strong clutching by the totally destabilized patient taking
individual therapy that he begins to fight his patient off, thus
immediately triggering delusions in him. Should the therapy then be
broken off entirely, the situation resembles one caused by a partner
who has followed the call of another love relationship. The dis-
couraged patient who returns to his parental home is headed for

trouble proportunately to the degree loving care is showered over him. Younger people tend to tie themselves to their mothers in a regressive-symbiotic way and find themselves hopelessly exposed to"emancipatory pressures" at their mother's death. Older people find shelter with older brothers and sisters where they lead exploited lives. In marital situations, too, former patients sometimes lead exploited lives, usually with considerably older partners and without children. In our study I would cite 26 women as leading such exploited lives within families of relatives or with partners. I am deliberately saying that it is I who regards them as exploited because they have never complained. It is therefore obviously that society seems to offer this chance for stabilization only to women reintegrated into families of relatives.

Summing up this study of 116 psychotherapeutically treated schizophrenics with a katamnesis of 3-30 years, we may say that the psychotherapeutical approach was effective in all age groups and improved contact readiness decisively so that the above-mentioned number of new relationships could come about. Isolation could be pushed back. Unusual relationships increased proportionately to the age at which treatment was first administered - both with regard to choice of partners and the type of relationship entered into. This can only partly be explained by the greater difficulties of finding partners in more advanced years. It must be taken into consideration that, as age increases, the psychotherapeutic help toward emancipation tends to be arrested in the phase of encouragement and that such help only strives toward structural changes without attaining them. As a result, this task is transferred onto the partnership which, however, cannot cope with it but adjusts to the structural characteristics, thereby reinforcing them; socially speaking, however, these structural characteristics are defused, the patient's live is going on rather adapted to social live. In terms of psychohygiene, such marital situations must be viewed as communal risks with a tendency to shift problems to the children involved.

REFERENCES

1. Boszormenyi-Nagy,I and Sparks,G.: The invisible loyalities. Harper & Row, New York 1973
2. Erikson,E.H.: Kindheit und Gesellschaft. Pan-Verl.,Zürich 1957
3. Kaufmann,L.: Familie,Kommunikation,Psychose.Huber-Verl.Bern 1972
4. Müller,Chr.: Über d.Senium der Schizophrenen.Karger-Verl.,Basel1959
5. Schindler,R.:Bifocal Group Therapy. In: Progress in Psychotherapy, p176-186,Editors:Massermann-Moreno,New York 1958
6.   "   :Bifokale Familientherapie. In:Familie und seelische Krankheit,p.216-235,Editors:Richter-Strotzka-Willi, Rowohlt-Verl.Hamburg 1976
7.   "   :Das psychodynamische Problem beim sog.schizophr.Defekt. II.Int.Sympos.zur Psychother.d.Schiz.,Proc.Bd.2,1960
8.   "   :Der pseudodement-euphorische Abwandlungstyp der Schizophrenie.Wr.Z.f.Nervenheilkund u.Grenzq.XXIV,70,1966
9.   "   :Rezidivverhütung im Zeitalter von Depotneuroleptika und sozialer Psychiatrie. Nervenarzt 47,347-350, 1976
10. Selvini Palazzoli,M.u.Mitarb.:Paradoxon und Gegenparadoxon. Klett-Verl.Stuttgart 1977

11. Stierlin,H.: Familie und Schizophrenie.Nervenarzt 34,495, 1963
12.   "   : Eltern und Kinder im Prozess der Ablösung. Suhrkamp-Verl.Frankfurt,1975
13. Watzlawick,P.-Beavin,J.H.-Jackson,D.D.:Menschliche Kommunikation. 4.Aufl.Huber-Verl.Bern,Stuttgart,Wien 1974
14. Watzlawick,P.-Weakland,J.H.-Fisch,R.:Lösungen zur Theorie und Praxis menschlichen Wandels.Huber-Verl.Bern,Stuttg.,Wien 1974

TABLE 1.

Age-group	Number	Catatonic	Paranoid	Procedural	Rejection	Search	Emancipatory Pressure
15-30	50	7			6	1	--
			38		13	20	5
				5	-	1	4
30-45	37	2			2	-	-
			34		12	15	7
				1	-	-	1
45-60	24	1			1	-	-
			21		2	8	11
				2	-	-	2
60-75	5	3			-	2	1
			2		-	-	2
				-	-	-	-
Sum.:	116	13	95	8	36	47	34

Column headers grouped: Clinical Development (Catatonic, Paranoid, Procedural); Release (Rejection, Search, Emancipatory Pressure).

TABLE 2.

Age-group		undisturbed	Children defective		Transfered Relationship	within family	isolated
15-30	Cat.:	5	1	4	1	-	-
	Par.:	17	12	9	7	2	-
	Proc.:	-	2	1	-	2	1
30-45	Cat.:	1	1	-	-	-	-
	Par.:	8	17	5	5	3	1
	Proc.:	-	1	-	-	-	-
45-60	Cat.:	-	1	-	-	-	-
	Par.:	3	18	7	-	-	-
	Proc.:	-	-	-	1	-	1
60-75	Cat.:	1	1	2	1	-	-
	Par.:	-	1	1	-	-	1
	Proc.:	-	-	-	-	-	-
Sum:		35	54	29	15	7	4

Choice of partners: undisturbed, Children defective, Transfered Relationship, within family, isolated.

TABLE 3.

Type of Relationship

Age-Gr.	undisturbed	Castrating	Jealous	sado-masochistic	exploited
15-30	14	12	8	5	10
30-45	8	8	9	3	9
45-60	-	7	7	3	6
60-75	-	3	1	-	1

PSYCHODYNAMICS OF OCCUPATION DEVELOPMENT IN 40 SCHIZOPHRENICS

Professor Dr. Dr. Paul Matussek
Director of the Research Center for Psychopathology and Psychotherapy in the Max-Planck-Society

The importance of occupational rehabilitation of the patients is being increasingly stressed in the treatment of schizophrenics. This may be due to a considerably broadened spectrum of social-psychiatric measures, on the one hand, and to the inadequacy of purely medicinal therapy on the other. However, occupational rehabilitation programs require an improved and differentiated knowledge of occupational capability, structure of management, and behavior in the working situation of these patients, as has been pointed out especially by Blankenburg (1970). Wing et al. (1964) emphasized that prepsychotic efficiency and social adaptability, to which older psychiatry paid too little attention, must also be taken into account. The ability to work was used as a rough standard for measuring improvement and making a diagnosis (Kraepelin 1913). Inability to work was itself considered an indication for the incurability of schizophrenia.

Recent investigations of various orientations offer a subtler picture. Bleuler (1972) points out long term courses of schizophrenics to be different, which take into account the most various models of occupational development and integration. Matussek and Triebel (1974) classify the group of schizophrenics from a psychodynamic point of view and refer to the relationships experienced in the family, psycho-social adaptation forms, occupational achievement and psychotherapeutic measures. Occupational reintegration can neither be separated from the kind of psychosis nor from the psychodynamics of schizophrenics' past history. Bovensiepen (1973) has analysed this relationship in detail in 40 schizophrenics in a dissertation.

DATA COLLECTION AND STATISTIC CALCULATION

The data for personal history were obtained by means of a semi-structured interview-scheme. The evaluation of the interviews resulted in a total of 1,421 dichotomized indications per patient. Distribution of the indications is numerically as follows, with respect to the areas identified: mother (42), father (45), interaction of parents (36), sibling relationships (29), sexuality and partnership (54), accomplishment level of family (51), pursuit of vocation (454), symptoms (267), therapy (26).

In order to obtain clinically identifiable types, Q-Analysis was carried out. Six factors were extracted by means of the Main-Component-Method. The number was determined according to the Screen-Test Gaensslen and Schubö (1973)

and rotated according to Varimax-Principles. The 6 factors comprise 52.7 %
of total variance with an intrinsic value of .97. The relative variance-proportion
explained by these factors is 25 % for Factor I, 20.5 % for Factor II, 19.3 %
for Factor III, 15 % for Factor IV, 13 % for Factor V, 7.2 % for Factor VI. The
split-half-reliabilities are correlations of factor-proportions which consisted of
2 accidentally extracted halves of the probands and which had to be corrected
according to the Spearman-Brown-formula for the total factor. The values are
.70 for Factor I, .60 for Factor II, .50 for Factor III, .54 for Factor IV, .53
for Factor V, .20 for Factor VI, respectively. Noteworthy is that Factor VI
shows a comparatively small value of variance fraction and split-half-reliabilities. The clinical Type VI corresponding to this factor will, therefore, receive
little attention in our description. As the result, 6 clinical types are described,
as they came out of computed factor-values of the individual indication (Hally
and Risberg 1971).

RESULTS

As with all types, irrespective of whether they are obtained intuitively
or empirically, the pure type is met only in rare cases. Nevertheless, in order
to enliven the type by means of a particular nomenclature and, by doing so, to
facilitate comparison in actual practice, the types will be named not only by
numbers but also on the basis of particularly significant mechanisms, even though
these labels by no means cover all the peculiarities, and the expression for some
representatives is certainly too drastic.

Typ I: The Occupation-dependent

The predominantly male patients feel neglected by their mother during
childhood but live with her. Most of them are separated from their rather
sociable fathers. They are mostly the youngest of all siblings and have a pro-
nouncedly cordial relations with their brothers and sisters, most of whom are
married. After primary school, like their father, such patients usually take up
a skilled trade. They finish their apprenticeship as clerk, technician or plumber
within the required time. They go to work willingly and can identify themselves
with the required achievement norm, and are very much concerned with earning
accordingly. These patients become financially independent. Before the outbreak of psychosis, they seldom change their job or occupation, are cooperative and good in team work, and prefer to work in a space together with many
others. They seek to resolve their conflicts through discussion with the colleagues of same sex. Outside their occupations, they are interested above all in
sports.

The illness begins acutely and assumes the course of "propulsive form".
When the patients first become psychotically susceptible to crises, they felt
strongly dissatisfied with the working atmosphere on the job. Despite the fact
that they work steadily, conflicts with their male colleagues become very
apparent. The patients blame the difficulties at work on external conditions,

feel insufficiantly appreciated and strive for a higher position with better income. Despite their illness, they remain financially independent by virtue of their own work. If they remain dissatisfied with their work, they begin to change their job more often. Contacts with fellow colleagues drop off. Despite hallucinations and delusions, social competence in long run is maintained. The psychotic symptoms suggest a tendency towards introverted movement. Delusions of being poisoned as well as delusions of persecution and of being influenced appear at times. The delusion is encapsulated, so that the symptom is difficult for outsiders to recognize. The mood is sometimes depressive, yet not self-destructive. Sometimes, it comes to thought-deprivation and thought-confusion.

Comments

This type is represented by those patients who stay with simple jobs, but as constant workers, quite competent and thoroughly conscientious of own occupational achievement. These patients seem to have received little affection from their parents, but all the more from siblings as they are the youngest. When it comes to rivalry at work, they can assert themselves at first, and a friendly situation at work is the one with which they are more familiar and which they aim at. Because of the strong emotional involvement in this field, they are also most vulnerable here. This is whown also in problems of rivalry at work which act as a trigger on the outbreak of psychosis. They obtain their job satisfaction through direct and quick recognition by their colleagues. Therefore, they try to hold their position in the world through solid performance at work.

Preference is given to practical activities, of which the use is immediately evident and through which direct feed-back regarding success or failure can be obtained. At the same time, work is the main source of their self-esteem. Failure at work or interruption of work in a critical period produces intolerable dependence. To avoid this, patients continue working even under strong "psychotic pressure". The fact that these patients can lean on the pattern of their fathers in occupational identity, as well as the partial intactness of ego-functions that makes possible separation of the delusional world from the experience of reality, are considered to be favourable for prognosis. When the patient undergoes psychiatric or psychotherapeutic treatment, this phenomenon should be taken into account for the reason that one brings these patients back as rapidly as possible into a work and/or psychotherapeutic group. These patients should be discharged from the clinic quickly, and their successful occupational activity should be confirmed. Individual psychotherapy will be necessary only in a few cases.

Type II: Highly talented victim

These patients are predominantly female and are the eldest of the siblings. They are the outspoken favourites of the mother who is experienced as intensely protective. The mother looks after her constantly and tries to further her daughter's dependence through excessive solicitude. The father is experienced as strong and consistent. His affection seems to dwindle when the daughter fails to achieve. The parents' marriage is experienced as lacking in feeling. The mother domineers in the family.

This type is characterized by achievement in school which is far above average in almost all subjects. These patients are especially interested in fine arts. Female patients prefer male teachers rather than female. The positive-transference relation to the male teacher plays an important role as a motivation to learning. A greater part of the patients begin their studies at college, whereby not rarely social and charitable motives determine their choice of occupation. At the first manifestation of psychosis, some of them are still in training for their occupation. Besides commercial employee, many of them are teachers of a wide variety of subjects.

In their work, they seek a great deal of contact with people and are relatively adjustable and flexible here. They work correctly and seldom have conflicts with colleagues of the opposite sex. They are extremely ambitious in pursuing their high intellectual and social goals. For this very reason, however, they become isolated outside their field of work. The disease breaks out acutely and develops propulsively. The female patients are largely free of symptoms between psychotic episodes, yet their work achievement level drops sharply. They are no longer able to be active in the occupations learned and to support themselves independently.

Hallucinations, especially expansive delusions such as of love, of grandeur or religion, and delusions of peacemaker, charakterize the psychotic symptoms. An elated, manic mood predominates, not rarely combined with compulsion to talk and constant search for contact. Aggression is directed not against others but against themselves and occasionally manifests itself in suicidal thoughts.

Comments

Despite very good premorbid social ability, these patients with predominantly above-average talent of type II are unable to work permanently. As the oldest child and the mother's favourite, they successfully fulfill the role of the ideal child in their adolescence. Through their favoured situation in the family, they do not learn, however, to face the problems of rivalry or to assert themselves aggressively, either with their siblings or later with their fellow-workers. As Binswanger (1955) described in the case "Ellen West", they seek their occupational satisfaction in "human love driven by ambition". The female patients who identify largely with their mothers try to overcome through projection their own vulnerability and disturbed interpersonal relations by altruistic abandon of drive-demands and the accompanying commitment. The background of this behaviour is a very emotional relationship to the mother and identification with the protecting and bestowing aspect of the mother who is experienced as over-solicitous.

This constellation has, despite some advantages for the development of certain ego-functions, the great disadvantage of promoting a clinging, symbiotic relation with the mother. Relations with men are then only possible at the level of the achievement, as these patients had learned from their fathers. Thus, the idea that work could be the source and the object of the struggle for possessions and of livelihood is shut off from consciousness by denial. Instead, the occupation is so ideologically and narcissistically over-emphasized that, in pursuing it, the patients are out of touch with reality and with the concrete world.

If the illusionary ideas are confronted with reality when the patient enters the practical world of work, she withdraws from real relations, and the illusionary ideas are restored in a distorted form in the delusion. Because of the strong narcissistic susceptibility to disease, psychotherapy for such female patients should begin with individual therapy at first and end with a combined individual and group psychotherapy. The development and enforcement of reality-testing ego-functions should be observed with special attention.

Type III: Occupation-negativist

The patients who are predominantly male almost always live separated from their fathers between the age of 5 and 15 years. Both parents are absorbed in their own occupations. These patients feel neglected during their childhood. Even in cases in which they are the only child, they do not experience the desired affection of at least one of their parents. Their fathers are ambiguous towards the patients. After the initially average level of school achievement, the level of achievement at school drops to below average following puberty. In school, they are interested above all in fine arts and reject mathematics and natural sciences.

It is not surprising that these patients, who are already recognized by marked aloofness in the schools, feel different from the others and often strongly oppose the usual achievement norms, rarely being able to complete vocational or professional training and support themselves. Once they do take up work, however, they are uninterested in the wage which is not high in any case. Yet, in return, they want to be "creative" and to realize their "childhood dream". In their jobs, they prefer places where they can work alone, and feel very much disturbed by noises, telephone or contact. Acoustically encapsulating themselves, they appear to develop neither positively not negatively in terms of emotional relations with their colleagues.

Prior to manifestation of the psychosis, work disturbance is revealed above all in form of unpunctuality, loss of interest and frequent absence from work, openly expressed dissatisfaction with their occupational situation and by own inordinate demands. Upon outbreak of the psychosis, they are failures at work and totally isolated. The psychosis develops slowly for the most part, but takes a propulsive course. The psychosis itself is characterized by a lack of productive symptoms. These patients give the impression of an encapsulating, emotionally blunted personality. Their interests and activities outside work fall off markedly. The disease becomes chronic, relieved by phases of adjustment to reality in which simple, occasional jobs are pursued. The rather inhibited-aggressive patients frequently suffer depressions and attempt suicide.

Comments

Contrary to the patients of type I and II who strive intensively for achievement, the patients of type III (and of type IV) are characterized by a marked inhibition of achievement, or, to be more precise, by achievement-negativism. True, the course of this schizoprenia is fairly free of clinical symptoms; but the patients are unable to work well long before the psychosis manifests itself first. More clearly still than in type I, these patients seem to have experienced little affection from their parents. Contrary to tpye I, they cannot compensate for this lack even by close sibling relations. They receive little approval from their parents. The father, frequently absend during the school period, takes a "double-bind" attitude towards these patients (Bateson et al. 1956), which exerts crippling effect on the development of initiative.

According to Erikson, school age is the period in which the child develops "identification with tasks" and by virtue thereof a sense of self-confirmation develops, which is confirmed in addition through identification with parental roles (Erikson 1970). There seems to be a causal relation between the work-block described above, which can increase to achievement-negativism, and these processes. Weak libidinous possession of the parental relation hinders the development of sufficient ego-strength as well as identification with socio-cultural achievement norms. This leads to the inability to concentrate energy on given tasks and to meet society's expectations regarding achievement. They withdraw negativistically and develop an overheightened demand for own achievement, which, as in type II, reveals itself in illusionary, unrealistic expectations about work.

Much more strongly inhibited than types I and II, in their expansive drive, they are unable to realize even a fragment of their ideas, either in the reality or in the psychosis. In order to liberate these patients from their isolation, an attempt can be made in group therapy to introduce identification with the goals of their peers. Individual psychotherapy often fails due to the patients' negativistic attitude.

Type IV: Occupation anxious

These patients, who are predominately female, practically never live apart from the mother. The mother is experienced as ambivalent. The later patients feel that, on the one hand, she urged them into the role of an adult too early and that, on the oiher hand, they were forced into strong dependency through permanent guardianship. The mother who is experienced as being courageous and capable of achievement supervises uninterruptedly. With the father, an oppressed feeling dominates. As to the education of these patients, the parents are experienced as being at variance.

These patients are the youngest of the siblings who attain occupational positions better than the patients. They originate from the upper middle class. Both parents work. In these patients, the failure in achievement is already manifest at the beginning of schooling. They frequently have feelings of failure in school, suffer anxiety over examinations and, despite massive support from their parents, do not finish school or professional training regularly.

Shy and lacking initiative, they have strong feelings of rivalry, especially with their sisters. They are irresolute in their choice of work and let their parents force them into activities to which they are not equal. They attempt work in social fields as well as in artscrafts, technical or administrative occupations. The mother is indefatigable in her ambition and in massive supply of help for the occupational progress of those who later become ill.

They work awkwardly and slowly. They often allow their thoughts to wander and only reluctantly engage in detailed work. Their self-esteem in terms of work depends strongly on kind acknowledgement from male superiors. The slightest criticism discourages them and activates depressive moods. The atmosphere at work bothers them little. They have no interpersonal contacts at work or privately. In the majority of the patients, the psychosis develops slowly between the age of 17 and 20 and becomes chronic. Psychotic symptoms which flare up repeatedly promote the deficient achievements which consist mainly of poor concentration, slower working manner, inability to make decisions, and lack of ability to make adjustments or changes. The patients respond to each failure with an increased desire to return to the parents' home. During their acute psychotic attack, they develop especially a delusion of love, delusional ideas with sexual contents, and also occasionally ideas of impoverishment, which can change into a manic mood. States of anxiety are frequent. The formal flow of thought is characterized by the disconnection of thought and the thought-deprivation.

Comments

This type is represented by the patients who are unable to pursue any long-lasting occupational activity. Together with type III, the patients of this type have the worst prognosis of all 6 types. In contrast to types II and III, these patients develop no solid ideals at the occupational level either. Inferior in performance, from childhood on, to the elder siblings who are successful at work, they dare not even get involved in rivalrous confrontations with colleagues. They are extremely unsure of themselves and anxious when it comes to achievement, and this has markedly phobic character during education (school anxiety).

The "double-bind" attitude of the domineering mother and the high level of parental demand promote the uncertainty of these female patients in their relations with colleagues ("How should I behave in relation to others?") and make them agents of parental demands. If the female patients of type II still restore the "Great-Self" in delusional form, delusion of love and of impoverishment could be considered in these patients as an expression of profound object-loss anxiety. Because of strong rivalry anxiety, a group therapy, too, is not advisable at first. Rather, building-up a practical, realistic behavior pattern should be attempted in careful individual therapy. These female patients can accept clear-cut and direct suggestions from the therapist and, protected by an idealizing transference, can slowly refill the deficit in their ego functions.

Type V: The business functionary

The patients, who are predominantly male are the favorite child of the mother who, mostly depressive in mood, is weak and little consistent to them. The introverted and contact-weak father is very ambitious and active as to the career of his son. Both parents share the patient's upbringing, but the father has the last word. The patients almost never live separated from the father. A particularly characteristic of the family atmosphere is the distinctly hostile attitude of both parents towards sexuality.

Pushed by the father, the patients, after finishing primary, middle or high school, take up work in a skilled trade like their father and aim at career-oriented positions. They work as bank employees, railway officers, post-office workers or forestry officers. They become financially independent. Their achievements are average, as they were in school. The patients are noted in school as being contact-weak and aloof who learn particularly out of fear of male teachers.

In their jobs, they lay special value on punctuality and correctness, avoid speaking about private affairs, rarely have conflicts with the superiors or co-workers and hardly ever see their colleagues outside work. If they do come into conflict with superiors, the patients are aggressive-inhibited and maintain "attitude" outsidedly. They prefer to work with colleagues of the same sex. They seek occupation fields with a clearly defined work order which leave little margin for initiative and require the least adaptability and flexibility. The patients succeed for a relatively long time in maintaining the over-flexible façade of adjustment. The disease becomes manifest generally after 30 years of age. It develops slowly.

Upon manifestation of the psychosis, it becomes clear that the patients have lost their pleasure and satisfaction in their work, feel exploited in their work and too little assured and appreciated in their activity. However, they cannot articulate this beforehand. The disease assumes a chronic course in which the work performance declines considerably. The patients remain capable of simple work which does not correspond to their education. They are able to earn their livelihood independently, however. Acute psychotic phases are rare. Inactivity, depressive mood, aggressive inhibitedness and eccentricity are the main features of these deficit-symptoms. During acute psychotic phases, ideas of guilt, delusional ideas with sexual and homosexual contents, occasionally also delusions of persecution, appear. However, it does not reach a point where formal thought patterns are distrurbed.

Comments

The patients characterized by type V develop, like those of type II, a stable social competence premorbidly, yet after the outbreak of psychosis suffer a serious drop in their performance level at work. For them, earnings and their work per se are not so much the main source of their self-esteem and satisfaction than the need for security and the social adaptation in society. Seen from the background of family dynamics, the patients reject their fathers as rivals. They identify themselves with the father's restrictive super-ego. By doing so, they internalize the parental achievement ideal with its compulsive-restrictive character. The lack of formal disturbances in thinking points to the relative intactness of the ego-functions and makes it possible to maintain a comparatively steady occupational adaptation for a long time.

Only in the psychosis is the archaically sadistic aspect of the super-ego projected onto men (delusion of guilt, homosexual delusions) for the first time. Corresponding to the forcibly nuanced achievement structure which is marked by compulsion, they behave over-flexibly, anxious-exact and aggressive-inhibited in relations with colleagues. They seek working situations which meet their compulsive structure, so that they can work adjustedly for a relatively long period. Occupational-therapeutically oriented rehabilitation programs should come first for these patients. Only in some individual cases would psychotherapeutic measures in the narrow sense be suitable, whereby what matters finally is to work through the restrictive aspects of the super-ego and consequently to free the way for a late ripening of the ego.

Type VI: Occupation ascender

As the variance fraction of 7.2 % in this factor is relatively small, and what is "typical" can thus only be presumed according to the tendency, a short sketch of some features should suffice.

Type VI contains both male and female patients who originate from families in which the marriage of the parents is disorganized, and quarrels occur frequently. Prior to the manifestation of the psychosis, the patients change their occupations and jobs frequently and show moderate achievement at work; nevertheless, they can earn their livelihood by themselves. Among them, we find commercial employees, female boutique owners, bankers and industrial merchants. The psychosis may begin acutely or insidiously, but develops propulsively. In some patients, the psychosis breaks out after starting new vocational training or taking up new work, while in others the trigger is the failure of a partner relationship.

During acute psychotic phases, delusions of persecution and of self-cure are frequently encountered. Just as frequently, the patients feel threatened with becoming annihilated. They are hyper-active. The intense aggressiveness is directed either against other, specific persons or against the patients themselves in form of suicidal thoughts. In the symptom-free phases, however, the patients are capable repeatedly of integrating themselves well occupationally and socially. The performance at work tends to improve in the course of the disease.

Comments

The family situation in this type corresponds to that of the "broken home". This is considered as prognostically favourable, according to Neumann and Matussek (1966). The psychotic ideas of self-cure as well as the actively preserved aggressiveness which derails only in the psychosis show further that these patients' splits are not "eternalized". They are, therefore, the only type in which the achievement curve even goes up. These patients will respond to differentiated, analytically-oriented psychotherapy most favourably. The ascendence of the occupational achievement level in schizophrenics, which cannot be observed in any case with more custodial, medicinal or other psychodynamically unspecific therapy, can presumably be explained also only by the application of psychotherapy.

DISCUSSION

In this investigation, fundamental hypotheses could not be tested and answered conclusively. Because of the small study material to begin with, that was not possible. Yet our hypothesis, already put forth in an earlier work, that the psychodynamically meaningful courseforms of life history are also to be found in schizophrenics, is reconfirmed, and this especially in the peculiarities of quite diverse occupational courses in the schizophrenics, each with "specific" difficulties of his own.

The problems which arise in selecting a vocation, in work itself, on the job, or in the family, or else in attempts at rehabilitation, cannot be judged separately from the events in the patient's life in its entirety. What follows as the important practical consequence is that, as soon as the clinical state of the patients permits, a detailed psychodynamically-oriented anamnesis should be obtained. In the anamnesis, lines of interpretation can be found which reveal connections between the characteristics of parent- and sibling-relations, of the way in which the patient comes to grips with work and achievement, as well as the characteristics of the symptoms. The types of courses here described or similar ones described by Matussek and Triebel (1974) could be used here as models.

In summarizing, therefore, let us point out the various psychodynamic connections once again, which in our opinion play a role in the behaviour of the schizophrenics in their chosen field of work and on the job. The constellation of the personal and interpersonal situation at the place where the patient works is frequently that of the old situation in terms of family dynamics, in which the patient grew up. If the sibling relation is still heavily invested with libidinal or aggressive energy, this is considered favourable for the prognosis and fruitful in terms of therapy. Achievement-demand as well as occupational identity are moulded strongly by father or mother or both parents, content-wise and quanti- tatively. Parental behaviour which is strongly restrictive and keeps the patient dependent fosters the development of illusionary ideas and excessively high expectations regarding work. They thus increase narcissistic vulnerability. The combination of the lack of affection, ambivalent behavior on the part of the parents and high achievement-demand seem to have a particularly inhibitive effect on achievement. A special form of compensation of the patient's inability to establish social relationships lies in his turning to vocations which require social commitment. In occupational rehabilitation should also be borne in mind to what extend the kind of work acts as temptation- or refusal-situation under drive-dynamic view point and makes corresponding drive- and/or defence-field labile. Along with other factors, the extent to which the occupational situation played a role in the outbreak of the psychosis should not be overlooked.

More differentiated indicative positions can presumably be obtained for the various therapeutic and rehabilitative measures with the help of the biographical anamnesis in individual cases. This can be decisive for the best possible referral of the patients by the psychiatrist to individual therapists who work analytically, group psychotherapists, social psychiatrists, or to the job site. The present investigation and that of Matussek and Triebel (1974) delineate clearly what kinds of schizophrenics should best be treated with which emphases by which therapists.

Bateson, G., Jackson, D.D., Haley, J., Weakland, J.H.:
Towards a theory of schizophrenia. Behav. Sci. 1, 251-264 (1956).

Binswanger, L.: Schizophrenie. Pfullingen: Neske 1957.

Blankenburg, W.: Zur Leistungsstruktur bei chronischen endogenen
Psychosen. Nervenarzt 41, 577-587 (1970).

Bleuler, M.: Die schizophrenen Geistesstörungen im Lichte lang-
jähriger Kranken- und Familiengeschichten. Stuttgart: Thieme 1972.

Bolte, K.M., Kappe, D., Neidhardt, F.: Soziale Schichtung.
Opladen: Leske 1966.

Bovensiepen, G.: Lebensgeschichte und berufliche Leistung bei
40 Schizophrenen (eine faktorenanalytische Untersuchung). Dissertation.
Technische Universität München 1975.

Bromet, E., Harrow, M., Tucker, G.J.: Factors related in shortterm
prognosis in schizophrenia and depression. Arch.gen.Psychiat. 25,
148-154 (1971).

Erikson, E.H. : Jugend und Krise. Die Psychodynamik im sozialen
Wandel. Stuttgart: Klett 1970.

Gaensslen, H., Schubö, W.: Einfach und komplexe statistische
Analyse . München: Ernst Reinhard 1973.

Gittleman-Klein, R., Klein, D.: Premorbid social adjustment and
prognosis in schizophrenia. J.psychiat.Res. 7, 35-53 (1969).

Harrow, M., Tucker, G.J., Bromet, E.: Short-term prognosis of
schizophrenic patients. Arch.gen.Psychiat. 4, 195-202 (1969).

Harrow, M., Bromet, E., Quinlan, D.: Predictors of posthospital
adjustment in schizophrenia. J.nerv.ment. Dis. 158, 25-36 (1974).

Holley, J.W., Guilford, J.P.: A note on the G-Index of Agreement . Ed.and.Psychol.Meas. 24, 749-753 (1964).

Holley, J.W., Sjöberg, L.: Some Characteristics of the G-Index
of Agreement. Mult.Beh.Res. 3, 107-114 (1968).

Holley, J. W., Risberg, J.: An analytical technique for obtaining
differential diagnoses on the basis of clinical data. Psycho.Res.Bull 11,
Lund University, Sweden 1971.

Kraepelin, E.: Psychiatrie. Ein Lehrbuch für Studierende und Ärzte,
Bd. III, 2. Teil, 8 . Aufl. Leipzig: Barth 1913.

Lienert, G.H.: Testaufbau und Testanalyse. Weinheim: Beltz 1967.

Matussek, P., Triebel, A.: Die Wirksamkeit der Psychotherapie bei
44 Schizophrenen. Nervenarzt 45, 569-575 (1974).

Neumann, Ch., Matussek, P.: Prognostische Kriterien bei der
Psychotherapie schizophrener Psychosen. Z.Psychother.med.Psychol.
16, 51 (1966).

Pollack, M., Levenstein, S., Klein, D.F.: A three-year posthospital
follow-up of adolescent and adult schizophrenics. Amer.J.Orthopsychiat.
38, 94-109 (1968).

Rosen, B., Klein, D.F., Levenstein, S., Shahaniar, S.P.: Social
competence and posthospital outcome. Arch.gen.Psychiat. 19, 165-
170 (1968).

Strauss, J.S., Carpenter jr. W.T.: The prediction of outcome in schizophrenia. II. Charcateristics of outcojme. Arch.Gen.Psychiat. 27, 739-746 (1972).

Wing, J.K., Monk, E.M., Brown, G.W., Carstairs, G.M.: Morbidity in the community of schizophrenic patients. discharged from London mental hospitals in 1959. Brit.J.Psychiat. 110, 10-21 (1964).

Ziegler, E., Philips, L.: Social effictiveness and symptomatic behaviors. J.abnorm.soc.Psychol. 61, 231-238 (1960).

Ziegler, E., Phillips, L.: Social competence and outcome in psychiatric disorder. J.abnorm.soc.Psychol. 63, 264-271 (1961).

THE ROLE OF THE FATHER IN THE FAMILY THERAPY OF A

SCHIZOPHRENIC

Hermann Lang and Satuila Stierlin

Abteilung Klinische Psychopathologie der Psychiatrischen Klinik der Universität Heidelberg; and Heidelberger Arbeitsgruppe für Familientherapie, Heidelberg, Federal Republic of Germany

In an interview with the house physician on the day after he had been admitted to the psychiatric clinic Gerd K., a secondary school boy aged 18, described himself as "sensitive, peaceable, and easily hurt", but when his parents arrived for their first visit Gerd exploded in foul abuse. "You dirty swine", he stormed at his father, "you twister, you lousy liar, you need your prick cut off". When the father replied that he thought he was right to have had Gerd admitted to hospital to prevent him meeting with the Heidelberg "King of Rock" and the mother added that Gerd seemed to be getting into bad ways, the boy roared at her, "You old cunt". She whimpered tearfully that he had always been such a good boy and wasn't he even now a senior altar server. The son raved on "Shut up. I'll kill the pair of you. I'll rip your cunt apart so a baby'll jump out. Go and fuck yourself you old cunt".

Compare this outburst, which was further interlarded with murder threats against his father, with an extract from the fifth therapeutic session with the family:

Mother: "Things are just fine with us now - really relaxed and straightforward".

Father: "Now when our son has problems he comes to me".

Son: "There's a much better atmosphere at home now. It's like this: when I came back from the course, the Siddhi Course on Transcendental Meditation, I realized how I'd been trying in so many ways to play my father up. And I knew what I was getting at then. And when I was with my friend Dagmar and suspected that she had had illicit sex relations with her grandfather when she was 13: I'd already filed a report on her and I wanted to see exactly what was happening in that family so as to get it sorted out"

When the therapists remarked that Gerd himself seemed to be acting like a family therapist now, but that it was hard to understand what provoking his father had to do with his relationship with his girl friend, Gerd K. replied:

Son: "I had to make my father take a tough line with me. I had to make him really put me through it".

Father: "And he did. The crunch came when he came back from
        the course".
Son: "My father should have said that he is boss here.
        He must be able to get tough. I fixed it that he
        got real mad. It wasn't enough though that he got
        so mad at me. Then I had to go so far that he might
        have got the gun out and had a go. That was kind of
        tricky. But I had to go that far with him".

Later in the interview the son remarked:

Son: "I can share things with others now - with my par-
        ents. It was different then, I didn't know that
        people's lives depend on this (the father's) work.
        The problems my father has in his business - well,
        a boss might have them! I've got my problems at
        school and my mother's in the middle. She's a house-
        wife - can't take responsibility like us two.
Mother: "The therapy's really helped".

To avoid misunderstanding, we must here point out that this
apparent happy ending to a family therapeutic idyll occurred
before the aggressive outburst described initially.
    These extracts indicate that the relationship with the
parents is clearly of primary importance. The passage from
family therapy mainly concerns the relationship with the
father. What the patient described-namely, that he believed
that the father was acting in earnest when he threatened to
reach for the loaded weapon and that from this action followed a significant change in family life and also in the
behavior of the son - we ourselves observed in the first
five sessions. In fact, when the father lost his reserve and
became a "strong father", the son's manic logorrhoea, which
often amounted to a state of mental confusion, immediately
improved. The position of the father has central significance
in this form of therapy and, of course, particularly in this
case of hebephrenia.
    Psychodynamic thinking finds such establishment of roles
neither selfevident nor relavant; it holds that experiences
of earliest childhood provide a sufficient etiological agent
for schizophrenic illness; obviously then the relationship
with the mother alone may be characterized as pathogenic.
Family therapy here contributes a new point of view that re-
directs and complements rather than contradicts the analytical approach; it hinges on the concept of the mother-child
relationship as part of the whole system of the family, and
not, as it has so long been considered in isolation. It must
follow that the father is a significant part of this system.
Lidz and his group (13, 97pp) in their paper on the fathers
of schizophrenics provide a first important example of the
use of this new approach.
    We must consider how the relationship of a mother to her
child depends critically on her side on her relationship
with her husband and his with her. Lang (10, 11) has suggest-

ed the name "structural triad" for this triangular relationship which supercedes the fundamental biological triad. The
physical presence of the father is not as important as his
indirect influence as a constituent of the marital relationship in the triad. From the beginning, the father, acting as
a third component, forestalls the development of the purely
dual union; the paternal structural factor is internalized
and representation of the father is achieved. Where this
primary structuring relationship of father to mother is absent and the child experiences only the mother a symbiosis
results leading to fantasized incest. It is no wonder that
Janzarik reports from an investigation of 100 schizophrenics:
"the theme of incest is unexpectedly frequent" (6). Similar
results are reported by Lidz et al. (13, 221 pp), L. Kaufmann
and C. Müller (7), and H. Stierlin (16, 114).

It is interesting to consider the case of Gerd K. in the
light of these results, especially in view of the incest-
uous tone of the aggressive outburst towards his mother.
Similarly suggestive is his otherwise incomprehensible, obstinate projective concern with incest in the family of his
girl friend. Gerd K. is the only child of a 40-year-old
father and somewhat younger mother. The father, originally
an unskilled worker, had through night school acquired enough
technical skill to be able to act as service agent for complex medical apparatus. He was barely able to cope with the
demands of this work, and it is characteristic of him that
he was unable to discuss within the family his anxieties,
arising, for example, from having to repair a heart-lung
machine while the operating team waited. It is also not surprising that his position within the family was one of an
outsider. Typically, shortly after the marriage, in the year
in which his son was born, he changed from work within the
firm's premises to work outside which meant that he frequently spent the whole week away from home. Here he was merely
repeating an already established pattern. One of a very poor
family with numerous children, he had as a child already
been sent to a family of wealthy farmers to seek his fortune
as a cowhand. When his own family was expelled from their
home in the former eastern German provinces, he was the only
child left behind. When at last he was allowed to follow he
was once again dispatched, this time to a farmer in a neighboring village.

It is also illuminating to consider Gerd's mother in
the light of such a multi-generational perspective (cf.M.
Bowen (3), I. Boszormenyi-Nagy (2) and others). Whereas the
father may be described as "expelled" (H. Stierlin) the mother had a "binding" relationship with her own mother; with
her father, who was often absent, she had a looser relationship. Gerd's father had had to turn down two jobs with good
prospects because his wife was unable to leave her mother
who lived near and shared the daily chores. During the first
four years of Gerd's life his family lived very closely with
his mother's parents; in fact the arrangement was only possible since the father was so frequently absent. From the

beginning the son was drawn into the binding relationship between mother and grandmother. He inevitably became a spouse substitute for the mother, who lacked the maturity to establish a partnership independent of her own family. Finally, Gerd became her "excitement provider" bringing variety into the dreary routine of everyday existence by his experiences in school, church, and Transcendental Meditation. A parentifying symbiosis developed which jeopardized and indeed made impossible the development of the patient's distinct individual subjectivity and identity.

As H. Stierlin has put forward, the family is "a relationship matrix, all the structure and movement of which crucially affect the individual's development and achievement of autonomy" (16, 108). This means that the relationship between mother (grandmother) and son could only become a symbiotic subsystem, if, as is frequent in such cases, "the father withdraws from contact with the children... the oedipal conflict is not settled" (19) and the son has, therefore, no chance to establish a representation of the father from which basis a barrier against the intrusive mother could be erected. During the family therapy it was established that father and son never did anything together, they never even spoke directly to one another, all communication being through the mother. This is shown in the extract quoted above: Gerd never addresses his father directly as "you", the "us" of the last sentence being the sole term of attachment.

That these manifestly disturbed relationships were caused by the fundamental failure to internalize the paternal authority owing to the inadequacy of the structural triad was revealed on the "Day of Reckoning". H. Stierlin (17) has described adolescence as the "Day of Reckoning" because it is then that "the work of individuation and separation of children and parents is at its most demanding". (18). Frequently, it is the confrontation with sexuality which provides the prologue to a drama with a psychotic ending, because the individual's personality structure is unable to meet this challenge. Mounting physical attraction in his relationship with a younger girl, Dagmar, made Gerd K. increasingly insecure. As Matussek has said, "for a schizophrenic such proximity represents danger" (14) and causes distance-seeking manoeuvers: Gerd K. had actually compiled a "dossier" about the girl writing about her in a cold and impersonal way as if she were a criminal psychopathological case. The less he was able to master the situation the more provocative became his behavior towards his father, who had suddenly taken on great and meaningful significance. What this already rather contactshy boy, who at the beginning of puberty was constantly occupied in drawing knights in armour, clearly sought was a figure with which he could identify and which could save him from the threatening danger of loss of personal boundaries which is implicit in sexuality. To cope with the situation with which he was confronted Gerd K. needed a father with whom he could identify. Instead he had a father who off-loaded the aggression he was not able to direct against his colleagues and employers on his son. This exploitation, made all to easy by the son's attempts to find a closer relationship with his father, pushed Gerd back into the diadic mother-child relationship.

That union with the love object presented a threatening danger for Gerd reflected nothing but his fear of the absorbing strength of the mother's engulfing image to which no appropriate paternal authority had set boundaries, so that, finally, the so-called Siddhi Course in Transcendental Meditation with its excercises in isolated meditation and expansion of consciousness occasioned a psychotic derangement. After three days of so-called "silence" (fasting, isolation from outside contact, silence, loss of time sense) Gerd K. became convinced that his thoughts were directing the course leader whose proximity he had constantly sought during the three days. Gerd sat on the raised chair provided for this "governor" and wanted to direct the course himself. He was convinced that he had made his girl friend pregnant, though a single kiss by the girl was all that had occurred between them. Back at home he imagined that a helicopter seen circling nearby was bringing the Maharishi Mahesh Yogi on a personal visit. Absolutely identified with the god figure and absorbed in the experience of divine awareness, he strew flowers around the university surgical clinic meanwhile talking in a confused and rambling way or wearing an ophelia-like smile. A psychiatrist who had diagnosed hebephrenia had referred Gerd K. and his parents for family therapy.

As already mentioned, a remission in the psychotic symptoms was noted as the father asserted himself. We, therefore, strove to bring the father into the family. During the fourth interview the father made a serious threat to destroy the family if nothing changed. As Hegel put it in Phänomenologie (5), he who can look death in the eyes is "master". As we have seen, the father was ready to "reach for the gun", and this step in a borderline situation marked the beginning of the remission phase. The father had "reached for the gun", and so the son need not fear being cast in the role of phallus to an omnipotent mother authority - according to the Freudian equation penis=child (GW XIV, 27). There was now another phallus to which the mother must refer. It would be interesting to explore this theme further in the light of Lacan's phallus concept, (8,9,12) however, that would be beyond the scope of this paper. The more the father came to occupy a central position in therapy - he was now able to discuss his work in the prescence of his family - the quieter and less problematic the son became. It is appropriate, as Bister would say, to see the change in the symptoms of the index patient in the light of the similarly changing interpersonal relationships (1). Gerd was able to return to school and performed so well that his teacher believed that he would be able to make up the lost ground and pass his exams. Immediately after the end of the therapy the father succeeded in changing his overdemanding job for a more congenial position as representative.

But too much school had been missed and the patient failed his exam. This narcissistic injury caused a hypomanic reaction and projective paranoid ideas directed against the "bad" teachers. With renewed family therapy the patient became quieter and no longer had ideas of persecution. Contrary to our expectation, however, there was an increase not in stability but in hypomanic activity: foolish, childish behavior; discussion of unrealistic career plans; furious attacks of rage characterized by foul abuse of the parents, particularly of the father. The cause of this deterioration was not clear until the father became able to admit that under the influence of alcohol he had caused a traffic accident and then fled the scene, for which crime he had not only lost his driving licence, but had been sacked without notice. Unable to come to terms with this self-sabotage he had once more used the son as a whipping boy, whose "difficulties" were actually welcome in providing distraction from his own misery. The son, his position undermined by this paternal failure and at the same time made the "waste bin" for the projections of his father's negative identity (H. Stierlin), reacted as described with attempted flight towards other father figures. His attempt to go to a party given by the so-called Heidelberg King of Rock was such a flight and caused the father, the therapists not being available, to have Gerd admitted to the local psychiatric clinic.

We have already noted the aggression this produced,"you dirty swine, you twister, you lousy liar, you need your prick cut off". Odysseus, bereft of the supporting mast, once more in danger, attempts to overcome the song of the mother sirens "I'll rip your cunt apart, so a baby'll jump out. Go and fuck yourself you old cunt". Discussion between the house physician and the parents, for whom the vacuum created by the son's admission to the clinic was intolerable, resulted in Gerd being sent home after two days. From the subsequent family interview, the last so far, it seems possible that through further work on the mutually interdependent difficulties of Gerd K. and his parents his mother's assertion that "the therapy's really helped" may be made true. The only feasible strategy is to create bonds between father and mother so that the father is brought into the family and the son is exploited neither as a phallus to the mother nor as "waste bin" to the father, so that Gerd, despite his undoubted regressive tendencies and constitutional biologically proven retardation, is able to some extent to cut loose from the family. It is possible to correct the fundamental deficit in the structural triad, the lack of primary identification with the father ? We cannot answer this here, although this deficiency was already apparent in the obstinate preoccupation of the 11-year-old with knights in armour, as it was in the prepsychotic and psychotic phases. It is interesting here to remember how the patient doggedly followed the course leader and reached a state of fused identity with him and with the Maharishi: signs of a bizarre search for a father figure and also certainly of a symbiosis in the mother-child diad which was on the point of breakdown. What possibilities of correction exist can only be realized if the therapeutic setting gathers all the components of the family system together in person. Slightly to adapt C. Müller's (15) concept, "orthopedically" this arrangement seems to us to hold out hope of success.

REFERENCES

1. Bister, W. (1965): In: Psychotherapy of Schizophrenia, p. 84. Editors: C. Müller and G. Benedetti. Karger, Basel/New York.
2. Boszormenyi-Nagy, I. and Spark, G.M. (1973): Invisible Loyalities, Harper and Row. New York, Evaston, San Francisco, London.
3. Bowen, M. (1960): In: The Etiology of Schizophrenia, p. 346. Editor: D.D. Jackson. Basic Books, Inc. New York.
4. Freud, S. (1940 - 1952): Gesammelte Werke I-XVII. Imago, London. (in neuer Auflage Fischer. Frankfurt/Main).
5. Hegel, G.W.F. (1952): Phänomenologie des Geistes. Editor: J. Hoffmeister. Meiner. Hamburg.
6. Janzarik, W. (1965): Arch. Psychiatr. u. Z.f.d.ges. Neurol., 207, 289.
7. Kaufmann, L. and Müller, C. (1969): Der Nervenarzt 40, 304.
8. Lacan, J. (1966): Ecrits. Ed. du Seuil. Paris.
9. Lang, H. (1973): Die Sprache und das Unbewusste. Suhrkamp. Frankfurt/Main.
10. Lang, H. (1977): Zur Rolle und Position des Vaters bei Schizophrenen. (Ungedruckte Dissertation. Heidelberg).
11. Lang, H. (1978): In: Das Vaterbild im Abendland I. Editor: H. Tellenbach. Kohlhammer. Stuttgart-Berlin-Köln-Mainz.
12. Lang, H. (1979): In: Kindlers Enzyklopädie. Die Psychologie des 20. Jh., Band X. Editor: U.H. Peters. Kindler. Zürich.
13. Lidz, Th., Fleck, S. and Cornelison, A. (1965): Schizophrenia and the Family. Internat. Univ. Press. New York.
14. Matussek, P. (1958): Arch. f. Psychiat. und Z.f.d.ges. Neurol., 197, 115.
15. Müller, C. (1972): In: Psychiatrie der Gegenwart, Band II, Teil 1, 2.Aufl. Klinische Psychiatrie I, p. 297.
16. Stierlin, H. (1972): Das Tun des Einen ist das Tun des Anderen. Suhrkamp. Frankfurt/Main.
17. Stierlin, H. (1975): Eltern und Kinder im Prozess der Ablösung. Suhrkamp. Frankfurt/Main, p. 154.
18. Stierlin, H. and Lang, H. (1978): In: Der Nervenarzt, 49, 53.
19. Tellenbach, H. (1977): In: L'Evolution psychiatrique, XLII Fasc. III/2 N$^{\circ}$ spécial, 901

SCHIZOPHRENIC AND SOMATIC SYMPTOMS AS MANIFESTATIONS

OF THE ILLNESS OF THE WHOLE FAMILY

Heimo Salminen M.D. Psychiatrist

Helsinki, Finland.

At the beginning of 1964 three persons contacted me simultaneously and wished me to start family therapy for the Smiths as soon as possible.

One of those contacting me was a psychiatrist who had treated seventeen-year-old Annie for schizophrenia. "Annie's therapy is stagnating, I don't think her treatment is possible without therapy for the whole family", he said. (Annie's doctor had made the diagnosis years ago and I don't know what the clinical symptoms were at the onset of the disease.)

The second person who contacted me was a physician whose patient was the sixty-one-year-old mother. "Mrs. Smith has been my patient for more than ten years, she suffers from severe diabetes and has had two heart attacks. I know the family and think that their problems are difficult. Family therapy must begin immediately", she wrote to me.

The third person contacting me was Mrs. Smith, the fat, busy, talkative mother of the family. She was a real chatter-box, talking all the time:

-" I've got a family estate, it is situated in the midst of lovely lakes and green forests. My husband was a veterinary, he was twenty years older than I. He died ten years ago of a heart attack and I have remained a widow with four children. Mike was 6 years old, Annie 11 years, Jack 14 years, and Helen was 16 years old at the time he died."

(At the time when I commenced treatment all the characters were 10 years older than the forementioned ages.)

-" Mike is very brainy at school,", the mother continues, " Annie loves horses, Jack studies economics and Helen is a music teacher. All the children have got their own flats. Annie goes to a driving school and is planning to buy a car of her own."

-" Why do you think you need family therapy?", I asked.

- "Why doesn't my mother's love suffice?", she replied and bursted out crying. "my children aren't able to live independently. Annie suffers from schizophrenia. Jack suffers with a peptic ulcer, he almost died of bleeding last year. It seems to me as

67

if Mike and Helen were accusing me of something too,
I'm an old woman and I'll die soon. Who will then take
care of my children and my farm?"
This was the way we began the therapy which consisted of 162 sessions throughout the course of four and
a half years.

THE PERIOD OF THE MOTHER'S DOMINATION

The family relationships with all their tragic
consequences are disclosed at the very beginning of the
first session. The mother domineers gravely. She talks
like a machine and interrupts everyone else. She introduces me to her children very proudly:
- " Annie, my dear horse-keeper; Helen, our music-
ian; Mike our egg-head, future scientist...; Jack,
the young head of our estate..... "
Schizophrenic Annie covers her face and ears with
her hands and kicks her feet into the air. She rushes
out of the room and back in again, buries her face in a
pillow and flings her arms about as if wanting to drive
away the others. As a rule she stands during the session
in a catatonic position with her hands raised up as if
in defence against somebody's attack. Every single word
from her mother affects her like a blow. The mother's
talk immediately becomes Annie's reality. Annie cannot
create a relationship based on dialogue, in which her
own reality would be in contact with another person's
reality and would simultaneously preserve its originality.
Her membership in the family is a constant fight for her
own existence. She has no place outside of the family and
inside it, she is in danger all the time of losing her
identity. She cannot express her distress verbally,
because the answer of other people, be it approving or
disapproving, makes her world come crashing down upon her.
Approval is an overwhelming obligation; disapproval
causes anguish for the loss of love. From this
point of view, Annie's so called schizophrenic behaviour
is quite normal. As her only place in the world is her
place in the family, she has to stick to it, like a
drowning man clutches to a straw, though it is extremely
difficult and distressing. Rushing in and out of the
room or covering her ears and eyes are simply a defence
against the threat represented by the contact with other
people. Aggressive outbursts and impulsive behaviour,
especially towards her mother, can be explained on this
basis too. They are inevitable, if she is going to maintain her own existence.
Jack and Helen were pale with anger after their
mother's introduction, Mike was seemingly embarrassed.
At the end of the session the mother took five white
envelopes from her huge black handbag and distributed
them to her children and myself. There were monies in
the envelopes. I suggested to them that thereafter each

68

of them would pay me in their turn, then I remarked that
the time was up.

During the first spring I told the children of the
fact that their mother assumes too much responsibility
and that their opposition is a consequence of that.
Furthermore, I told them about their lack of mutual
confidence, their difficulty to take into consideration
one another's views, their insecurity, depressed hate,
excessive dependence, and living off of one another.

In the last session before my summer holiday,
Helen asked her mother:

-"What do you think of Heimo Salminen?"

-"I hope he will take this burden of responsibility
from me." , her mother replied.

THE ANT AND THE CRYSTAL LAMP

In the autumn of 1964 the mother's monologue is still
going on, but has changed insomuch that she tells about
her own feelings too. The story about the ant is one of
the mother's monologues. The mother relates, very moving-
ly, that the ant is now learning to walk. It seems to me
that she is talking about herself in this story.

Another topic of the mother is the crystal lamp.
For ages she has been planning to buy such a lamp.
Buying has however, come to no avail.

I think that the crystal lamp, that the mother has
failed to buy is the part of her life that has not been
fulfilled. Eventually the mother allows other members of
the family to speak, but she often takes a nap whilst the
others speak. Once, when Helen spoke about her own feeling
of hate aroused by mother's endless chattering, mother
fell fast asleep and snored noisily. The snoring mother
in the arm-chair, with her hat and coat on and
handbag on her lap, made me think of a person fallen
asleep on a train.

A week later the mother had an apoplectic stroke
losing her power of speech and movement . She was permanently hospitalised. I almost wept when recalling the
story about the ant.

THE PERIOD OF JACK'S DOMINATION

Jack remarked, " Now I am your closest relation,"
in the first session after their mother's stroke.
Life was going on tranquilly. Jack had taken his mother's
place and started domineering the others, as their
mother had done before, and the others were in opposition.
The principle of the reorganisation seemed to be,
as few changes as possible. Although the 'constellation'
remained the same as before, there were important
nuances which were different from the previous situation
or constellation. Jack was very aggressive towards me

if the others turned to me for guidance. His relationship towards me was on a more equal level than that the mother's had been. Also the others' opposition was modified, Annie ceased being schizophrenic.
Her outbursts of rage were gone and she stood no longer during the sessions. Her schizophrenia presupposed mother's presence. Mike was clearly relieved, he did not have to protect his mother any longer and became more active. Helen had hitherto been withdrawn but she now began to fight for leadership with Jack.

The mother's stroke and the beginning of Jack's period of domination aroused an ardent wish of independence in everyone, but at the same time there was a fear of the dissolution of the family and being left alone. The fear won; the farm was restored to such a condition that the children could live there as they had done in their childhood. There was a room in the attic where Jack and Helen had lived as children. Their struggle for the leadership of the family now appeared as a quarrel for possession of this room. The quarrel was not settled.

At this phase , Jack was taken ill with sciatica. He has to bear mother's burden and that is too much. Surely, he would like to share it, but this is impossible, because he does not dare rely upon the others. At the same time his dictatorship is collapsing.

The fact that Jack's illness is sciatica, not the previous ulcer recurring, is in my opinion a step forward.

Living together on the farm turned out to be, as one could imagine beforehand. All wanted to be children, nobody wanted to perform the duties of a parent. There was no one attending to the shopping, cooking or cleaning. Jack was the one whom mostly assumed the role of an adult.

A NEW CHILDHOOD

As none of the children had had the possibility of being a child in their childhood , everybody now tried to be as childlike as it is possible for an adult to be. The farm was their home and I was both father and mother.

The farm was their home and I was both father and mother. Annie and Helen both brought their puppies to the sessions and babble to them like babies. It is very difficult for Jack to play the role of a child. He only knows how to exercise his authority over the others. However, his domineering turns out to be less perfect than that of his mother.

The turning point of the period of Jack's domination is disclosed in Mike's dream:
- "We are all on the farm and ardently desire that mother would take care of us. However, mother leaves us and goes to work. I think that I could never be so cruel."

In my opinion each of them is inconsistent, everybody wants to remain a child and, simultaneously, wishes to grow up. The mother's position in the dream corresponds to the therapist's position in the therapeutic process. The others succeeded somehow in acknowledging the child in themselves, but for Jack it was difficult. His need to be a child manifested mainly in somatic disturbances.

CHARLIE'S CAR WITH AUTOMATIC GEAR-CHANGE

A lively picture of mutual relations in this stage of the therapy is given by Helen's monologue in the May of 1966. Charlie, a family friend, had parked his car with automatic gear-change in front of the garage. Helen's car was in the garage. She relates:
- " I cannot drive a car with automatic gear-change, so I was unable to move Charlie's car I got furious. I cursed, kicked the car and tried to push it away, but all in vain. I called to Charlie for help but he didn't hear me. I tried to find someone else who knew how to drive the car, but I didn't succeed. I even thought of crashing at speed into Charlie's car to get it aside. Fortunately, I came to my senses only just in time."
Helen's story is an analogy of the relationships that existed within the family. Everybody already exists, though the experience of democracy is faint.
Another person is a menace and an obstacle, not a co-operating and interacting partner. Human relations require subjection and being subjected violently. Long, torturous pauses and sudden outbursts of hate are characteristic of this phase of therapy.
Jack's comment was:
-" When there are four mothers together, this kind of atmosphere will prevail."

DREAMS AT THE END OF JACK'S PERIOD OF DOMINATION

Helen's dream reflects the situation at the end of Jack's period of domination:
- "We are all in the smoke sauna on the farm. I have warmed it up myself. Heimo Salminen is washing little children. Annie wants to take a breath of fresh air, the others also grumble at bathing in the smoke sauna. Suddenly, there appear men dressed in black coats departing from father's room."
The therapist is more a mother than a father, for he is washing little children. The thought of a father is unknown and threatening because the men dressed in black appear from their father's room. Their father was a man constantly involved with his work.
In the same session Mike relates a dream too:
- "We are all in Heimo's office, and you, Heimo,

are standing in the middle of the room shaking your finger at us and demanding that each of us must know, why we are here."

The dream illustrates the challenge of therapy as well as the challenge of life. A reorganisation is evidently occuring in the family's life. They have started monthly meetings, where they discuss problems connected with farming. Each of them is chairman in their turn.

Better co-operation and a more democratic atmosphere brings forth fears too. Mike's dream testifies to this:

- " We are all on the farm. Helen's dog Spot bites me. I'm afraid of being infected with rabies. You, Heimo, are there too, and assure me that Spot hasn't got rabies and that there is no danger of infection."

The situation of the members of the family, resembles that of people on board a wrecked ship. Firstly and foremost everyone has to save one's own skin. Another person's touch is a threat rather than a protection. That is why Spot's bite signifies a danger of being infected with rabies.

The growth of security and equality brings forth yet more new aspects. These are disclosed in Helen's dream:

- " I am going to a party and want to give Heimo the key to my flat, but, he doesn't want to take it. Suddenly, I see that Heimo's wife has arrived at our farm and is hustling there. I am surprised."

The dreamer is growing as a woman, they are all getting more independent and grown-up. Besides Jack, none of them have love affairs.

Democracy is difficult for Jack. The peptic ulcer recurs once again. He cannot accept equality. He is so alienated from his self that he is only able to live by domineering other people. If this turns out to be impossible, he falls somatically ill. His mother did also. Jack had a dream concerning this:

- " A glass-blower shapes a dame-jeanne and puts it on a shelf. Jack comments on his dream in the following way:

- " Being an authority to others, that is my spine. If I give up the task I'll become an amoeba."

Jack's period of domination is coming to an end. In a session Mike sits down in my chair. We all accept it, with the exception for Jack. To him this deed is terrible.

- " If Mike takes Heimo's seat and everyone here accepts it, I must change into an amoeba- and that is impossible. I shall have to discontinue therapy if Mike won't return to his old seat."

Mike does not return to his old seat, Jack takes part in a couple of sessions, then gives up and begins individual therapy.

THE PERIOD OF HELEN'S DOMINATION

After Jack had left, a process familiar to us all
was repeated. Helen is a queen and the others are her
subjects. Annie fights against Helen but is also very
dependent upon her, as she had previously been upon their
mother. However, the psychotic symptoms are absent from
her behaviour.

Though the system of relationships is the same as
it had been earlier, Helen's period of domination has
got its own characteristics. They are perhaps best disclosed in an episode that took place at the very beginning of this period.

- Mike's car was broken down, so only Annie and Helen
arrived at the therapy session. A pillow war broke out
at once. First they threw pillows at each other. When
I remarked that they were competing for my attention,
they formed an alliance and both started to throw
pillows at me.

Subjecting and being subjected had earlier supp-
ressed competition and aggressiveness. Now that atmosphere had changed, they are evident.

Mike's dream tells of new features too:

- " We are going with Annie and Helen on holiday
to Brazil. My master there is a Brazilian engineer. The
passionate temperement of Brazilians seems to me to be
vey menacing. We are all thinking of taking part in the
Rio carnival despite this fact."

I said that   I heartily welcome the dream because
it is an expression of a rousing joy in life.

THE PERIOD OF AUTONOMY

The period of autonomy begins with a large announce-
ment of news.

- The farm will be sold!
At one of the monthly meetings Jack had suggested it
and all had agreed. They had come to this conclusion
because nobody was interested in farming, nobody had been
trained to be a farmer. Helen had had a dream also.

- " Mother suffers from breast cancer and dies.
The puppies get drowned but after a while they are again
jumping safe and sound on the shore."

Life based upon old engagements is going to
disappear, something new is coming into being.

In the last year of therapy, we have come to a
situation where everybody is getting along on one's own.
Mike studies law and has a girlfriend, he has moved into
a house of his own. Jack has graduated from the School
of Economics and is going to be a shop keeper. Helen,
who is a music teacher, lives a hermit's life but
has begun to take part in trade union activities.
Annie has bought her own house too, and lives there alone.

She judges her situation at the end of her therapy in
this way:
- " Life is difficult, because I cannot make up my
mind and choose a profession."
In the last session Mike tells of a dream:
-" Three children are walking down a busy road.
One of them fearlessly goes to dangerous places, another
is helpless and cannot yet walk well, I am holding both
by my hands."
I answered in reply to this:
"Each of us is made up of childishness, courage,
helplessness as well as other human qualities. It is of
great importance that these elements are in constant
dialogue with one another."

THEORETICAL SURVEY

Family therapy can be stressed in three different
ways:
1) by emphasising the experiences of one member of
the family and outlining the family process from his/her
point of view.
2) by emphasising the relationship between two
family members e.g. mother-daughter relationship and
outlining the whole family process from this point of
view.
3) by emphasising the family process as a whole.

The therapy described above belongs to the third
group. The working method can be called holistic and
integralistic.

Bion (1) distinguishes four kinds of processes in
a human group: dependence, pairing, fight-flight and work.
Dependence is a dominant process in the therapy of the
Smiths. It is characteristic during the period of
domination of the mother, Jack and Helen. The therapist
is the leader of the work process. Throughout the period
of dependence he must make the patients recognise their
dependence in order that they gain maturity as human
lbeings. Only in the period of autonomy were the patients
able to maintain the work process without the support of
the therapist.
Whitaker and Lieberman (2) use five basic concepts
whilst analysing a human group: focal conflict,
disturbing motive , reactive motive, restrictive solution,
and enabling solution. Dependency upon authority was
a focal conflict in the periods of the mother, Jack and
Helen. The need for independence was a disturbing motive,
fear of losing the security given by an authority was a
reactive motive. In the course of the therapy a
restrictive solution changes into an enabling solution.
In the mother's period, the solution was mostly
restrictive. The mother was in charge of all power and

responsibility, the othersadapted themselves completely.
In Jack's and Helen's periods a solution enabling independence and self-responsibility matures and this
solution is established in the period of autonomy.

Ezriel (3) is of the opinion that there is a threefold field of tension in a human group. Required
relationship, avoided relationship and calamity. In the
mother's, Jack's and Helen's periods, dependence on
authority was the required relationship, a revolt
against authority was the avoided relationship, and being
left alone was the calamity. In Jack's period the situation began to change to the contrary. When we come to
the period of autonomy, everybody's own autonomy is the
required relationship, dependence upon authority is
the avoided relationship, andthe loss of independence
is the calamity.

Rekola (4) characterises the common outlines of
illnesses as follows:

" Some forms of illness can be understood on the
basis of human situations, other forms come forth as a
somatic disturbance connected with strong psychic
defence."

Looking upon the case of the Smiths in this light,
the relationships between Annie and the rest of the
family can be understood on the basis of human situations
For the rest of the family, Annie's schizophrenia was
the most effective weapon against the domineering mother.
The mother's diabetes and heart-attacks, as well as
Jack's ulcer and sciatica are diseases of organs and
organisms connected with strong psychic defence. The
mother's story about the ant and Jack's impossibility
to turn into an amoeba make one think that defence often
hides orphanhood and insecurity within itself.
It is a little child's compulsion to live without mother,
father and home.

Siirala (5) outlines the initial onset stages of
illness in this way:

'' There is some disintergration- which I call a
historic constellation' , some failure has intruded
between the community and the individual. This failure
to intergrate is one that cannot penetrate into awareness
nor communal responsible consciousness. It prevails as a
latent communal crisis. Certain types of individuals are
particularly vulnerable to this crisis. For them the
crisis becomes crucial, the dilemma in the whole
'constellation'is transferred to them, becomes a burden
for such an individual. Perhaps this person who has been
made soley responsible will be able to develop a
crisis at semi-communal, semi-personal levels, let us
say a neurosis or at the price of destruction to his
social entity, a psychosis. Such crisis are indirect

appeals to the community. But physical illness also, is, in a certain sense a way of expressing the dilemma- but a more concealed, muffled and inarticulate alarm."

What is the communal crisis in the case of the Smith family then? In the periods of the mother, Jack and Helen the basic structure of communal crisis is similar. One domineers and the others submit grudgingly. The development of the family as a whole and of every single member, individually is in danger of stagnating. The dilemma is transferred to an individual.
Annie must be a child on behalf of the others, whilst mother, Jack and Helen assume the role of an adult in turns, even though they are children. The mother is a child too. Where growth is not possible, there will be distortions. Annie's schizophrenia is a sort of distor- tion as well as the mother's diabetes and heart-attacks, Jack's ulcer and sciatica. All the members of the family, including the mother, seek the care of a father, mother and home. Nobody is able to recognise this or experience it emotionally. That is why the family is missing a responsible consciousness. The mother cannot get help anymore because her existence is too fundamentally deviated.

SUMMARY

The therapy process of the Smiths has been presented and investigated in the light of the theories of Bion, Whitaker & Lieberman, Ezriel, Rekola and Siirala.
The group processes described by Bion (dependence, fight-flight, pairing and work.) aim at the nutrients necessary for human growth.
Whitaker & Lieberman consider the actual important conflicts of a human group and its solution (focal conflict, enabling solution, restrictive solution) as the crutial process of every new stage in development.
Ezriel illustrates the levels of reality (requir- ed relationship, avoided relationship, calamity.) which human beings have to take into account in search of a genuine contact.
Rekola gives a psychosomatic model for the analysis of illnesses and its adaption to the therapeutic dialogue. (Some forms of illnesses can be understood on the basis of human situations, others as somatic disturbances connected with defence.)
The viewpoint is very fruitful in all forms of psychotherapy.
Siirala brings forth an aetiological hypothesis of the interaction of illness and communal life (communal crisis, lack of responsible consciousness, neurosis, psychosis, physical illness). The observations made in therapeutic work give support to this hypothesis.

REFERENCES

1. Bion,W.R. Experiences In Groups.
   Tavistock publications, London 1961

2. Whitaker, D.S. & Lieberman, M.A. Psychotherapy
   through the Group Process. Aldine, Chicago.

3. Ezriel, H.A. Psycho-analytic Approach to Group
   Treatment. Brit.J.Med.Psychol. 23 , 1950

4. Rekola, J.K. , Nivelreuma ja antropologinen
   safauskäsitys. Psykoterapeuttinen aikakauskirja 1
   Helsinki 1968.

5. Siirala, M. , Medicine in Metamorfosis.
   Tavistock Publications, London 1969.

ASPECTS OF SCHIZOPHRENIC REGRESSION: DEFECTS, DEFENSE, AND DISORGANIZATION

Daniel P. Schwartz, M.D.

Medical Director, Austen Riggs Center, Inc., Stockbridge, MA., U.S.A.

Patients having had a schizophrenic episode often disown, but never forget this experience (27). Therapists, deeply chilled as they witness this human event, mark it as of central importance (15). Called quite properly "Regression," its essential data are often explained and grouped by two conceptual emphases--called either Defect theory, or Defense theory (19), (2), (32), (9). Various "Defect" conceptions stretch in their range and honor from those extraordinary early observations of Bleuler, and Freud, to current studies of Pious, and Wexler, of Freeman, and London (5), (12), (24), (33), (8), (20). Concepts of Schizophrenic Regression as "Defense," each quite differently shaped begin systematically with Freud and Abraham and extend today through Arlow and Bion, through Searles and Will and Burnham, through Lidz and Fleck (11), (1), (3), (4), (30), (34), (6), (16). Viewed often as concepts requiring a disjunctive choice, defect and defense may, in fact, be regarded as two different descriptive dimensions of a schizophrenic regression. Defect theories typically locate as of prime importance that data of the episode which involves loss of contact with reality. ("The world has changed," the patient says noting the beginning operative slippage in their own capacities for reality contact.) And they regard as one resultant of this loss, the disproportionate shift of energy and focus upon the patient's self. Defense theories locate the vulnerability to regression as the primary data, with a resulting return to earlier levels of adaptation of the id, ego, superego, and reality (self-object) integration. ("There is an evil within me," the patient says--using early introjective defenses.) These earlier levels of adaptation are regarded as being the products of this vulnerably defensive regression, or in their own separate various forms are used in the service of the continued necessities of defense.

A third area of description I would like to include, and call it "Disorganization." Let me focus upon this third dimension. In this dimension of disorganization I would include those "new" (to that person) phenomena which are a regular part of that schizophrenic episode of regression. These "new" phenomena are in their operation and experience not reasonably seen as previously existing organizations of growth in that person's developmental processes. They are not, for example, simply a repetition of a stage of libidinal orality, not simply a return to an introjective-projective developmental state of defense. They include such a phenomenon as that referred to by Freud in his comment in the Ego and the Id about those patients who "deserted by all the forces of protection...(the ego) lets itself die" (13). That, I would regard, as one of the "new" phenomena. "New" here is again something different from the ordinary developmental processes of a person's psycho-social growth. I would include those dimensions of that schizophrenic regression where pain in its various affective forms floods that person's ego functions and experience, where options for action seem and are experienced as unavailable, where perception and thought are fragmented. All this does not appear to be fully describable in a language which emphasizes the shift in libidinal cathexis resulting from the loss of an invested reality, its mental representation, and a cathectic retreat to a narcissistic stage of development with grandiosity, autoeroticism, and homosexuality (7). Nor does fragmentation, for example, seem describable simply as a defensive regressive return to an earlier level of developmental adaptation.

An example may clarify.

Bright and charming, a "recovered" schizophrenic boy excellently completes his first semester of work at college. He packs his suitcase, leaves the house in which he has been boarding, and asks to be readmitted to the psychiatric hospital in which he had been previously treated. He states that he has become very frightened. His college career has been launched. He has felt grown now. There is, in fact, no place for him at home--where he was not the son for whom his father wished, and could never become the cure of his mother's glacial depression. First success at college in its quality is too lonely, too guilt-ridden and fragmentary for him to use as a focus around which to organize a life. The therapist on whom he had come to depend is unexpectedly moving to a distant city. He walks into the hospital, will talk to no one of his many pressing concerns--his despair, his anger--though the patients and staff of this hospital know him well and attempt to share and know his position as best they might. Within a week he is acting more and more bizarrely. He is running up and down the halls, disrupting meetings, going into rooms where he does not belong. He progressively restricts himself. He is progressively restricted by the patients of the hospital and staff until he sleeps in the seclusion area and is constantly accompanied by an aide. His therapist, who sees him regularly, walks one day through the door into his presence in the seclusion room. The young man screams at the sight of him, "Dr. Black" (the therapist's name) "is dead!" Panic stricken, he hallucinates bullets and other deadly things radiating from the lights in the seclusion room ceiling. He tries his best to beat his head against the wall. He bites himself, tears his hair and flesh, looks in constant terror, pupils dilated, hyperventilating. He acts as if he does not hear the words his therapist or others say. His screaming repetitively pierces the seclusion room and area barriers, it

frightens people down the length of the halls of the
hospital. His rage is continuous, he uses attempts
to restrain him as a rack on which he lies prone and
tortured. He is incontinent, mute, staring fixedly
at the blank wall whenever he rests. He never weeps.

Such an eruption has the quality of an avalanche. It has a
momentum which is formidable, a change and discontinuity of state
which is awesome. A slow start, a directionality, a gradually increasing pace, and a thunderous inundation of an ordinary human
being's capacity to function.

No evocation of previous developmental levels of adaptation
appear to encompass this data. There is the real success, the
sought out retreat, the "letting go," the frantic search for, and
avoidance of actions options. There is the escalating disruption
of ego functions of behavioral control, of affect modulation, of
thought organization, or pain modulation, of boundary clarity.
There is the therapist as real object responded to as present, and
represented as murdered and destroyed. There is fear, pain, and
aggression which flood the behavior and experience of this human
being's inner and outer disorganization.

The data of psychoanalytic observation of developing children,
the data from reconstructive information about childhood, from the
memories of adults and the understanding of their transferences to
their analysts, do not to me indicate that ordinary children in
their wildest and most frantic anxiety or temper tantrums contain
anything near the dimension of this psychotic experience (10), (29),
(22), (25). It is closer to, but very different than children's
nightmares (21). In particular, I do not find it believable that
the fragmentation of thought, the flooding disruption of ego functions control of behavior, affect, memory, sequence, perception,
and the experience of "ego death" are a part of the normal child's
experience (17). Let us entertain this descriptive hypothesis--that
this schizophrenic episode's experience is in part descriptively
"new" for a psychiatric and psychoanalytic observer and functionally
and experientially "new" for the patient, in its dreadful and disorganizing dimension. Does such an hypothesis simply push that patient and those data toward a neurological view of this disorder? I
think not, though in fact it is possible that a clearer psychological
view may help establish psychological-neurological bridges even
there. I believe it helps us to organize our data psychologically,
and helps us to understand and respond to our patients psychologically as well. Those patients who say in describing such an experience
"Something in me died then (when I had that disorganizing experience)." Or, "I'll never go back there (to that state or experience)."
"It was too painful, too terrifying, even now for me to think of that
time," or "Thoughts hailed me," or "I could not tell an hour from a
week," require from us as psychotherapists and in fact often obtain
our respect, our belated understanding and acknowledgment of the new
and discontinuous changes involved for that patient and their disorganized state.

Therapy must--and at best does--reflect that knowledge. It
acknowledges that no schizophrenic patient forgets that disorganizing
episode, that like the other crucial parts of their experience, it
has become a part of their self, of their mind's memories, their

ego's capacities. It not only is something which can be remembered, but it can be frighteningly reproduced. Such acknowledged capacity of the real and frightening dangers within one is paradoxically re-assuring--as is much truth! The "hopeless and psychological un-treatability" views of past and some current opinions regarding schizophrenia is thus better understood--though not accepted (31). For a portion of that "hopeless" view of schizophrenia rests on the reality of that perceptual experience of the observer, which notes this new and disorganizing change in that other human being; and in fact upon the experience of the reality of that change by the patient himself. One young mute schizophrenic woman whom I worked with said her first words--when I had finally acknowledged that she must re-gard herself as hopeless, as forever damanged. She spoke then-- after months of silence--and said her first words. She said, "Dr. Schwartz, it's like slowly going blind."

Schizophrenic patients regularly respond to all three of these dimensions of their own regressive episodes, respond to their de-fensive, defective, and disorganizing aspects. They respond in at least two separable, but probably functionally related fashions, by attempting to represent their current inner state, and by attempts to do something about that state. It is no surprise to the thera-pist of such a schizophrenic patient, therefore, to hear that she is spending much time in the occupational therapy rooms pouring out plastic molds, pots, and as they harden, taking these regular pots and "accidently" dropping them and breaking them, so that much of the time she spends attempting to glue back together pieces of these "cracked pots." Such a patient arrived at her therapist's office with her arms loaded with "junk"--old books, partially read maga-zines, half-used appointment calendars from previous years, empty brown paper bags, etc.--and by word and gesture indicated that this "junk" is, as she says, to be "burned, buried, or destroyed!" There is in this context the strong suggestion that this "junk" is her gift of herself, her view of her relationship to the world, her conception of herself, her representation of her inner state. This is not simply a part of a defensive regressive state--though its defensive components of discarded anality, of degraded femininity are clear enough. It is not simply a demonstration of a shift to cathectic grandiosity, though that is touched on by the nature of the data. It is a response to that regression which attempts to represent itself--its fragmented inner state, its flooded disorganized posi-tion--with whatever conceptual media are personally available.

The patient's attempt to "do something" about that regressed state must also be separated from the nature of the regressed state itself. In its simple forms this involves attempts to achieve inner organization, and to modulate the pain and constrain one's own be-havior in some fashion. Freud, of course, noted these attempts to cure one's self. In his observations of Schreber's delusions, Freud thought these were "restitutive" efforts, attempts at recovery through recreating a representation of that patient's outer world with which they had lost contact (14). Today, we extend that view and note that any inner organization achieved after such a regressive episode is often clung to with extraordinary tenacity. Often that achieved organization is linked inextricably with whatever has func-tioned (or the patient has believed has functioned) as a modulator of their pain as well. Thus, we understand that running until one is exhausted, masturbating relentlessly and frantically, engaging in violently restrictive diets, and compulsively writing down each thought in a journal, are not simply regressive phenomena, but best efforts--best available attempts--to modulate, damp down, shape and control, and rid one's self of those impulses which that regressive episode has unleashed. When one talks with a young man repetitively sitting cross legged on the floor, eating barely enough for his own survival, praying repetitively for the fate of the world which he believes will be destroyed should he alter his behavior, one talks with the understanding that this conception of imminent catastrophe, this representation of the to be achieved moral mission, those constraints against malice, against impulse expression and gratification, all modulate pain and attempt to evolve an inner structure in the face of a regressive experience real and perceived in its peril by that patient.

This knowledge, too, guides our therapy so that with a patient who risks modifying such newly achieved organizations, such modulating structures, such represented views of themselves and the universe, we are prepared to understand what he struggles with in that risk. He has to venture to contend with greater disorganization and pain, with real and experienced fear of his own operable controls when he reaches that point of growth within a therapy, where his delusions are about to be left aside and behind. It is a part of himself he is trying to leave behind--and one that may have been life sustaining in its own time (26). One organizes and identifies as one's self not only one's external accomplishments and failures, but those various and complicated inner organizations of intrapsychic thought, memory, and structure. We regard ourselves as at one with-- and identified with--our own memories, as well as our own behaviors, our loves and our traumas, our previously normal and variously achieved and lost ego states and conscience formations. In schizophrenic states, which are in that regard not very different from normal states, whatever is achieved as structure becomes precious and a part of themselves is given up only with grief. Schreber published his memoirs, I would think, not simply for the sake of his own grandiosity, but among many other reasons in order to hold for himself as valuable his experience and his representation of achieved inner organization (23).

Finally, in a schizophrenic regression reality as defined by significant action plays a multi-faceted pivotal role. Not only must the new phenomenon of inner disorganization and personally discontinuous change in experience and function be noted and acknowledged. Not only must the patient's attempts to represent that inner disorganization and to evolve a modulating holistic structure be respected. But crucial actions inextricably linked with the precipitants, the processes, the historical predisposition, and the psychotherapeutic relatedness in such a schizophrenic episode must be explicated and their place understood (28).

A last example.

A quiet young man at college suddenly flies into a rage over a seemingly minor matter and physically attacks his roommate. His roommate flees, and the young fellow is later found in an ice cold shower, muttering inco-

herently to himself, apparently hallucinating.
Attempts to talk with him by professionally-
trained personnel seem simply to provoke his rage.
He makes it plain that he will hit anyone who
approaches him. A force of men is marshalled,
they walk into his presence, the patient is told
that he is going to be taken to a local hospital,
it is evident that his behavior will be contained.
The student then turns off his shower himself, his
muttering stops, he sits down and without much ado
and in apparent calm, allows himself to be carried
out to a local hospital where he is admitted. He
then organizes himself and returns to his parental
home for that weekend. He returns to college with
no evident signs of regression and begins to see a
local therapist.

Note the reality of action in the assault, the apparent regressive psychotic episode, the relation of the action of others which
signals their readiness to act and contain his assault, and care fo
him as well, the remission of his overt regressive manifestations.

Some months later the college infirmary staff
are called. This same young man has been found
groggy, drugged with psychoactive medicine in
apparent overdose in his room. An open notebook
by his bed reveals a scrawled "I am sorry..." which
trails off illegibly.

The college psychiatrist acts in the commonplace helpful task-related fashion. He determines
that the medication overdose is not physically
dangerous, puts the patient in the infirmary until
the toxic medication effects are worn off, he
evaluates the suicidal risk as not imminent, and
gathers from talking with the assembled patient,
suitemates, nearby sisters, mother, the following
information.

Long a shy person, this young man has lived
in a family which has moved often and in many
foreign lands. His very successful father has
mostly been away from home, on business trips,
and when around seemed somehow to be personally
unavailable to his son. The young man has not
felt "at home" in his family. He had, however,
high hopes for this college in which he was now
living. He had hoped to make friends in a way
which he had not been able to do before. Common
interest, time, and close living opportunity
might help him, he thought. He had, however,
been severely disappointed in this matter. The
previous fall his roommates had all been invited
to make plans to join social fraternities which
had not included him. This move of his various
roommates, in fact, would probably signal the end
of his friendship with the roommate that he particularly felt at home with. It was this room-

mate whom he subsequently attacked. He had felt
unable to act in any way which remedied this painful separating situation. The attack itself had
frightened and surprised the patient himself as
much as it had the roommate.

The current episode seemed to involve similar
phenomena. His teammates in the school rugby team
had all been planning to take a vacation and attend
a sports camp during that period. These plans fell
through because of various financial difficulties
of some of these teammates. His friends were not
able to attend this rugby camp. The patient felt
utterly without recourse, unable to act. He could
not think of what he could do to get a ride, who to
ask, or how to find a roommate during the vacation
at that camp, from among those other people who
were going and who were his peers. Simultaneously,
he had written a short story of special importance
to him, given it to one of his teachers in a course
on science fiction writing, and had been waiting
fruitlessly for a number of weeks for a response
from his teacher to that story. It was difficult
for him to approach his teacher about this matter.
In fact, he became more confused and blocked in his
thinking as he tried to discuss this story and its
importance with the college psychiatrist.

The psychiatrist, of course, did not press for
this information. He talked instead in banal fashion (ego functions in action often seem banal) with
this young man about what he, in fact, might do to
arrange rides for himself to the camp, what vacation roommates he might obtain at the camp, and how
he might discuss with his suitemates, mother, and
sister, their appropriate concern and anger over
his suicide gesture. They discussed what he might
be doing unwittingly himself, to make friendships
more difficult for himself, how to get an early
appointment with his own therapist, and how to
rouse his teacher to respond more rapidly to the
piece of science fiction writing he had submitted.
His father's repetitive absence was also noted as
annoyingly troublesome.

This was all then managed rather well by the
patient and the patient returned and said he would
like to see the psychiatrist once more before his
regular therapist returned, and this was arranged
for a day or two to follow.

Note in this the lack of seeming options for action explored
and explicated, the rather commonplace nature of the therapeutic action of the psychiatrist, the opportunity to move toward the future,
the historical (developmental) background of implied family actions
of rootlessness and societally supported abandoning actions by his
father (18).

On the patient's final visit, he explained that his short story was indeed a very important one to him. It was a story based on his own nightmare, recurrent these past few years. In it, he (the patient) was sent from another planet to visit the earth. His job was to teach the earthlings to communicate with one another. He was terrified in this nightmare, both because of the magnitude of the task for one person, and because he himself did not speak the same language as those earthlings. As he described this nightmare, he felt and looked extraordinarily anxious. All of his life, he said, he had felt alone. He had hoped to change that here at college but had not been able to do so as yet successfully. At times he felt himself detached from people. It was as if he was floating through the world. He would, on occasion, walk out into the night and sink his fingers into the soil so that he might hold onto the earth; so that he might feel connected to the ground. The night hid the shame he felt at this degrading act and this to him demeaning loneliness.

Communication here, as is most often true, <u>follows</u> the coping action. The patient has taken action in managing his vacation, his roommates, his ride to the camp, his story, his relationship to his psychiatrist. The psychiatrist's action has involved his availability and focus upon the patient's task.

And the nightmare—is it a fantasy only, in a boy whose family has been for him without roots, with a present-absent father in historical development action? And as he grabs the earth to hold on to connectedness and reality, is that a defect in cathectic strength, or an action which defines inner and outer reality? Is that floating feeling only a regressive defense against his aggression—in a boy whose father is lost in the empty reaches of psychological space?

If much of this is defect—in that cathectic strength, in that mental representation—is that equipmental or learned? What does it do to a mental representation when the central figure in your life is never there? If much of this is vulnerably responsive regression—what does it do to one's regressive capacity, when the central figure in your life cannot communicate or engage one in focused action?

Finally, what does it signify—that a schizophrenic regression is so often precipitated by an action defining reality, about which the patient can only wish to say in pain, "Not really again, not again, and again?"

REFERENCES

1. Abraham, K. (1949): In: Selected Papers, p. 418, Hogarth Press, London.
2. Arlow, J. A. and Brenner, C. (1969): Int. J. Psa., 50, 5.
3. Arlow, J. A. and Brenner, C., Ibid. 2
4. Bion, W. (1957): Int. J. Psa., 38, 266.
5. Bleuler, E. (1950): Dementia Praecox or the Group of Schizophrenia. Int. Univ. Press, New York.

6. Burnham, D., Gladstone, A., and Gibson, R. (1969): Schizophrenia and the Need-Fear Dilemma. International Universities Press, New York.
7. Fenichel, O. (1945): The Psychoanalytic Theory of Neuroses. W. W. Norton, New York.
8. Freeman, T. (1958): Psychoanalytic Study of the Psychoses. International Universities Press, New York.
9. Freeman, T. (1970): Int. J. Psa., 51, 407.
10. Freud, A. (1958): In: Psychoanalytic Study of the Child, Vol. 13, p. 92. International Universities Press, New York.
11. Freud, S. (1954): In: The Origins of Psychoanalysis, p. 109. Editors: M. Bonaparte, et al. Basic Books, New York.
12. Freud, S. (1958): Psychoanalytic Notes on an Autobiographical Account of a Case of Paranoia, Standard Edition, Vol. 12. Hogarth Press, London.
13. Freud, S. (1961): The Ego and the Id., Standard Edition, Vol. 19. Hogarth Press, London.
14. Freud, S. Ibid. 12
15. Hill, L. (1955): Psychotherapeutic Intervention in Schizophrenia. U. of Chicago Press, Chicago, ILL.
16. Lidz, T., Fleck, S., and Cornelison, A. (1965): Schizophrenia and the Family. International Universities Press, New York.
17. Lidz, T. (1968): The Person. Basic Books, New York.
18. Lidz, T. (1978): In: Schizophrenia: Science and Practice, p. 69. Harvard University Press, Cambridge, MA.
19. London, N. (1974): Int. J. Psa., 54, 197.
20. London, N. Ibid. 19
21. Mack, J. (1970): Nightmares and Human Conflict. Little, Brown, Boston, MA.
22. Mahler, M. (1975): The Psychological Birth of the Human Infant. Basic Books, New York.
23. Niederland, W. (1974): The Schreber Case. Quadrangle, New York.
24. Pious, W. (1961): In: Psychotherapy of the Psychoses, p. 43. Editor: A. Burton. Basic Books, New York.
25. Rosenfeld, H. (1965): In: Psychotic States, p. 155. International Universities Press, New York.
26. Schwartz, D. P. (1975): In: Psychotherapy of Schizophrenia, p. 23. Editors: J. Gunderson and L. Mosher. Jason Aronson, New York.
27. Schwartz, D. P. (1978): In: Schizophrenia: Science and Practice, p. 197. Editor: J. C. Shershow. Harvard University Press, Cambridge, MA.
28. Schwartz, D. P. Ibid. 26
29. Searles, H. (1962): J. Amer. Psa. Assoc., 10, 22.
30. Searles, H. (1965): In: Collected Papers on Schizophrenia, p. 114. International Universities Press, New York.
31. Shershow, J. (1978): In: Schizophrenia: Science and Practice, p. 3. Harvard University Press, Cambridge, MA.
32. Wexler, M. (1951): Int. J. Psa., 32, 157.
33. Wexler, M. (1971): Psa. Quart., 40, 83.
34. Will, O. (1961): In: Psychotherapy of the Psychoses, p. 3. Editor: A. Burton. Basic Books, New York.

CURRENT STATUS OF THE FINDINGS OF THE SELF-REPRESENTATION-OBJECT-REPRESENTATION DIFFERENTIATION (SOD) SCALE

Clarence G. Schulz

Senior Psychiatrist, The Sheppard and Enoch Pratt Hospital, Towson, Maryland, U.S.A.

The purpose of this paper is to summarize the development of the SOD Scale, elucidate the scoring system in current usage and to report the early findings. Much of this will be in outline form and details may be found in the various references cited.

The Scale initially was an outgrowth of meetings begun in 1971 of members of the Washington group of the NIMH Study Group* on schizophrenia. The needs for the Scale grew out of the concept that schizophrenic patients showed a tendency to a threat of fusion, with loss of identity and sense of boundary, upon intimate involvement with another person. This loss of boundary was thought to be directly related to the concept of the differentiation of self-representation from object-representation. It was postulated that patients showing a persistent proclivity toward fusion or the need to defend against the fear of fusion would be vulnerable to schizophrenic pathology. Hence if a scale could be developed which would measure the degree of fusion versus differentiation, one would have something akin to a "xray", in contrast to other rating scales which would measure more "surface" phenomena. The theoretical underpinnings of this concept can be found in a recent paper entitled "The Contribution of the Concept of Self Representation-Object Representation Differentiation to the Understanding of the Schizophrenias."(3) The work draws heavily on the previous writings of Mahler (2) and Jacobson (1).

The SOD Scale together with a clinical descriptive table of the scoring of the Scale can be found in the attached appendix to this paper. In brief, it will be noted that there are 16 items to the Scale. Items representing fusion or defense against fusion are on the left hand column while polar opposite items of differentiation are on the right hand column. Therefore, any items scoring one, two, or three would represent fusion. We score the same patient at intervals over a longitudinal period of time during the course of treatment and then compare any shifts from fusion to

*Drs. Marvin Adland, David Feinsilver, John Fort, John Gunderson, Clarence Schulz, Helm Stierlin, and Lyman Wynne.

differentiation. Initially we made independent ratings of a group of patients by two senior clinicians who did not know the patients but interviewed them independently for about a half hour each. In addition, we obtained a rating by the chief of service and another rating by the patient's therapist. In that initial project the ratings of the two senior people were almost identical and were uniformly toward the side of differentiation. The chiefs of service rating were closest to those of the senior raters but more toward fusion and the therapist were furthest from the senior raters and uniformly toward greater fusion than the chief of service. At first, we concluded that the nearly identical ratings of the senior raters meant that these were more accurate because the clinicians had a great degree of experience, with the chief of service who was next in amount of experience being in the middle, whereas the least experienced therapist, usually residents, scored more toward pathology. Later on, I came to see that the exact opposite was true. The therapists were closer to knowing the patient and picking up nonverbal cues. Therefore, their ratings toward fusion were more accurate than the chief of service who knew the patient somewhat better than the senior raters. The senior raters missed a number of features about fusion because they could not pick up many of the signs in the brief interview.

At one time, we designed a self rating system of a forced choice series of items which turned out to be completely useless because the self rating scale required that the patient already have conceptualized and recognized many of the features of fusion. Instead these patients often selected a response indicating a healthy differentiation in accordance with what was expected of them.

Our present project is as follows. About a month or so after the patient is admitted, since it requires that period of time for the therapist to be able to carry out an initial scoring, patients are scored initially and then periodically throughout the hospital stay at about every four to six months until they are discharged. In addition to the therapist scoring ratings on the patient, I, as a senior person, rated the patients independently. Concurrently the NOSIE (Nurses Observation Scale for Inpatient Evaluation) was made on each patient. (See appendix for NOSIE) We tried to select patients who would be in the hospital for a while as well as patients who would demonstrate some features of fusion although occasionally the patients selected did not show any elements of fusion on the scale or only a very few. It was our plan then to do a follow up a year after discharge to ascertain the outcome of hospitalization and treatment. We postulated that a shift in scoring from fusion to differentiation would be correlated with good outcome whereas a persistent fusion would predict a poorer outcome. The means of ascertaining outcome consisted of a brief form filled out requesting information concerning the patient following discharge. Any patients who were readmitted

to a hospital or committed suicide were regarded as poor
outcome. The returned questionnaires were rated independently
by three clinicians according to poor outcome and good outcome. The agreement of these independent raters is as
follows: As of August, 1978 with 20 returns there was
complete agreement in 15 cases (75%), divided opinion in
four cases and one inconclusive.

SCORING OF THE SCALE

It became apparent with clinical usage of this Scale
that items registering fusion were much more compelling of
fusion than the absence of fusion reflecting differentiation.
For example, in clinical medicine if a patient has a fever
we have a strong sense that some type of illness or pathological process is present. However, in the absence of fever
one cannot with the same conviction conclude that the
patient is therefore healthy. Consequently, there was concern that by simply totalling the scores, any uncertain items
erroneously scored as not present, and therefore reflective
of differentiation, might cancel out or erase the convincing
items scored as fusion. It was therefore decided that we
would simply score the Scale by taking any items scored as
one, two, or three and register this as indicative as fusion.
We would ignore items on the right hand side of the scoring
and merely total the number of items indicating fusion. It
would then be possible to have a maximum score of 16 (in
which case either one, two, or three would have been scored
on each of the 16 items) or a minimum score of zero.
    With this method, we combined the score of the senior
rater with that of the therapist in order to obtain a more
accurate rating. We decided to not count the same items
twice. Hence, if the therapist rated five items as indicating
fusion, and three of these five items were in common by the
raters then the total integrated score would be seven. Thus,
the combined ratings of the two would register fusion on
seven out of the 16 items. It became apparent that adding
the senior ratings did not appreciably change the population
division regarding fusion and differentiation. Consequently
the senior rating was dropped altogether. The results of
the present report are based on therapist's ratings alone
in this study.
    A scoring system was developed in order to take into
account both the change in the score of fusion and differentiation as well as the final rating result of the degree
of fusion just prior to discharge. Thus, a patient might
change a substantial number of points but still end up with
a quite high score indicative of fusion. By contrast
another patient might start with a very low score of fusion
and the resulting change might be only one or two points.
This had to be taken into account to reflect a final score
representing differentiation. The following formula was
arrived at to reflect differentiation or fusion:

Differentiation
  S.O.D. decrease 4 or
  more/final 2 or less

Fusion
  S.O.D. decrease 3 or less/
  final 5 or more

Similarly, the NOSIE was calculated as follows to reflect either an improvement in the NOSIE or a lack of change of the NOSIE:

NOSIE+ gain 10 or more/final   NOSIE- decrease or gain 9
  150+   or less/final below 100

TABLE 1

RESULTS OF THE FOLLOW-UP AS OF AUGUST, 1978

	Differentiation	Fusion	
Good outcome	12	1	S.O.D. predicts
Poor outcome	4	7	correctly 79% of 24 cases

	NOSIE+	NOSIE-	
Good outcome	12	1	NOSIE predicts
Poor outcome	6	5	correctly 71% of 24 cases

Clinical Ratings (1 = poorest   7 = most favorable)

	1	2	3	4	5	6	7
Good outcome	0	0	0	3	3	6	0
Poor outcome	1	1	1	6	2	1	0

ANALYSIS OF PATIENT VARIABLES OF FUSION VERSUS DIFFERENTIATED GROUPS[x]

Variables which were compared across the two groups included the following: Patient history items, suicide attempts, previous outpatient treatment, previous inpatient treatment, number of prior psychiatric hospitalizations, symptoms on admission, symptoms on discharge, symptoms present both on admission and discharge, treatments of choice, evaluation conference diagnosis, discharge diagnosis, whether or not there is a change in the diagnosis, estimated optimal length of stay; evaluation conference ratings of psychological adjustment, precipitating factor, maladjustment, readiness for psychotherapy and prognosis; type of discharge,

[x]This analysis and report was provided by Gerald Whitmarsh, Ph.D., Head of the Department of Research, The Sheppard and Enoch Pratt Hospital.

92

condition on discharge; discharge ratings of change in condition, general psychiatric condition, final prognosis; length of stay.

For the non-continuous variables, differences in proportions for the two groups were tested, while t tests were used for the continuous variables.

Only five variables were found to be associated with group membership, and all of these were discharge variables.

1. Fifty-eight percent of the fusion group and eighty-nine percent of the differentiated group obtained straight discharges. (P < .02)

2. Of those patients in each group who came in with a thought disturbance, 62% of the fusion group left still with a thought disturbance, whereas only 20% of the differentiated group left under such conditions. (P < .02)

3. The mean change in condition on discharge rating was 5.12 for the fusion group and 6.00 for the differentiated group, with the fusion group having shown less of a positive change in condition. (P < .01)

4. The mean ratings for general psychiatric condition on discharge for the fusion and differentiated groups were 3.04 and 4.75 respectively. The differentiated group showing a higher degree of adjustment. (P < .001)

5. Prognosis on discharge was also significantly different in terms of mean rating on discharge, with the fusion group having a poorer prognosis than the differentiated group, with means of 3.19 and 4.61 respectively. (P < .001)

REFERENCES

1. Jacobson, E. "Contributions to the Metapsychology of Psychotic Identifications", Journal of the American Psychoanalytic Association, II, 242, 1954.
2. Mahler, M.S., Pine, F., and Bergman, A. The Psychological Birth of the Human Infant. Pp. 220-230. Basic Books, Inc., New York, 1975.
3. Schulz, C. The Contribution of the Concept of Self Representation-Object Representation Differentiation to the Understanding of the Schizophrenias. (In press, NIMH)

Appendices on page 94-97.

C. G. Schulz, M.D.
Revised 11/24/72

THE SHEPPARD AND ENOCH PRATT HOSPITAL

SCALE FOR SELF-REPRESENTATION — OBJECT-REPRESENTATION DIFFERENTIATION (SOD)

Patient _____ Sex _____ Age _____ Diagnosis _____ DSM # _____

Date ____ / ____ / ____ Weeks of Therapy with this Therapist _____

Person filling out Scale _____ Years in Psychiatry _____ Profession _____

1. Manifestations Apparent in Patient's Interactions with all Staff.

   a. Excessive stimulus input needed to main-tain sense of body identity.   1 2 3 4 5 6 7   Relative freedom from physical contact need.

   b. Pre-ambivalent (split) view of others / self as "good" / "bad".   1 2 3 4 5 6 7   Fusion of "good" / "bad" into ambivalence.

   c. Inability to see self as separate from the surroundings.   1 2 3 4 5 6 7   Capacity to see self as separate from surroundings.

   d. Over-reaction to loss of body parts.   1 2 3 4 5 6 7   Acceptance of loss as natural function.

   e. Gender identity confusion.   1 2 3 4 5 6 7   Stable sense of sexual identity.

   f. Patient's experience believed to be the experience of the other person.   1 2 3 4 5 6 7   Privacy of body and mental experience.

   g. Pre-transference (autistic, symbiotic).   1 2 3 4 5 6 7   Transference relationship.

   h. Patient avoids close / intensive relation-ships or has many superficial relation-ships.   1 2 3 4 5 6 7   Capacity for intimate relationships.

   i. Confusion / disorganization / paranoid response to separation from others or change in patient's situation.   1 2 3 4 5 6 7   Feeling (grief / guilt / anger / tenderness) responses to separation from others or change.

   j. Misidentification of self / others.   1 2 3 4 5 6 7   Clear perception of self / others.

2. Manifestations Primarily Related to Patient-Psychotherapist Transactions but also Ratable by other Staff.

   a. Agreement / consensus / closeness with therapist associated with engulfment / being swallowed up / negativism.   1 2 3 4 5 6 7   Agreement / consensus / closeness with therapist enhances sense of self-identity.

   b. Patient oversensitive to intrusive aspects of therapeutic situation.   1 2 3 4 5 6 7   Readily discloses information.

   c. Inability to agree / disagree with thera-pist in a discriminatory way.   1 2 3 4 5 6 7   Able to agree / disagree with therapist in a discriminatory way.

   d. Patient confuses role with that of thera-pist.   1 2 3 4 5 6 7   Collaborates with therapist with clear delineation of roles.

   e. Countertransference fusion of patient and therapist.   1 2 3 4 5 6 7   Clear delineation of patient and therapist.

   f. Accentuation of great gulf of inequality between therapist and patient.   1 2 3 4 5 6 7   Permits closer approximation of patient-therapist status.

DETAILED TABLE OF SOD CATEGORIES

FUSION	1	2 & 3	4	5 & 6	7	DIFFERENTIATION
1a. Excessive stimulus input needed to maintain sense of body identity.	Head banging, cutting, shouting, smoking excessively with coughing, gorging or starving.	Patients sometimes scratch selves or occasionally get into fights to feel real. Exercise until tired. Reach out to touch and be touched. Hot and cold baths.	Patient experiences relief from feelings of depersonalization or unreality by pinching self.	Only occasional transient depersonalization relieved by picking at his skin, scratching himself or jiggling extremities.	Nothing beyond ordinary environmental stimuli needed to feel real.	1a. Relative freedom from physical contact need.
1b. Pre-ambivalent (split) view of others/self as "good"/"bad".	Splits staff in good and bad. Sees self as good or bad or alternating from one to the other. Staff divided in attitudes about patient.	Some selecting of some good guys and bad guys. Uncertainty about patient's self-concept with sometimes feeling totally good and sometimes bad. Splitting used as defense to keep categories in awareness as separate and non-interacting.	Some relationships split in terms of good and bad but there are also ambivalent attitudes toward others on occasion and toward self.	Ambivalence toward self and others predominates with occasional use of splitting defense.	Attitudes of ambivalence with repression and other higher level neurotic defense.	1b. Fusion of "good"/"bad" into ambivalence.
1c. Inability to see self as separate from the surroundings.	Personalizes many ordinary environmental stimuli with delusions of reference. Outside events have direct message or connection with patient's activities or thoughts.	Patient attentive and preoccupied with noticing extraneous events. At times delusional about relating to self but also has substantial doubts about the reality of it.	Occasionally patient thinks that some events possibly relate to him initially but then appraises situation realistically.	Patient rarely notices stimuli in a personalized sense and momentarily connects with self but appraises it realistically.	Clearly sees self as separate from surroundings.	1c. Capacity to see self as separate from surroundings.
1d. Over-reaction to loss of body parts.	Marked reaction to blood samples, fingernails trimmed, hair cut, giving up feces and urine. Saves menstrual pads.	Relinquishes body parts with some opposition.	Uneasy about giving up body products but complies.	Willingly lets go of body products with only twinges of anxiety.	Fantasied loss of body parts would be in the form of oedipal level castration anxiety.	1d. Acceptance of loss as natural function.
1e. Gender identity confusion.	Marked confusion about whether male or female. Half of body is one sex, the other half the opposite. Frequent slips of tongue mixes gender pronouns.	Some uncertainty about gender identity but also periods of clarity about what sex patient is.	Sometimes refers to self as opposite gender via dreams or slips of the tongue.	Shows some slight anxiety about identifications with the opposite sex.	Has well established gender identity and is comfortable with feelings of bisexuality.	1e. Stable sense of sexual identity.
1f. Patient's experience believed to be the experience of the other person.	No feelings of body or mental privacy. Delusions of mind reading, thought transmission. As though patient and others are siamese twins physically/psychologically.	Reactions to revealing secrets and thoughts with concerns about therapist knowing too much. Might border on delusions of having mind read but no absolute conviction about it.	Thinks therapist ought to know what he is thinking without having to specifically say what is on his mind.	Thinks that his thoughts show in his expressions or gestures but knows the therapist cannot read his mind.	Fairly comfortable with secure feelings of privacy of body and mental experience.	1f. Privacy of body and mental experience.
1g. Pre-transference (autistic, symbiotic).	Intense, immediate reactions to others involving projection leading to instant prejudicial attitudes.	At initial meeting a mixture of intense attitudes with some delay in responding to them.	In initial contacts sometimes projects but more often experiences transference distortions.	Reactions are primarily of transference variety with only rare use of projection.	May have intense transference feelings but able to connect these with earlier attitudes toward significant others.	1g. Transference relationship.
1h. Patient avoids close/intensive relationships or has many superficial relationships.	Total avoidance of threat of intimacy. Lack of emotional attachment or commitment to any one person or many quite superficial relationships as protection against involvement.	In relationships the possibility of intimacy leads to occasional ventures or risk of emotional involvement followed by quick erection of barriers out of anxiety in the face in intimacy or commitment.	Able to initiate brief intimate involvements with others but this is followed by pulling back or reinstating some distance.	More sustained intimate relationships but always accompanied by a mixture of doubting, anxiety, uncertainty.	Shows capacity for durable intimate relationships and values these highly.	1h. Capacity for intimate relationships.

95

FUSION	1	2 & 3	4	5 & 6	7	DIFFERENTIATION
1i. Confusion/ disorganization/paranoid response to separation from others or change in patient's situation.	Separations - even as minor as loss of eye contact or ending a session - leads to regressive disorganization or paranoid response. Same for any change including progress in patient.	Tolerates occasional and brief separations but in longer separations or moderate change there are intense reactions of delusions, paranoid ideas or confusion. There may be some reluctant acknowledgement of the connection between the reaction and separation or change.	Patient tolerates lapses of attention on part of therapist. Response to separation with anger, depression, guilt mixed with some denial, disorganization or transient confusion.	Reacts to separation predominantly affectively with rare denial or extremely brief confusion.	Experiences grief, anger, sadness, or affection in response to separation or change.	1i. Feeling (grief / guilt / anger / tenderness) responses to separation from others or change.
1j. Misidentification of self / others.	Delusionally misidentifies himself or others. Believes he has known others from the past with disregard for time or geography.	Misidentification of self and others; when it occurs does not have the conviction of certainty about it.	Situations of anxiety and insecurity are relieved by momentary feelings of being like the therapist.	Patient rarely feels like he is the therapist but does use the therapist's phrases or body gestures.	Clearly delineates self from others yet able to identify with others. Retains self-identity even during transient de-differentiation in the service of the ego.	1j. Clear perception of self - others.
2a. Agreement / consensus / closeness with therapist associated with engulfment / being swallowed up / negativism.	Slightest closeness including being understood or in agreement threatens patient and evokes negativistic reaction. Warmth, concern, tenderness aggravates.	Brief attempts at closeness / agreement / being understood are followed by distancing processes and/or negativism.	Experiences of closeness tolerated to some extent but most often eventually lead to anxiety, opposition or withdrawal.	Experiences of closeness and warmth are welcomed in a tentative way of daring to risk involvement.	Agreement and closeness is welcomed and enhances sense of self-identity.	2a. Agreement / consensus / closeness with therapist enhances sense of self identity.
2b. Patient oversensitive to intrusive aspects of therapeutic situation.	Patient tries not to reveal anything of thoughts or past. Physically avoids meeting with therapist. Complains of living in goldfish bowl. Intense and prolonged secretiveness.	Patient meets with therapist but is still quite guarded and does not readily reveal things to therapist. Patient feels it important to retain some secrets.	Partial disclosure of secrets followed by guardedness and withdrawal.	At times withholds secrets but on second thought discloses in the interest of therapy.	Shows no voluntary withholding of thoughts even though feeling anxiety, guilt and shame about expressing these.	2b. Readily discloses information.
2c. Inability to agree/ disagree with therapist in a discriminatory way.	Disagreement with everything therapist says or excessive compliance. Absence of listening, weighing and deciding things independently. May imitate movement of others in an automatic way.	For the most part patient compliantly agrees or tends to repeatedly disagree but occasionally has an independent attitude.	Patient mostly discriminates in relation to agreement or disagreement but occasionally gets caught up in stubborn disagreements.	Is frequently able to agree or disagree, sometimes feels guilty about it, but mostly feels stronger as a result.	Clearly able to be autonomous about expressing opinions to therapist and others. Able to listen with discrimination.	2c. Able to agree / disagree with therapist in a discriminatory way.
2d. Patient confuses role with that of therapist.	Confuses role. May interview therapist or ask questions in manner of therapist. May sit in therapist's chair.	Occasionally patient might think he is being therapist to the therapist or helping him with his problems.	Patient will attempt to interpret dreams of staff or other patients or be the therapist to other patients.	Occasionally feels like he is being a therapist.	Clear delineation of role as a patient.	2d. Collaborates with therapist with clear delineation of roles.
2e. Counter transference fusion of patient and therapist.	Symbiotic phenomena by therapist. Slips of tongue mix up patient and doctor. Affects vaguely and diffusely referable to either party.	Therapist seen as over-involved by other staff. Occasionally lets the session run over after losing track of time.	Therapist shows less frequent confusion of himself with patient. More "objective" about patient.	Patient experiences therapist as less involved with him and sometimes complains that therapist has changed.	No evidence of symbiotic counter-transference, although therapist still experiences feelings about the patient.	2e. Clear delineation of patient and therapist.
2f. Accentuation of great gulf of inequality between therapist and patient.	Patient repeatedly and almost constantly emphasizes difference in gender, religion, value system, intelligence, competence, approach to treatment and medications. Especially prominent when moving closer together.	Patient regards himself and therapist as being of quite different backgrounds though occasionally sees how they could come together on more equal footing in some characteristics.	Patient more frequently allows some equality with the therapist but unable to tolerate this for any extended time.	Seldom emphasizes differences between self and therapist.	Closer approximation of patient and therapist status which enhances the feelings of patient's self-esteem.	2f. Permits closer approximation of patient therapist status.

NURSES' OBSERVATION SCALE FOR INPATIENT EVALUATION (NOSIE-30)

SUBJECT'S NAME_____ DATE_____

RATER'S NAME_____ TITLE_____

DIRECTIONS

PLEASE RATE THIS PATIENT'S BEHAVIOR AS YOU OBSERVED IT <u>DURING THE LAST THREE DAYS ONLY</u>.
INDICATE YOUR CHOICE BY FILLING IN ONE BLOCK FOR EACH ITEM, USING THIS KEY:

0 = NEVER   1 = SOMETIMES   2 = OFTEN   3 = USUALLY   4 = ALWAYS

USE NO. 2 PENCIL.   MAKE YOUR MARKS HEAVY AND BLACK.   ERASE MISTAKES COMPLETELY.

0=== 1=== 2=== 3=== 4===   (1) IS SLOPPY.
0=== 1=== 2=== 3=== 4===   (2) IS IMPATIENT.
0=== 1=== 2=== 3=== 4===   (3) CRIES.
0=== 1=== 2=== 3=== 4===   (4) SHOWS INTEREST IN ACTIVITIES AROUND HIM.
0=== 1=== 2=== 3=== 4===   (5) SITS, UNLESS DIRECTED INTO ACTIVITY.
0=== 1=== 2=== 3=== 4===   (6) GETS ANGRY OR ANNOYED EASILY.
0=== 1=== 2=== 3=== 4===   (7) HEARS THINGS THAT ARE NOT THERE.
0=== 1=== 2=== 3=== 4===   (8) KEEPS HIS CLOTHES NEAT.
0=== 1=== 2=== 3=== 4===   (9) TRIES TO BE FRIENDLY WITH OTHERS.
0=== 1=== 2=== 3=== 4===   (10) BECOMES UPSET EASILY IF SOMETHING DOESN'T SUIT HIM.
0=== 1=== 2=== 3=== 4===   (11) REFUSES TO DO THE ORDINARY THINGS EXPECTED OF HIM.
0=== 1=== 2=== 3=== 4===   (12) IS IRRITABLE OR GROUCHY.
0=== 1=== 2=== 3=== 4===   (13) HAS TROUBLE REMEMBERING.
0=== 1=== 2=== 3=== 4===   (14) REFUSES TO SPEAK.
0=== 1=== 2=== 3=== 4===   (15) LAUGHS OR SMILES AT FUNNY COMMENTS OR EVENTS.
0=== 1=== 2=== 3=== 4===   (16) IS MESSY IN HIS EATING HABITS.
0=== 1=== 2=== 3=== 4===   (17) STARTS A CONVERSATION WITH OTHERS.
0=== 1=== 2=== 3=== 4===   (18) SAYS HE FEELS BLUE OR DEPRESSED.
0=== 1=== 2=== 3=== 4===   (19) TALKS ABOUT HIS INTERESTS.
0=== 1=== 2=== 3=== 4===   (20) SEES THINGS THAT ARE NOT THERE.
0=== 1=== 2=== 3=== 4===   (21) HAS TO BE REMINDED WHAT TO DO.
0=== 1=== 2=== 3=== 4===   (22) SLEEPS, UNLESS DIRECTED INTO ACTIVITY.
0=== 1=== 2=== 3=== 4===   (23) SAYS THAT HE IS NO GOOD.
0=== 1=== 2=== 3=== 4===   (24) HAS TO BE TOLD TO FOLLOW HOSPITAL ROUTINE.
0=== 1=== 2=== 3=== 4===   (25) HAS DIFFICULTY COMPLETING SIMPLE TASKS ON HIS OWN.
0=== 1=== 2=== 3=== 4===   (26) TALKS, MUTTERS, OR MUMBLES TO HIMSELF.
0=== 1=== 2=== 3=== 4===   (27) IS SLOW-MOVING OR SLUGGISH.
0=== 1=== 2=== 3=== 4===   (28) GIGGLES OR SMILES TO HIMSELF FOR NO APPARENT REASON.
0=== 1=== 2=== 3=== 4===   (29) IS QUICK TO FLY OFF THE HANDLE.
0=== 1=== 2=== 3=== 4===   (30) KEEPS HIMSELF CLEAN.

0===	1===	2===	3===	4===	5===	6===	7===	8===	9===	PROJECT NUMBER
0===	1===	2===	3===	4===	5===	6===	7===	8===	9===	
0===	1===	2===	3===	4===	5===	6===	7===	8===	9===	
0===	1===	2===	3===	4===	5===	6===	7===	8===	9===	SUBJECT CODE NUMBER
0===	1===	2===	3===	4===	5===	6===	7===	8===	9===	
0===	1===	2===	3===	4===	5===	6===	7===	8===	9===	
0===	1===	2===	3===	4===	5===	6===	7===	8===	9===	TREATMENT GROUP
0===	1===	2===	3===	4===	5===	6===	7===	8===	9===	RATING PERIOD
0===	1===	2===	3===	4===	5===	6===	7===	8===	9===	RATER

*GILBERT HONIGFELD, PH. D., BEHAVIOR ARTS CENTER, 77 LYONS PL. WESTWOOD, N. J. 07675
© GILBERT HONIGFELD 1966

INTEGRATIVE PSYCHOTHERAPY IN SCHIZOPHRENIA -- 25 YEARS LATER

David Rubinstein, M.D.

Clinical Professor of Psychiatry, Department of Psychiatry,
Temple University School of Medicine, Philadelphia, Pennysylvania
U.S.A.

I began to treat schizophrenic patients 25 years ago. This
presentation is an integrative view of my experience in psycho
therapeutic management in schizophrenia. I will discuss successful
and unsuccessful strategies, their rationale and my present position.
When we began this journey we felt that a psychoanalytic
orientated modality in psychotherapy would be a sufficient technique
to cure schizophrenia."Schizophrenigenic mothers", the fixation
at oral stages of development, the need to create a new nurturing
relationship with the patient and the analysis of a symbolic-
autistic world, were of primary concern in my early career.
Sometimes we were very successful -- often inadvertently. In
many other cases, however, patients reverted to old patterns of
schizophrenic behaviour and became immovable.Chronic hospitalization
and use of phenothiazines, in addition to psychotherapy, or as a
substitute for it was offered as an alternative by some colleagues.
I also pursued this avenue with my patients and, as a result,
discovered the slumbering schizophrenic who may cope with the
culture of a hospital but cannot deal with outside reality. We
also used long term electroshock treatments and insulin
comas pretending that we were able to dialogue intelligently,
psychotherapeutically with those patients.
New understanding of schizophrenia and the discovery of the
family system as a possible etiological element and as a therapeutic
milieu led us to this treatment. Again, our initial enthousiasm
created the illusion that family psychotherapy was the exclusive
answer to the very complex problem of treatment. We have learned
that although the application of family psychotherapy is important
in the treatment of schizophrenia it must not be the exclusive
method of therapy for patients and, perhaps, for some it is not
even applicable. (3) (5)
Family therapy seems to contribute to progressive recovery
from schizophrenic illness for some, for many others the involvement of the family in treatment offers observations explaining
the lack of improvement. I have asked myself why we fail with
these families and how we can be more creative.

DYNAMICS OF THERAPEUTIC FAILURE IN SCHIZOPHRENIA

During the last symposium (7) I discussed some of the elements
in the family which facilitate or prevent recuperation from the
psychotic process. Positively, I listed: 1) ability to tolerate

psychosis, 2) mutual support, 3) ability to reach decisions, 4) ability to understand primary process, 5) ability to resolve conflicts, 6) ability to define a"self" position. Among the negative elements in the family which interfere with the recovery process from schizophrenia I observed: 1) overprotectiveness and mutual overdependence, 2) pathogenic functions by the patient to maintain homeostasis in a pathologic family system, 3) pathologic defensive operations in the family system which deny existential characteristics in the patient, 4) severe pathology in the communicational patterns in the family system, 5) role expectations held by the family towards the patient during permorbid periods which are unfulfillable and non-negotiable.

THE THERAPIST

A therapist may fail with these families because of his/her cognitive exhaustion. The variety of levels, the amount of incongruencies, and the simultaneity of multiple messages during particular periods become insurmountable for the therapist's ego capacity and attention span. The therapist is pushed defensively into an autistic position and threatened with possible ego disintegration or ego incompetence. Often autistic fantasies manifest in the therapist who continues to grope for links and meanings in the family's disorganized processes, instead of recognizing that the system is operating at a primary process level and that verbalization shared are only autistic ruminations by each member of the family group. The therapist's autistic defenses add to the highly chaotic process of the family session.

As the therapist fails to organize the chaos countertransference phenomena such as anger, hopelessness and the conviction that the family is "incurable" surfaces. It is highly probable that this "ego exhaustion" is similar to the ego processes observed in children in such families when their maturing ego attempts to organize and process information in their systems; the ego incompetence would make the child vulnerable to the family system's pathology and thus to overidentify with the family's cognitive style. Hence, the high incidence of overt schizophrenia in offsprings of families at risk showing subclinical evidence of this illness.

COGNITIVE CHAOS

Although normal ego functioning is capable of screening out information which is not relevant to the individual's purposes in a primary process level of functioning humans have difficulty in ignoring information. Children, for example, are continuously distracted because they accept all information and stimuli. A schizophrenic, with severe ego deficiencies, is also continuously assimilating excess information and, thus, his behaviour becomes distractible and disorganized. Interruptions may become so intense and frequent that they block all behaviour.

100

Iconsider that schizophrenics are <u>hypersensitive</u> to the environment and at the same time, the patient is not able to organize all that he overincludes. In the family the patient may get more disorganized due to unlimited and unorganized information being transacted among family members as s/he gets trapped by the system's transactions from which s/he cannot differentiate. Family members who may be functioning at a borderline level suffer similar phenomena, i.e. difficulties in screening out information. Therefore, the family operates as a group of individuals with poor differentiation and permeable ego boundaries. In this system the patient's behaviour serves as an input to the family providing a mass of disorganized, unscreened, primary process level stimuli.

The system of the family and the patient's behaviour become epigenetic to each other, escalating the other's pathology and regression. While attemptong to organize the patient's behaviour and communicational patterns, the family fails and further regresses as a group. Symptoms of this regression are explosions of primary affect. communicational pathology and thought disorganization.

ROLE RELATIONSHIPS

The hypersensitive patient is frequently the best guide for the therapist to learn meanings of behaviour in the family because s/he is the most sensitive amplifier of the family system and its conflicts. The patient may also be able to make correct readings of the underlying and unverbalized emotions in the family members and in the therapist.

In many families, the patient serves as a vehicle to discharge personal preoccupations, personal conflicts, and unresolved maturational deficiencies and also s/he fills the gap in interpersonal relationships. In the absence of a "patient" the family is pressed into serious interpersonal confrontations and to the dramatic awareness that meaninglessness pervades their interpersonal field. In order to secure the binds and the family contract a patient is necessary or pathologic interpersonal defenses will be utilized. The first alternative is safer as the second choice may lead to excessive narcissistic injury. Whether the patient's role is a by-product of the system's dynamics or a contributory cause of its development. when the family seeks help years have passed and the roles are fixed. This is a crucial problem in the treatment of schizophrenia.

Formulations and observations describing the mother-child relationship in schizophrenia abound. Although these observations are generally correct for the premorbid period and for some phases of symptomatic development in the patient, around the tenth family session, when the patient demonstrates signs of recovery the father who is generally passive-aggressive, becomes a crucial figure in the binding process. At this point, he gets more involved in the offspring's life but his attitude is one of ambivalence. The father double-binds the recovering offspring through impatience with his progress, angry demonstrations about past psychotic behaviour and by imposing inflated expectations upon the patient's behaviour. While the father sustains the binding service in the

family,the mother becomes soothing and more distant. The parents
establish a partnership in binding the schizophrenic offspring,
each operating according to the presenting level of pathology --
the rules shift but the system is unalterable. As a consequence
of these binding mechanisms. the patient develops a paralyzing
amotivational syndrome. If the anxiety in the family becomes too
difficult for the patient s/he regresses to a new psychotic episode
and the cycle begins again with the mother reinitiating her binding
processes. The shifting balance of expectations and binding mechanisms fixates the family utilizing the patient as a narcissistic
object in a pathologic system of relationships. In sum, father's
active intervention provide ultimately for mother and offspring
to continue a pathologic narcissistic relationship.

The patient amplifies the shifting parental role by splitting
object relations. At times one of the parents is the "good" one
while the other is projected as the "bad" object then the shift
takes place and the reverse becomes operational. I have speculated
that, from the perspective of the patient, the parents are representatives of the split image of the "good" and "bad" mother which
saves the patient from confronting conflict-ridden ambivalence
toward the same object. This splitting phenomena in object relationships may also be projected unto the therapist by the patient and
other family members.

PRIMARY PROCESS GOVERNING POWER STRUCTURE AND DECISION MAKING

To allow the family new alternatives flexibility is necessary.
The family of the schizophrenic is impeded in reaching decisions in
the face of crises, dilemmas or joint tasks due to looseness and
undisciplined thinking or due to rigid and constricted thinking
styles (9). This deficiency in the decision making process leads
to a chronic accumulation of unsolved issues and when decisions
are made, frequently they are on basis of impulsiveness. One
person in the family must make decisions for the entire group.

In these families the patient sets the rules through the
activities of the primary process and utilizing the axiom that
the person who sets the rules in a system is invested with power --
the patient controls the power role. This is manifest in
therapy sessions when the patient often sets guidelines, agenda
and decisions are made unpredictably to comply with the patient's
narcissistic demands. As a result. the family seems to be functioning in erratic ways. For example, the family begins to discuss the
treatment for the chronic patient. This theme is abandoned in a
few minutes and they begin to respond to the looseness of the
patient's thinking and to his/her bizarre behaviour. Thus, power
in these families follows the economy of primary process functioning not rational, cultural traditions. It may shift from moment to
moment, according to whom in the family group is capable of most
regressive mechanisms.

AN INTEGRATIVE PSYCHOTHERAPEUTIC APPROACH

Presently, the best results in treatment of schizophrenic

patients is an <u>integration</u> of various therapeutic methods.

Schizophrenic families cannot be managed exclusively by isolating the individual patient from the patterns of recurrent interpersonal situations that transform his/her behaviour nor by involving the family exclusively. It has become clear that the phenomenology in a schizophrenic system is a result of the integration of the original psychological stress in the family, the effects on the individual and the impact created on the various eco-systems within which the individual grows and develops. In order to reverse the malignancy of the schizophrenic process the therapist must integrate and synthesize resources from various hierarchical levels which contribute to human behaviour. A system's perspective views behaviour as an integration of biochemical, psychodynamic, familial, social and cultural levels, Each of these are governed by principles which interlock functionally with hierarchical rules. Conflicts amomg various subsystems are reflected in behaviour which gets characterized as "maladaptive" or "abnormal".

Specifically, our approach relates to the ecological substratum assuming that symptomatic manifestations in behaviour are an expression of maladjustement among various systems centered around the patient or are a result of transitions from one system to another. The disappearance of symptoms is a result of having found a better adjustement or a more adequate negotiation among various systems. To organize behaviour into more adaptive manifestations the therapist must acknowledge the contributions of various subsystems governing the schizophrenic's life patterns.

Our approach utilizes the benifits of individual, family and group psychotherapy. Pharmacotherapy may be utilized. An initial target of our treatment program is the alleviation of anxiety because we consider that anxiety in the patient and in other family members, operates as the primary trigger for individual and system decompensation. Whenever we utilize phenothiazines they are prescribed in minimal amounts, sufficient to counteract malignant anxiety in the family. Abuse of phenothiazine therapy interferes with psychotherapeutic work, creates a <u>slumbering schizophrenic</u> but does not resolve the schizophrenic process in the family system nor in the individual.

It is my belief that not only the patient but other members of the family system are at risk and may require medical attention. The psychiatrist, as a family physician (6) is in an ideal position to provide continuous and comprehensive care for one or more family members. Our program consists of:

    a) an initial meeting with the patient and/or family to help them enter a therapeutic program;

    b) an evaluation phase of the patient's and family's psychological needs and resources:

    c) a phase of therapeutic approaches to mobilize interpersonal and transactional relationships in the family system to achieve maturation of the individuals.

FAMILY SESSIONS

We initiate the therapeutic program with a series of family

sessions to aid the therapist in getting acquainted with the ecological system of the patient. If the patient is experiencing
overwhelming psychotic manifestations, anti-anxiety medication
is indicated and family sessions are postponed. Because family
sessions may increase psychotic regression in the patient,a result
of the exposure of system defenses, individual treatment in conjunction with family sessions without the patient may be indicated.

When family therapy is utilized the role of the therapist
becomes crucial. S/he has to deal with multiple levels and meanings
generated during the family sessions. The therapist's stance will be
neutral, reflective, observant, directive and sufficiently healthy
to be able to process relevant information during the session.
The therapist must be competent in understanding primary process
phenomena and its manifestations. (4) S/he should be aware of their
narcissistic needs so that counter-tranference phenomena is recognized and dealt with immediately. The therapist may benefit from
the presence of a co-therapist who adds an element of reality testing to this enterprise.

Primarilly, the therapist must be in control of the session
to neutralize the malignancy of the family's tendency towards
chaotic thinking. S/he will select the themes to be dealt with
despite the temptation to allow the process in the session to run
uncontrolled. (4) This limit setting establishes him/her as a role
model and a leader of the session.

The therapist may function as an auxiliary ego to the family
system as s/he translates primary process symbols into secondary
process language. S/he directs the economy of narcissistic needs
demonstrated by members of the system. At this point the therapist
sets the rules of the family session and thus established his/her
power. The tendency of the family to be ruled by the most regressed
member, by primary process principles, is reversed creating a healthier environment for the patient and protective defensive, operations
for the group. As each member is encouraged to develop autonomy
in the context of the family the tendency of the parents to secrifice
their individuality for the sake of the schizophrenic child is
counteracted.

When families seek help for a sick member they come with the
unconscious belief that the therapist will validate their role
structure and preconceived explanations for the patient's sickness.
The role structure is generally fixed and centered around the patient
as a narcissistic object and scapegoat with the underlying thought
that there are other scapegoats in the family that will be uncovered
by the therapist. The stategy is to restructure the role system
amd make corrections in the mythical explanations espoused by
the family.

INDIVIDUAL PSYCHOTHERAPY

A goal in individual therapy is to understand the symbolic
world of the patient and to get acquainted with his/her paleologic
style of thinking.(1) The patient is helped to deal with stressful situations which precipitate overwhelming anxiety and is helped not to respond with primary process behaviour.

It is useful to train the patient to identify stressful situations which precipitate psychotic symptoms. For example, a
patient was able to learn that whenever she heard "voices" it was
correlated with arguments, decisions she had to make or impending
difficult situations. Whenever she reported having experienced
auditory hallucinations we would screen, in detail, events or subjective experiences which preceded that bout of hallucinations.
This technique educated her to an awareness of the meanings of her
psychotic experiences. This knowledge can be shared with other
family members in conjoint sessions correcting the belief in the
family and in the patient that schizophrenic symptoms are mysterious and beyond understanding.

A genetic approach in individual psychotherapy sessions help
the patient to understand the specific roles s/he have played in
the family system, as well as their unusual personality organization.
A young woman, was able to trace her auditory hallucinations as a
representation of her superego and as a manifestation of her close
identification with her mother whom she was serving as a super-ego
delegate. (8) The pseudo-solution of premature sexual activity
facilitated further binding with her mother's and her own super-ego
now expressed through hallucinatory messages.

I often use the metaphor that a psychotic break is like a
fractured leg and the person should not attempt to run while the
bone is still fragile. The patient and the family must understand
ego capacities and sensitivities and learn that symptoms of psychosis are expressions of forceful maneuvres on the patient's fragile
ego and should be avoided. The therapist sets limits for the
patient and the family in reference to unrealistic expectations.
One of the most difficult realities to accept by the family is the
reality of the patient's sensitive ego and psychosis. I have found
that a total denial of the patient's psychosis has been maintained
for a long period of time -- this denial is still continued when
a psychiatrist is consulted. This lack of acceptance of the
psychotic experience is shared by the patient, contributing to an
absence of insight and perverting the experiential meanings of
the patient as an individual.

GROUP PSYCHOTHERAPY

In addition to individual and family psychotherapy the patient's
participation in a group of peers introduces reality testing in his/
her life. Group psychotherapy is organized with peers matched for
ego resources, age, both genders and in limited series of 12 sessions.
Patients may attend several successive series. I have observed
that it is more profitable for the patient to participate in a
group where other members have healthier ego resources, rather than
an exclusive group of schizophrenics. The latter alternative fosters
the maintenance of primary process functioning while the first
alternative introduces reality testing to the patient's psychotic
bahaviour, and forces him/her to a more reality orientated approach
to their lives. The group process thus generated keeps a strong
check on the patient's psychotic solutions and helps him/her to
initiate a genetic exploration of his/her conflicts.

The group process also extends an essential belief that permeates all of these modalities of psychotherapy i.e.. the development of self-responsibility to counteract tendencies to maintain binding mechanisms, dependancy needs, pathological narcissism, and delegate functions.

The group leader is crucial to the effectiveness of this therapy. S/he must understand psychodynamic processes in schizophrenia and have a very clear knowledge of what it means to grow in our present society and culture. As a facilitator, the leader has to be sensitive to topics raised in his/her group. The group leader is a person with a mature ego functioning who has acquired over a long period a sense of self and individuation through personal insights.

Schizophrenic patients and their families do not follow an even, progressive course in therapy. There are periods of progress and then of no progress when some regression may be observed. It seems that during those periods the individual and the system absorb and integrate what they have learned up to that point in therapy.

Progress in therapy follows a dialectic principle with a continuous setting of anthithesis and synthesis. Every new phase of development constitutes a new baseline from which the patient may differentiate and develop further. Patients and their families may avoid therapy during those plateaus until they are ready for the therapist's intervention. Another family member may temporarily become an index patient during this time.

Psychotherapy must be an opportunity for psychological growth and to grow implies the acceptance of one's frailties and the recognition of others' capacities and responsibilities. To mature means to find new alternatives, utilizing various resources available to the individual. Growth is not an accidental potpourri of events but an integration from several hierarchical levels which determine behaviour. The psychotherapist esentially catalyzes the integration of such learning.

ACKNOWLEDGEMENT

The author acknowledges with gratitude the grateful assistance of Joan F. Timmins in the preparation of this paper.

REFERENCES

1. Arieti,S. Interpretation of Schizophrenia. New York., Basic Books, 1974. Second Edition.
2. Rubinstein,D. Family Dynamics and Prognosis in Schizophrenia (1966) In: Proc.lV World Congress of Psychiatry, Amsterdam, Excerpta Medica.p. 2972-2975.
3. Rubinstein,D. (1971): Clinical Issues in Family Therapy of Schizophrenia: In Psychotherapy of Schizophrenia: Proc.lVth Int.Symposium, Turku,Finland 1971: Amsterdam, Exerpta Medica.
4. Rubinstein, D. (1974) Techniques in Family Psychotherapy of Schizophrenia: In: Strategic Intervention in Schizophrenia:

REFERENCES

Editors:R. Cancro,N.Fox and L.Shapiro. Behavioral
Publications, New York.

5. Rubinsteib,D. Family Therapy of Schizophrenia -- Where to?--
What next?--(1975) In: What is Psychotherapy? Proc.9th
Int.Congr.Pschother.,Oslo 1973. Psychother.Psychosom.
25: 154-162

6. Rubinstein, D. The Psychiatrist as a Family Physician (1975)
presented at Hong-Kong Symposium on Psychosomatic Medicine.
World Psychiatric Association -- in publication.

7. Rubinstein, D. Ecological Aspects in Psychotherapy of Schizo-
phrenia: A challenge to the Therapist (1976). In:
Schizophrenia 75, Psychotherapy, family studies and research.
Proceedings of the Vth International Symposium on Psychotherapy
of Schizophrenia, Oslo, Norway. Editors: J.Jorstad,
E.Ugelstad, Lie & Co., Oslo Norway.

8. Stierlin, H. Psychoanalysis and Family Therapy:
Jason Aaronson, New York, 1977.

9. Wynne,L.D. and Singer, M.D. (1963) Thought Disorder and
Family Relations of Schizophrenics. 1. A research stategy.
11. A classification of forms of thinking. Arch.General
Psychiatry;9:25.

FUNCTIONS OF MILIEU THERAPY

John G. Gunderson, M.D.

Assistant Professor of Psychiatry, Harvard Medical School,
Boston, MA

Director of Psychotherapy, McLean Hospital, Belmont, MA

The current status of milieu therapy indicates a
confluence of two major developments. The first is that
milieu therapy has rapidly become much more diversified
and ambitious in its clinical practices during the past
twenty years. The second development is that research has
documented that milieu therapy can have relatively powerful effects on outcome (13). This has largely been
evident in the last ten years and represents a turnabout
from previous research which had indicated that milieu
therapy had minimal or even negative effects on outcome
(31). Recent research has shown that specific active
types of milieu therapy can be effective with specific
patient groups but it does not allow any generalization
of the value of milieu therapy.

Both the diversity of clinical practices and the
specificity of research results indicate a need for a
better understanding of the underlying active therapeutic
activities which milieu therapy is capable of. This
paper attempts to conceptualize five major therapeutic
processes which commonly exist in a broad range of
milieus independent of size, length of stay, staffing
and philosophy. These five functions are: containment,
support, structure, involvement, and validation. It is
hoped that defining these functions is a step towards
identifying the critical processes which explain why one
milieu is therapeutic for a given patient, while another
is not. This is important since the proper design of the
milieu must depend upon knowing what therapeutic activities within it are intended to be maximized.

In this paper I will first describe the historical
development of these five different functions and then
discuss their implications in terms of their applicability
for different patient groups and their implications about
staffing. Finally, aspects of the sequence in which
these functions are employed and their interrelationships
will be discussed.

EARLY DEVELOPMENTS

Until 1800 most psychotic people were provided with
milieus solely intended to keep them from grossly hurting

themselves or others. The first and only therapeutic
function was <u>containment</u> of the patients -- to prevent
unacceptably destructive behaviors and sustain their
physical health.

Containment remains an important ingredient in the
care of mentally ill. The more exclusive dependence upon
this function can still be found in large state hospitals
such as those about which Goffman (12)   and more
recently Braginsky (4) have written. It is also the
principle therapeutic function of maximum security and
crisis intervention wards. Containment functions to
remove the unaccepted burden of self-control or omnipotence in psychiatric patients. Some means by which
containment is provided is through food, shelter, wet
packs, seclusion, screened windows, locked doors, medical
care, etc. Its effect is to temporarily reinforce the
internal controls of patients and to reality test their
omnipotent beliefs concerning their destructiveness.
Unfortunately, given too much emphasis containment can
suppress initiative, and hope, and reinforce isolation.

The belief that the environment in which a patient
lives can have positive effects on the course of his/her
illness is traceable to the pioneers in psychiatric
reform at the end of the eighteenth century. The early
proponents of moral treatment had in common the belief
that psychiatric patients would profit from being treated
with warmth and respect within the confines of a relatively stress-free environment (21). This introduced
the second major therapeutic function of psychiatric
milieus -- <u>support</u>. Support refers to conscious efforts
by the social network to make patients feel better and
enhance their self-esteem. The concern with how patient
feel and how they view themselves was a major departure
from past concerns. Support is a major aspect of many
milieus today. It can be provided by actual behavioral
provisions such as food, escorts, cigarettes and attenti
or it can be provided verbally by direction, advice,
reality testing and education. Efforts to support self-
esteem are provided by praise, reassurance, and encourag·
ing patients to do things within their range of expected
competence. Self-disclosures by staff and ongoing
availability after discharge are other forms of support.
The effect of support is to relieve self-accusations and
to make patients more tolerant of the limitations of
others. Too much support, however, can reinforce unrealistic dependency and imply that personal problems
are externally created and solved. The supportive
elements of moral treatment were adopted and employed
in a group of private mental hospitals established in the
United States in the early nineteenth century. The
emphasis upon the therapeutic function of support is stil
evident in some of these private hospitals (11, 28) where
the milieu is considered an asylum in which patients are
encouraged or directed to participate in other more

specific types of therapy, e.g. psychotherapy, rehabilitation programs, etc. It is also a major component of
milieus within the Veterans Administration system.

The prevailing optimism about moral treatment of the
insane in the nineteenth century provided a persuasive
rationale for governments to construct new mental hospitals for the care of the mentally ill. In the United
States, these original government financed hospitals were
small and patients remained there for a limited time after
which, if they didn't improve, they were expected to
leave. However, even as Dorothea Dix's perservering
efforts led to the establishment of a state hospital
system, the original small asylums had been transfigured
into large custodial institutions to house chronically
ill patients (24). Once again, the therapeutic function
provided by the milieus reverted to containment. The
mandate of moral treatment to provide safety and support
and thereby allow natural healing processes to occur, had
changed into a mandate simply to provide safety and
security. In the process, the mentally ill patient was
once again isolated from relationships which may have
been therapeutic. By 1925 over 50% of the patients admitted to state psychiatric facilities were never discharged!

In this bleak period more systematic approaches to
the study of the design and the effects of milieus upon
patient outcome were initiated. Sullivan (30) began such
experiments with a unit for the treatment of acute young
schizophrenic males and inspired a more hopeful approach
to the treatment of schizophrenia through the use of
specifically designed milieus. In the 1940's Rowland (27)
and Caudill (6) initiated the first careful descriptions
of the staff and patient subcultures within psychiatric
milieus. They illustrated how differing expectations and
belief systems of patients and staff led to therapeutic
impasses. In 1954, Stanton and Schwartz (29) taking a
microscopic view of the staff and patient interactions
within the milieu at Chestnut Lodge described how problems
in communication and social organization can enhance or
interfere but in any case directly influence the behavioral course of treatment for psychiatric patients. While
these investigators and in the same tradition later,
Edelson (7), carefully analyzed the characteristics and
complications of psychiatric milieus, their contributions
were largely descriptive. In the literature during the
1940's and 50's, psychiatric milieus were still largely
considered from the viewpoint of their ability to cause
or prevent dangerous regression. These early investigators did not, in themselves, elevate the milieu to a
therapeutic modality in its own right, nor did they develop the idea that the optimal milieu can provide therapeutic
functions for patients which go beyond those first introduced by the ideas of moral treatment, namely, support
and containment. Nevertheless, the conception of the
milieu as a potentially more active positive force was

developing during this period.

ACTIVE MILIEUS

Traces of a more active attitude within and about milieus can be found in elaborate and explicit treatment programs advocated by Menninger (19) and Bettelheim (3). Such programs recognized the value and importance of organizing the time, space and activity of each patient's environment, i.e., of providing structure. The value of this third therapeutic function was somewhat lost on account of Menninger's ill-fated efforts to prescribe attitudes by staff and because of the inimical style of Bettelheim's leadership.

Structure acts to make the environment less amorphous and allows a non-invasive attachment to it. Within the milieu the function of structure promotes changes in symptoms and action patterns of patients which are considered maladaptive. It helps people to consider consequences and to delay acting upon dysphoric feelings or impulses. Some ways in which this is done is through hierarchical privilege systems, uniforms or name plates, use of contracts, desensitization, regulated censure and praise, mandatory meetings or drugs, and regulation of sleeping, eating, isolation and hygiene patterns of patients. Structure is especially evident in milieus where there are fixed role definitions, high order and organization, and hierarchical responsibility distribution. Structure is readily recognizable in milieus which heavily invoke a medical model or which are intent upon early discharge. Without question the most extensive and purest examples of the use of structure in milieus are found in behavior modification units. Such units have drawn attention to the refined and creative ways in which structures can be implemented and manipulated to alter unwanted social behaviors. Their effectiveness in so doing was first described and provided with a conceptual basis by Ayllon and Azrin (2). Although token economies have been employed almost exclusively in large state hospital units for chronic patients, the principles of operant conditioning are a central ingredient of many psychiatric wards which are often employed unknowingly. The effect of structure is to promote internal organization and improve frustration tolerance. In its extreme, it can also dangerously mask psychopathology, encourage compliance, and stifle assertiveness.

Structure can be provided to patients because of staff's perception that it is required (e.g., a room schedule for a manic patient) or can be provided in collaboration with patients about mutually perceived problems (e.g. desensitization for a phobic patient). In the latter instance, the patient's active involvement in his/her treatment program is required, i.e., it cannot be legislated or prescribed by staff to the patient.

Involvement refers to milieu activities which address and utilize a patient's ego by insisting that they attend to and interact with their social environment. Involvement particularly combats patients' passivity, i.e., their wish to have others do things to or for them. The purpose of involvement is to strengthen a patient's ego and to modify aversive interpersonal patterns. The function of involvement was largely embodied in the concepts of the therapeutic community introduced by Main (18) and Maxwell Jones (16). Unlike its predecessors this milieu approach is not prescriptive but requires active collaboration by patient members. Critical elements of the therapeutic community include: 1) flattening of the hierarchical distribution of authority with distribution of decision making power, 2) blurring of role definitions, 3) emphasis on group participation and sharing of personal problems. Means of facilitating involvement include open doors and open rounds, patient led groups, the identification of shared goals, mandatory participation in milieu groups, community activities, verbalization of problems, and self-assertiveness experiences. High recognition to the interpersonal meaning to symptomatic acts conveys the belief that they are within patients' control and thus their responsibility. Patients who talk about their unmet "needs" will have them restated as unrealistic "wants". The effect of involvement is to develop social competence, diminish dependence upon narcissistic gratifications, and reinforce ego strengths. For this, patients are expected to relinquish or subordinate private, asocial, or unrealistic wishes. Too much emphasis on involvement may frighten patients into thoughtless conformity or belligerant negativism. It can also beget exclusivity and scapegoating. Wards which emphasize involvement are recognizable by the patients preoccupation with each other's problems and their generally intense, busy atmosphere. Involvement has been a central feature of many medium-length-stay wards in community mental health centers and teaching hospitals.

An important fifth ingredient of active milieus, entitled validation, has its origin in the psychoanalytic tradition. Bullard (5) for example urged "an environment in which the patient may be sick and unpunished for it". The affirmation of this principle can be found in those milieu programs which emphasize non-coercively "being with" schizophrenic patients such as Kinglsey Hall (17) or Soteria House (22), and within psychoanalytically oriented settings such as described by Foster (11) and Alanen (1). It is also common in day care or halfway house settings. This therapeutic function refers to processes which affirm a patient's individuality. This may be evident in attention to individualized treatment programming, respect for a patient's right to be alone or to have secrets, frequent exploratory one-to-one talks, allowing patients to fail, an emphasis on loss, and encouraging individuals to operate at the fringe of their known capacities. This function requires the milieu to accept incompetence, regressions, and symptoms as meaningful expressions of that person's inner-self which needn't be terminated or ignored but should be understood. Validation can help patients develop a greater capacity for closeness and a more consolidated identity. As discussed below, the principle danger of too much emphasis on this function is the sense of neglect which can develop.

DISCUSSION

The introduction of structure, involvement and validation into modern psychiatric wards has elevated the milieu from a form of treatment provided as the background for more specific therapies into a definable and specific form of therapy in its own right. An active therapeutic milieu, however, is still not the modal hospital environment for psychiatric patients. The vast majority of psychiatric patients are still treated primarily with containment and some supplementary support and/or structure. Such milieus are unquestionably needed and useful but they are limited by modern standards.

Eldred (8) notes that recent research on the milieu has gained in utility and believability, but these advances have been made at the expense of the results having broad explanatory power. Nowhere is this more apparent than in the area of studying milieu processes. The outline of five major types of therapeutic function described in this paper offers a means of identifying therapeutic milieu processes but it lacks the measurable basis by which it could be reliably employed in studies of milieu outcome. In contrast, two major instruments for assessing characteristics of milieus reliably have evolved in recent years: the Perception of Ward (POW) by Ellsworth (9) and the Ward Atmosphere Scale (WAS) by Moos (20). Both of these major investigative instruments have now been utilized to assess wards, to indicate needs for change, and to assess whether changes have occurred. Nevertheless, since they do not specifically focus on the processes within wards which are responsible for therapeutic effects, they can be expected to have only a weak relationship to outcome and cannot illuminate the reasons for a milieu's effectiveness or lack of it (14). This paper is an introductory effort to provide some definition of those activities which are closer to the heart of a milieu's effectiveness.

The varying responses of different patient groups to similar milieus (10) and the varying responses of similar patients in different milieus (25) draw attention to the fact that it is almost certain that patients will fit better into some types of milieus than into others. It is my impression, for example, that each of the five functions described above is particularly and differ-

entially needed by different patient groups. Containment
is most important for incorrigibly assaultive and self-
destructive patients but is also needed for actively
psychotic persons who are confused and dnagerously impulsive. It is most harmfully overemphasized whcn employed
for long periods of time with chronic schizophrenics.
Support should be maximized for frightened and depressed
patients. It can have harmful effects for paranoid and
borderline patients who become frightened or negativistic
in this type of setting. Structure is most useful to
chronic schizophrenic, manic, and impulsive patients. I
find it hard to identify any major patient groups for
whom too much structure is harmful. It can, however, be
unnecessary for the occasional hospitalized neurotic or
be the reason for unnecessary struggles with borderline
patients. Involvement is particularly valuable for withdrawn, sociopathic, and nonparanoid schizophrenic patients.
Actively psychotic patients are overstimulated and disorganized by the demands for community involvement. Manic
patients are especially likely to be ostracized in such
milieus. An emphasis on validation is especially helpful
to paranoid and borderline patients. It can, however, be
dangerous to suicidal patients and may cause passive or
nonverbal patients to be neglected. Although such refined
hypotheses are still within the realm of clinical opinion,
further studies are greatly needed to address these and
other specific questions of fit between milieu design and
patient pathology.

An encouraging implication of the recent developments
in milieu therapy is that the traditionally low level
staff on inpatient services can -- in addition to providing a warm and reasonable environment -- learn specific
skills such as operant conditioning (25) or "being with"
psychotic patients (22, 26), or the empathic skills
required for exploratory one-to-one talks (1). Since
such skills could add appreciably to the therapeutic
efficacy of a milieu, this is a promising development in
terms of cost effectiveness.

In addition, there are probably particular personality characteristics which can work more effectively
with different types of patients (15, 23). It is my
impression that there are different qualities in staff
members which would be well suited for the delivery of
the five forms of therapeutic activity outlined here.
Physical strength, reliability and self-control are
especially valuable characteristics for staff providing
containment. Support is often provided most comfortably
by staff members who are stable, patient and shy. Often
this is easier for staff members who are older than the
patient population. Ideal qualities in staff who are
providing structure for patients are compulsvity, and
comfort with aggression. Compulsivity refers particularly
to such qualities as punctuality and orderliness, whereas
comfort with aggression is manifest in tolerance of anger,

ability to set limits and firmness. Involvement is facilitated by staff who are energetic, enthusiastic and are of
similar age to the patients. Validation depends on the
empathic skills, sensitivity, and tolerance of uncertainty
by staff. Such staff should combine introspectiveness and
comfort with passivity in themselves and, unlike for
involvement, be comfortable with this quality in others
as well. The use of more specialized skills in staff or
the advantages of special personality qualities mean that
greater attention needs to be given to the training,
selection and supervision of every staff member.

The same sequence which was evident in the historical
development of the five functions can be seen in the
progressively greater complexity each of them involves
and in that each requires more participation and initiative by patients to make a function usable. Each function
depends to some extent upon the successful incorporation
of all those prior to it. Thus, within a given milieu at
times of crisis, the milieu will normally regress toward
the more simplified and clarified security of the earlier
functions.

The five functions can also help to conceptualize
the changing needs of a given patient during the course
of a hospitalization. Thus the grossly psychotic patient
who is dangerously impulsive may initially profit from a
simplified milieu which keeps him safe (containment). As
the psychosis recedes this patient will frequently feel
depressed and the patience and encouragement (support) of
his environment become essential. Emergence from this
period may reveal the need to learn social skills both in
terms of consequences of actions and the impersonal nature
of reality (structure). This period will frequently
include learning about his effects on other people and
the advantages of more sensitively recognizing their
potential to hurt or assist him (involvement). As the
patient plans to leave the hospital he must resume fuller
responsibility for his life and suffer the knowledge that
a safer world is being left behind (validation). There
may be other sequences by which these functions are
required for the hospitalizations of other patients.

SUMMARY

Milieu therapy has grown enormously in its complexity
and ambitions during the past 200 years. It is clear
that within the common rubric of milieu therapy there
now is found a broad diversity of programs. It is also
clear that these various milieus can exert a strong but
variable influence on patients. Available instruments
for assessing milieus can help to evaluate and engineer
milieu programs. Yet, these are limited by the absence
of a conceptualization of the critical therapeutic
activities within milieus which need to be assessed and
engineered. This paper develops a conceptualization and

description of five major therapeutic activities which are commonly found in a broad cross section of modern milieus. The five functions of containment, support, structure, involvement and validation offer a means of understanding how and why milieus work.

REFERENCES

1. Alanen, Y. (1975): The Psychotherapeutic Care of Schizophrenic Patients in a Community Psychiatric Setting, in: Studies of Schizophrenia, Brit. J. Psychiatry Special Publication No. 10, pp. 86-93, Editor: M.H. Lader.

2. Ayllon, T., Azrin, N.H. (1965): The Measurement and Reinforcement of Behavior of Psychotics. J. Exp. Anal. Behav., 8:357-383.

3. Bettelheim, B. (1950): Love is Not Enough, Free Press.

4. Braginsky, B.M., Braginsky, D.D., Ring, K. (1969): Methods of Madness: The Mental Hospital as a Last Resort, Holt, Rinehart & Winston, New York.

5. Bullard, D.M. (1940): The Organization of Psycho-analytic Procedure in the Hospital, J. Nerv. Ment. Dis. 91:697-703.

6. Caudill, W. (1952): Social Structure and Interaction Processes on a Psychiatric Ward, Am. J. Orthopsychiatry, 22:314-324.

7. Edelson, M. (1964): Ego Psychology, Group Dynamics, and the Therapeutic Community, Grune & Stratton, New York.

8. Eldred, S. (1979): Research and the Therapeutic Milieu, In: Principles & Practice of Milieu Therapy, Editors: Gunderson, J.G., Mosher, L.R. & Will, O.A., Jason Aronson, Inc., New York. (in press)

9. Ellsworth, R.B., Maroney, R., Klett, W., Gordon, H., Gunn, R. (1971): Milieu Characteristics of Successful Psychiatric Treatment Programs, Am. J. Orthopsychiatry 41:427-441.

10. Fairweather, G., Simon, R., Gebhard, M., et al, (1960) Relative Effectiveness of Psychotherapeutic Programs, Psychol. Monogr. 74: whole #492.

11. Foster, B. (1979): The Psychiatric Milieu Combined with Psychotherapy in an Open Hospital, In: Principles & Practice of Milieu Therapy, Editors: Gunderson, J.G.,

12. Goffman, E. (1961): Asylums, Doubleday & Co., Inc.
     New York.

13. Gunderson, J.G. (1975): Recent Research on Psycho-
     social Treatments of Schizophrenia, In: Schizophre-
     nia '75 Psychotherapy, Family Studies, Research,
     Universitetsforlaget, Oslo, Norway.

14. Gunderson, J.G. (1978): Defining the Therapeutic
     Processes in Psychiatric Milieus, Psychiatry
     (in press).

15. Gunderson, J.G. (1978): Patient-Therapist Matching:
     A Research Evaluation, Am. J. Psychiatry (in press).

16. Jones, M. (1953): The Therapeutic Community, Basic
     Books, New York.

17. Laing, R.D. (1967): The Politics of Experience,
     Ballantine, Inc., New York.

18. Main, T.F. (1946): The Hospital as a Therapeutic
     Institution, Bull. of the Menninger Clinic, 19:66-70.

19. Menninger, W. (1936): Psychiatric Hospital Treatment
     Designed to Meet Unconscious Needs, Am. J. Psychiatry
     XCIII:347-360.

20. Moos, R.H. (1974): Evaluating Treatment Environments:
     A Social Ecological Approach, John Wiley & Sons,
     New York.

21. Mora, G. (1967): History of Psychiatry, In: Compre-
     hensive Textbook of Psychiatry, p. 2, Editors:
     Freedman, A.M. & Kaplan, H.I., Williams & Wilkins
     Co., Baltimore, MD.

22. Mosher, L.R., Menn, A., Matthews, S.M.(1975):
     Evaluation of a Home-Based Treatment for Schizo-
     phrenia, Am. J. Orthopsychiatry 45(3):455-467.

23. Mosher, L.R., Reifman, A., Menn, A. (1973): Charac-
     teristics of Non-professionals Serving as Primary
     Therapists for Acute Schizophrenics, Hosp. & Comm.
     Psychiatry, 24:391-396.

24. Ozarin, L.D. (1973): Moral Treatment and the Mental
     Hospital, In: The Therapeutic Community, Editors:
     Rossi, J.J. & Filstead, W.J., Behavioral Publica-
     tions, New York.

25. Paul, G.L., Lentz, R.J. (1978): Psychosocial Treat-
     ment of Chronic Mental Patients: Milieu vs. Social

118

Learning-Programs, Harvard University Press, Cambridge, MA.

26. Rappaport, M., Hopkins, H.K., Hall, K., et al. (1978) Schizophrenics for Whom Phenothiazines may be Contra-indicated or Unnecessary, In: Controversy and Psychiatry, Chapter V, Editors: Brody, H.K.H. & Brady, P., W.B. Saunders Co., Philadelphia, PA (in press).

27. Rowland, H. (1938): Interaction Processes in the State Mental Hospital, Psychiatry I;323-337.

28. Rubenstein, R. (1974): Crticial Elements of a Psychiatric Hospital Treatment Program, Proceedings of the International Conference on Milieu Therapy, Oct. 14, 1975, Stockbridge, MA.

29. Stanton, A.H., Schwartz, M.S. (1954): The Mental Hospital, Basic Books, New York.

30. Sullivan, H.S. (1931): Socio-psychiatric Research: Its Implication for the Schizophrenia Problem and for Mental Hygiene, Am. J. Psychiatry, X:977-991.

31. Van Putten, T., May, P.R.A. (1976): Milieu Therapy of the Schizophrenias, In: Treatment of Schizophrenia Progress and Prospects, Editors: West, L.J. & Flinn, D.E., Grune & Stratton, Inc., New York.

PSYCHIC EFFORT, DRIFT AND REALITY STRUCTURES:
OBSERVATIONS FROM PSYCHOANALYTIC WORK WITH NEUROTIC,
BORDERLINE AND SCHIZOPHRENIC PATIENTS

John S. Kafka

George Washington University School of Medicine and
Washington Psychoanalytic Institute, Washington, D.C.,
U.S.A.

There is madness in my method.   There is method in my
madness.   There is madness in my method.   First, listen
to this:
    "We find ourselves in a department store:
    we want to use the escalator
    to get to the toy department
    where we want to buy building blocks
    but since the escalator has at this moment stopped
    the stopped escalator
    on which we were going upstairs, transforms itself
    into our suspended breath, and our suspended breath
    which we now exhale
    because the escalator suddenly moves again
    collapses into a pile of building blocks--"
Also listen to this:
    "Somebody sees so many objects
    that the objects become indifferent to him--
    somebody sees so many indifferent objects
    that by and by he loses his awareness of himself--
    then he sees an object
    that he does not wish to see
    or that he wishes to see longer
    or that he would like to have
    so that the object becomes an object of
    his curiosity
    his wish to
    his wish not to
    and he looks at it
    or he averts it
    or he wants to have it:
    and he again becomes aware of himself--"
    There is method in my madness of starting with these
two quotations from Peter Handke's "The Innerworld of the
Outerworld of the Innerworld" (4, pp. 128, 131-132, my
translation).   Handke describes, among other things, the
shift in tension when awareness of something overlaps--
or does not quite overlap--with awareness of self.   There
are states of mind, for instance, in which aggression is
in the air, but in which it is a moot question who is the
aggressor.   The size of the organic unit in question is
not defined at that moment--for example, it might be a

121

dyad; if in an analogous therapeutic situation the therapist is too preoccupied with who is who, at the expense of full contact with the quasi-Platonic idea of, say, diffuse aggression in the atmosphere, contact with the patient is at least temporarily lost.

Before going farther I should point out here that my experience has not led me to a cult of loss of boundary in the therapist, even in work with the most psychotic patients, but to a striving for a comprehensive stance-- rather than an understanding one. In the therapeutic situation it must be possible for the therapist to have a wider stance than the patient. I emphasize that at any one moment that does not necessarily mean greater understanding. It may mean greater tolerance of not understanding, greater tolerance of paradoxical realities. Such tolerance in turn is related to a suspension of some fixed notions of object constancy and of causal connections tied to those constancies. I have elaborated these issues in several other papers (7, 8), but will focus here on the experience of effort in therapeutic situations as it relates to the structuring and restructuring of realities.

Pertinent here are some observations on my own fatigue and on the time of my awareness of different degrees and qualities of fatigue with various kinds of patients. These observations have had some corroboration in the experiences of colleagues. During a period when I was dividing my time between psychoanalytically based therapy with psychotic (mostly schizophrenic) patients and "borderline" patients, and the psychoanalysis of neurotic patients, I found the day-to-day work more fatiguing with the neurotic patients than with the flagrantly psychotic ones. However I found some reversal of this situation upon returning from vacation; often, prior to meeting with psychotic patients for the first time after a vacation, I was particularly aware of my expectation of hard work. "Borderline" patients tended to be on both sides of the fatigue spectrum. I will gradually try to place these observations in the context of a broader discussion of effort in therapeutic work.

Effort makes no sense if we do not believe that it will produce something. Effort is thus tied to the idea of causality. If there is no causal linkage between events, they occur in a haphazard fashion. The idea of the unconscious shrinks the world of the haphazard since linkages are established or are presumed to exist where previously there seemed to be none. Perceived linkages determine our world, our psychological realities. In Tanner's movie "Jonas Who Will be 25 in the Year 2000," a history teacher brings an enormous blood sausage to class to illustrate the course of history. Giving his students different perspectives on a drawing of the sausage, he demonstrates that it can be seen either as a chain of links or as separate and broken parts. Later the teacher is fired, largely because of his unorthodox teaching methods. Obviously he has not dealt effectively with the problem of at least somebody's resistance to a change in perspective! In our work we have to deal with our perspectives and our patients' perspectives (and, especially in hospital work, also the perspectives of the families) on the various aspects of multidimensional blood sausages, and not being fired is part of our job.

In addition to the problem of seeing separate parts, apparent lack of continuity, where actually there is unseen continuity, there is the opposite problem--seeing continuity, a chain of causal connection, where actually there is none. This has been illustrated in an experiment by Bavelas (2). The subject of the experiment is told there is a correct sequence of punching a group of buttons. A bell will sound, he is told, when he hits upon the correct pattern. The subject's work is rewarded with increasingly frequent bell sounds until the experiment is interrupted. When asked about the correct pattern, the subject describes it and explains which hypotheses he formed, discarded, and modified in the process of becoming convinced that he has discovered the right sequence. He is totally incredulous when the experimenter explains that there is no correct pattern and that the timing of the bell sounds followed a theoretical learning curve. The subject gives up his conviction only after he becomes the experimenter with another naïve subject, who becomes equally convinced of the correctness of a different pattern.

It is necessary in a sense to become "another person" in order to abandon a conviction concerning continuities and causalities that do not in fact exist. However, for the same person only a position change is necessary to abandon a mistaken conviction of discontinuity and lack of causal relationships--the patient gaining such insights can, so to speak, move around and stay within his own skin (which is analogous to recognizing the overarching "skin" that holds together the disparate parts of the blood sausage). In contrast, a change from subject to experimenter means that one has gotten out of one's own skin. Neurotic patients--i.e., patients whose skin is more or less intact--in a basically benevolent nonjudgmental atmosphere which fosters therapeutic alliance, find it relatively easy to move around more freely than they had previously. But in order to get out of their own skin and explore a world in which connections that carry a heavy charge of previous conviction may not exist, they need transference countertransference fluidity.

If those whose skin is less intact are even to move around somewhat more freely, transference must be established. The recognition of the intense transference phenomena of psychotic patients, associated with the name of Frieda Fromm-Reichmann among others, remains of major importance for therapeutic approaches to these patients. These patients must borrow, to use Bion's word, the "container" before they can move around as a piece. When the boundaries are fragile, movement increases the danger of oozing out, and thus, especially for such patients, transference developments are a necessary ingredient of early movement attempts in the treatment (6, p.578). (On a very concrete level, I have placed some mute catatonic patients in cold wet sheet packs at a time when they were not moving. My crude reasoning was that if all their energies were absorbed in not moving in order not to destroy, perhaps some energies would become available for verbal communications if they received some external help in not moving. In several instances this hoped for result occurred.)

In returning, however, to the treatment of patients in states of less fragility--and especially to the question of who makes and experiences effort, and when--I need to elaborate further some of my reasons for selecting the quotations from Handke. My primary reason is his description and induction of the tension between the not quite overlapping awareness of "something" and awareness of self-- for instance, the quality of suspendedness, the center of which cannot be quite located in the halted escalator, the halted breath, or somewhere in the "halted atmosphere." Those of you familiar with Rorschach scoring methods will recognize at least a partial similarity here to the "small m" symbol ("m") for inanimate movement (e.g., the response "There is a wind blowing"). Such responses are generally discussed in the context of "ego weakness," or "loss of impulse control," but they are also included in the context of "regression in the service of the ego," particularly when protocols of patients in analysis are studied and their "loosening of ego boundaries" is related to the psychoanalytic process. In previous work (esp. 6) I have developed the idea that such a quality (here the quality of "haltedness") can have an "object constancy" of its own, a greater constancy, for instance, than is connected with the mental representation of a person, of the "self", or even of more traditionally thought of "part objects".

Handke also gives us, in the two quotations, indications of two "resolutions" of the tension. The expelled breath and the suddenly again-moving escalator become transformed into the collapsing pile of the sought-after building blocks. This is the catastrophic resolution of the tension, the analogue--available to all of us--of the world destruction fear against which the catatonic defends by freezing the universe into immobility. The other resolution of tension which Handke illustrates is contained in the passage moving from the indifferent object--associated ultimately with the loss of awareness of oneself, with the loss of consciousness--to the object of desire, the wishing to possess, with all that this implies about the existence of an inside and an outside. (This sequence also gives rise to additional questions that may be related to the etiology of pathology: How indifferent or significant an object was the individual at different times to his parenting figures?)

In Handke's work there is an endless mirroring of the mirror involving the reflection of content in form and vice versa. It is tempting to discuss in detail the relationship of his ideas to the psychoanalytic notions of projection and projective identification, but that would lead us too far afield. Suffice it to say in the present context that the collapse of either content or form as stable end points is a psychoanalytically important concept related to the "object constancy" characteristics of such qualities as, for instance, "suspendedness" or "aggression," in which there can be constant oscillation between content and form. In an earlier paper I attempted to depict this experience by extending the concept of synesthesia "beyond the usual sensory synesthesia to include in addition to seeing, hearing, tactile sense, kinesthesia, and temperature sense also mood, emotion, space, and time..." (10, p. 238).

It is incumbent on me to more clearly emphasize the connections between a discussion of expulsion of breath, world destruction fantasies of catatonic patients, "atmospheric" object constancies, and the treatment of neurotic patients--the analysis of "patients with less fragility." It would be easy here, but not entirely fruitful, to get involved in a general discussion of the levels of regression which must be reached in ordinary psychoanalytic work, or a discussion of what kind of analyst's interest in pregenital material vitiates the analytic process and what kind of analyst's fear of and avoidance of pregenital material has different but equally vitiating results. There is, of course, agreement among analysts that the more advanced, genital levels of conflict, from which preoccupation with more primitive material may be a defensive escape, should not be neglected. The point that I wish to underline here is that each perceptual act may recapitulate the development of perception. It is of clinical interest that experimental observations support this idea. Adult experimental subjects to whom Rorschach cards are presented for a small fraction of a second "see" in the cards what young children report seeing when they have unlimited time to look at the cards (14). The adults, not so incidentally, may be quite reluctant to commit themselves to reporting their impressions. The act of "organizing" the "flashing" impressions--in which raw color and inanimate movement frequently predominate--in order to "translate" them into a statement, requires considerable EFFORT. There may be a degree of similarity between such an effort and that of the hardworking neurotic patient in psychoanalysis, who goes back and forth between the flashes of his internal perceptions and more or less organized statements about them.

The observing ego is indeed a hard-working ego. The work often involves either or both of the changes which I described (I deliberately avoid the terms "role" and "role change" because they frequently carry sociological meanings

that are not intended here)--the "position" changes leading to the perception of continuities where there seemed
to be none, and the "becoming another person" changes,
which involved transference proper and the discovery of
discontinuities where there was a previous conviction of
causal linkages. In active periods, often the mid-phase
of analysis, these changes are worked through to organized
statements which may be closely followed by, or simultaneous with, an opening to the internal perception of a
"flash". (The extent to which such "statements" have to
be explicitly verbalized in psychoanalysis is sometimes a
matter of debate.)

In general the analysand's (ego) experience of work
has its countertransference reflection in the analyst's
day-to-day experience of hard work. This is usually the
case even when the patient seems to be doing it all by
himself and the analyst makes few explicit verbal interventions. The patient who previously may have complained
about the analyst's relative degree of silence may now
find almost any comment disruptive, disagreeable, intrusive. Not getting into the analysand's way is now a significant part of the analyst's effort. Rather rapid judgments about how to avoid getting in the way--or how to
quickly shift again and reintervene--may frequently be required of the analyst. Of course, transference and countertransference of degrees and qualities of effort may themselves sometimes move to the foreground as topics for analytic scrutiny. In addition, I have noticed that at such
times of active effort by the analysand, information about
and problems related to the patient's work life--often a
previously neglected area--may become more visible.

The range and rhythm of oscillation between "primitive"
and "organized" (often probably primary and secondary process) material in patient and analyst tend to have a relatively high degree of correspondence, and this accounts
for the day-to-day level of the analyst's work, effort,
and fatigue experience. The opened-up issues often find
some resolution during the day's therapeutic work, or at
least resolutions are in the field of the probable or the
possible, so that the accumulation at the end of the day
is moderate and manageable. As much as this is possible
for what Freud called the "impossible profession," the
day's work resembles other kinds of work.

With respect to a presentation of aspects of therapeutic work with schizophrenic patients, ideally one should
spell out those speculations about etiology which produced
the working hypotheses that formed the basis of the therapy. Although my focus here on the issue of effort somewhat limits the discussion, in this context I find that a
central etiologic position is occupied by the idea introduced earlier--that perceptual acts recapitulate the development of perception. The contributions of "external"
and "internal" elements to what one "sees" in perceptual
"flashes" are particularly difficult to sort out. Since

each perceptual act which unfolds sufficiently thus seems
to accommodate the development of a boundary between inner
and outer, one could reasonably talk of perceptual acts
as recapitulating individuation. As I have indicated in
my earlier papers (8, 7, 6) that discuss aspects of these
matters in detail (object constancy, time experience,
drive derivatives in perception, and reality construction),
I believe that premature ego demands, leading to avoidance
of paradoxical and transitional experiences, are more
likely candidates for an etiologic role in   schizophrenic and borderline pathology than overexposure to certain
kinds of paradoxical communications, as envisaged by
double-bind theorists (1, 7). The point to be emphasized
here is that the effort--if that is even an appropriate
word--to tolerate ambiguity is qualitatively and quantita-
tively different from the effort "to straighten things
out."

For practical working purposes I do find that I function as though I believed that trauma was etiologically
more important for some patients than for others. I think,
for instance, of a patient who had her first psychotic episode after she had obeyed her mother's request and arranged to be present in the operating room in which the mother
was "opened up" and found to have a widespread malignancy.

I would further propose that the concept of the reca-
pitulation of development in the perceptual act, when applied to the study of schizophrenic patients, can also ten-
tatively accommodate various so-called "deficiency" and
conflict hypotheses concerning etiology (13) and also the
idea of "perceptual defense." Neurotransmitter studies
employing a conceptual framework that includes consideration of the forming, timing, and spreading of perceptual
organization might be a starting point for meaningful confluence of different areas of research.

Focusing again more specifically on effort, I find that
therapists of schizophrenic patients--some publicly and
some only privately when they are not afraid of sounding
naïve--do think of some patients as trying very hard at a
particular time "not to be crazy" and of others as "deciding" at some moment (often one which is perceived as
"crucial") to be psychotic. I recall with particular clarity a young, brilliant philosophy student hospitalized
with a diagnosis of schizophrenia, catatonic. While he
could engage in what seemed to be genuine, meaningful, interesting conversations, with give and take about esoteric
intellectual matters, he often would react to the introduction of a topic concerning his daily living by locking himself into a "lotus position", rolling back his eyes, and
staying "locked" for days despite physical efforts of several strong male aides. The catatonic episode would continue for a long time even after he came out of a three-
or four-day lotus "exercise." Such apparently voluntary
aspects of the behavior of the patient who is "trying
hard" despite his severe thought disorder," the patient

who "gives up," the patient who defiantly seems to choose or flaunt his psychosis, all have profound countertransference consequences related to the experience of effort. But before considering these further, I wish to say a word about my current working hypothesis concerning these "voluntary" aspects of the schizophrenic patient's behavior and communications.

Like many others, I think of "voluntary" psychotic behavior as a major defensive operation. Defensive against what? Among other sources of information, some reports by users of psychedelic substances may be informative. Some hint at two kinds of "ego death." One includes fusion, becoming somebody else, or even transformation into an inanimate object (which may, however, be suffused with energy, atoms, electrons). The other may be referred to as an unspeakable void, a nothingness against which death pales. I believe that Fromm-Reichmann in "Loneliness" (3) and Lichtenstein in "The Effect of Reality Perception on Psychic Structure" (12) deal with these states. While I cannot say more about the void, I can communicate my belief that the area of the relative degrees of completion of the perceptual act, an area perhaps roughly corresponding to a major area of activity of the preconscious, is also the one in which the voluntary and the haphazard meet. It is the area for the position changes from which the blood sausage of history looks different and the area for transference, for "becoming another person."

Our discussion of effort in work with schizophrenic patients will remain somewhat incomplete because it will not consider in detail the motivations of therapists who choose to spend some of their energies in such work. Here I will simply refer to the rather obvious strong motivation to make contact and "to make sense" where sense may not be readily apparent. Sometimes these two motivations can be talked about somewhat separately; more often they are blended. Most amusing stories about work with schizophrenic patients have to do with seeming collapse, or in a peculiar way, with a degree of success of efforts at contact or understanding.

Let me illustrate: I had been impressed with Fromm-Reichmann's description of an episode in which she had sat for many hours with a mute patient until finally one day he lifted one finger. Fromm-Reichmann "understood" his communication about the degree of his loneliness and she lifted two fingers to indicate that he was not alone. This example of nonverbal communication impressed me sufficiently during my residency so that after sitting for many hours during several months with a totally mute patient, I told him, in some desperation, the story of a famous psychiatrist who had sat with a mute patient like him who one day lifted a finger--"Like this," I demonstrated. I said that the doctor had seemed to understand the gesture, and I then asked the patient what he thought the patient meant. However, either for unconscious reasons which still elude me, or because as an immigrant I lacked complete understanding of American sign language, I had lifted the middle instead of the index finger. The patient looked at me without changing expression and answered my question clearly and distinctly. "Fuck you," he said. He never spoke to me again after this monumental breakthrough connected with my effort to make contact.

At another time, I was sitting with a gesticulating patient--a patient on whom people had "given up"--who repetitively drew an angle in the air and then looked at me questioningly. I finally said, "You mean, what's my angle?" The patient's gesticulating behavior immediately diminished and changed in nature, and there was some increase in verbal communication. I did not think then and I certainly do not think now that I had understood his gesture correctly. I do think, however, that the intensity of my effort to understand him did in the long run have a slight impact, even though he improved only moderately during the time I worked with him. The same patient, some months later, was saying some incomprehensible things about which I ventured some guesses. He said "louder" and I raised my voice. Again he said "louder," and again and again until I was shouting. He looked at me more intently at that point and said rather paternalistically, "Not you!" Some time later, when I was asking him questions about his hallucinations, he explained to me how absurd certain questions seemed to him. For example, some of his utterances had led me to ask if he was hearing father or God, and he clearly communicated that he considered this a rather pedestrian concern which he could answer either way. He taught me that he was dealing with a certain kind of majestic atmospheric quality.

One of the main things that the therapist of schizophrenic patients learns in his first five to ten years of such work is the absurdity of most of his efforts to make contact with and to understand the communications of many deeply "regressed" patients. From day to day one's conscious expectations are reduced, compared to those in psychoanalytic work with neurotic patients. In addition, processes of repression and denial of one's impotence play a part in the countertransference picture. The combined effect is that from day to day one feels that one does not have to work so hard with the schizophrenic patient. However, the processes of repression and denial specifically linked to such treatment are loosened during a vacation. The therapist's more ordinary expectations of being able to make contact and to make sense are in the foreground, and just before or during the first postvacation session with the schizophrenic patient he becomes aware of derivatives of the unconscious efforts, the "work" related to his repressions and denials. These, too, of course must be seen in the context of countertransference, as a reflection of the significance of the patient's areas of impotence or as residuals of the patient's omnipotent delusions.

As I indicated earlier, "borderline" patients tend to be on both sides of the fatigue spectrum. A recent major compendium on borderline personality disorders edited by Hartocollis (5) reveals how differently the term is used by different authors, with a special divergence between those who consider such disorders as "soft schizophrenia" and those who see them as "stable instability." In focusing on the "effort" theme in relationship to borderline patients, I will not discuss the diagnostic concept in detail, but I would like to refer you to my review of the Hartocollis volume for a more thorough analysis (9).

When I consider characteristics of patients whom I think of as having marked borderline features, their investment in maintaining "discontinuities" moves into the foreground. This is, of course, consonant with Kernberg's elaborate theory of the significance of "splitting." Recalling again the image of the blood sausage, I think of these patients as characterized by great "resistance" to changing or reexamining their perspective so as to be able to see obvious links. However, since these patients may be psychologically quite mobile (especially in contrast to the immobility of some schizophrenic patients), and since they demonstrate a "stable instability" by avoiding or sliding out of those specific positions that would seem to be the keys to movement, the therapist's countertransference picture frequently contains a certain exasperation and confrontational mood. Kernberg's paper "Structural Change and Its Impediments" (11) illustrates this with considerable poignancy. The magnitude of the day-to-day therapeutic effort and fatigue (Kernberg specifically recommends that one should have only a few of these patients at any one time) is related to an undercurrent of feeling that such patients' overall functioning SHOULD make it possible for them to develop therapeutic insights, and that aggression--including a primitive level of oral aggression--is part of the picture.

Kernberg warns against the therapist's acceptance of stalemate, his sinking into lassitude in an interminable unproductive situation. He points to the necessity of "facing" issues, accepting limitations, and confronting aggression. Thinking about the clinical atmosphere Kernberg describes, I believe that my own tendency currently is to "confront" later--that is, not to avoid contact with rage, but to encounter it on another level. Schematically, I now think that some patients with whom I previously thought early confrontational work was necessary would be too gratified by the sadomasochistic aspects of such an atmosphere. Even with meager supportive genetic evidence, I am more likely to offer interpretations along this line, despite the fact that any "response" to such interpretations is sometimes delayed for a strikingly prolonged period. Eventually, however, it may become clear to the therapist and to the patient that the resistance against being in a position from which continuities could be seen is only an advance defensive line, behind which the more tenacious clinging to connections where there are none represents the transference aspects which have to be engaged. At this point "psychotic" transference elements are likely to become a prominent part of the picture. Even in work with those borderline patients with whom the risk of overt psychosis is not great, the analyst's effort and fatigue distribution and its timing may now resemble those of his work with psychotic patients more than those with which he is familiar from the psychoanalysis of neurotic persons.

I might also add a word here about the therapist's resistance to moving into areas in which intense negative--I am inclined to say "bloody"--transference elements are likely to come into the foreground in work with hospitalized borderline patients or schizophrenic patients. It is reported that families--supposedly to maintain an internal equilibrium or (pathologic) status quo--frequently agitate for the removal of the patient from the hospital just when he is beginning to show striking signs of improvement. While I do not doubt that this sometimes occurs, I have observed the following when I was involved as a consultant in establishing a program for the families of hospitalized patients. Often at the beginning of the program, when considerable EFFORT in working with the family was successful to the extent that an improving patient was not removed from the hospital, the response from administration and/or therapist was much less enthusiastic than I had expected. In retrospect, it was as if there had been some peripheral awareness in the therapist that the improvement might represent temporary positive transference, beyond which loomed troubled times. To put it strongly, when the family was induced to keep the patient in the hospital, an element of unconscious collusion between therapist (and hospital), patient, and family may have been exposed. Where the family and the hospital system are fairly explicitly involved, the therapist's scrutiny of effort--and attempts to be released from effort--in himself and his patient can thus also be an interesting and perhaps useful therapeutic activity.

In psychoanalytic work with patients of various degrees and kinds of pathology, the study of who makes what kind of effort when, throws some light on the shifting scene of the focusing and resolving of those linkages which determine the nature of personal realities.

REFERENCES

1. Bateson, G., Jackson, D.C., Haley, J. and Weakland, J. (1956): Toward a Theory of Schizophrenia. Behav. Sci. 1, 251.
2. Bavelas, A. (1970): Description of experiment on persistence of erroneous convictions regarding "causality."

In: Problem-Solving and Search Behavior Under Non-contingent Rewards. J.C. Wright. University Microfilms, Ann Arbor, Mich.

3. Fromm-Reichmann, F. (1959): Loneliness. Psychiatry, 22, 1.
4. Handke, P. (1969): Die Innenwelt der Aussenwelt der Innenwelt. Suhrkamp, Frankfurt am Main.
5. Hartocollis, P., Editor (1977): Borderline Personality Disorders: The Concept, the Syndrome, the Patient. Int. Univ. Press, New York.
6. Kafka, J.S. (1964): Technical Applications of a Concept of Multiple Reality. Int. J. Psycho-Anal., 45, 575.
7. Kafka, J.S. (1971): Ambiguity for Individuation: A Critique and Reformulation of Double-Bind Theory. Arch. Gen. Psychiat., 25, 232.
9. Kafka, J.S. (1977): On Reality: An Examination of Object Constancy, Ambiguity, Paradox, and Time. In: Thought, Consciousness, and Reality, Vol. 2 of Psychiatry and the Humanities, p. 133. Editor: J.H. Smith, Yale Univ. Press, New Haven, Conn.
9. Kafka, J.S. (in press): Review: Borderline Personality Disorders. Editor: P. Hartocollis. J. Amer. Psychoanal. Assoc.
10. Kafka, J.S. and Gaarder, K.R. (1964): Some Effects of the Therapist's LSD Experience on his Therapeutic Work. Amer. J. Psychother., 18, 236.
11. Kernberg, O. (1977): Structural Change and Its Impediments. In: Borderline Personality Disorders, p. 275. Editor: P. Hartocollis. Int. Univ. Press, New York.
12. Lichtenstein, H. (1974): The Effect of Reality Perception on Psychic Structure: A Psychoanalytic Contribution to the Problem of the 'Generation Gap.' Annual of Psychoanal., 2. Int. Univ. Press, New York.
13. London, N.J. (1973): An Essay on Psychoanalytic Theory: Two Theories of Schizophrenia. Part I: Review and Critical Assessment of the Development of the Two Theories. Part II. Discussion and Restatement of the Specific Theory of Schizophrenia. Int. J. Psycho-Anal., 54, 169 and 179.
14. Stein, M.I. (1949): Personality Factors Involved in Temporal Development of Rorschach Responses. Res. Exch. and J. Proj. Tech., 13, 355.

AN APPROACH TO UNDERSTANDING PSYCHOSIS THROUGH VARIOUS TECHNIQUES IN GROUP WORK

Georges   Abraham, Philippe Bovier and Jacques Dubuis

Clinique Psychiatrique Universitaire, Bel-Air, 1225 Chêne-Bourg Genève (Switzerland)

At the University Psychiatric Clinic of Bel-Air (Geneva) we have created a research group on the psychotherapy of psychotics. Our purpose has been to try to reach a better understanding of the functionning of the psychotic subject and for this purpose to see how one might enter into communication with him. Rather than apply a theoretical model, our idea was to put ourselves in a situation of "encountering" one or more patients, living together a certain lapse of time, calling upon various techniques but just as much upon our "spontaneity" and our counter-transfer. In fact it seemed to us that the utilization of a given technique represented a priori an imposed and therefore limiting model of communication. Thus the inner disponibility of each group member became the characteristic mark of the informal relationship we offered to the psychotic pa-tient. A discussion at the end of each session aimed at trying to understand what had happened and to pick out various clues.

The group, composed of members of the Clinic staff, has now been in existence for three years. Its development during this time seems to us to show an increase of flexibility and a redisposition of our identity as therapists, rendered necessary by our premises. What actually happened was that we started out, without intentions of orthodoxy, simply by being a group which was going to see a patient hospitalized in one of the units; and, full of the desire to understand this person's discourse, we spoke with him; referen-ce to the analytical model was established quasi spontaneously; and we thus improvised psychodramas or conversation (among therapeutical personnel) about the patient. There followed a period of diverse attempts, concentrating on two or three patients seen regularly in company with their staff team, with the intervals occupied by a patient in a more acute situation. We tried some hypnosis, we introduced marionettes, and we also used a contract system, a kind of written agreement between us and the patient, covering specific ward activities, obligatory thoughts, or even the audition of taped voices inspired by their hallucinations. Most frequently it was we who invited the patient into "our" room. The third period was characterized by the closing of the group, which gave it an outward stability, thereby probably permitting greater freedom and scope inside each weekly session. Progressively we invited several (two to four) patients together. The techniques included the waking dream, role-playing, transactional analysis, paradox, music therapy and, above all, various physical approaches: corporal

expression, group games, massage, relaxation, bio-energy, but
without any strict codification; moreover we introduced "passivity":
doing nothing, proposing nothing, waiting to see what would happen.
During the course of this development the leader's role was by turn
that of guide - whether supple, authoritarian, or invested in the
expectation of reassuring activities - and that of catalyst.
Psychotic mechanisms were often at work inside the group itself,
visible for example in the oscillation between fusion and cleavage,
and once even by the exclusion of the therapists.

CLINICAL EXAMPLES

We have chosen to describe several sessions, in view of the
discussion to follow.

1. Two Sessions with One Patient

We know of this patient that he is a young catatonically
decompensated schizophrenic with long periods of block finishing
by masturbation, rocking, and repeated rubbing of his hands. The
group is already set up in a circle in the room. The patient enters
and sits down in one of the chairs in the circle, next to the door,
and stays there rigid, motionless, silent. We speak about him
among ourselves, each saying what he thinks or feels. At this
point he states, "I am caught in the gears". Several staff members
act out symbolically the meshing of gears, coming close to him,
touching him, hugging him, etc.   He wishes to leave this encircle-
ment with the help of a woman - and we act that out. The couple is
at the center of the group. He blocks again, stops speaking, turns
in upon himself. Some one says, "You are fine like that and we
accept you like that". Then the notion of the belly occurs and the
patient declares that he wants to get out. From that point on there
is a discussion with him, turning upon his mother and father; bit
by bit he becomes more rigid. He unblocks when the group tells him
they like him all the same, closed in on himself. We authorize him
not to communicate with his parents during the interval between the
two sessions.

In the follow-up discussion, we take note that he is more at
ease in physical relationships and we suggest being less verbal
the next time.

In the following session, his doctor recounts that the patient
did not participate in the Christmas festivity and that he did not
receive any presents; nevertheless he went around to all the other
patients wishing each one a Merry Christmas, and then relapsed into
silence. The patient enters and we propose a Christmas celebration.
He remains silent and rigid. Some one says, "He doesn't feel like
talk; we'll come up to him and wish him Merry Christmas but without talking". Each member comes up to him and communicates his
wish in his own way. When one of the staff massages his trapezius
muscles, he becomes distrustful and moves, eliciting the following

comment: "Ah. He is getting ideas. This is my way of wishing him
a Merry Christmas. Now I shall rock him, he is scared, it is understandable... We are caressing him instead of making him work, like
his parents... We could pick him up, all together". At this point
the patient gets up and goes to sit facing the group. We improvise
group games (walking blind, rocking in a circle...), gradually
integrating him and finishing by lifting him up on our hands. At
the end we are all sitting in a circle. He says, "I, I...".
Some one suggests acting like him. We all go immobile. Bit by
bit he starts rocking. We all rock. Then each of us goes up to
say goodbye to him.

During the discussion we note that for the time being the
physical approach is best. Furthermore he seems better when he
is not in a privileged position, whence comes the idea of having
several patients at the same time. Some one brings up the problem
of the start of the session: if an activity had already begun,
the patient would be more at ease. Another interesting element is
that of the patient's unknown reactivity: one never knows how he
will react, what is going to happen, what will be understood.
Finally, facing a case of block, we feel the temptation to use a
specific method for obtaining a deblock. For example, a woman
patient said, "I breathe out thoughts when I breathe out heavily";
an interpretation comes immediately to mind and closes off the
possibility of observing otherwise what is going on interiorly.

2. One Session with One Patient

One of the staff lies down while the others stand around her
and wait for the situation to develop. The patient, a woman,
enters and each of us says what he might do with the person lying
down. The patient says, "Leave her alone, let her dream", whereas we had been proposing to "do" something (encircle, move, massage,
speak to, etc.). We then take off on a dream voyage with theme and
symbolism given by the patient: wall, sand, tempest, weather,
danger from the outside, treasure at the bottom of the sea, flying,
etc. At the end we delegate our guest to be the group's Dreamer,
putting value on her capacity to do it alone; we ask her to dream
by herself every day of the week.

3. One Session with Four Patients

The staff and patients arrive one or two at a time. Ball games,
rythm games begin spontaneously. One patient proposes the exchange
of personal belongings: a scarf, a sweater, necklaces, keys,
watches... This exchange turns into games with streamers and cushions
becoming more and more disorderly and noisy. Some one yells very
loudly, and every one responds to this stimulus by doing the same.
Calmness slowly returns. Then one patient suggests making a film.
He tries to organize a group of "actors", without managing to do so.
The group falls into marked passivity, then some of the patients
start doing whatever comes into their heads, whether or not the

others join in: talking, moving, emitting cries or other noises, etc. Several come, go, go out, come in again. The session come to an end when one patient declares, "Fine. But as for me, I'm getting out of here".

During the discussion we take up the fact that every patient wants to be the center of interest and drops out whenever some one else starts something with part of the group. They are better integrated, but passive, when the leader and the group act more directively. On the other hand they are more at ease and definitely more coherent in a formless group, hazy, and crazy. Finally a notion of containment comes out, a containment realized by the group members looking at others doing or experienced something.

4. <u>One Session with Two Patients</u>

One of the patients declares that he launched the war between the Chinese and the Japonese, and he demands a punishment. We hold a trial. The second patient plays the public prosecutor: a judge, a defense attorney, and defense and prosecution witnesses are improvised. At one point witness confirms the accusation, because he has seen a light come out of the accused's head and disappear very quickly. The patient is much struck by this testimony and integrates this new element into his system of a delirium: that is exactly what had happened. The Judge condemns him to a week of thinking about something unpleasant. The convicted patient proposes thinking about the second patient, the prosecutor of the trial. The latter becomes angry, saying, "I am not a murderer". The doctor-Judge offers the choice of thinking of him either as a murderer or not. The patient chooses: "Murderer".

The discussion, which we tried to have in the presence of the two patients, proved to be difficult because they were continuing the game. Nevertheless we are struck by the intensity of a whole scheme of communication established and encouraged to flourish by the specific atmosphere of our group.

<u>DISCUSSION</u>

As long as psychosis and particularly schizophrenia still remain a mystery, however relative, medical modesty is de rigueur.

Thus our group preferred to make its observation of the patients as devoid as possible of structural or nosographic assumptions; in place of therapeutic projects or curative impulses the group substituted efforts at understanding and making contact. Our one therapeutic aim can be expressed in terms of seeking out a psycho-emotional mobilization of the patient and hoping to be able to offer him alternatives to his own defensive stereotypes. Therefore there can be no question here of relating either results due to remedial measures of the efficacity (or non-efficacity) of a clinical application of a given vision of psychosis.

As for the different techniques utilized, even when they intrinsically imply a therapeutic model, we used them only as tools capable of facilitating communication or the provocation of material for later observation.

At all events we sought to accord equal importance to the imaginary and the real, to expressions both phantasmal and corporal, to speech and all its possible equivalents. We tried to be as incoherent, irrational, and spontaneous as possible. When the atmosphere of a session seemed to be getting heavy or stagnating, we quickly changed our method of approach or of relational orientation - very passive or very active and directive, very silent and unobtrusive or noisy and agitated. On the other hand, since some members of the group sometimes acted in one way while others at the same time were turning towards a different attitude (either the opposite or simply with a shade of difference), the leadership of the group moved to define and assert itself for several instants and at other times dimmed and dissolved.

Above all we were pleased to feel ourselves greatly accessible. Our counter-transfer served as our guide, particularly through collective or majority sensations of ease or on the contrary through perceptions of uneasiness that could penetrate all of us or sometimes only just a few members of the group.

If, from time to time, an explanatory model seemed to come to light, we used it only as a working hypothesis ready to be replaced or modified. In any case the construction of such a model never preceded observation but either parallelled it or followed it. Furthermore we did not experience the explicatory polymorphism coming out of our observations as upsetting or possibly confusing, but interpreted it as the result of the complexity and overdetermination of the target phenomena of our observation.

On the other hand, in approaching patients, we also assumed the existence in ourselves of several possible personalities of varying reciprocal predominance and of there being different parts of ourselves - including "mad" parts - that could constitute the most valid interlocutor for our research.

At the level of basic observation, it seemed to us that in all the patients studied there were at least four openings for communication or, if one prefers, four fundamental functional fulcra.

(1) The first could be described as a vectorial perception of the presence of others, capable of modifying - sometimes to a minimal degree - reactional comportment and defensive dispositions. Whether it be a question of delirium, hallucinations, mannerisms, etc., the presence of others, invasive or not, always interferes with the patient's supposed autism. The autism in question thus becomes a datum that is relative, not absolute.

(2)   The second functional fulcrum could be described as the persistance, despite perturbations and deficiencies in the patient's personality, of a need for estimation and confrontation of the value of the self; a sort of inalienable narcissistic nucleus that is therefore maintained over and beyond the most serious symptomatology. Thus, for example, if two patients are simultaneous objects of observation, each tries to polarize on himself the full attention of the group.

(3)   The third basic functional fulcrum is the maintenance of an aggression function, generally rather tonic despite the patient's apparent apathy or withdrawal into himself. Aggressive energy seems in fact to form an inexhaustible energy capable of exploitation oriented in a different way.

(4)   The fourth fulcrum and the one that seems most interesting to us is the evidence of a certain pleasure (even though combined with anguish) in incoherence. All of these patients seem to like to push their incoherence to its extreme limits. Even when this brings them anxiety and, on occasion, guilt.

If the observers try to "rave" along with the patients or even outdo them, the patients often react with attempts to "return to reality" or to a certain kind of coherence or, after a whole session of incoherent dialogue, they express a great fatigue or exhaustion as if in short the delirium was only a limited and controlled form of incoherence, whereas the induced extension of possibilities for delirium would cause with the patients a "rebound" or else an activation of a supplement of defensive energy.

In conclusion, and despite the fact that our experiments in their entirety still seem fragmentary to us and not sufficiently worked through, we can establish the following hypotheses:

1.   Instead of raising a veritable communication barrier or breaking off all possibility of dialogue, the psychotic seems simply to put to work a particular form of language which proves to be not impossible to learn.

2.   A pluridimensional and polymorphic approach to the psychotic, whether through a variation of techniques or through the form of a group, seems to work by a very effective complementary reciprocity instead of constituting an element of communication "jamming".

3.   An attitude of great accessibility, both conceptual and emotional, seems to open the possibility of recognition of variables and unknowns in psychotic manifestations.

Our present closed conceptualizations threaten to partialize or freeze the approach to this kind of patient.

4. By trying to push to excess a certain symptomology of delirious types or the deformation of reality and the incoherence which stems therefrom, the psychotic seems to react by a "rebound" inducing a kind of momentary reconsideration of his own comportment.

FAMILY TREATMENT OF PSYCHOTIC DISTURBANCES IN CHILDREN AND ADOLESCENTS

Daniel Masson and Odette Masson

Institut Universitaire d'Hygiene Mentale, Lausanne,
Switzerland

Based on a study of 6 families, this paper seeks to demonstrate the value of the family approach in the treatment
of psychotic crises in children and adolescents.

The difficulties encountered in the treatment of these
patients have led a number of researchers to seek approaches
other than the classical individual psychotherapy. The Paris
psychoanalytic school developed psychodrama (Lebovici et
al., 1958). Anglo-saxon researchers have, since 1950, developed various methods of family therapy which take into
account the great interdependence between family members,
and the position occupied by the child or adolescent in the
hierarchical structure of the family. Therapists working
either with individuals or with families have a common goal,
to alleviate psychological suffering both in the patient
himself and in those around him. Disparities in the methods
of individual and family treatments occur on theoretical,
etiological and technical levels. Instead of the deductive
analysis used in cases of individual psychotherapy, family
therapists have developed a method of study based on the
observation of relationships through communication. All behaviour is communication and all communication affects behaviour (Watzlawick et al., 1967). M. Selvini et al. (1975)
consider the family a 'natural group with a history' which
during its development has established rules peculiar to
itself or which are rooted in the family origins. This family group represents an open and self-regulating system
which oscillates between tendencies towards stability
through negative retroactions, and tendencies towards change
by modification of norms and rules under the pressure of internal or external events through positive retroactions.

The most severely affected families are those most re-
sistant to the necessary changes which make up the process
of the life cycle. 'In the face of stress (they) increase
the rigidity of their transactional patterns and boundaries,
and avoid or resist any exploration or alternatives' (Minuchin, 1974). Thus are the families considered here. They
illustrate what a large number of authors have observed in
psychotic contexts, with their blurred generational boundaries (Lidz et al., 1965), chronic 'parentification' of the
children (Boszormenyi-Nagy, 1973), and interactional modes
such as binding, delegation and rejection (Stierlin, 1973).

From the systemic viewpoint, the symptoms appear as redundancies in the specific interplay which characterizes the interaction and 'not as the result of an unresolved conflict between assumed intrapsychic forces' (Watzlawick et al., 1967). The very fact that the symptoms seem to move between hosts within the family, though the interactions remain unchanged, gives full weight to this view. The symptoms of the person identified as the patient in addition to certain behavioural manifestations in other members of the family, equally symptomatic but rarely presented as such, serve to maintain the homeostasis. At the same time, it is these very marked symptoms which represent the opening up of interactional vicious circles to the extent that they bring about the entry of the therapist into the family. This entry is threatening and is feared by all the protagonists which are actively maintaining the vicious circles. Understanding this fact underlines the risk run by the therapist of becoming caught up in these transactions and of merely becoming a supplementary element in the circuit. Technically, the therapist joins the family without allowing himself to be drawn into judgements or criticisms about the group or any of its members (Selvini et al., 1975). He practices a multidirectional partiality (Boszormenyi-Nagy, 1973) which allows him to set up contact with each member of the family. Once the therapist has established a relationship with the members of the family and understands the nature of the system adequately, he can see the symptoms of the identified patient as help brought to the family. It is the 'positive connotation' (Selvini et al., 1975) which reveals the function of the symptom in the family transactions

This has been a brief summary of the theoretical options which underlie our work with these 6 families. The families have the following characteristics in common:

1. One or more of their members presented a psychotic episode triggered when the family moved into a new phase in its life cycle: in one family, at the prospect of adoption of a one-year old daughter; in a second, when the two eldest girls started school; and in 5 families, at the onset of adolescence in a child aged between 13 and 16 years. The total of 7 crises in 6 families is accounted for by the reoccurrence of schizophrenic decompensations alternating between mother and daughter in one of the families.

2. These families are members of institutional cohorts and are therefore selected according to the severity of the symptoms presented by the identified patient and by the rigidity of the familial organisation. We bear in mind that the natural history of young patients presenting psychotic reations, carries the risk of transition to a chronic psychosis with secondary mental retardation in the case of a young child, or to schizophrenia in the case of an adolescent.

3. The identified patients in these families were all referred by third parties, sometimes after the repeated failure of earlier treatments.

4. These 6 families are still in contact with the therapists at present, even if treatment may have ceased. The length of contact varies from 8 to 72 months.

5. Several of these treatments were difficult to conduct as they sometimes called for the assistance of a number of institutions, including: the Day Hospital for Adults, Child Guidance Counselling, the Psychiatric Hospital for Adults, Pediatric clinics, the Children's Day Hospital as well as contact with school psychologists, private pediatricians and teachers who were also involved in the lives of these families. We often encounter with psychotic families this multiplicity of participants, used by the family members in an attempt to diminish the growing emotional tensions within the group by implicating third parties.

6. The psychotherapeutic methods used, refer to the General System Theory, even if at certain intermediate phases of treatment, contact has only been tenuously maintained with the family via a single member.

In observing the progress of the treatment, we may divide these 6 families into 2 groups, I and II:

I. Group One is made up of families A, B, and C, who were able to pursue conjoint treatment with regular sessions. In these 3 families the lengths of treatment needed to produce a change in the interactional patterns together with a disappearance of the symptoms in the identified patient were relatively brief, 2, 7, and 8 months for A, B and C respectively (Table 1).

II. The second group consists of families X, Y and Z who were unable to pursue a conjoint therapy and offered substantial resistance to change, using classical manoeuvres - either the absence of certain members of the family, or the temporary stopping of treatment (Table 2). In these 3 families a change in the patterns of interaction was slow to occur. In family X it did not occur at all, though the symptoms switched hosts; the identified patient is now free of them but the mother has taken them on. The 10 months of treatment have consisted of 5 family sessions and 30 individual sessions with the adolescent who, for the present, is the only one prepared to meet with the therapists.

The relational patterns of family Y are currently in the process of changing very slowly after 27 months of treatment.

In the case of family Z, the therapeutic contacts have been intermittent, extending over 72 months. It was 69 months before any significant change in the family system was seen.

We should like to emphasize that we do not consider the simple disappearance of the symptoms in the identified patient as a positive outcome of therapy, but insist, as a condition of successful treatment, on a tangible change in the interactional patterns amongst the members of the nucleus family and also, if possible, those of the enlarged family.

Amongst the variables accounting for the differences

TABLE 1

Family	Child's symptoms	Length and form of treatment
A	Autistic withdrawal from the age of 18 months	7 family sessions over 6 months
B	Apragmatic crises, delusional thinking from the age of 16 years	12 family sessions over 13 months
C	School phobia, autistic withdrawal from the age of 13 years	11 family sessions over 8 months

TABLE 2

Family	Child's symptoms	Length and form of treatment
X	School phobia from the age of 13 years, auto- and hetero-aggressions	6 family sessions, 30 individual sessions with the adolescent, over 10 months
Y	Panphobia, hallucinations from the age of 13 years	17 family sessions, 20 individual sessions with the adolescent. Current resumption of therapy: over 27 months
Z	Psychotic crisis of catatonic aspect at 12½ years	9 family sessions, 6 couple sessions, 15 family and couple sessions, over 72 months

in the outcomes of treatment in these 2 groups of families, one must, of course, include the technical and strategic errors which the therapist may make in his approach: the adoption of symmetrical behaviour, abandoning the rule of no criticism; failure to maintain multidirectional partiality; loss of the systemic perspective at certain times.

There are other variables which may be recognized as sources of technical or strategic difficulties: an only child: this favours extreme system rigidity and is found in 2 of the 3 families in Group II; social isolation, in the cases of families X, Y and Z; the presentation of the conjugal relationship as something idyllic, unchangeable and untouchable, which was apparent in 3 families in Group II; a long-term lack of information from the parents regarding their relationships with their own families.

We will now summarize the process of two treatments. The first account is brief and deals with family C, a member of Group I, including the less rigidly organized families, which responded to short-term treatment.

Family C consists of the parents, a daughter aged 16, and a son of 14 who is the identified patient. Over a period of 1 year the boy had demonstrated a gradually deteriorating school phobia, and for several months psychotic symptoms which included confusion, dissonance, an atypical hemiparetic syndrome and a door-cleaning compulsion.

In this case, 11 joint sessions, spread over 8 months, led to the disappearance of the symptoms and the adoption by the family of a new functional equilibrium with respect to the adolescence of the 2 children. The therapists used the technique of positive connotation; they were able to observe attempts to maintain the dysfunctional homeostasis originating from different members of the family and alternating with every change. Thus the identified patient was replaced in his role of symptom-bearer first by his mother, and later by his sister. All these movements were connoted positively up to the appearance of functional alliances between brother and sister and then between husband and wife. Up to that point, no such alliances had been seen.

The second example deals with family Z from Group II. This family consists of a father and mother with 3 daughters, all 3 born by caesarian section within a space of 30 months. The husband is 8 years younger than his wife. During his childhood he had been beaten by his alcoholic father. His elder brother had always been odd and had been unable to pursue a normal education. The mother is the eldest of 5 children and harbors terrifying memories of her father's periods in a psychiatric hospital. She herself suffered acute schizophrenic crises, hebephrenic and later paranoid, during adolescence and again at the ages of 33, 37 and 42.

We became aware of this family 6 years ago, during the mother's most recent admission to the psychiatric clinic, during the course of a preventive consultation with children of psychotic parents (Masson, 1976). We thus found a family group in functional chaos in almost every area: relationships, education, housework, finance. The enmeshment was maximal and was apparent in verbal communication. The following is an example: The mother, wishing to talk about her second daughter who was annoying her said: 'She loses my temper'. This 7-year-old child was still being spoon-fed by the mother, was wetting the bed, was anorexic and very contrary. The eldest daughter, aged 8, presented a picture of chronic deficit psychosis appearing in early infancy. Work with this family started in 1972. During 1973, the therapeutic effort consisted of introducing all the members of the family to treatment. At first, we only succeeded in meeting with the mother, invariably the identified patient in the eyes of the family, as well as the second daughter, who was working hard to maintain her position as scapegoat. The youngest was described as the 'well sibling' and the eldest, destined like the paternal uncle, to 'dwell in the clouds'. The father, at the onset, refused all involvement claiming that his vocation as a mechanic made it impossible for him to understand any exchange with the therapist. It was up to her, he maintained, to decide on solutions for the children. Little by little, the father started joining the therapeutic sessions. On the first few occasions, he stayed only a few minutes. During the following year, the eldest, who had completely lost her grip at school, was attending a day hospital. In this same period, the family was able to come together for 9 sessions with a team of 4 therapists. During these sessions we observed a tableau of psychotic transactions; the members of the family showed that they were indissolubly bound up in a network of permanent chaos. With the full complicity of their parents, the daughters forcefully displayed scenes of disconnected theatre; there were some disguised messages to the therapists in their dialogues: 'You're not coming into our cottage', 'I am only pretending to be ill'. Alliances were confused, leadership unassumable, communications heavy with disqualifications. No one member of the family offered to support another. This first series of family sessions broke up without any change in the interactional patterns.

The preliminary contacts did, nevertheless, make it possible to set up a fairly firm relationship between the family and one of the therapists, thus breaking into the social isolation in which the group was living. The disturbances which the children were continuing to suffer, induced the parents to attend several sessions during the next year, and these revealed the persistence of the same morphostatic balance within the system. The mother was thinking more and more about her wish to take up a part-time job and have more contact with the outside world, but at the same time she was perfectly willing to put up with her husband undermining all her attempts to do something for herself. As on the first occasion, we were careful to approve resistance to treatment. Then in 1977, a major incident occurred - an acute psychotic crisis in the second duaghter which took a catatonic form. She was 12 years old, and throughout the preceding months, as the onset of adolescence approached, there had been rows of ever-increasing intensity between mother and daughter, which was affecting them both, more and more. The symptomatic balance between these two members of the family was openly expressed by the mother. She knew, she said, that one of them would lose control during the autumn: 'It's her or me'. The daughter was losing ground at school, until 4 days before Christmas when she went into a catatonic state with inertia and psychomotor negativism, inability to eat or drink, mutism, and double incontinence; she could not get up, and displayed remote and discordant paramimicry. She was fed intravenously for a week. The parents requested the therapist at the pediatric clinic where the child was hospitalised and the family sessions, including both child and parents, took place daily.

The positive connotation of the major regression in the child, i.e. that the catatonic crisis was intended to reassure the members of the family as to the absence of risk of the girl's onset of adolescence, induced a progressive change in the parents. Since then, the husband has been able to allow his wife to resume her relationship with her own parents, with whom she had been careful, with the active participation of the husband, to play the role of a vapid, incompetent and sick girl. We then watched this 42-year-old mother, weighing 115 kg, living out a veritable adolescent revolt in respect to her own parents. This took place in the presence of her own daughter, whose symptoms rapidly regressed. After 4 weeks, the girl asked to return to school and recovered her intellectual powers. Thumb-sucking still continued, unusual in a well-developed 13-year-old adolescent. We told the girl that she was quite right to go on sucking her thumb so that she could remind the whole family that despite everything, she was still a baby, and that a girl who sucks her thumb runs no risk of being taken too seriously. There was a double response, she immediately stopped sucking her thumb and snapped at her mother - 'It's fine for you to nibble away all day and get fatter and fatter'. The mother who was dangerously obese, started to think about her physical condition, and realising that she was likely to kill herself, began with her husband's help, to take care of herself, nagging her daughters less, and taking up a job outside the house.

In fact, it is only during this latter period of treatment following the serious crisis, that we have been able to observe a notable change in the family interactions. This takes the form of a separation of the 3 generations, with the establishment of genuine alliances between husband and wife, who brought their conflicts to the surface instead of, as previously, presenting themselves in a mythical and idyllic relationship.

In conclusion: Family therapy is an important form of treatment in adolescent and child psychiatry. We think it is particularly indicated in the case of minors presenting psychotic disturbances.

Those families consulting psychiatric institutions after the failure of earlier treatment are the most rigid, and sometimes need to be approached over a long period before they are able to accept family treatment. Quite often, they leave the identified patient in the hands of the therapist who, during certain phases of the treatment, is forced to resort to individual treatment. We think it important that the therapist, whatever the stage and nature of his relationship with the family, continually realign his activity and position in the light of the systemic perspective.

If, over a certain period, contact is restricted to individual sessions or is addressed to a sub-system, the therapist, nevertheless, takes into account the feedbacks from his treatment. To neglect this aspect runs the risk of a consequential breakdown or stagnation of treatment, a deterioration of the condition of the patient, or decompensation in another member of the family.

We suspect that there is great variation in families operating in psychotic transactions. Some of these families find themselves in this situation temporarily, at key moments in their development or at times of particular stress. Others seem to live chronic schizophrenic transactions such as our family Z. In these cases, short-term treatment of 10 to 20 sessions may not be enough to change the psychotic transactional patterns established since the previous generation. While treatments for families of the first type are more often in the nature of crisis interventions, their effects also appear more rapidly. The aim is to prevent the symptoms from becoming chronic and the long-term installment of psychotic transactional patterns with all the prognostic significance that this implies for the various individuals, especially for those of the youngest generation. The onset of psychosis, as Beels (1976) describes it, must be capable of being lived out by the members of the family as a crisis of group development, and as part of the process of change that all the protagonists must undergo.

This leads us to reflect on the concept of the schizophrenic condition which we cannot hold to cover a nosological entity, but rather represents a transactional way of functioning which occurs or is created in certain natural-groups-with-a-history (which need not necessarily be families, they can also be social, religious or work groups). The reversibility of this functioning has been demonstrated by individual schizophrenia therapists. We believe that this reversibility can also be demonstrated by family therapy, which can thus contribute to the broadening of our understanding of the etiological problems.

REFERENCES

1. Beels, C.C. (1976): Family and social management of schizophrenia. In: Family Therapy, p. 249. Editor: Ph.J. Guerin. Gardner Press, New York.
2. Boszormenyi-Nagy, I. and Spark, G. (1973): Invisible Loyalties. Harper and Row, New York.
3. Lebovici, S., Diatkine, R. and Kestemberg, E. (1958): Bilan de dix ans de pratique psychodramatique chez l'enfant et l'adolescent. La Psychiatrie de l'Enfant, Vol. I, t. 1, p. 63.
4. Lidz, T., Fleck, S. and Cornelison, A. (1965): Schizophrenia and the Family. International University Press, New York.
5. Masson, O. (1976): Réflexions sur les possibilités d'approches thérapeutiques et préventives chez les en-

fants de mères schizophrènes. Rev. Neuropsych. infant., 1-2, 5.

6. Minuchin, S. (1974): Families and Family Therapy. Harvard University Press, Cambridge, Mass.

7. Selvini, M., Boscolo, L., Cecchin, G. and Prata, G. (1975): Paradosso e Controparadosso. Feltrinelli, Milan.

8. Stierlin, H. (1973): Interpersonal aspects of internalisations. Int. J. Psycho-Anal., 54, 203.

9. Watzlawick, P., Helmick-Beavin, J. and Jackson, D. (1967): Pragmatics of Human Communication. Norton and Company, New York.

PRIMAL FANTASIES, PROMOTER OF FAMILY HOMEOSTASIS

by E. Gilliéron, médecin-adjoint of the Policlinique psychiatrique universitaire (Director: Prof. P.-B. Schneider)

> "In the beginning was the Deed"
>
> Totem and Taboo

Introduction

The ideas which I will present here are extracts of a paper I delivered in 1973 (La famille, fantasme ou réalité?) of which certain passages have been published [1].

The confrontation of my individual psychoanalytical practise with so-called family therapies induced me to grant a central place to primal fantasies in the study of the functioning of the family as a whole. At the time, it concerned conclusions resulting from an essentially clinical experience. In 1964, Dr. Laplanche and Pontalis amply discussed the problems of the place of primal fantasy in Freud's work [2]. Closing in upon the ambiguity of this concept they debated the relationships of these formations with the external reality as well as with the biological reality. However, the conceptual psychoanalytical apparatus was developed based on the experience; the importance of the "setting" of the treatment for the development of the transfer (see Lagache, for example,[3]) or the active role of the analyst in the construction of the "analytical space" (Vidermann,[4]) have already been pointed out. Furthermore the analyst, in order to understand his patient, must go through a gesture of identification before returning his image. By doing this he sees "through the eyes of his patient", the same reality - psychic as well as external - as his patient sees: this is a crucial moment - where he feels what the other feels and perceives what the other perceives. In this manner the analyst is able to have access to the psychic reality of his patients; but he will find that the moment he becomes interested in the relationship of his patient to his significant others he risks finding himself in a similar position as the man in Platon's myth of the cave - all he can make out is the shadows. In fact, he knows this perfectly well and this causes him to implement a strict technic aimed at not allowing the external reality to come into his interventions. However, as Laplanche and Pontalis remind us, it is very difficult to define the fantasy without calling upon what is named "reality".

For my part, I asked myself what we could learn about the fantasy by changing the setting, that is by examining the family as a whole: the patient and his relatives. This would consist of seeing the way in which the fantasies of the child meet with the fantasies of the parents - from a psychoanalytically-inspired point of view, but in a different setting. My point of view would be above all groupal and systemic-"groupal" insofar as I will try to examine those fantasies shared by the family group, and "systemic" because I will try to see the dynamics of the interactions. Moreover, the systemic point of view seems to me to have been very close to Freud's own outlook: this can be seen by simply seeing the ease with which Anzieu, for example, or

151

Racamier were able to integrate the paradox dimension into the psycho-analytical practise [5,6].

We could consider, as some authors have done[7,8], the family to be a small group with particuliar characteristics (for example: hierar-chical structure due to the presence of at least two generations - the intensity of the daily affective ties - what distinguishes them from so-called therapeutic groups, etc.) Now it is known that a group en-sures its cohesion by sharing certain fantasies, and I asked myself whether a related phenomenon doesn't crop up within the family. Influ-enced by Winnicott's view [9], I started by accepting the hypothesis of an "intermediary family space", gathering ground of the fantasies of each of the family members.

Now the families which we as therapists come to examine are gene-rally confronted with insurmontable conflicts which are stagnating in the swamps of inhibitory fantasies. The designated patient simply re-veals their problem. The family thus finds itself in an extremely co-hesive situation which could be named "homeostatic" in the systemic terminology. This homeostasis, of neurotic or psychotic origin, seems to be connected - similarly to what happens in groups - to fantasy problematics which are deeply buried in the family's unconscious. It is a known fact that in the Freudian theory the symptom was first of all considered as a mnemonic symbol of a trauma and in time was des-cribed as the "mise en scène" of an underlying fantasy. However, the question concerning the origin of the fantasy remains unanswered, and Freud did not seem to have given up the idea of basing it on an histo-ric reality (Totem and Taboo, for example). For my part, it seemed to me that we could pick up on this Freudian idea without refering to a genetic explanation going back to the pre-history of mankind; namely, by studying the dialectics which occur between the concrete actions and the fantasies of individuals in face of each other; in short, the dialectics real experience - fantasy - symbol.

We know that the fantasy life is structured by the Oedipus complex - the triangle around which the primary fantasies hinge. The fantasies, according to Laplanche and Pontalis, are fiction - a Freudian inven-tion which claims to give a picture

"of the exact time when the desire appears (...), the mythical moments of the separation (...) between both times of the real experience and its hallucinatory reviviscience, between the ob-ject which fulfills and the sign which at the same time registers the object and its absence". [2].

This definition thus brings in the three dimensions which we are con-cerned with: the myth, the real experience and the sign: it can thus be understood why the primal fantasies have taken on such an important place in my elaborations. As an onlooker of the family situation, I intend to show that not only is the family structure the producer of these fantasies - which would certainly be willingly agreed to - but also that the functioning of the family as a whole can aim at avoiding their formation in the intrapsychic world of the child.

Lack of time forces me to take a number of short cuts for which, I hope, the listener will kindly forgive me. Above all it is my inten-tion to stimulate the discussion by submitting to you some reflections rather than an elaborate theory.

Relational Dynamics, Primal Fantasies and Family Structure

"Among the wealth of unconscious fantasies of neurotics, and
probably of all human beings, there is one which is seldom
absent and can be disclosed by analysis, concerning the watching of sexual intercourse between the parents. I call these
fantasies, together with those of seduction, castration, and
others, primal fantasies; and I shall discuss more fully elsewhere their origin and the relation of them to individual experience".

This is how Freud expressed himself in 1915 concerning a paranoic
case [10]. This was the first text where the term primal fantasy is
used.

From the point of view proposed by Freud, fantasies are hence intrapsychic organizing structures. In my opinion, when observing the
family, fantasies may be seen to modulate the interactions in the bosom
of the family similarly to the way it happens in groups where the verbal and non-verbal communications of the participants express common,
underlying fantasies in such a manner that it is difficult to determine the real source of the behaviour of the members. To illustrate
the spirit with which I approach this problem and before coming to the
heart of the matter, I would like to call to mind that Luc Kaufmann
gave an interpretation of the Oedipus myth in 1967 which would permit
us to speak just as well of a Laios complex as a Jocasta complex [11].
But this is not my purpose: the outlook which I present aims at not
isolating Oedipus' behaviour from that of Laios or Jocasta, nor even
from that of the given oracle.

In the same way, the primal fantasies are film-scripts reciting relational structures which, according to my hypothesis, can either be
interiorized in an individual in the form of a fantasy, or "acted out"
in the family in a mise en scène where each fantasy takes on a more or
less defined role which only an on-looker is able to perceive. The
"producer" of this "mise en scène" stands outside the nuclear family;
in order to understand the plot of this drama it is necessary to resort to a genealogy going back three generations, as will be seen below. Oedipus' trajectory cannot explain itself without reference to
the oracle given to the parents and their subsequent reaction. But who
pronounced the oracle? Wouldn't it, symbolically, have been the grandparents? It does not seem necessary to go back to the primitive horde
of Totem and Taboo to explain the Oedipus structure.

As I have already said, the Oedipus myth may be regarded as a relational, dynamic complex as well as a complex which structures the intrapsychic life. Likewise the primal fantasies. We must go one step
further yet: we are aware that therapeutic and T-groups are soldered
together around common, usually very primitive, fantasies because of
the loosening of the boundaries of the individual Self. This regression is provoked by the group situation. All interactions occuring in
the core of these groups can therefore be understood in terms of these
common, basic ideas. Moreover it is the presence of the leader which
allows the group to structure itself and gradually evolve. In this

sense. the family group also obeys a law it has not made itself; this law is symbolized by the mute presence of the grandparents in the family.

It is necessary to add another aspect: the family, unlike the other groups mentioned above, is structured in a very particular manner from the beginning: it indeed comprises a groupal aspect which encourages primitive fantasies to appear, but it also comprises an aspect which is hierarchical from the start and in which each member has a very definite function. As a matter of fact, every nuclear family originally comprises three biologically distinct members: a man, a woman and an immature new born child. These are the three external elements in the Oedipus' structure: two strong adults of opposite sex, who are theoretically capable of being independent, and a child, who is unfit for survival without the assistance of the others. On the biological level sexuality underlies the emotional nature of the parents' relationship, and dependency, on the other hand, underlies the relationship of the child to the parents. Meanwhile the forces facing each other are conflicting. In a way, each one, in his own way and of course the child in particular, needs the others. But each one also has to be able to go without: the child must come to maturity and become independent but the bonds to the parents are also made up of a mixture of, on the one hand, acceptance of a certain reciprocal dependence, and, on the other, a certain freedom of movement. However, from the start sexuality underlies the main expectations of the parents, and dependence underlies those of the child. With the evolution connected with maturation, the child's bonds to the parents will become more and more marked by sexuality. Of course, here we rejoin the Freudian idea of anaclisis of the sexual drives on ego instincts. I am unable to dwell on this subject. I believe that this simple, real life situation sufficiently explains the forming of primal fantasies in the child.

Stressing the biologically structured aspect of the family comes back to asking oneself what is the impact of this reality on the psychic apparatus of the individuals in view of each other. Now the biological reality, which imposes the problematics of dependence and sex--ual complement, comprises one obvious anti-narcissic aspect which permitted Racamier to say that from the onset reality has a traumatic quality [12]. At the time of birth, the psychic apparatus of the new-born child would risk being subjected to a very traumatizing excess of excitement connected with brute reality. This is what prompted Freud to postulate the existence of a protective shield which insulates the child until the progressive make-up of the psychic apparatus allows him to integrate this excitement. Since writing "Traumdeutung" in 1899 Freud has pointed to the importance of the dialectics between the experiences of satisfaction and frustrations for the build-up of this apparatus. More recently, D. Braunschweig and M. Fain admitted that in the beginning, it is principally the mother who takes on the role of the protection shield. Consequently, as his Self takes form, the child takes back the responsibility for this role whereby he is assisted by the mother, who pulls back from the child and again progressively chooses the sexual object cathexsis with the father. In this manner, she exercises a progressive censorship on the child which is named the "lover's censor"[13]. However, this description does not sufficiently allude to the active role of the father, whose penis seems to wait patiently until the mother becomes interested in it! In effect, due to his action, the father can also either be too partial to the fusing mother-child relationship, or else violently intervene in this relationship, which would thus cause a dangerous breach in the protective shield system described above.

The organization of the child's fantasies, resulting from coming into contact with the primal objects, will depend as much on the mother as on the father, for different reasons, of course. I think that no one will contradict me when I say that the child will be nursed differently depending on whether the mother-father relationship is good or bad. I knew a mother who was having a major conflict with her husband at the time of her child's birth. Being perhaps a little more candid than most, she later told the child, "You suckled poisoned milk!" In this manner, she summarized the consequences of her marital conflict upon the child. The future of the child will thus strongly depend on the harmonious parental relationship. Now the affective bond, which is particularly based on their complementary sexuality, will, in my opinion, strongly depend on their ability to confront the problematics of the primal fantasies. It is either by unconsciously sharing certain fantasies or else by fighting against them that the family ensures its cohesion, sometimes risking to go from simple cohesion to a dangerous homeostasis, which is liable to hinder any evolution. The primal fantasies are therefore border structures between the biological reality and the psychic reality and are at the same time formed by the family equilibrium and responsible for maintaining this equilibrium.

Schizophrenia and Primal Fantasies

In what concerns the topic of these days, we can be interested in the manner in which primal fantasies are handled by the family of a schizophrenic. Observations of such families permitted me to perceive a phenomenon I believe to be characteristic and specific, which sets them off distinctly from other forms of pathology: it is the intense fear of sexual differenciation - fear of the castration fantasy. All transactions in the bosom of the family aim at fighting against the appearance of this fantasy and at maintaining the Kleinian myth of the "combined parent". The following schematic example illustrates this point: I asked the parents of Esther, who for years has been clinically suffering from schizophrenic decompensation of a paranoid nature, "Which one of you most desired the birth of your daughter?" Mother and father, turning towards each other with an ecstatic smile, answered in chorus, "Both of us!" The father went on to say, "As proof, I looked forward so much to having a child that I had said, as early as one month before our marriage, that even if I have five boys, I would not give my first name to any one of them!" The mother showed her approval and upon hearing her daughter grunt, added, "Furthermore, here is a pretty funny anecdote which Esther doesn't like very much: Shortly after our marriage, I met my sister-in-law who was four months pregnant, and told her that I, myself, would be very afraid of being preg-

nant. And can you imagine, the funny thing was that I already was
pregnant." At the time the father, somewhat surprised, said to his
wife, "But you never told me that!" The mother brushed away this remark with a careless wave of the hand, adding the comment "it is so
unimportant". In this particular case, the father's history showed his
reasons for not wanting to become a father: it so happened that one
younger sister, Sophia, died because of the carelessness of an older
brother, Jack, who was known to be jealous at Sophia because of her
relationship to the father. Jack was also the first name of his father,
the patient's grandfather. Within the family, each one knew of Jack's
responsibility, but no one ever spoke of it: the implict instructions
of the grandparents was "not to speak about Jack".

Esther's father seemed to live with the idea that to be the representative of his father could bring about death. He thus had to eli-
minate from his being any resemblance to his father. Allthewhile affirming that he would do everything for his daughter, he could never
bear the fact that the latter needed him even just a little bit. This
expressed itself through eminently contradictory behaviour, for example, insisting that she go to university but refusing to pay her
way, or declaring her to be a big, independent girl at a very young
age and then reproaching her for not showing interest in the family
etc., etc. For different reasons than the father, the mother had an
absolutely symetrical attitude which left the father without the
slightest worth. The parents never had the least difference of opinion
but nor did they show any gesture of tenderness to one other. They in-
sisted that Esther be independent.

This example is only here to show the original position of the parents. The "idea" which the couple shared could be summarized as
follows: The father's outlook - it is very dangerous that my daughter
be in any way attracted to me. The mother's outlook - it is very dangerous to be sexually attracted to a man. In the past, the mother
couldn't count on her father, who was seriously depressive. The consequences of this idea, which both parents share, are simple to deduct:
the family transactions aim at keeping any idea concerning the differences between the sexes, sexual exchanges, the primal scene and seduction theory out of the family's semantic field. For example, seduction does not exist because there is no difference between the sexes;
there is no incest taboo; sexual intercouse will not be experienced as
an exchange between two different sexes. In my opinion, the typical
and well-known transactions of the schizophrenic families (pseudo-mutuality [14], the double-bind [15], the struggle for the defining the
relationship [16]) must be understood from this point of view: their
aim and function is to persistently keep primal fantasies, especially
the castration fantasy, out of the family's semantic field. In fact by
maintaining the myth of the "combined parent", all primal fantasies
are thus rejected, that is to say, kept outside the family's symbolic
field. The need to keep them "at distance" is so great that it leads
to homeostasis - sometimes a stormy homeostasis, of course - characterized by a stability rarely found elsewhere. It goes without saying
that very quickly the child will learn to maintain this homeostasis
through a sort of empty structure - through fantasies which are the

156

opposite of fantasies, exchanges which are not exchanges, ideas which are not ideas. And in this sense, I think return to P.-C. Racamier's theses on "paradoxes of the schizophrenic" [6]. The primal fantasies are jammed in the family of the grandparents, which nevertheless has important   practical consequences on the therapy. It was indeed very long ago that the idea was brought up which said that to "produce a schizophrenic" three generations were necessary. To me it seems impossible to understand the symbolic functioning of a schizophrenic's family without taking the grandparents into consideration.

Allow me to go back to the original greek myth: when Gaéa the Earth, all-powerful mother, perhaps encouraged by Eros but without his interference, took a form in order to bring some order and stability to the chaos, she very soon felt the need to bring her own flesh and blood into the world in the form of Uranus, a being hardly different from herself. Both remained all but glued to each another, and the children born of this union stayed unborn in the warmth of the mother's womb. Gaea very soon became angry and asked her children to castrate the father, Uranius in order to put some distance between them. Father Time, Chronos, took the matter in hand: a certain distance thus was created between Uranus and Gaea, who from then on only met at infrequent intervals. A certain differenciation gave place to sexual confusion. Nevertheless, as we know, Chronus' action, inspired by Gaea, did not have only beneficial results. It succeeded in stirring up all sorts of hostile powers (the Furies, for example), who were opposed to the harmonious forces symbolized by Aphrodite, born of Uranus' sperm which had fallen into the sea! When Chronos married Rhea, the situation was still not more stable, for Chronos, fearing that his children would make him undergo the same fate as Uranus, ate up his children. Not until the appearance of Zeus, who was protected by his mother from Chronus' misdeeds, and after titanic conflicts that order, light and stability appeared on the Olympus. The light appears for the third generation.

It was greatly due to the experiences of Zeus' parents, Thea and Chronus, with their own parents, Gaea and Uranus, that Zeus, after first having victoriously fought with Chronos' fears, was able to establish a certain harmony on the Olympus. In the same way, it is the relationship of the parents to the grandparents which will allow the child to learn to bring some harmony and order into the interiorized, relational constellation of his parental imagos.

In the same manner as it is within Gaea that Chronos can reach his father and separate the latter from his mother,   the child starts to discover his father by distinguishing himself from the mother (the lover's censure). But if a child has no other choice than to constantly remain confronted with one "combined parent", a mother-father, then he has no other point of reference than chaos to explain their origin. This is the fate of the schizophrenic.

From Myth to Ritual

I have just called to mind the dimension of the collective myth in the description of the functioning of the family of the schizophrenic. Now I don't think that this is sufficient: it is said that the myth is an allegorical explanation of a problem which is difficult to express otherwise, and the fantasy is the vivid expression of the pleasure principal according to the Freudian theory. Thus a myth can be considered to be an a posteriori explanation of a historical problem. Whether the story of Adam and Eve is true or not is, in fact, unimportant - what is important is that it gives an explanation of an obsolete problem. The same applies to Totem and Taboo. In my description of the functioning of the family of a schizophrenic, I have spoken of a very particular "ritualized" behaviour aimed at maintaining in the present what for the spectator is a myth. Namely, the idea of a union of the parents so perfect that it is the negation of all differences, negation of complementary sexuality, negation of all conflicts, and negation of the narcissic wound. In this sense I believe that for the actors, the myth is not a myth but nothing less that a sacred thing, probably in the sense of what G. Bateson meant [17], in that the actors of the tragedy being played do not have the right to doubt the reality of what is being played. In such cases, we would not be able to speak either about a sort of "taboo" of sexuality. It is rather a matter of a ritual which is respected by all the members of the family and aimed at proving the absolute value - the reality - of the absence of any difference between the members of the family. It is, in short a hymn to each one's omnipotence narcissism, to the denial of needs and desires. But this is only visible to the trained eye of the psychoanalyst, who wishes to understand the hidden meaning of what happens on the family stage. Obviously the transgression of the rules in such a case is extremely dangerous and can only result in the rejection of the transgressor by the others in a similiar manner as an act of ex-communication.

It must be added that every society, without our always being conscious of it, soulders itself by means of a number of acts made sacred which are not to be betrayed. This can easily be seen by observing the reactions of social groups to attempts to introduce any change in the group, such as new schools of thought (see Copernicus, for example). This phenomenon is found in the families of neurotics, but time does not allow me to dwell on this subject.

On the Subject of Family Homeostasis

The Palo-Alto school has amply discussed the problem of homeostasis, which is expressed by a sequence of exchanges on the basis of the well-known "endless game". I believe I have shown above that the problematics of the origins can almost always be found to be behind this game - at least, this is my hypothesis. In the families of schizophrenics, symbols of the origins are avoided in the family semantic field through the maintenance of the combined parent myth by ritual exchanges. This seems to explain why the individual schizophrenic has no coherent intrapsychic life. The latter is sometimes able to tell the truth, but in crisis situations; when they do tell the truth, they discredit it right away for it is only by being mad in the eyes of the others that they can express themselves. It's a matter of the "insanisation" movement as described by Racamier (6). The total derelection of schizophrenics is explained by the fact that they have no other point of reference than chaos with which to explain the origins of the parents.

As opposed to this type of functioning, neurotic families display
a much more differenciated behaviour: these families also seem to organize themselves around a myth, a shared fantasy, destined at avoiding full confrontation of the Oedipus problematics. The fantasies
circulate more freely, in the sense that certain differences are admitted, such as difference of generation, sexual difference, etc. However in these families certain critical fixation areas can be observed, where all the conflicts are focused, and around which, at the
same time, the family homeostasis is organized. Underlying these conflict areas, the problematics of the origins can always be discerned:
the organization is more supple than in schizophrenia, in that certain
fantasies are authorized to circulate; but homeostatic tendencies, organized around one of the myths of the origins and varying according
to the family's degree of maturation, can be discerned. In my opinion,
the actions of such a family, aimed at the homeostasis contained in
such a mythology, lead to the distortion of the child's fantasy organization through the constantly repeated "mises en scène". This obviously touches the dialectical problem between the deed and the word
- the process of fantasizing and of symbolisation within the family.
Conclusions

Laplanche and Pontalis connect the advent of primal fantasies to
the appearance of auto-erotism in the child at a time"when sexuality
detaches itself from every natural object and is abandoned to the fantasies..." (2). By trying to show that, seen from a different angle,
they are formed in the child at the time when the need progressively
gives way to desire, I rejoin this conception.

I wanted to point out that they are directly connected to the stand
which the parents and the children will take in respect to the problematics of the origins. It seems to me that in the child they reveal
the different stages of maturation; and in the family, the different
levels of the instinctive family life.

I watched how the family as a whole adapts itself, on the one hand
to the maturing of the child, and on the other, to the very particular
dynamic situation, the family nucleus, composed of three members with
very distinct characteristics (sexual difference - dependence). Originally registered in the very structure of the father - mother -
child triangle, the primal fantasies express different maturation levels of the child as well as of the functioning of the whole family.
It could be said that before being fantasies they are family myths,
and before being myths they are family structures. The actions of the
parents, the subtile game of their exchanges will, or will not, allow
the child to forge his inner world. They hinge on the almost divine
powers - the grandparents - and it is in respect to these grandparents
that they should take on their true sense, unknown by he who acts. The
parents' actions integrate themselves into an order which is beyond
the individuals in view of one another and beyond their comprehension.

The intrapsychic process of the parents is as active as that of
the child in the structuration of the latter's fantasies. The parents
must be able to discover, within themselves and at the right time, the
same fantasy which the child is building up in respect to the evolu-

tion of his pulsional equilibrium. It is in this manner that their mutual understanding and enrichment will be forged. Nevertheless fear, provoked in the parents by the developping impulses of the child and reinforced by the regressive movements necessary for the understanding of the latter, sometimes seems so strong that it leads the members of the family to repeated behaviour which has no other aim than to hinder certain fantasies from appearing in the space which unites and separates them. This results, then, in homeostatic situations based on myths - myths of the origins - which must be maintained and reinforced by ritualized acts and not by enriching exchanges. To me, it seems that in this manner the family thus becomes a neurotic or psychotic flavoured brew.

References

1) E. GILLIERON: Névrose et Famille. in: Group therapy and social environment, H. Huber, Berne, pp. 189-197, 1973.
2) J. LAPLANCHE & J.-B. PONTALIS: Fantasmes originaires, fantasme des origines, origine du fantasme. Les Temps Modernes, 215: 1833-1868, 1964.
3) D. LAGACHE: La doctrine freudienne et la théorie du transfert. J. Int. Psychother., 1954.
4) S. VIDERMANN: La construction de l'espace analytique. Denoël, Paris, 1970.
5) D. ANZIEU: Le transfert paradoxal. De la communication paradoxale à la réaction thérapeutique négative. Nouv. Rev. Psychanal., 12: 49-72, 1975.
6) P.-C. RACAMIER: Les paradoxes des schizophrènes. Rapport présenté au XXXVIIIè Congrès des psychanalystes de langues romanes à Florence. PUF, Paris, 1978.
7) A.C.R. SKYNNER: A group-analytic approach to conjoint family therapy. J. Child Psychiat. Psychology, vol. 10, 1969.
8) H. STIERLIN: Group fantasies and Family Myths - Some theoretical and practical aspects. Family Process, 12, 2, pp. 111-125, 1973.
9) D.W. WINNICOTT: Playing and Reality. Tavistock, London, 1971.
10) S. FREUD: A case paranoia running counter to the psycho-analytical theory of the disease. Collected papers, II Hogarth Press, London.
11) L. KAUFMANN: L'Oedipe dans la famille des schizophrènes. Rev. franç. Psychanal., 31: 1145-1150, 1967.
12) P.-C. RACAMIER: Propos sur la réalité dans la théorie psychanalytique. Rev. franç. Psychanal., 26: 675-710, 1962.
13) D. BRAUNSCHWEIG & M. FAIN: Eros et Anteros. Payot, Paris, 1971.
14) L. WYNNE & M.T. SINGER: Thought disorders and Family relations of schizophrenics. Arch. Gen. Psychiat., 9: 191-206, 1963.
15) G. BATESON, D.D. JACKSON and al.: Toward a theory of Schizophrenia. Behavioral Sci, I, 251-264, 1956.
16) M. SELVINI & Coll.: Paradoxe et contre-paradoxe. ESF, Paris, 1978.
17) G. BATESON: "Why a swan ?". in: Steps to an ecology of mind. Ballantine books, New-York, 1972.

PSYCHOTIC INCLUSIONS IN THE SELF : THE PSYCHOTHERAPEUTIC MANAGEMENT
OF THE MORROW OF THE PSYCHOTIC CRISIS.

Antonio Andreoli, Philippe Giacobino.

Centre Psycho-Social Universitaire de Genève.

Introduction

It generally seems very important to establish whether one is
dealing with patients of a nevrotic, psychotic or borderline structure. Then again the coherent complex of reactional mode, defensial
organization and instance relations which define psychic
structure is generally considered to be the most decisive factor
for clinical evolution and type of reaction of the patient in
difficulty.

   We find this point of view unsatisfactory. For in psychotherapy the structure, and the structural point of view are soon found
to be but a surface wrapping soon to be abandonned for it covers a
deep nucleus far more significant and meaningful for us (the nevrotic's repressed, what we call psychotic inclusion). Likewise, we
feel in clinic that it is the personal experience of madness which
determines the future of the person and is an irriducible element
from which operates a radical change in the clinical evolution of
the patient. When the psychotic episode is important, when it takes
place in difficult interpersonal conditions, when it lacks adequate
management and care it seems destined to leave in the patient's
personality and in his relations something which will insidiously
disorganize his whole psychological life often independantly of the
structure which could be fixed at the outset.

   From the point of view which we propose one must agree to make
the distinction between psychosis and that which is within us and
makes us mad. Psychosis thus becomes but the manner proper to each
one of dealing with his own source of madness. The way in which
shall ach cope with the moments of madness in our life. Behind the
architectures woven by splitting and denial how often do we manage
to grasp the "blank" left by the autistic episode, the "overflow"
of the confusion, the fine breaking up in which is dissolved the
unbearable anguish of a depersonalization crisis. But further still
one sometimes has the impression of finding a common element : the
oncoming of an interior constellation announced not by the worring
strangeness of repression giving way, but by the confusion and more
profound bursting which corresponds to the intrapsychic arrival of an
experience too violent to have been submitted to a symbolic inscrip-
tion however primitive. It is here that part of the self where con-
densation is stretched to the limit, its most corporal side, here
where the dream thought has been unable to establish even oneirical
outlines of its domination. Here where the tissue of the personality
becomes flesh, emotion, matter. These distant nebulae have therefore
no psychic reality. This part of the self (we feel obliged to have
recourse to this notion because of the dilatation to the non

psychological which is imposed on us by the existence of the unnameable and non-symbolic parts) is that which Bion called psychotic part of the personality. Our concept of psychotic inclusion corres - ponds to the attempt to situate more explicitly the psychotic part of the personality and its genesis in the intersubjective movement of experiences and relations which make up the history of investment of the individual.

All that we have exposed here brings us back to a more psychoanalytical vision of the transformation of the psychotic world and of its psychotherapy. The madness - psychosis relationship thus becomes a reference not to the notion of phase or structural maturation (as would have it the concept of psychotic nucleus for example) but to the originality and discontinuity typical of everyone's relations. Which seem to us to contest as much any pedagogical approach of the psychotherapy of the psychotic as any notion of substitutive therapeutic whether institional or not.

Psychotic inclusion and transference.

"It was more than anxiety, it was as if the membrane which held in all my anxieties was torn... since then I've got used to it but I feel that they are still there and this fear has never left me. It is something that I feel but which I cannot describe to you". These are the words used by a patient to describe his psychotic experience and his relation with it.

All his psychosis, and all the psychosis of other patients amounts to an attempt to dam up the abyss of confusion which lies in wait for the pervert behind the apparent clarity of a certain play of light, a certain turn of syntax, for the paranoïac behind the scotoma which excuses him, for still others behind the dressing of a delirious idea, an hallucination or a reasoning by rationalisation or the deformation of the character.

Visceral nucleus, encystement, agglomeration, inclusion so many descriptions to emphasize one or another of the characters of the confused, heterogenic experiences which occupy the patient. It is a question of formation made up of intermingled layers for the material of which it is constituated relates to more recent experiences (going back to adolescence or the patient's adult life) as well as more remote infantile experiences. We find ourselves in a situation similar to that of an archeologist excavating a site previously occupied by a town destroyed and buried by an earthquake. Even if a stratification has been constituated through the years the chaos which meets the eye will have been determined by a particular event : the recent natural catastrophe. In short, the clinical evolution seems once again more in relation with the telluric shock(s) than with the more or less long process during which the structure has been put in place.

The status of psychotic inclusion is like that of an internal object : linked indissolubly to the world of the self, there is no way in which it can depart from the patient's universe and cannot be forclosed. One can no more extricate oneself from it than one could guarantee that one's structure will keep one from madness.

The natural catastrophe to which this patient brings us has been described by Winnicott in the notion of breakdown : this author hereby takes up a concept of Bion, that of the projective explosion, that is to say the experience of an acute overload of the thought apparatus by its content or the experience of foundering in a limitless container. In this situation not only is it impossible to portray the emotional experience but it undergoes an extreme fragmentation and the residues of this solar explosion as it is called by Hautmann will be reintemorized in an indiscriptable pell mell, in an agglomeration thus held together without any real integration and without losing any of the destructurating potentiality of the affects which are attached to it.

This agglomeration must be kept seperate from the self as it would develope an action of attack, of "unbinding", of pullution just as the plague which raged at Thebes and which marks the fatal destiny of Oedipus. Here is the vital function of clivage and of its particular prostheses which aim at the reinforcement of the parti - tion which it establishes in the self - the fetish or psychotic formations in the first place.

On the other hand the transfer unfailingly tends to subvert the splitting and favour the return of the psychotic inclusion by reactivating the desire and the need to live from the psychotic part which occupies it. This does not prevent the patient from trying desperately to defer this moment : eg. in taking the language literally or by presenting us with too real images which astonish us or by very crude somatisations.

On other occasions it is the extreme idealization which take over from the defenses planing down certain areas of transference.

When such a type of idealization broke down one of our patients, who had begun psychotherapy after a serious psychotic crisis, presented a dilusion with themes alternatively erotomaniac and persecutional. She called these oscillating movements black or white magic through which everything took on meaning according to the angelic or satanic influence of the therapist. In this way she tried to restore the splitting in the face of the confusing sexualisation of the therapeutic relationship. In these situations the symbolic equation   established by the therapist and the members of his family all of whom bccome members of a persecuting gang, of a sort of syncytium of an amniotic state of the self which lay within her and which had been constituated in previous psychotic crises.

In trying to resituate that which belonged to the body of the patient and that which belonged to the therapist and the members of his family, we slightly reduced a little of the mass of this syncytium and the patient immediately walled up the entances (to wall up the entrance to Alice's wonderland) in making by identification of this mass to a very rigid superego. We are satisfied with the treatment for it is not impossible that the situation at the outset could have exposed the patient to a schizophrenic type morrow whereas today although can be considered severy depressive or seriously sensitive she remains capable of sufficient contact with reality.

Sometimes the psychotic eclipse which marks the approach or the entering into the area of psychotic inclusion is revealed by a different phenomenon although always secondary to the attack on the patients thought capacity which is triggered of by the inclusion. Suddenly the affective and fantasmic depth dissolves. It gives way to a kind of hypertransparency through which the external reality becomes acting in in the session. One then has the impression that the patient becomes a group. To this effect one of us spoke of the existance of symbiotic windows, that is to say passage points between the intrapsychic and interpersonal levels of the conflict. This dimension of the psychotic inclusion is particularly important to us in order to explain the contagion of the psychotic crisis of and by the group and therefore the establishment of a chronic condition in the patient. As one advances in the analysis and one goes beyond the different types of symbolical eclipses and at the same time one obtains a diminution of the confusion one finds that at the centre of the agglomeration there is something other than the overlapping of fragments of experiences and parts of the self. It is as if at the centre of the insane material thus liberated there were particles of reality, but reality with a small "r", burning matter, unfiltered or tamed by the conscience which torments by its burst and its glare. In definitive there is a sort of indigestion of the reality beyond the symbolic equations, the stare of Medusa or the apparition of the Sphinx which leads the patient to his loss. First of all it is the reality of the body which breacks down by psychosomatic crises, by psychosomatic reminders which can come to us only at that moment. Then in the middle of the inclusion the tactile sensations, smells, shapes come to us in an extremely striking spot pattern. In this fine unbleached sand, product of the destruction of the capacity to render the elements of experience capable of establishing bindings, one can feel the very essence of the psychotic part of the personality.

Such is the reality when the capacity for psychic perception is rendered void. Occasionally one will have a presentiment of this when in a totally cold discourse the attention is seized by an extremely illuminating detail. It is the body as a sensoriel psychic organ of the ego which is anulled, which disintegrates and leaves in its place an eyeless, earless psychically skinless flesh. Denial is the telescoping of the body as a dimension in which the consciousness takes on form throught the fact that the body is able to function as a sensoriel organ of the ego. In traumatic nevrosis, and even more so in acute hypochondria secondary to narcissistic trauma one finds a model of corporal heretism which constitutes the nucleus of psychotic inclusion. The cleft which then opens on the surface of the psychic apparatus by regional destruction of the capacity to perceive psychically explains how the indigestion of the reality could be considered as the consequence of the creation of particular conditions of incorporation during the psychotic crisis. One thus believes that one has grasped this amalgam of opacity and hypertransparency residue of the experience of madness. Further more as well as the post oneiric ideas of traditional psychiatry there are other models of the genesis of a confused nucleus close to our psychotic inclusion : night terror, hallucinogenetic psychoses. The awakening from delta sleep or psychodysleptic intoxication create the conditions of a direct contact between the ego and the reality.

It is at that moment that the sensorial plenitude of the reality becomes at the same time distinguishable in its brilliancy and sensuality. It becomes penetrating and terrifying like the stare of Medusa. Every baby experiences such indigestions each time his capacity of mentalisation and the maternal care do not keep pace with the maturation of his neurological perceiving apparatus, every time that the sensoriel psychic organ is unable to put on a skin, a neurological receptacle, and leaves the ego bare. The creativity of thought can be understood as the capacity to give shape to the incitement created by an excessive innocence of the perception. It is to know how to sustain and, unlike the psychotic, transform the real.

Alice's wonderland

Some clinical examples will illustrate this notion of psychotic inclusion corresponding to our impression that one can localize and sometimes demarcate a material which is closely linked to a previous psychotic experience. This material is made up of a pell mell aggregate of present fantasms recollections and symptoms. It is probable that this material is situated in the periphery of an inclusion, itself unable to be transcribed into thought, which appears in negative like an eclipse of the symbolical discourse or like a blurring of its articulations when certain themes are approached, bringing about a sudden inability for the patient and therapist to work together.

In one of the first sessions, this 31 year old woman described pictorially a psychotic decompensation which occurred in the form of a paralytic illness which kept her bed-ridden between the ages of 20 and 27. She clung to a concret discourse made up of morsels of her past of which the links were missing, which made it difficult for me to follow the sequence of events, evoking for me a sequence of slides in "fondu-enchaîné", sharp and immobile images between which the links remained vague. Then she stopp and adds "it seems artificial to talk about all that... I don't know what I was going to say anymore... my head aches". As if in resituating herself in the therapeutic relation she removed herself from this discourse in which at that time she could only perceive the subjacent confusion which precipitates separation anxiety into the body with the sudden apparition of a pain.

In another session, speaking of the same period, she describes a masculine personage, friend of her mother, who was distant and unapproachable and I feel around this evocation a zone in which the symbolical relation with me is lost. I myself feel distant and unapproachable until she speaks of the marvelous dresses which she made for herself at this time and was never able to wear and which she has recently started to make again and I feel in the evocation of this long work something like the search for a contact on a skin level in the session which she suddenly abandons and says "there are still a lot of things missing I should like to know what there is underneath". But this sudden distance uncovers her and confronts her with the solidity of a too raw material which troubles her sight and makes her confused.

In a following session, having announced that she had a host of things to tell me she adds :"I received a letter from my mother and it has blocked everything" announcing the continuation of her discourse in which she speaks of her mother, incapable of living the present moment, of her conviction of having been raped by one or the other of her parents, of their sexual disharmony, of their separation and of her mother since then "like Sleeping Beauty... she fell asleep and everyone with her... I want to scream but I daren't... I'm afraid it would hurt". She seems effectively blocked on the superficial level of the expression of a destructive aggressivity, that of which she is conscient and at a deeper level in the confusion of a language which cannot succeed in maintaining the appearance of a superficial oedipian symbolism and which slides towards the elementary language of the body, the cry, the pain which she strives to contain.

This material is included in the session like a morsel of raw material which contrasts with the ground of a behavioral discourse. It reminds me of her drawings which she claims not to like, resenting the foreign influence of her parents, and the way in which she presented them to me in one of the early sessions : she arrives with a portfolio which she places behind her requesting me to remind her five minutes before the end of the session to show me her drawings. In effect, she seems to forget about them and after my reminder hands over a series of familiar objects (packet of sweets, coffee-pot, chair) placed without support on an absolutely white background, impressive by the poorness of volume and by the sharpness and precision of the outlines which seem to want to hold in the shading made of a violent and disorganized graphicism. Like certain artistic productions of the hyperrealistic trend, they seem to attempt a primary symbolic transformation of an interior pollution by fragmented elements of the reality of the exterior and the reality of the body. She shows me these beautiful pictures rapidly one after the other without seaking any commentary from me and closes her portfolio. Like the disorganized violence of her graphicism the insoluble residues of the psychotic experience seem to be outlined by the sharpness of a visual perception which draws dazzling and useless things and vacates "whitens" the surrounding space.

One must emphasize the importance of vision for this patient as the principal sensorial mode of construction of the transferencial world and as the defensive mode of distance creation and immobilisation. The visual architecture of the edified transferencial relation has certainly a character of strangeness for the therapist accustomed to a different mode of perceptive integration, which makes it more difficult for him to distinguish between that which in the regard is function of integration and that which, on the approach of inclusion notably, is function of gripping on, of immobilisation and of negation of the distance.

The whole of another session was taken up by a hysteriform crisis which corresponds with the apparition of a corporal world, intil then split, in which intermingle the present needs to touch and be touched and the cutaneous and mucous touch shattered in the past. I felt then that my voice, rather than being the carrier of the word, essentially had a function of shoring up after the trembling of the visual architecture and abo a tactile function of enveloping. The confusion manifests the acute insufficiency of splitting based on visual predominance and thus appears as a sensorial destructuration.

This vision appears to compensate for an over-fragile skin. That which the patient feels as her proper delineation is a sort of visual skin assuring a function of protection against a rule of all or nothing but containing badly and devoid of tactile qualities. It is more like a garment, and a borrowed garment at that in which she feels stored :"I am never quite right even in jeans, I have never got quite the right way of wearing jeans".

The image of an insensitive envelope, alien to her own flesh, is exteriorized in the many jewel boxes, portfolio and envelopes of her mother's letters which she manipulates during the sessions, and when she compares me to a pot which perhaps she would very much like to smash, I feel myself becoming a sort of pachydermatous skin, a too impervious container of her madness. What she asks of me is often that of containing in a sort of skin and alluding to the well-being that she feels when I speak to her, regardless of the meaning of my words, she tries to reduce my presence and discourse to this function :"I would like you to talk and I should listen". Moreover, this search for an adhesive identification seems to constitute a necessary stage in the containing of inclusion before dealing with it's sexed content. Little by little she tries to thicken, by impregnating it with non-visual perceptions, this thin skin which badly covers over the inclusion flush beneath it. The transference effectively begins then to develop on a tactile level which also confers on her regard another character.

The transferencial relation helped the establishment of bearable links between the sensations for this patient, which at the same time relieved the vision of its function of a containing of a raw material from which it remained split in favour of its plastic creative function.

The patient, between moments of confusion which indicate the proximity of the ever-present inclusion little by little feels "more full... more alive" even her visual perception is modified : "I feel I see things more in depth... people like my drawings because the perspective is wrong but this angered me because I didn't realize it" as if one is present at the beginning of an integration of senses formely split, this touch of the regard suggesting a three dimensional perception of the world.

This indication of progress allows us to deal veritably with a part of the included content. The patient's sudden loss of the capacity to establish symbolical relations follows non-fortuitously the evocation of events concerning a period of late adolescence, soon after the patient had her first sexual relations and attempted to seperate from her mother. These events refer her to a rape, badly situated in time, and to different masculine personages revolving in the orbit of her mother. A last sequence will illustrate this : she is waiting for me in the corridor, afraid of a large man in the waiting room who reminds her of one of her uncles. She tells me that I look well, that she likes the colour of my clothes. "I've got a lot of things to tell you... I can see perspective much better" thus reassuring herself that the representation apparatus functions properly she goes on :"I saw the film "L'amour violé" (raped love) and it reminded me of my own rape". She then tells us precipitously of the episode again, which does little to enlighten me. She then associates with her first sexual partener of whom she shows me a photo, and soon after tells me that she had sexual relations the previous week end that she didn't feel well afterwards. She comes back to her mother who wanted to turn her out when she (the patient) reproached her this rape (which she discovered on the occasion of her first sexual relations) and that it was then that she fell ill. She adds that people reject her when she talks of this rape. As this sequence shows, all the internal space occupied by masculine perso-nages is undified and shifting, these images blend with and overlap each other. This confused and fragmental area of the internal world this shows itself to be the seat (at once the source and the target) of a very intense projective and introjective identification which caused upheaval there where the oedipian type internal object rela-tion should be situated and on the border of which the patient indulges in a game of approach and retreat in which she finally feels confused and rejected.

The confusion of the discourse seems to us to be the conse-quence of an extreme rapprochement of sexuality and separation in an early oedipian situation which prevented the development of a sexed relation with the father. At present sexuality and separation are amalgamated in an apparent simultanity of experience where, on the border of psychotic inclusion, is to be found that deficiency of the temporal dimension, which the immobility of images uninserted in duration suggested earlier. There one has a defensive immobilisation of the elements of inclusion which in themselves are generations of change under a two dimensional membrane where time is simultanity. All sexual movement, as prospect of change therefore risks to preci-pitate separation and become immobile or else entail confusion and somatic illness.

After having seen me by chance in the corridor she tells me in the following session :"With you it is very difficult because you are a man and what is more you are nice". Then she describes her tendance to break off when she forms a relation too close and adds : "I don't feel well... I can't think anymore... it is as if my mind is encircled by tight thongs, it doesn't move any more".

The recognition which she progressively makes of the sexuality and mental functioning of the therapist permits a sexualisation of the transferencial relation, sexualisation to which the psychotic inclusion reveals itself to be closely linked. This recognition entails successive crises of splitting which are manifested by confusion, short delirious episodes, somatic symptoms when during the session any allusion is made to sexuality, change, separation (eg. the intrusion of a third person in the office, a phone call during the session as well as the separation of vacations or the intervals between sessions). It is doubtless the fruitful paradox of this relation to be able to contain a certain uncontaining of the madness and to allow it, one day, access to thought.

Conclusions

We have tried to demonstrate the impossibility of reducing the psychotherapy and the clinical approach to psychoses to the evolu - tion of the psychotic structure. We believe that psychotic realiza- tion is the moment of a qualitative change which will leave in a patient's world of interpersonal relations and his intrapsychic object universe which will provoke, if left to themselves, a progres- sive destruction of his psychological world. The morrow of a psycho- tic crisis thus seems to us to be a particularly important moment for the psychotherapeutic approach. Placing in the foreground the problematic of psychotic inclusion in respect to the problematic of the structure, we have thought to propose a less normative approach to the psychotic patient and a mode of intercourse with him which does not refuse an attempt to open the dialogue also with his madness.

In a way our point of view can be resumed by a displacement of the accent on childhood onto adolescence considered not as an ortho- genetic entity but as a dimension of the object relationships. One of our patients asserted that that which characterized his former suffering was never to find at any time, with anyone or in any place the comfort and the respite which the envelope of our relation could now offer him. That occurred on one of our returns from vaca- tion and the patient continued in affirming that during his period of crisis he had functioned like a machine with the wires crossed : for example he felt completely deformed and distorted by the presen- ce of someone in the next appartment or completely invaded by the pressure of noises from the street.

Projective explosion is an acute experience of uncontaining, a narcissistic shattering related to a breaking through of sexual drives. Only in this way can we understand the continual double movement to which our countertransference is called. On one hand there is the patient's need for reembodiment which we find in his sadistic or libidinal attachment to the setting, in his need to come and associate, to find an identity in adhering to our presence, a narcissistic need for contact for which we become a sort of psychic pillow. But beyond this narcissistic work of containing which is a task of weaving a surface and the reconstruction of the bounderies of a surface, inclusion calls us to the patient's hope to give psychic life, to put in thought the suffering of the shattered part which occupies the depth. It is there the work of containing of which the object finally seems to us to be always the same : the breaking down due to an unbearable sexualisation of the body and of the relational worls.

Indeed, almost always when by the psychotherapeutic work the formless content of the psychotic inclusion tends to reconstrict itself, it seems to take form round something concerning the primal scene. In addition the opening of the crypt which encloses the inclusion always takes place at the moment when, because of the "absence" of the therapist, the transference begins to take on a sexed form. This sexualisation of thought is the opening onto a world which leads the patient towards the psychic space. In defini- tive inclusion is constitued by a destroyed Oedipus.

If psychosis can be considered the successful narcissistic attempt to prevent the opening of this psychic space then madness represents the crumbling of this world in the great vertigo which seizes he who is unable to give form tn a premature explosion of the oedipian world. To have tasted this fruit is a puberty which changes irrevocably the life of those who were and those who were not prepared to face it.

BIBLIOGRAPHY

1. ANDREOLI, A. : "Vertiges : forme de la pensée, psychose et créativité en psychanalyse". Rev. Franç. Psych. No 5-6 (1978) in press.

2. ANDREOLI, A. : "Les démons dans le corps". Rev. Med. Psychosom. et Psych. Med. No 2 et 3 (1977).

3. ANDREOLI, A. : "La crise psychiatrique : lorsque le patient devient un groupe". Med. et Hyg. 35:2972-8, (1977).

4. BICK, E. : "The experience of the skin in early object-relations". Int. J. Psycho-Anal., 49 : 484-486(1968)

5. BION, W.R. : "Transformations". Heinemann, London, 1965.

6. BION, W.R. : "Second Throughts (Selected Papers of Psychoanalysis". Heinemann, London, 1967.

7. BION, W.R. : "L'attention et l'interprétation. Une étude de la connaissance intuitive en psychanalyse et dans les groupes". Payot, Paris 1974.

8. HAUTMANN, G. : "Les aspects asymboliques du psychisme et leurs rapports avec le narcissisme dans la formation du Soi, à partir de l'analyse de l'organisation borderline". Rapport au XXXVIII Congrès des Psychanalystes de Langue Romane. Rev. Franç. de Psych. No 5-6 (1978) in press.

9. MELTZER, D. et coll. : "Explorations in autism", Clunie Press, Strath Tay, 1975.

10. PALACIO F. : "Les états psychotiques infantiles et la relation d'objet précoce". A paraître.

11. ROSENFELD, H.A. : "Clinical approach to the psychoanalytic theory to the life and death instincts : an investigation into the agressive aspects of narcissism". Int. J. Psychoan. 52 : 168-178 (1971).

12. SEGAL, H. : "Introduction to the work of Melanie Klein". The Hogarth Press Ltd., London, 1964.

ON PSYCHOTHERAPEUTIC GOALS, STRATEGIES AND THE RELATIONAL
REALITY OF THE SCHIZOPHRENIC

Helm Stierlin

Department of Psychoanalysis and Family Therapy, University of Heidelberg, Germany

AN EXPLOSION OF VIEWPOINTS

Today, we witness an explosion of information and,
along with it, an explosion of perspectives within which
this information is organized. Schizophrenia - or more
correctly: that which we call schizophrenia - exempli-
fies such explosion of viewpoints. The book "The Nature
of Schizophrenia", (11) recently published under the
editorship of Wynne et al., is a case in point. Its more
than 60 chapters spread before us arrays of data about
such diverse subjects as genetics, neuropharmacology,
child-development, family studies, anthropology, etc. At
the same time, they employ widely differing concepts, set
differing emphases, establish differing hierarchies of
importance, in brief: open up different perspectives. A
synthesizing genius, i.e. a "Hegel of psychiatry", seems
needed to cope with this diversity.
     But while such genius - or whoever feels called upon
to sift and synthesize the accumulating information -
struggles along, therapy cannot wait: as therapists we
need to act (and often need to act fast) in the face of
the misery, tragedy and human waste which the word
schizophrenia implies.
     And here is the problem: to a therapist it makes a
difference as to which data he holds important and which
perspective he adopts. It makes a difference whether he
views schizophrenia foremostly within a medical model
which directs him to interfere with hypothetical neuro-
transmittor derailments; it makes a difference whether
he focuses on presumably faulty genetic mechanisms which
direct him toward eugenic consultation; it makes a difference whether he sees the schizophrenic (or the person so
labeled) as stunted by ego-defects and growth deficits
which he must help him to correct; whether he sees him
torn by inner conflicts or a need-fear dilemma which he
must help him to understand and resolve; or whether he
sees him victimized by, and in need of, liberation from
an exploitative, double-binding family or even society.
In brief: Differing models of schizophrenia make a difference, because they imply differing goals and differing
strategies of treatment.
     Such differences might encourage a pragmatic "wait-
and-see-stance" - one that lets the differing models and

strategies compete with each other and waits to find out what works. Thus, therapeutic success would measure, confirm or disconfirm the given model and strategy. But differing models, we find at closer inspection, imply also differing notions of mental health, and hence imply differing yardsticks by which to define and measure therapeutic success. A schizophrenic may under massive thorazine medication loose his bizarre ideas and, therefore, within a medical model, qualify as therapeutic success. But he may no longer so qualify when, within a wider perspective and different model, his lost of zest, liveliness and whimsy is taken into account and his over-all performance and relatedness is considered.

Our yardstick for measuring therapeutic success changes again once we look at the whole family and focus here on dynamics of delegation. Such focus may alert us to how a given schizophrenic's recovery and discharge from the hospital may set off a suicidal depression in his mother, a depression she could control as long as her son acted as her "bound delegate", i.e. as a target for her agitated worry and as an ever available container for her disowned badness and madness. Within this model, then, her son's schizophrenia would seem to have warded off, and his cure to have triggered, her own collapse and, within this model, therapeutic success would, thus, have to encompass not one but several family members. In sum: Differing models of schizophrenia imply not only differing therapeutic goals and strategies, but also differing notions and value-orientations as to what constitutes mental health and therapeutic success.

To find here our way, a dialogue - between therapists and therapists, researchers and researchers, and researchers and therapists - is needed. While such dialogue sifts, clarifies and, if possible, integrates the different models and orientations, it requires as well as creates a realm of discourse, of shared meanings, expectations and values, in brief, requires and creates a common, similarly perceived and jointly sustained reality. But such common reality seems ever harder to come by as the perspectives continue to explode.

THE CONCEPT OF A RELATIONAL REALITY

I submit now that our difficulties in creating and sharing such reality have relevance to how many a schizophrenic struggles to create and share his (or her) reality, and, further, that they have relevance to how we, as therapists, may help or hinder such struggle. To make this clearer, let me turn to a conceptual distinction I recently suggested - the distinction between "hard" and "soft" reality.

Within this distinction, hard reality refers to what we usually mean by material reality, i.e. to concrete and easily visualizable reality. To this reality belongs the stone which hurts me when I hit it, the street car which knocks me over unless I step aside, my body which weakens unless I eat and which, inevitably, will one day die and decay whatever I do. Such hard reality contrasts with a soft reality that is less easily visualizable and appears more dependent on, i.e. sustained and created by, our perceptions, interpretations, emotions and fantasies. It includes the opinion and expectations which my mate, parents, friends or superiors - overtly or covertly - hold of me, the loyalties which tie me to certain persons or groups, the desires, fantasies and prohibitions which govern my sexual conduct.

As of today, we lack a good name for this second type of reality. We could speak of psychological, experiential, social, interpersonal or interactional reality or, with Hegel, of the reality of the objective spirit. I myself prefer to speak of "relational reality", taking Gregory Bateson as my guide. The shaping and understanding of one's relationships is, according to Bateson, man's most central and pervasive endeavour. In the intended meaning the term relationship covers my relations to myself, i.e. to my inner life, my needs, my body - as well as to others, their inner lifes, their expectations, their bodies, as well as to given social institutions. Together with our hard reality such soft or relational reality provides the matrix of what we experience, suffer, hope, expect, what makes us sick or well, makes us survive or perish, in brief, it constitutes our world.

Often this relational reality cannot easily be distinguished from hard reality, as hard reality, too, is subjectively mediated and becomes accessible only through perceptions and a language which we must learn and/or share. (Thus, even a piece of wood exemplifying the visualizable concreteness of hard reality dissolves at a physicist's closer inspection into a dance of atoms or something of that sort.)

And yet such distinction - between hard and relational reality - makes sense: Our relational reality grows in importance as basic needs for food, clothing and shelter are satisfied. Much more than hard reality it appears man- and culture-made, and subject to historical change. And to the extent that such change accelerates - as happens presently - it becomes less and less a matter of adaptation than of a constant intersubjective evaluation and confirmation of our perceptions and interpretations, of our joint commitment to given values and worldviews, of our sharing a common focus of attention, in brief: becomes a matter of negotiations, of a dialogue, or, as I put it elsewhere, of a positive mutuality. Therefore, the concept "adaptation to reality", well known from psychoanalytic usage, suits chiefly our dealings with hard reality. It does not do justice to our handling relational reality. Rather, a concept such as Harry Stack Sullivan's "consensual validation", implying an ongoing intersubjective sharing, confirmation, dialogue and negotiation, seems here appropriate.

With the above in mind, we turn, next, to the child's early development. How, we ask, does such consensual validation and negotiation of one's relational reality evolve? And how can it derail?

Increasingly, we have come to focus here on the child's individuation and separation, during the course of which he or she learns to distinguish between me and not-me, inside and outside, good and bad, thoughts and events, one's own motives, wishes and expectations and the wishes, motives and expectations of others, etc. Thus, the child, step by step, stakes out and differentiates what becomes his or her relational reality.

Yet despite such structuring endeavour, this reality is not of the child's making. On the contrary: In myriad ways it reflects, and interlocks with, the "stronger reality" of his parents. To this stronger reality the small child - so I wrote in a paper in 1959 (8) - must adapt lest he or she perish. And such adaptation to the parents' stronger reality, I showed then, can be wrought with difficulties that may account for a vulnerable child's sooner or later becoming schizophrenic.

Today, nearly 20 years after this was written, some of these difficulties stand out more clearly. In particular, there stands out a seemingly paradoxical task with which each child must grapple in order to avoid a schizophrenic fate.

I refer to the fact that this child must acquire and yet must transcend fundamental categories and distinctions and that he or she, in so doing, must not only adapt to, but also must challenge and make negotiable, the stronger person's reality.

Ted Lidz (5), above others, alerted us to the importance of early category-formation. Through categories our experiences can be communicated, a dialogue becomes possible, our relational reality is ordered. To quote Lidz:

"... a person's experience unfolds in a ceaseless flow and in order to perceive, understand and think about experiences they must be divided into categories. Experience, we may say, is continuous, whereas categories are discrete. There are innumerable ways of categorizing experiences and each culture does so differently; and to some degree all persons categorize slightly differently depending upon their education and their experiences. To form categories, boundaries or hiatuses are established by repressing what lies between them. In particular, tabus are placed on material that would obliterate fundamental categories such as between the self and non-self upon which all further categorization rests, on such matters as fusion between child and mother, on fantasies of fusion in incest, and similarly on what might blur the basic categories of male and female - such as homosexuality and transvestite behavior."

Thus, into early category-formation there seem to enter those processes of infantile repression, denial and splitting on which psychoanalytic investigators of schizophrenia and borderline states have increasingly focused. And such repression and splitting they found, exacts a price. Edith Jacobson (4), for one, pointed to "the enormous and rather disruptive influences which the processes of infantile denial and repression exert upon the formation of the self and the object world". And among such enormous disruptive influences we must now also count the ways in which the splitting and denial inherent in rigid category-formation threaten to make our relational reality non-negotiable. By cutting this reality into sharply polarized entities, such categories easily turn into traps: By the uncompromising use of "hard" categories such as goodness versus badness, maleness versus femaleness, strength versus weakness, mine versus thine, etc. we can quickly lock ourselves into a corner, into unresolvable (intrapsychic as well as interpersonal) conflict, and into hopeless estrangement from self and others.

Therefore, we must learn to gradually transcend and qualify our early bedrock categorizations and, to this end, must learn to shift our attention flexibly and to change our perspectives. This then allows for ever new vantage points and for transitions between extremes to emerge. And yet, despite such needed shifts in attention and perspective, we must keep our bearings within our relational reality, and must continue to feel safely rooted within a cosmos of reliably shared meanings.

It is these meanings which our parents' stronger reality centrally represent and which, in order to allow for a safe anchorage in a common human and culturally shared cosmos, must at first be quasi sacrosanct and non-negotiable. And yet there must come a point (and must come soon) where such unquestioning acceptance of sacrosanct meanings must give way to their questioning and where the adaptation to the parents' stronger reality must give way to negotiations about this reality, in brief, there must come a point where a true dialogue can begin.

We still understand too little how the above developmental, or perhaps better: relational task - to acquire bedrock categorizations, and yet to transcend them; to adapt to, and yet negotiate about, the stronger person's reality - can be mastered and how a dialogue can start. Yet a key to such mastery and facilitation of a dialogue can, I believe, be found in the word trust.

I refer to that kind of trust which guarantees that my relations - my relations with myself and my relations with others - again and again will open up to a successful dialogue. Hence, I see such trust unfolding in two interconnected relational axes, as it were: in relation to myself where it implies trust in my senses, trust in my (inner as well as outer) perceptions, trust in the solidity and adequacy of my linguistic tools, and in the categories and meanings thereby staked out; and in relation to others, in particular to the parents with the stronger reality, where such trust implies trust in their essential fairness and goodness as well as trust in the coherence, meaningfulness and justice of the human order into which I, as a child, am introduced. This trust encompasses the "basic trust" which Erikson has described. It makes it possible that there can and will be a safe and fair dialogue, a dialogue in which a common focus of attention is shared, the (initially) weaker person is respected and listened to as a person in his or her own right, in which conflicting positions can be articulated and endured, weakness and vulnerability be revealed, anger as well as tenderness expressed, mutual rights and obligations ascertained and negotiated, and reconciliation occur.

TRUST, TRUTH AND CONCERN

I submit that such experience of trust has much to do with how we commonly experience truth. The archaic meaning of the English word truth is fidelity, constancy. The German word wahr (true) and the Latin verus have a common indogermanic root and mean basically trustworthy, vertrauenswert. Thus, in so far as we equate being true with being real, trustworthyness and fidelity can be viewed as underlying truth and reality, and, in particular, relational reality.

Yet another key to a mastery of the above task and the facilitation of a dialogue I find in the word concern with which the late Winnicott described a certain developmental stage (Melanie Klein's depressive position) of the child. Winnicott refered here to an emerging capacity of the child - to see his mother, the person with the stronger reality, as a separate, important yet also vulnerable being and thus, as one who may suffer from the child's (real or fantasied) actions. Hence for Winnicott the capacity for concern implied also the capacity to experience guilt.

Here I would like to submit that the child and his parents can only begin to have a true dialogue and to negotiate about their common relational reality once there is mutual concern - i.e. not only concern of the parent for his or her child, but also of the child for his or

176

her parent.

Now, when I searched for the best possible German translation of concern I came upon several older German substantives, now almost extinct, which in earlier times were often used synonymously - the substantives Wahr, Acht and Hut. Today, these words live on in such derivatives as beachten, achtsam, behüten, behutsam, bewahren or gewahr werden. The root meanings are each time abiding interest, care, protection and respect. And here I found of special interest the old substantive Wahr (old high German bi-waron, old English warian, old Islandish vara) which signifies a protective and caring bond with people or things. Where such a bond is lacking, we still speak in German of Verwahrlosung, i.e. waywardness.

But further: this old German word "Wahr" - and this accounts for my special interest in it - can also be found in the current word Wahrnehmung, the German equivalent to the English perception. Hence, to perceive would mean in German to take something into the mind's protective custody, or, to take it into one's concern.

For most German speaking people, though, who are not versed in etymology, the word Wahr in Wahrnehmung evokes primarily the meaning true or truth and to them wahrnehmen means, accordingly, "to take for true (or real)". Therefore, the word "Wahrnehmung" can be said to contain two key meanings, one sanctioned by etymology, the other by common, though unreflected usage. And these happen to be the meanings which we found most essential to the facilitation of the early dialogue and the negotiation of one's relational reality - the meanings of "truth", implying mutual trust and loyalty, and of concern, implying mutual care and respect for the other's otherness.

In keeping these meanings of "Wahr" in mind, we can now take a new look at schizophrenia and discern here a disturbance of Wahr-Nehmung. Such disturbance would, first, reflect a cognitive or epistemological dimension: The schizophrenic takes to be true that which is (at least in the eyes of most others) not true, i.e. he misidentifies bodily signals, attributes ideas and motives to others which should be attributed to himself, develops Wahn-Wahrnehmungen (delusional perceptions) etc. and thereby reveals those actions or characteristics which Kurt Schneider has captured in his first rank symptoms and Clarence Schulz in his SOD (Self-Object-Differentiation)-Scale. Within the framework here proposed such disturbance would then derive from, as well as reflect, a lack of relational trust, as outlined above.

At the same time, a disturbance of Wahr-Nehmung would here signify a lack of mutual concern, i.e. a lack of care for the other as a person in his or her own right. Both these lacks - of trust and concern - would then make better understandable why the all-important dialogue derails or even fails to get under way, and why a relational reality which is binding for, and sustained by, all partners, cannot be negotiated.

But further: In any such dialogue we can - if we stick for a moment to the meaning of Wahr as "true" - differentiate between the Wahr-Nehmer, the person who nimmt "wahr", who receives or takes over the truth, the truth-taker, as it were; and the Wahr-Geber, the giver of truth (or at least of what most other people hold to be the truth). Thus, we can visualize an interpersonal dialectic in which, over time, several persons of different generations, functioning as truth-givers and truth-takers, create and consensually validate a shared relational reality. Within this dialectic the positions of Wahr-Geber and Wahr-Nehmer appear at first separate and fixed: the parent with the stronger reality is the Wahr-Geber, the dependent child - the one with the weaker reality - the Wahr-Nehmer. But to the extent that a dialogue and negotiations get under way, these positions shift, and the roles of Wahr-Geber and Wahr-Nehmer can alternate.

Such notion of an interpersonal dialectic, unfolding over time, in which "Wahr-Geber" and "Wahr-Nehmer" change roles while they jointly negotiate and validate their shared relational reality, opens another angle on schizophrenia. For we note here that diagnostic and therapeutic endeavours have for a long time focused almost exclusively on the Wahr-Nehmer, the person with the weaker reality, as it were, i.e. the one who mis-perceives, mis-interpretes and mis-handles certain aspects of relational reality and therefore one day comes to be labeled as schizophrenic. Then came, some 25 or so years ago, a shift in focus - away from the Wahr-Nehmer to the Wahr-Geber, a shift that was pioneered by such authors as G. Bateson, L. Wynne, T. Lidz, R. D. Laing, H. Searles and others. This Wahr-Geber - the person (or persons) with the stronger reality - came to be seen as the one (or ones) who prevented the sharing of a common focus of attention, mystified the dependent child, misdefined this child to himself, attributed to him weakness or badness, exposed him to double-binds, tried to drive him crazy, made him into a bound delegate, etc. Occasionally, such hapless Wahr-Geber was labeled "schizophrenogenic", but, as of today, we are still lacking a good name for his or her contribution to the above dialectic.

Increasingly, though, it became apparent that neither focus on Wahr-Nehmer or Wahr-Geber, on the distorting receiver or the distorting provider of one's relational reality will do. Rather, we need to focus on how all contributing partners, as well as the system they share, block the negotiation of a viable and shared relational reality.

SYSTEMS ASPECTS OF CONFLICT

And here, I believe, we must, first of all, look at those deep and explosive conflicts - between the partners and within the system - that may block a needed negotiation of one's relational reality.

Such conflicts, I showed elsewhere, frequently build up over long periods of time. They are often rooted in missions and legacies that are transmitted over the generations and set different families and/or different members within one family on collision courses. A conflict may finally explode when parents who have been burdened by conflicting missions bequeathed on them by their own parents, once more pass on these burdens to a vulnerable child. This child may then, at one and the same time, have to become an academic superstar, remain a dependent infantilized baby as well as an ever-present container for the parents' disowned badness or weakness, i.e. may have to fulfill tasks so overtaxing yet also so conflicting that they cannot but steer him toward a schizophrenic breakdown (9).

But conflicts - and this compounds an already complex picture - frequently derive also from epistemological and cognitive errors, as it were. They derive from misperceptions, from falsely and too rigidly employed categorizations, from restrictive inner schemata, from erroneous inferences and inacurate generalizations which often are collusively entertained.

Both factors then - these families' excessive, transgenerationally bequeathed conflict load and their erroneous epistemology - make for an especially vicious circle: they make ever more urgent a family-wide-dialogue and negotiation of a shared relational reality, yet also strain ever more the family's resources of trust and concern on which such dialogue and negotiation must build.

In this situation the family's ability to cope with conflict is likely to falter rapidly. Typically, the members seem either stalemated in open, but unresolvable hostility or they collusively deny or sidestep _any_ conflicts. Depending on whether conflict seems overt or covert, we may speak of pseudo-hostility and family schism, or of pseudo-mutuality and family skew.

But whether there is schism or skew, pseudo-mutuality or pseudo-hostility, on closer inspection we find a desperate, unabated struggle is raging on. Typically, this struggle has the earmarks of what G. Bateson (1) described as "symmetrical escalation", i.e. of a competitive power struggle in which "the complex gamut of values is inevitably reduced to very simple and even linear and monotonous terms". Only winning or loosing counts, everything else becomes irrelevant. J. Haley (3) and M. Selvini (7), among others, have described how such

struggle unfolds in "schizo-present" families. Also in
such families, these authors showed, the terms of the
struggle are simple and monotonous - it's all a matter of
either winning or loosing - yet the strategies employed
seem often bewilderingly complex: they frequently include
what has come to be known as mystification, as the dis-
qualification of meaning, as the imperceptible shifting
of one's focus of attention, the subtle undercutting of
the other's statements, the disclaiming of agency and
hence of responsibility for one's actions and statements,
etc. But whatever the strategies, they amount all to a
manipulation (or attempted manipulation) of the relational reality, and they all lead nowhere. For by its very
nature, such power struggle - or perhaps more correctly:
such struggle for the power of the stronger reality - can
neither be won or lost. Rather, it locks the protagonists
into a malignant clinch, in which it becomes ever more
desperately necessary yet also ever more difficult to
have a dialogue, i.e. to negotiate or re-negotiate a
viable relational reality.

THERAPEUTIC IMPLICATIONS

What, then, are the therapeutic implications of such
failure to have a dialogue and to negotiate one's relational reality?
Within the above model, a therapist faces two major
and interrelated tasks: to break the malignant clinch,
and to facilitate a new dialogue so that a viable relational reality may be negotiated. Both tasks require him
or her to bring to bear on his patients or families his
or her stronger reality and to rekindle and/or redirect
trust and concern.
At this point we might well look at the work of
Hans H. Strupp (10) who, like no other researcher, over
decades has examined and compared the workings and effectiveness of different forms of individual psychotherapy and of different psychotherapists. In summing up this
work, Strupp emphasizes a therapist's - any therapist's -
enormous interpersonal power. This power, Strupp writes,
"is deployed more or less deliberately in all forms of
psychotherapy regardless of the specific techniques that
may be utilized. In other words, if a symptom, belief,
interpersonal strategy, or whatever is to change, a
measure of external force must be applied". But for this
force to become beneficial, the patient needs to have
trust and hope, and experience the therapist's concern.
"Thus", to quote Strupp again, "psychotherapy is a series
of lessons in basic trust, together with the undermining
of those interpersonal strategies the patient has
acquired for controlling himself and others". And further:
... "the touchstone for these changes is the experience
that, in a profound sense, the therapist has the patient's

best interest at heart. ... The therapist has to care; he must have a deep and genuine commitment to the patient and a pervasive dedication to help. Without these, the patient could never carry through the arduous and painful work of therapy."

The above key elements - the therapist's dedication to the patient's interests, the judicious use of his interpersonal power, and the patient's experience of trust and concern - operate, so Strupp tells us, in the individual therapy with all kinds of patients, be these called neurotic, borderline or psychotic, and with all kinds of therapists. Yet they seem most important - and most difficult to come by - in the therapy with those patients whose clinch seems the most malignant, whose betrayal of basic trust the most serious, and whose expectations and capacity for genuine concern and care the lowest, namely in the therapy of many of those patients that have come to be called schizophrenics. Still, even in their therapy notable success can be achieved as is now proven beyond doubt through the work and testimony of such pioneers as Frieda Fromm-Reichmann, Christian Müller, Gaetano Benedetti, Otto Will, Harold Searles, Clarence Schulz and many others.

At the same time, though, we have become more aware of the limitations of most individual psychotherapies with schizophrenics, limitations which - so I tried to show in my paper held at the last Schizophrenia Symposium in Oslo three years ago - have much to do with our neglect of systems forces, and, in particular, family dynamics operating in these situations. Within my present perspective, I would like to emphasize only one consequence of many a schizophrenic patient's hidden captivity or loyalty to his family: Often this patient cannot have a dialogue with his therapist as long as his dialogue with his family remains blocked. This means, as Ivan Boszormenyi-Nagy (2) has so well shown, he will experience any awakening trust and openness toward his therapist as a betrayal of hidden loyalties, causing him fierce breakaway guilt for which he must punish himself by staying sick and unresponsive. And this means then that the leverage of the therapist's interpersonal power and the reservoire of trust and concern which reside in the given dyadic relationship cannot overcome the power of the malignant clinch which blocks the dialogue within the family and between the generations.

It follows that the strategic place to break the malignant clinch and to rekindle the dialogue is the schizo-present family itself. And we must ask: How can the therapist deploy his interpersonal power - i.e. the power of the stronger reality - and the given resources of trust and concern to achieve this goal?

We thus conceive of the therapist as a kind of "clinch breaker". And here we may well think of the

referee in a boxing match who might have to use all his
moral as well as bodily power to tear apart the protagonists who, while pummeling each other, fight on without
really fighting, and without deciding anything. I believe, this referee has much in common with a family
therapist who deploys his superior "moral power" to break
a family-wide clinch. Such comparison is, for example,
suggested by Napier's and Whitaker's (6) account of
a family therapy, as recently published in the book "The
Family Crucible". In this family the index patient, a
very troubled and apparently suicidal adolescent girl
had been diagnosed as schizophrenic. But in the book's
story the focus shifts soon away from her to the bitter,
at first covert, then ever more overt struggle in which
the parents and the whole family appear deadlocked, a
struggle which turns out to be rooted in strong and conflicting family legacies and missions. In this struggle
the family therapists, and most notably Carl Whitaker,
the senior therapist, impress us as highly successful
clinch breakers and facilitators of an overdue dialogue.
Thus they commit the members, again and again, to what
Ivan Boszormenyi-Nagy has called the basic rule of family
therapy: to talk about all that which till now had seemed
too dangerous to talk about - such as shameful family
secrets, long held grudges, real or imagined injustices
suffered a long time ago but still acting as festering
wounds, unsettled accounts, accusations of exploitation
and counter-exploitation. The therapists facilitate such
dialogue and confrontation because of their demonstrated
concern, their (relative) freedom from anxiety, their
conciliatory humanness, their shown ability to cope with
conflicts in their own co-therapist relationship. Thus,
the dialogue expands, the family members negotiate anew
their relational reality and they all get a new lease on
their lifes and growth.

But there are different ways to break a malignant
family clinch. Napier's and Whitaker's way, as just outlined, is one way. Another is demonstrated by therapists
who rely chiefly on paradoxical interventions. And here I
think, particularly, of Dr. Selvini-Palazzoli and her
Milanese team whose work - I had a chance to watch it -
has greatly inspired our Heidelberg group. Today I am
convinced that paradoxical interventions can be a - maybe
the - most elegant as well most powerful method to break
many a malignant clinch, and particularly so in schizo-
present families.

Many analytically trained therapists, though, (and
I speak here from personal experience) find paradoxical
strategies still hard to digest. To them, they smack of
manipulation and, by their very nature, appear to negate
what seems so central to a positive mutuality: trust,
concern and an open, honest encounter. And I must admit,
it took me some time to find here my way; yet if I found

it and am now groping toward a reconciliation I must
again give credit to Hegel.

For Hegel advocated making concepts fluid, liquidizing them, as it were. And, I believe, we follow such
advocacy when we, through paradoxical interventions, help
to liquidize a relational reality that has so hardened
that it locks the protagonists into futile and tragic
power struggles. In liquidizing this hardened relational
reality, a therapist shakes up the family's whole epistemology, the basic categories, distinctions, schemata
and assumptions which direct the members' perceptions,
expectations, even their account-keeping. Thus, old
battle lines, old alliances, old causes for divisiveness
collapse, become meaningless - just as on the present
political arena only, a few years after the end of the
Vietnam War, old alliances, battle lines and causes for
divisiveness become meaningless.

Closer inspection shows now that key elements in such
shake-up of the family's epistemology are here, as in
other therapeutic settings, the therapist's judicious
use of his interpersonal power - i.e. the power that goes
with the stronger reality - yet also (and this may at
first seem strange) the family members' receiving a
lesson in basic trust and concern. The therapist gives
this - admittedly brief but concentrated - lesson by
taking utmost care not to endanger the family members'
self-esteem, already so low, nor to add to their anxiety,
shame and guilt, already so great. He does so by exer-
cising a multidirectional empathy, by refraining from
even the slightest hint of an accusation, by accepting
all their positions, and by giving these a "positive" -
i.e. non-accusing - "connotation". Thus, he emphasizes,
for example, the members' self-sacrifice where others
might emphasize a guilt-inducing ploy, emphasizes hidden
loyalty where others might emphasize stubborn defiance,
emphasizes positive attachment where others might emphasize tyrannical overprotectiveness, etc. All this contributes then to a liquidization of the family's relational reality and works toward the break of the clinch.

Optimally this amounts then to a re-opening of a
dialogue which derailed a long time ago when the dependent, trusting child turned to his parents, the persons
with the stronger reality, both for safe anchorage as
well as for a share in the making of their common relational reality - yet, along with these parents, became
entrapped. Now the paradoxical intervention may serve as
the key that springs open the trap - and thereby frees
all family members for further growth, individuation and
new forms of relatedness.

But finally a note of caution: With many schizophrenics, I believe, springing of the trap will not be
enough. Often these patients need further help in over-
coming the lack of skills, lack of experiences, the

cognitive distortions or even defects, etc. which are consequences of their deprivations and uneven developments suffered during their long family-wide developmental and relational stagnation. Also, these patients often will need further help to confront, understand and cope with the conflicting missions and legacies, the unmourned losses, the split loyalties which we typically find at the root of schizophrenic tragedies. Thus, clinch breaking, in whatever manner it is done, can only be part of our therapeutic endeavours, but certainly a central part, in fact one, that affects whatever we do as therapists and, very possibly, affects how we view all human development, conflicts and relations.

REFERENCES

1. Bateson, G. (1973): Steps to an Ecology of Mind Paladin, Frogmore.
2. Boszormenyi-Nagy & Spark, G. (1973): Invisible Loyalties, Harper & Row, New York.
3. Haley, J. (1959): The Family of the Schizophrenic. A Model System. In: J. Nerv. Ment.,Dis. 129, 357-374.
4. Jacobson, E. (1957): Denial and Repression. In: J. of the Am. Psychoanal. Ass., 5, 61-92.
5. Lidz, T. (1978): Egocentric Cognitive Regression and the Family Setting of Schizophrenic Disorders. In: The Nature of Schizophrenia, p. 531. Editors: L.C. Wynne, R.L. Cromwell, S. Matthysse. J. Wiley, New York.
6. Napier, A.Y. & Whitaker, C.A. (1977): The Family Crucible. Harcourt & Brace, New York.
7. Selvini Palazzoli, M. et al. (1978): Paradox and Counterparadox. J. Aronson, New York.
8. Stierlin, H. (1959): The Adaptation to the 'Stronger' Person's Reality. In: Psychiatry, 29, 143-152.
9. Stierlin, H. (1978): Delegation und Familie. Suhrkamp, Frankfurt.
10. Strupp, H.H. (1973): Psychotherapy: Clinical Research and Theoretical Issues. J. Aronson, New York.
11. Wynne, L.C. et al. (1978): The Nature of Schizophrenia. John Wiley, New York.

INDICATIONS FOR DIFFERENT FORMS OF PSYCHOTHERAPY WITH NEW SCHIZOPHRENIC PATIENTS IN COMMUNITY PSYCHIATRY

Yrjö O. Alanen, Viljo Räkköläinen, Riitta Rasimus and Juhani Laakso

Psychiatric Department, University of Turku, Finland

In the treatment of schizophrenia in community psychiatry, the role of psychotherapy is still relatively secondary. Intensive individual psychotherapy in particular is presumably viewed by many as a treatment mode which requires too much time and too much special training to be used on a larger scale. Considerable effect has evidently been exerted by certain studies carried out in the United States in the 1960s, in which comparisons were drawn between the results of drug treatment and psychotherapy, emphasizing the superiority of drug therapy (14, 15, 16, 8, 9). In our view the results of these studies are not particularly relevant to the assessment of the possibilities of psychotherapy; due to their rigid research design, they do not justice to an individualized (cf. 24) psychotherapeutic approach linked more closely to the patient's life environment.

It is clear, for instance, that the patient's motivation for confronting and trying to deal with his problems and even for entering treatment has significance in appraising the possibilities for psychotherapy in each particular case. Psychotherapy, particularly in the area of the psychotic disorders, can never be a universal remedy applicable to all patients in the same way. It is therefore not possible to gain an accurate view of the possibilities of the psychotherapeutic treatment orientation on a larger scale when the patients are randomly allocated into different treatment categories following the methodological approach of the natural sciences, as was the case in the Camarillo State Hospital study carried out under the direction of Philip May. It should be also pointed out that neither May's study nor the project conducted by Grinspoon and his coworkers at the Massachusetts Mental Health Center encompassed any family therapy. The great importance of the family environemnt and disturbances in it - in terms of pathogenesis, treatment and prognosis - has been generally recognized among psychotherapeutically oriented investigators and therapists working in the field of schizophrenia.

Accordingly, psychotherapy can never be a panacea given to all psychotic patients. Nor should it be the exclusive right af a few socially and economically privileged patients, who are by no means always the ones best suited for treatment. Likewise it need not always be intensive in character; less intensive therapy, provided be less highly trained staff who are supported by supervision and guidance, can bring about highly significant results in the case of many patients. At our own hospital, for example, over a period of nearly ten years we have obtained very favorable experiences of this. The successful establishment and maintenance of a lasting, reliable and open treatment relationship may already in itself constitute an important goal. In many cases a family-oriented approach is helpful in achieving a successful outcome; besides an   actual family therapy, this may involve contacts established with the patient's family already at the beginning of therapy and continued in the later phase of treatment.

THE PLAN AND OBJECTIVES OF OUR RESEARCH PROJECT

The research project in which our team is involved has as its objective the development of forms of treatment for patients with schizophrenic disorders in the frames of community psychiatry.   Our approach follows three main principles: firstly, it is psychotherapeutically oriented; secondly, the emphasis is on the family as a whole; and thirdly, it corresponds to the needs of community psychiatry and the resources available. The study is being carried out in Finland, in the Mental Health Care District of the City of Turku. Our data were gathered over a period extending from April 1, 1976 to October 31, 1977 and consist of 100 consecutive patients, aged 16 to 45, who lived in Turku and who entered treatment for a schizophrenia-type disorder for the first time in their lives at an outpatient or inpatient treatment unit operating in the sector of community psychiatry. Psychiatric interviews with these patients, as well as interviews with their close relatives, were conducted by two members of our team, a psychiatrist (V. Räkköläinen) and a nurse specialized in psychiatry (R. Rasimus). A psychological examination was also carried out (J. Laakso). In this connection the research team also laid out for each patient a treatment plan that was regarded as optimal for his needs, and we have also tried to stimulate the actual realization of these plans by means of action research.

The second phase of the study consists of a follow-up investigation of each patient and his family members, carried out two years after the beginning of treatment. In this phase the outcome for the patient as well as his family, and the effect of the treatment given, are assessed. This follow-up study is currently under way, with a research psychiatrist not associated with our original team as one of the participants. In this part of the study, the original treatment plans will be reassessed and the patient's current need for treatment will be examined. The investigation does not involve a concurrent control group, but the effect of the development of this treatment orientation can be assessed by comparing the present findings with those obtained in earlier prognostic studies carried out both in Turku and elsewhere in Finland. The third phase of this study, as planned, will consist of another follow-up survey of our patients, taking place seven and a half years from the entrance into treatment. Here comparisons can be drawn between the outcome in these patients and the results obtained in a follow-up

survey of schizophrenic patients who entered treatment for the
first time ten years earlier, during the years 1965-1967, and
who likewise had a follow-up period of seven and a half years
(21). The development of the psychotherapeutic treatment
orientation in Turku has taken place on a larger scale during
the ten-year period separating these two patient samples.

In the following, a summarized account of indications for
different psychotherapeutic treatment modes in our sample will
be presented, based on the first phase of the study. Our results
should be considered preliminary in nature; the final estimates
as to the accuracy of the indications can be presented only
after the completion of the follow-up study. These results,
however, may be of interest even at the present stage, if only
because such estimates as to the need for psychotherapeutic
treatment, based both on the personality of the psychotic patient and the nature of his disturbance on the one hand and
on his life situation and environment on the other, have not
as far as we know been previously reported in the area of
community psychiatry.

COMMUNITY PSYCHIATRY IN TURKU

In keeping with the aims of this study, we tried to determine the indications for different forms of psychotherapy in
such a way as to take into account the realistic possibilities
available to community psychiatry, "in conditions regarded as
optimal". As elsewhere in Finland, our manpower resources, particularly in the outpatient sector of community psychiatry, are
considerably less than adequate. This is somewhat compensated
by the extent of the private sector. With the latter taken into
account, it was possible, in an up-to-date study af all available outpatient services (22), to regard Turku as an area of
abundant outpatient services, given Finnish conditions. Adjusted
for the population as a whole, and including all those 15 years
of age and over, there were 8.7 outpatient visits a week per
1000 inhabitants. Only 40 % of all outpatient visits were accounted for by the treatment units belonging to the system of community psychiatry services (including the community mental health
centers, the psychiatric policlinic of central hospital, and
the aftercare of discharged patients, taking place in our own
hospital). It may be noted,however, that in this figure the private sector is considered to include the so-called A-clinic, with
its unit for young persons; this clinic operates as a treatment
facility for persons with drinking problems, and is financed
by a private foundation, but in practice its operations may be
regarded as forming part of community psychiatry. Approximately
80 % of outpatient visits by psychotic patients were paid to
the treatment units belonging to the sector of community psychiatry.

THE STRUCTURE OF THE PATIENT SAMPLE

Age	Schizo-phrenia	Paranoid psychosis (near schizo-phrenia)	Acute schizo-phreni-form psychosis	Schizo-affective psychosis	Border-line psychosis	Total
16-25	20	1	2	3	8	34
26-35	17	1	9	9	10	46
36-45	7	2	7	1	3	20
Total	44	4	18	13	21	100

Table 1. Distribution of patients by age and diagnostic group

The structure of the sample, by diagnosis and age, is presented in Table 1, which shows that we included in the study patients between the ages of 16 and 45, who are divided in the table into three ten-year groupings. The diagnostic criterion was that the patient should belong to the category of schizophrenic psychoses in the broader sense of the term. This means that, in addition to typical schizophrenia and the para-noid psychosis closely related to it, we also included patients with acute schizophreniform or paranoid psychosis (the category usually referred to as "reactive schizophrenias" in American terminology) as well as schizo-affective psychoses, and finally those borderline psychoses in which schizophrenic thinking and behavior were at least episodically clearly manifested. This diagnostic classification corresponds to that outlined already by Eugen Bleuler (3) in his classic monograph.

The diagnostic and age structure shown in the table is in keeping with our expectations, also in the sense that quanti-tatively it corresponds quite closely to our comparison group, with the onset of the illness ten years earlier. Nuclear schizo-phrenias and borderline psychoses are heavily represented in the two youngest age groups, while acute schizophreniform and paranoid psychoses are more frequent in the older patients. Of interest is the concentration of schizo-affective psychoses in the intermediate age group. In subsequent comparisons we have combined on the one hand the groups with nuclear schizophrenia and paranoid psychosis, on the other those with acute psychoses and schizo-affective psychoses, while a third, separate patient group consists of borderline psychoses.

Among the patients there were 48 men and 52 women. Our subject differ from the general population in terms of educa-tion: the proportion of patients with a relatively high level of basic education is fairly large compared to the average population. This is due to the fact that Turku has several important schools and universities; in addition to the normal population of 165 000, it has some 20 000 students, half of

them at university. These and other backround data will appear
in subsequent tables, in which comparisons will be drawn between them and the treatment modes indicated.

THEORETICAL FRAME OF REFERENCE

Our views concerning the nature of schizophrenic psychosis,
and the factors relevant to its genesis, are based on psychodynamic theory, which has taken shape on the basis of influences from the area of individual therapy on the one hand,
family dynamics and family therapy on the other. The effect
of different modes of psychotherapy, and the indications for
them, can be both understood and justified on the basis of
such a theory.

We consider the schizophrenic psychosis as a disorder
which varies in duration and extent, and which affects the
basic psychic structures - the 'self' following Kohut's usage
(11,12) - but which is in principle restorable. The onset of the
psychosis is often associated with challenges to growth - in
principle often quite normal - occurring in the life situation,
or with stress factors (cf. 19) while a particular proneness to
psychotic disintegration is also involved.

The critical pathogenesis of vulnerability takes place
in the first two or three years of life, particularly in a
disturbance of the interaction between the mother and the child
during its first two phases, the symbiotic and the separation-
individuation phase. In our view this increased vulnerability
also varies in extent, and it may also center on different
phases of the early interactional processes. Studies in the
field of family dynamics (e.g. 1,13, 26) show that it is also
influenced by other intrafamilial interactions even extending
beyond the boundaries of the nuclear family (e.g., at the
intergenerational level). This vulnerability is ameliorated or
aggravated by successes or failures during later developmental
phases, particularly during adolescence. The proneness to disintegration may thus be connected with different personality
structures, and the form the manifest psychosis takes in the
clinical picture may accordingly vary extensively, as indicated
also by our diagnostic classification.

A common feature in the prepsychotic development of most
patients is a multiform adaptive disability, which often leads
to an avoidance of the growth challenge situations normally
encountered in life; the patient builds up external protective
structures which compensate for deficiences in the internalized
psychic structures (20). Most commonly these are intensive,
regressive and overdependent relationships, directed particularly to the members of one's own family, the parents or the marital partner. Often the overdependence is reciprocal, due
more primarily to the other person concerned. At its most
typical this is seen in those parent-child dependence relationships, described e.g. by Stierlin as a transactional mode of
binding, in the genesis of which the parent's own separation
problems play a crucial role (cf. 26).

The psychotherapeutic treatment of schizophrenic psychosis may be viewed as the restoration of that developmental failure which led to the manifest psychosis, and also the prevention of further disturbance. This includes a study of underlying disintegration vulnerability and the supporting structures protecting it, and also an effort to enhance psychological growth by means of the therapeutic process. These therapeutic objectives are differentially weighted from case to case, according to the disturbance of the personality of the patient as well as the individuals in his immediate environment and, on the other hand, according to the favourable potentials they present.

DETERMINING THE INDICATIONS FOR DIFFERENT MODES OF PSYCHO-THERAPY

In the following, the groups whereby a given mode of psychotherapy was considered to be indicated, and the number of patients falling to each treatment category, are presented. The latter figures are also shown in Table 2.

	N (%)
1. Individual psychotherapies	
Intensive individual therapy	25
Other individual contact	71
2. Family therapies	
Conjoint family therapy, intensive	6
" " " , supportive	10
Marital or couple therapy, intensive	13
" " " , supportive	13
Separate support to members of primary family	24
" " " secondary "	12
Other contacts with the patient's family	19
3. Group therapy (Open care)	10
4. Psychotherapeutic community in the hospital ward	63

Table 2. Number of patients indicated for different forms of psychotherapy

1. Intensive individual psychotherapy

This type of therapy was regarded as indicated for those patients whose development and life situation showed such a current disturbance in psychological growth, or such a developmental lag or arrest, as could best be corrected by means of psychotherapy provided in a two-person relationship and working towards conscious developmental goals. Perhaps the most important determinant in the case of this treatment mode was the investigators' view as to whether the patient would be able to benefit from a therapeutic process, that would

deal with deep-rooted developmental problems, and whether such
a process would be possible to be motivated in his particular
case. By intensive individual psychotherapy we do not necessarily mean a strictly analytic, insight-directed therapy, although
this kind of treatment relationship is assumed to include aspects
which clarify and enhance the patient's own insight into his
problems. The minimum intensity of treatment is considered to
be one session per week, over a period of several months at
least, and generally therapy is provided on a long-term basis.
In practice, the nature of the therapeutic process, and the
integration of various forms of activity, is left to the thera -
pist and is worked out by him according to his own resources
and the patient's special characteristics and life situation.

Intensive individual psychotherapy was regarded in our
sample as indicated for 25 patients, or one-fourth of the total patient body.

2. Other individual contacts

In the case of this form of treatment, we have a considerably more heterogeneous category. This indication occurred
most typically when it was considered beneficial for the patient
to have an opportunity for a human relationship providing support
and security. In these cases the original plan may already have
involved the establishment of a fairly long-continued, supportive
treatment contact. This was combined with the control of drug
therapy, which constituted a relatively important task in the
treatment of many of these patients.

In this setting the patient can also examine his feelings
and reactions relating to the onset of his symptoms or the
course of his own life history, without, however, aiming at a
long-term explorative therapeutic process in the first place.
In certain cases this relationship may prepare the way for
actual intensive individual therapy; in other words, the possibility of individual therapy is not entirely excluded. In some
other cases - in our estimate, 27 patients out of the total 100-
this type of treatment represents a form of crisis intervention;
it is short-term in nature, but often involves frequent contact,
and in addition to the patient members of his family and other
persons in his immediate environment are also seen. Except crisis intervention, the frequency of supportive contacts is generally lower than in the intensive individual therapy;no distinctive
line, however, can be drawn between the two on the basis of
contact frequensy. The principal difference lies in the degree
of their explicit developmental aims.

Our sample included only four patients for whom no individual therapeutic contact was considered necessary after the phase
of the initial psychiatric axamination. The treatment plan for
those patients centered on either group or family therapy.

3. Conjoint family therapy

The term "conjoint family therapy" denotes family therapy
provided in the form of joint sessions with the patient and
members of his family of origin. This type of treatment was

considered indicated when the basic disturbance of the patient, and the onset of his illness, appeared to be so closely related to intrafamilial relationships, and the mutual dependency of the family members was so intensive, that it was felt to be impossible for the patient to emancipate himself without an active psychotherapeutic intervention directed into these actual intrafamilial interactional processes. It was also assumed that interviews with the patient and his parents had given some grounds for concluding that conjoint family therapy would be possible and useful, and that the motivation for it could be aroused.

In the course of this study, we have experienced that conjoint therapy of the family of origin is often possible only after a relatively prolonged preliminary period. It was probably due to this that, while conjoint family therapy was considered indicated for sixteen families, in only six of them a more intensive long-term therapy could be initiated right away. In the remaining ten cases, less frequent conjoint sessions often supporting the patient's individual therapy were indicated, sometimes preparing a more intensive family therapy.

4. Marital therapy

Joint participation of the patient and his or her spouse in family sessions was regarded as indicated when the illness of a married patient appeared to be related to mutual problems of the marital partners. In certain other cases the indication for marital therapy was based above all on the view that the support provided by the spouse would be of central importance in the treatment of the patient. Intensive marital therapy was indicated in our sample in thirteen cases and infrequent, supportive interviews together with the patient and his or her marital partner likewise in thirteen cases. The category of supportive interviews also included a few couples who had recently been separated, in which case the joint sessions dealt with the clarification of the divorce situation. Joint marital therapy was considered indicated for nearly 80 % of the married patients in our sample. The number is high and reflects the very crucial role played by the marital situation in the psychodynamics of the onset of the illness and the treatment of these patients.

5. Other contacts with family members

Indications for this type of care were present in various situations:
- when a family member appeared to need help as an individual
- when the relatives appeared to need support in order to prevent the patient's illness or its treatment from becoming too heavy a burden on them
- when the patient's treatment would possibly fail without such contact with the family
- when the patient's lack of treatment motivation actually led to a situation in which sustained contact with a family member constituted the only possibility for providing care

- when these contacts with the family were seen to serve as a
  preliminary ground work for the subsequent family therapy

In the present sample there were only three patients in
whose case there was in our view no indication for any contacts
with family members. This demonstrates the emphasis that our
experience has led us to place on the role of intrafamilial
relationships in the psychodynamics and treatment of schizophrenia. When these patients are married and have children,
we also take into account the position and the involvement
of the children in the family pathology. This may take place
by means of visits to the family in a home-care setting, which
makes it possible to see the children. In our experience, however, joint sessions with the marital partners often also
provide good opportunities to support the healthy development
of the children's mental life.

6.Group therapy

In the experience of our team, the importance of group
therapy in the treatment of psychotic patients is not as great
as that of individual and family therapy if the treatment involves relatively far-reaching developmental aims. Group therapy, however, often has an enhancing effect on the interpersonal relationships of the patients (cf. 6). In our own sample
we considered group-therapeutic activities indicated particularly in the case of a lonely, socially isolated person, in whom
motivation for therapeutic work in a group can be stimulated.
In some cases group therapy was chosen as the primary mode of
treatment, while in others it was considered to provide support
for individual therapy.

Group therapy in an outpatient setting was considered to
be indicated for ten patients. This figure, however, would be
considerably higher if it included those   patients for
whom participation in the therapeutic community operating in
the hospital ward was indicated, since these patients nearly
invariably took part in groups. It turned out to be impossible
to assess at the time of the initial examination the subsequent
need for group therapy following discharge from the hospital.

7. Therapeutic community in a hospital ward

During the 1960's and the early 1970's, the importance of
outpatient treatment of schizophrenic patients has been strongly emphasized in community psychiatry; this has been related
to the efforts aiming at shortening the duration of hospital
stays (e.g. 4, 5 ,10). In Finland, for instance, the average
duration of the first hospitalization of schizophrenic patients
in Helsinki dropped from 148 days in 1960 to 38 days in 1970
(17).

In the view of our team (e.g. 2)   the quick discharge of schizophrenic patients from the hospital should not
be taken as a primary goal compared to more long-term objectives.
Particularly among the more severely disturbed schizophrenic
patients there are many persons who need relatilevy long-continued hospital treatment, in order to establish a therapeutic

relationship which will make it possible to help them in a more profound and more permanent way. It may be symptomatic that many writers in recent years have stressed some of the disadvantages of short hospitalizations (e.g.25, 7,18). In particular the study by Glick and his coworkers (7) showed that hospitalizations lasting three to four months led first-admitted schizophrenic patients and their environment to accept the need for treatment and to permit better arrangements with a view to long-term outpatient care, more easily than did stays lasting three to four weeks.

Our team holds the view that therapeutic community repre-sents a "maximal" offer of treatment provided by community psychiatry with severely regressed patients. In our hospital we have characterized the wards of psychotic patients as "psy-chotherapeutic communities", in which one important objective has been the development of an empathic and "parental" therapeu-tic attitude (cf.2). In addition to the commonly shared attitude of "holding" (23,27) and social situations stimulating more open and unstrained communication, we also aim in our therapeutic community at developing the individual therapeutic relationships as well as contacts with family members.

Of the 100 patients in our sample, we assessed treatment in a therapeutic community as indicated in 63 cases. This phase of treatment formed at the same time a basis for the development of an overall treatment plan, including the sub-sequent outpatient care. The optimal length of hospital treat-ment has to be determined individually for each patient.

8. Drug therapy

Although the indications for neuroleptic drug therapy in our sample are outside the scope of this paper, it may be worth noting that mild or moderate use of drugs was indicated for over 80 % of our patients, with the purpose of reducing anxiety, facilitating the establishment of contact with the patient and alleviating gross psychotic symptoms. Our sample included only four patients in whose case massive doses of drugs aimed at bringing the symptoms rapidly under control, played a fundamen-tal role in the initial treatment plans .

INDICATED TREATMENT MODES IN RELATION TO CERTAIN BACKGROUND VARIABLES

The percentual distribution relating to the patients' age and indicated mode of treatment is seen in Table 3. It shows that the assessed need for intensive individual psychotherapy declines with increasing age; in the patients aged 16 to 25 the figure is three times higher than for those aged 36 to 45 years. Indications for therapeutic community are distributed in a parallel way. In the case of family therapy, including both conjoint family therapy and jointly attended marital the-rapy, in both intensive and less intensive forms, there is a reverse trend, which is due to the large incidence of marital therapy in our sample. Of those for whom joint therapy for the

194

patient and his parents was indicated, nine fell in the youngest, six in the intermediate and only one in the oldest age group.

Forms of therapy

Age group	intens. individ. therapy (N=25)	other individ. contacts (N=71)	family therapy (N=42)	other family contacts (N=55)	group therapy (N=10)	therap. community (N=63)
16-25 N=34	32.3	70.5	32.3	64.7	14.7	74.4
26-35 N=46	26.0	69.5	41.3	52.2	6.5	60.9
36-45	10.0	80.0	55.0	45.0	10.0	40.0

Table 3. Indicated forms of psychotherapy in relation to age groups, percentage

Forms of therapy

Sex	intens. individ. therapy (N=25)	other individ. contacts (N=71)	family therapy (N=42)	other family contacts (N=55)	group therapy (N=10)	therap. community (N=63)
Female N=52	29.1	68.8	54.2	48.8	4.2	70.8
Male N=48	21.1	73.1	30.8	63.5	15.4	55.8

Table 4. Indicated form of psychotherapy in relation to sex, percentage

In the distribution of the patients by sex (Table 4), attention is primarily drawn by the fact that most intensive modes of treatment were indicated somewhat more frequently for women than for men, with particular reference to family therapy and treatment in the therapeutic community. The difference is accounted for the greater prevalence of character disturbances and drinking problems in men than in women.

In the distribution by marital status (Table 5) individual therapy and treatment in the therapeutic community are particularly pronounced in the group of single patients. In the married group, the proportion of actual family therapy is predictably high, whereas group therapy is not recommended for them and the need for therapeutic community is also markedly low.

Forms   of   therapy

Table 5.

Marital status	intens. individ. therapy (N=25)	other individ. contacts (N=71)	family therapy (N=42)	other family contacts (N=55)	group the- rapy (N=10)	therap. commu- nity (N=63)
single N=57	33.3	64.9	28.1	66.7	14.1	73.7
married N=28	17.6	78.6	78.6	21.4	0.0	25.0
widowed divorced, separated N=15	6.7	80.0	20.0	73.3	13.3	33.3

Table 5. Indicated forms of psychotherapy in relation to
marital status, percentage

Forms   of   therapy

Social group	intens. individ. therapy (N=25)	other indiv. contacts (N=71)	family therapy (N=42)	other family contacts (N=25)	group therapy (N=10)	therap. commu- nity (N=63)
I-III N=73	30.1	67.1	47.9	50.9	5.5	67.1
IV N=27	11.1	81.4	25.9	66.6	22.2	57.9

Table 6. Indicated forms of psychotherapy in relation to
social group of the primary family, percentage

The relationship between the social group of the patient's family
of origin and the mode of treatment is shown in Table 6.
Families representing social group IV, the lowest class (unskilled workers), who accounted for somewhat over one-fourth
of sample, are distinct from the rest. Patients from the other
social groups i.e. I, II and III, have intensive individual
psychotherapy and family therapy indicated clearly more frequently than those from class IV; in the case of group therapy the relationship is the reverse, and in the case of
treatment in the therapeutic community there is no actual difference. The distribution according to the patient's basic
education (Table 7) shows a similar difference in the case of

individual psychotherapy, but not family therapy. It may be noted that, while these educational and social class distributions were fairly distinct particularly in the case of intensive individual therapy, there were also six persons with the lowest level of basic education for whom intensive individual therapy had been indicated.

F o r m s   o f   t h e r a p y

School education	intens. individ. therapy (N=25)	other individ. contacts (N=71)	family therapy (N=42)	other family contacts (N=55)	group therapy (N=10)	therap. community (N=63)
basic school N=60	10.0	85.0	43.4	56.4	13.3	56.7
more than basic school N=40	47.5	50.0	40.0	60.0	5.0	72.5

Table 7. Indicated forms of psychotherapy in relation to the patients' education, percentage

F o r m s   o f   t h e r a p y

Diagnosis group	intens. individ. therapy (N=25)	other individ contacts (N=71)	family therapy (N=42)	other family contacts (N=55)	group therapy (N=10)	therap. community (N=63)
nuclear sch+par. psychosis N=48	31.2	66.7	41.7	58.3	8.3	75.0
sch-form + sch-affect. psychosis N=31	9.7	80.6	54.8	38.7	9.8	19.4
borderline psychosis N=21	33.3	66.7	23.8	71.4	14.2	38.0

Table 8. Indicated forms psychotherapy in relation to diagnostic groups, percentange

197

The distribution of indications according to the clinical diagnosis is shown in Table 8. It is fairly easy to understand that indications for treatment in a therapeutic community are clearly most frequent in the group with nuclear schizophrenia. These patients, if only because of their more extensively damaged ego, need a more holistic approach to treatment as well as support from external structures. The need for intensive individual psychotherapy, however, is also great in this group as well as among the cases of borderline psychosis, in contrast to those with schizophreniform and schizo-affective psychoses. In the latter groups, family therapy is prominent, due to the fact that the majority of the married patients for whom marital therapy was indicated belonged to these two diagnostic categories. Indications for actual family therapy, however, were also present for more than 40 % of the patients with nuclear schizophrenia, while in borderline psychosis this mode of treatment was indicated less frequently.

In addition to psychotic symptoms, neurotic symptoms were found in our sample in 25 patients, depressive symptoms in 64 patients, acting out in 27 and a tendency alcohol problems in 35 patients. Table 9 shows that the presence of neurotic and depressive symptoms showed a positive correlation with intensive individual psychotherapy, group therapy and treatment in therapeutic community. Potential acting out and excessive drinking, on the other hand, are often associated with a character pathology which contraindicates long-term psychotherapies. For the acting-out patients, however, intensive family therapy was often the indicated form of treatment.

F o r m s o f t h e r a p y

Other symptoms	intens individ. therapy (N=25)	other individ. contacts (N=71)	family therapy (N=42)	other family contacts (N=55)	group therapy (N=10)	therap. commu- nity (N=63)
neurotic N=25	40.0	60.0	36.0	56.0	24.0	72.0
depressive N=64	29.6	64.1	45.3	50.0	12.5	70.3
acting out behav. N=27	11.1	81.5	66.7	37.0	11.1	63.0
alcohol problems N=35	17.1	80.0	31.4	62.9	8.6	57.1

Table 9. Indicated forms of psychotherapy in relation to other psychiatric symptoms

F o r m s   o f   t h e r a p y

Insight capability	intens. individ. therapy (N=25)	other individ. contacts (N=71)	family therapy (N=42)	other family contacts (N=55)	group therapy (N=10)	therap. community (N=63)
denial or externalization N=49	10.2	83.7	46.9	51.0	4.1	55.1
at least partial internalization N=51	39.2	58.8	37.3	58.8	15.7	70.6

Table 10. Indicated forms of psychotherapy in relation to insight capability

Finally, it is interesting to see to what extent our estimates as to the patients' capacity for insight into their own problems were correlated with the treatment indications as assessed by us (Table 10). Approximately one-half of our patients used extensive denial as a defence or tended to externalize their problems, while the other half was partly able to integrate their problems and also their illness. The difference was greatest in the case of intensive individual psychotherapy, which was indicated four times more frequently for those patients who showed insight into their problems than for the other group. The same trend is seen also for group therapy, while family therapy was considered suitable in many cases in which the patient's own capacity for insight was poor.

DISCUSSION

The results of this kind of study can never have universal applicability, since they are always dependent on local conditions, e.g. on the attitudes and the educational level of the population, on the quality of training of care-taking personnel and undoubtedly also on the views of the investigators concerning the treatment of psychotic patients. The available resources also have an effect, even though in our own study they were assumed to be greater than they are in reality, i.e. they were assumed to correspond to "optimal" community-psychiatric conditions.

It is our view, however, that the number of cases indicated for the different modes of treatment would not be much higher in the present sample even under ideal conditions, because limitations to treatment were in most cases imposed by various clinical and psychodynamic factors and those relating to the patient's life situation more than by other factors.

In our study we tried to compensate for the shortage of manpower in the outpatient sector of community psychiatry, by referring patients for treatment also to private practice when this was possible. In addition, our team provided supervisory guidance of therapeutic work in outpatient treatment units. Actual therapy was also provided by members of the team, though only one, Mrs. Rasimus, the specialized psychiatric nurse of the team, was employed full time in work relating to our project. More intensive treatment could thus be provided for the patients of our sample and their families, compared to the average conditions of community psychiatry in Turku, while treatment resources nevertheless remained below the level we consider optimal.

According to our preliminary data, intensive individual therapy has actually been received by approximately two-thirds of the patients for whom this was initially indicated. The role of the private sector seems to be relatively important here. In those cases in which intensive individual therapy was regarded as indicated or was attempted in any case, the impediment to treatment was caused by the patient's life situation turning out more unfavorable than assessed at the outset, or by a lack of treatment motivation, at least as often as by a lack of treatment resources. Conjoint family therapy and marital therapy have been realized in somewhat lesser degree, according to our current figures in approximately 40 % of the cases for whom they were indicated. The role of the private sector has been slighter in these cases. The training of therapist by us in family therapy is that of a nurse or a social worker more frequently than in individual therapy, where the therapist is more commonly a psychiatrist or a psychologist. The impediment of family therapy was in many cases due to a lack of motivation on the part of the families. A readiness for an ordinary family therapy evidently by us requires on the average more time than in the case of individual therapy. This is apparently true both for the families and for the therapists, who may likewise consider family therapy a more demanding and anxiety-arousing task than individual therapy. The lack of tradition and training in family therapy is also relevant here.

The final results concerning the implementation and effects of different modes of treatment can be reported only after the completion of our follow-up investigation, at which time the indications can be reassessed. Already now it seems evident that often the situation at the time of the follow-up has changed for both the patient and his family, and a reassessment of treatment possibilities is necessary if only because of this. Much more attention than at present should be paid in community psychiatry to a continuously open and active attitude in working out and reshaping treatment plans for the patients.

In our opinion, these preliminary data on the realization of the original plans of treatment still are encouraging. They show at least that a psychodymanic concept of psychosis functions in practice in the field of community psychiatry as well. Psy-

chotherapeutic activities can be adequately developed in this
field relative to the indications, without an undue increase
in treatment resources. A central role is played not merely by
an increase in the number of care-taking personnel, but above
all by the development of widely-based supervisory work and
training, in which particular attention is paid to an adequate
understanding of the specific nature of the problem area represented by psychotic patients and to a family-centered approach
to the work.

REFERENCES

1. Alanen, Y.O.(1958): The Mothers of Schizophenic Patients,
   Acta psychiat. Scand. Vol. 33. Suppl. 124.
2. Alanen, Y.O. (1975): The psychotherapeutic care of chizo-
   phrenic patients in a community psychiatric setting. In Studies of Schizophrenia, ed. by M.H. Lader, Brit. J.Psychiat.
   Spec. Publ. No 10.
3. Beuler, E. (1911): Dementia Praecox oder die Gruppe der
   Schizophrenien. Deuticke, Leipzig u. Wien. (engl. transl.
   1950).
4. Brown, G.W., Bone, M., Dalison, B.&Wing, J.K. (1966): Schizophrenia and Social Care. Institute of Psychiatry, Maudsley
   Monographs 17, Oxford.Univ.Press, London.
5. Caffey, E.M., Galbrecht, C.R., Klett, C.J.&Poit, P. (1971):
   Briefhospitalization and aftercare in the treatment of schizophrenia, Arch. Gen. Psychiat. 24,81.
6. Cleghorn, J.L., Johnstone, E.E., Cook, T.H.& Itschner, L.
   (1974): Group therapy and maintenance treatment of schizophrenics Arch. Gen. Psychiat. 31, 361.
7. Glick, I.D., Hargreaves, W.A., Drues, J. & Showstack, J.A.
   (1976): Short versus long hospitalization. A prospective
   controlled study: IV. One-year follow-up results for schizophrenic patients. Amer. J. Psychiat. 133, 509.
8. Grinspoon, L., Ewalt, J.R.& Shader, R. (1968): Psychotherapy
   and pharmacotherapy in chronic schizophrenia. Amer. J. Psychiat. 124, 1645.
9. Grinspoon, L., Ewalt, J.R.& Shader, R. (1972): Schizophrenia:
   Pharmacotherapy and Psychotherapy. Williams & Wilkins, Baltimore.
10.Gruenberg, E.M. (1974): Benefits of short-term hospitalization. In Strategic Interventions in Schizophrenia, ed. by
   R. Cancro, N.Fox & L. Shapiro. Behav. Publ. New York.
11.Kohut, H. (1971): The Analysis of the Self. Internat. Univ.
   Press, New York.
12.Kohut H. (1977): The Restoration of the Self. Internat.Univ.
   Press, New York.
13.Lidz, T., Fleck, S. & Cornelison, A.r. (1965): Schizophrenia
   and the Family. Intern. Univ. Press, New York.
14.May, P.R.A. (1968): Treatment of Schizophrenia. Science
   House, New York.
15.May, P.R.A. (1969): The hospital treatment of the schizophrenic patient. Internat. J. Psychiat. 8, 699.

16. May, P.R.A., Tuma, A.H., Yale, C., Potepan, & Dixon, W.J. (1976): Schizophrenia - a follow-up study of results of treatment. Arch. gen. Psychiat. 33, 474.
17. Niskanen, P., Lönnqvist, L. & Achté, K.A. (1973): Schizophrenic and paranoid psychotic patients first admitted in 1970, with a two-year follow-up. Psychiatria Fennica 1973, 103.
18. Reybel, S. & Herz, M.I. (1976): Limitations of Brief Hospital Treatment. Am J. Psychiatry 133, 518.
19. Räkköläinen, V. (1977): Onset of Psychosis. A clinical Study of 68 Cases. Ann. Univ. Turkuensis, Ser. D:7.
20. Räkköläinen, V. Salokangas, R.K.R. & Lehtinen, P. (1978): Protective constructions in the course of psychosis, a follow-up study. This symposium.
21. Salokangas, R.K.R. (1977): Skitsofreniaan sairastuneiden psykososiaalinen kehitys.(The Psychosocial Development of Schizophrenic Patients). Kansaneläkelaitoksen julkaisuja, sarja, AL:7.
22. Salokangas, R.K.R., LehtinenV., Holm, H. & Laakso, J. (1978): Preliminary information.
23. Salonen, S. (1976): On the technique of the psychotherapy of schizophrenia. In Schizophrenia 1975, ed. by J. Jorstad & E. Ugelstad. Universitetsforlaget, Oslo.
24. Schulz, C.G. (1975): An individualized psychotherapeutic approach wit the schizophrenic patient. Schizophrenia Bull. 13, 46.
25. Schwartz, C.C., Meyers, J.K. & Astrachan, B.M. (1974): Psychiatric labeling and the rehabilitation of the mental patient. Arch. Gen. Psychiat. 31, 329.
26. Stierlin, H. (1974): Separating Parents and Adolescents. Quadrangle/ The New York Times, New York.
27. Winnicott, D.W. (1960): The theory of the parent-infant relationship. Internat. J.Psycho-Anal. 41:585.

THERAPY OF PSYCHOTIC TRANSACTION FAMILIES: AN EVOLUTIONARY PARADIGM

E. Fivaz
Centre d'Etude de la famille, Hôpital de Cery, 1008 Prilly,
Switzerland

R. Fivaz
Laboratoire de Physique appliquée, Ecole Polytechnique Fédérale,
1003 Lausanne, Switzerland

L. Kaufmann
Centre d'Etude de la famille, Hôpital de Cery, 1008 Prilly,
Switzerland

1. INTRODUCTION

It is well known that families with a psychotic member present
prevailing characteristic transaction modes commonly called
"psychotic". Their essential role seems to be the safe-keeping at any
cost of the established family structure, which then takes the
appearance of an intrinsicality inherent to this type of family. They
thus tend more and more rigidly to repeat solutions learnt to be of
service to the homeostasis (1), in spite of the changes occurring
with time and in spite of the poor and stereotyped functional relationships which these families tend to establish with their environment. These highly homeostatic features have found a useful model in
the general theory of closed systems, or systems close to equilibrium.
Indeed, this theory explains how a set of norms of preestablished
structure determines the behavior of a system when internal negative
feedback mechanisms can be activated to return to zero any detected
divergence from these norms. Thus the interactional structure of a
family can be apprehended through the conscious or unconscious norms
and rules which it obeys when in its state of equilibrium (2). In the
same way, the negative feedback mechanisms put into play during
crises which deviate the family from equilibrium can be listed and
analysed, including those mechanisms used to frustrate therapeutic
attempts at destabilizing the homeostasis.

Indeed, these interventions aim primarily at altering the rule
network which binds individuals in their stereotyped behavior, in the
hope that a development will proceed as well as new functional
relationships. This process, however, requires that the basic interactional structure of the family be modified and some of its functions be abandoned, while at the same time cohesion should be protected for vital functions to be preserved: qualitative structural
changes are to be provoked in a permanent system. The dynamic laws of
such changes obviously elude the theory of closed systems which are
ideally stable and non-evolving systems.

The general problem of qualitative changes in permanent systems
recently found a new expression in the general theory of open systems
far from equilibrium: beyond a certain level of complexity, some
systems are liable to spontaneously increase their internal order.
There exists an unexpected but explicit paradigm in the physics of
irreversible processes: this domain accounts for the organisational
changes occurring in physical, chemical or biological systems

subjected to <u>external forces</u> sufficient to remove them significantly from their state of equilibrium (3). In this type of transformation, several structures called "dissipative" may be reached successively so that a development takes place in which the order increases in successive stages; in principle, not only the structure of the stages can be described, but also the processes which destabilize them and lead to the structuring of the next stage. The dynamics of these dissipative structures accommodates also for invention and creativity insofar as it does not prejudice either the ulterior structures which will materialize or the time when they will occur.

To summarize, the proposed paradigm is apt to represent in detail complex development processes under the influence of appropriate external agents. Obviously, this situation is similar to psycho therapy in the special settings conceived for it. For this reason, the paradigm may be useful for formalising and analysing a therapeutic treatment. It may also allow us to approach the difficult problem of etiology in dysfunctional systems and of the progressive stabilization of psychotic transaction systems.

Such an aim is naturally extremely ambitious, since change processes tend to be rapid and elusive and there is yet no reliable method of observing them. However, the evolutionary paradigm can have an immediate use: from the knowledge of the mechanisms of qualitative change, certain rules can be derived which favour evolution in making it <u>more probable</u>. The enforcement of such rules does not require detailed knowledge of the structures or of the transformation processes. The paradigm is thus liable to guide the therapeutic treatment in making more intelligible the specific functions and mutual interactions of the various foreseeable procedures: therapeutic settings, interpretations, prescriptions, etc. In that perspective, the first step is to establish a dictionary relating the notions brought into play in the paradigm and those which clinical practice has shown to be useful. One will moreover notice the close relationship existing between that practice and the rules which favor evolution in the paradigm.

Thus, having described the paradigm and its epigenetic perspective, we will propose a classification of family types in terms of its main variables, stability and resilience. The paradigm will then be applied to therapy; a specific classification of known therapeutic strategies will follow as a first example of formalisation in terms of the paradigm. Finally, we will also use it to find out how a few specific strategies operate, namely the positive connotations and paradoxal prescriptions: the processes which necessarily lead to structural change will be identified. This second example involves the detailed dynamic properties of the paradigm and constitutes a first demonstration of its considerable explanatory power.

2.   DISSIPATIVE STRUCTURES

The structures appearing in complex systems subjected to external force fields are called "dissipative structures" (4). A simple physical example is represented by the convective motion in a gas (an ordered rotary structure of the velocity distribution) subjected to a sufficiently high temperature gradient (external field): these structures are dissipative because they dissipate a part of the energy provided by the applied field; they only exist if the field exceeds a critical value and they disappear if the field vanishes; they are of a higher order than the structure without field (in the example, a purely random velocity distribution) and are thus less likely to occur in the thermodynamical sense.

The change from a structure without field to a dissipative structure with field constitutes a transition: this is a process involving the entire system and which arises from the cooperative behavior of all subsystems (in the example, gas molecules) that are coupled in the system (in the example, coupling by collisions between molecules). The transition is initiated by one of the random fluctuations which always occur in a complex system (thermal fluctuations in the physical example, mutations in biology, etc). Thanks to these small deviations from the average, the system is capable of permanently "probing" the different states which it can attain in the force field. Normally, the coupling between subsystems dampens all fluctuations, so that the system regains by itself its original average stationary state: these couplings act as negative feedback mechanisms. It may happen, however, that a fluctuation reproduces an optimal state, i.e. of total lower energy, in a large enough volume; a new process may then take place called "nucleation": instead of being dampened, the random fluctuation is amplified by other internal mechanisms (e.g. in the physical example, Archimedean forces) and the whole system necessarily passes into the privileged state. The system complexity condition thus includes the existence of such nonlinear positive feedback mechanisms, which are the agents of the transition to the superior order contained in the optimal state. After the transition has occurred, and the new functions associated with the new structure have been established, the system may envisage new transitions which were previously unforeseeable, according to Prigogine's evolutionary cycle

$$\text{structures} \rightleftarrows \text{functions} \rightleftarrows \text{fluctuations}$$

The existence of such a cycle, which can be traced repeatedly and in either direction, as momentarily required by the demands of adaptation, obviously opens perspectives of complex system transformations. It is thus possible to represent these transformations in abstract terms which are independent of the nature of these systems and of the applied forces. Before discussing these epigenetic perspectives, five remarks have to be made concerning the potential contribution of exact sciences to evolutionary problems.

1) Physics distinguishes between two types of transition which seem to be found also in the application proposed below:

    a) The first order transitions pass through intermediate states of low probability, which more or less represent a "barrier" to be crossed: they are thus generally more difficult to achieve and may demand the application of a strong field. On the other hand, they are discontinuous, rapid, insensitive to ulterior fluctuations and irreversible in the sense that the applied field can decrease without immediately destabilizing the new structure (hysteresis effect).

    b) The second order transitions pass through successive states of equilibrium representing a continuous series of probable states; the applied field may be weaker, but the transition is relatively slow, sensitive to fluctuations, and reversible as soon as the field decreases.

2) In the exact sciences, there exist many systems which are liable to exhibit transitions but they are characterised by different sets of parameters. It is known, however, that the dynamics laws are general and applicable to most of these systems, and the study of these laws is called "synergetics" (5). Therefore simple systems may hopefully act as significant paradigms for more complex systems, such as those relevant to social sciences. Such attempts have already been made in sociology, for example to gain insight into the phenomena of sudden polarisation in public opinion (6).

3) Thus, as an example, there is a ferromagnetic system where a process of selection among various substructures occurs according to a criterion of usefulness (7). This selection is made possible because the function fulfilled by the system has a feedback on the distribution of its substructures (Prigogine's cycle traced in the direction: functions ⟶ structures ⟶ fluctuations). Thus, for an adequately chosen external field, the most efficient substructure can be automatically selected so that the functional productivity of the system is maximalized. The relative functional superiority of a substructure, which we will call differentiation, is a critical variable in this selection process. It determines the nature of the transition by which the substructure is chosen: if the differentiation exceeds a critical value, the transition is of first order and irreversible when the field decreases; on the contrary, when the differentiation is weak, the transition is of second order and reversible as soon as the applied field decreases. This model illustrates the well-known relationship between the permanence of a structural change and the functional output it produces (substitution of the hoe by the plough (4)).

4) Physics shows that if loss of information occurs in the feedback loops, on the one hand the regulations are less accurate, and on the other hand, the transitions are more difficult or even impossible to achieve.

5) According to the physics of irreversible processes, the transitions are accompanied by increasing energy dissipation at the external force field's expense: this additional dissipation preserves the thermodynamical principle of the increase of total entropy in spite of the entropy decrease within the system.

3.   EPIGENETIC PERSPECTIVES

The problem of development naturally emerges from the idea of an evolutionary cycle where each achieved state is the starting-point of a transition to an ulterior state of superior order: in the "phase space", which contains the set of all the possible states of a system, the development is described by the series of points reached at each revolution of the cycle and which trace a certain trajectory in that space. The trajectory is not arbitrary and the various constraints to which it is subjected are the subject matter of development theories. For instance, Piaget's school elaborated a theory for cognitive development (8) which displays a complex and necessary series of successive stages as well as some of the mechanisms involved in their succession. The constraints which influence the developmental trajectory go from the limits imposed by progressive maturation of nervous tissues to an ultimate constraint which probably depends on culture. In our culture, this constraint is expressed by the requirement to represent not only the structures and processes observed in nature, but also the very necessity of their existence.

In the presence of a large number of constraints, the system may move along various trajectories, the choice of which constitutes its history: the phase space contains various "attracting centers", where the states are more probable, and separated from one another by sets of less probable states or "repelling centers" and the trajectory meanders between these centers. This space may thus be symbolized as an epigenetic landscape (9) consisting of valleys, or "chreods" (necessary paths), which are more or less wide and separated by more or less high walls. In this image, the profile irregularities of the epigenetic landscape represent the intensity of the negative feedbacks which ensure the stability of the trajectory. From the point of view of long term viability, the most favorable circumstance is when the system evolves in a wide chreod with small irregularities and surrounded by high walls: in plains with small irregularities, the stability of the system is low because the negative feedbacks are weak; the fluctuations may be large; the accessible states are many and diverse, even though their essential structural characteristics are identical because they are particular to the chreod; the transitions between states are mainly of second order and as a result the adaptation to a changing environment is relatively easy. On the other hand, the high walls determine intense negative feedbacks and the system rejects the fluctuations which would make it pass through a first order transition in another chreod where the state's structure would be completely different: the system is thus endowed with high resilience. On the contrary, the adaptation becomes impossible for a system caught in a deep and narrow chreod: the negative feedbacks are always intense and instantly repress all fluctuations which thus remain of negligible size; the accessible states are few and differ only slightly from one another; the system is both stable and resilient. The selection will operate against such a system unless, under its pressure, the system succeeds, by a first order transition, in jumping into a neighboring chreod, which is larger and richer in diverse functional modes.

Of course, the assumption that especially conceived fields might induce such transitions in a more secure manner is the basis of education in general, and of therapy in particular. However, by definition, the dissipative structures represent a superior order state which has a low probability from a thermodynamical point of view: their permanence depends on the durability of the external field which assisted their appearance. Consequently, these models, as they stand, do not contain the mechanisms which would ensure the permanence of the achieved structures once the field is withdrawn, as is generally the case in educative processes or when a successful therapy has been completed. It is however agreed that living systems have the specific feature of partially controlling the epigenetic landscape in which they realize their adaptation (teleonomy): not only do they actively seek novelty (fluctuations) but they experience

it (transition) and afterwards choose the experiences which favor
their symbiosis with environment. This last operation results in a
modelling of the epigenetic landscape according to the evolving
system's own judgement; it is independent of the applied fields and
determines the long term stability of the structures put into
place by the temporary application of these fields. This notion is
also found in the principle of evolution by experimentation and a
posteriori vindication (10), and is included in the constructivist
theory of cognitive development (8).

4.   CLASSIFICATION OF FAMILY TYPES

From the paradigm point of view, families are considered as
dissipative structure systems and are defined by their elements,
individuals and groups. A family system is characterized by a set of
parameters which include :

a)   coupling between elements of the system

This parameter measures the reciprocal influence which people
or groups of people have on one another. In families, it may be more
or less strong, going from one extreme in the most "enmeshed"
families where the boundaries between individuals are blurred, to the
other extreme in "disengaged" families where the boundaries are
impenetrable (11). The two extremes are known to be of unfavorable
prognosis for individual development. In the paradigm, the first
corresponds to a coupling which is too strong and tends to limit the
amplitude of fluctuations in instantly dispersing them in the system,
that is before they have an opportunity to establish themselves in
their entire extent. The second extreme corresponds to a coupling
which is too weak and which transmits the fluctuations too feebly
and too slowly, so that they remain punctual. The critical dimensions
for the nucleation are not reached in both cases. This is similarly
the case in therapy: for example, individual treatment of a schizophrenic may fail while being shared with the mother, or on the
contrary the treatment of a disturbed child may fail if his family
is insufficiently concerned.

b)   system structure

This term designates the hierarchic organisation of people and
groups of people in the system. This organisation is well known for
families (12) and is reflected by a network of rules and metarules
(13) which command the dynamics of the system. The higher metarules
are characteristic of the chreod in which it evolves, in particular
those which spell out the conditions in which the lower rules can be
changed.

c)   differentiation of the substructures

This parameter measures the difference in efficiency of the
different substructures that are available to fulfil a given function
and whose dynamics is determined by the lower rules of the rule network. According to the model mentioned above, highly differentiated

208

substructures are immediately put into play, exemptive of all the
others, by first order transitions. In this way, the output of the
system remains high for a large variety of functions: thus, the
extensive set of relationship definitions which are available to a
differentiated person. In the opposite case of low differentiation,
a substructure of mediocre output is selected by a second order
transition; consequently, the selection may be slow and sensitive to
fluctuations. It appears that the therapists' experience is unanimous
on this point for which various concepts have been proposed:
differentiation (14), clarity of relationship definitions (15),
degree of coherence and of complexity of the rule network (13).

As a dissipative structure system, the family evolves under the
influence of various external fields available in the socio-cultural
environment, under the condition, of course, that it entertains
significant relationships with this environment. The evolutionary
processes may be divided in three stages which the observer can in
principle identify :

a)   fluctuations

This term designates all the divergences from the rules
observed by the system in its state of equilibrium. Fluctuations can
be considered as perceived when they are recognized by at least two
members of the system, and they initiate each time a conflict which
calls for a regulatory response from the system. Fluctuations may
originate within the family: casual events, developmental crises,
alliance attempts or manipulations, symptoms, etc. They may also have
an external origin and penetrate the family system through the interactions which its members have with the socio-cultural environment;
they may have many forms, such as informations, value systems, laws,
rules and instructions of groups containing these members, etc.

b)   nucleation

In the course of this phenomenon, the size of a fluctuation
remains constant or grows, whereas the normal coupling between
elements of the system should dampen the fluctuation by diffusion.
The reason is that an internal positive feedback process enters in
competition with the dampening effect, according to the rule network
prevailing in the family.

c)   transition

This term accounts for the system evolution during the amplification of the fluctuation. This amplification is generally rapid for
first order transitions. The selection of highly performing substructures or the passage from one chreod to another are examples of
first order transitions. On the other hand, the evolution within a
given chreod more often represents a series of second order transitions, where the amplification may be relatively slow.

When a fluctuation occurs an evolution may take place under the
condition that one state of adequate structure is accessible amongst

all the possible states of the system. In the image of the epigenetic
landscape, this condition expresses itself in terms of the amplitude
of the fluctuation and of the width of the system's chreod. Among all
the possible cases, we examine three variants which can be clearly
distinct from the clinical point of view:

1) the functional family is a system evolving in a wide chreod, such
   that the fluctuations do not reach the limits of resilience which
   maintain the fundamental structure of this system.

2) the family in crisis is the intermediate case where the fluctuation
   and the width of the chreod are of the same dimension. If the
   system does not break up, it should evolve by transition to
   another chreod accompanied by a fundamental change in the family
   structure, or else it remains in the same chreod and evolves
   towards the following variant.

3) the psychotic transaction family evolves in a narrow chreod where
   the fluctuations often exceed the limits of resilience. They
   result in symptomatic behaviors of one or more members who attempt
   to obey simultaneously the metarule and the contradictory lower
   norm contained in the fluctuation (16).

These three family types may be described in terms of dissipative
structures in the following way :

1)   The functional family

The functional family is a system which is both barely stable
and resilient, and largely open to the exterior. The possibilities of
adaptation are many since the following conditions are united :

a)   hierarchically superior systems

The functional family has many relationships with its socio-
cultural environment. Therefore, hierarchically superior systems
are always available as external fields, providing it with
energy equivalents in the form of information, ideas, or
motivations.

b)   fluctuations

Apart from the fluctuations which originate from biological
organisers, many fluctuations penetrate in the family system
through its various relationships with the exterior. Internal
fluctuations often take the form of analogous communications,
which represent experimentations in the range of interpersonal
relationships. When the transition succeeds, these fluctuations
are formalized as digital communications (17).

c)   negative feedbacks

The negative feedbacks are moderate and permit the exploration
of small new variations (fluctuations) (18), their experimentation (transitions) and the eventual integration of the corresponding possibilities in the epigenetic landscape. Moderate

210

feedbacks thus accommodate for the "play space" (19) which is
necessary in order to protect the members of the family,
specially the children, from the pseudosocialisation by preco-
cious and forced accommodation.

d)   the chreod of evolution

The chreod of evolution is wide and deep. It is dominated by
a general metarule which is resilient because it explicitly
anticipates the mobility which the adaptation to development
and to variation will demand, for instance of the sort :
"parents are competent to change certain rules without relating
to external referees and when the needs and the actual means of
the family members require it". Clinically speaking, the system
seems to be both "tolerant" and "resilient"; it is open to
experimentation ("curiosity") and able to select the transitions
realized under temporary fields. Under these conditions, the
chreod's epigenetic landscape is rich although specific to the
family, since it accedes to most of the individual potentiali-
ties of its various members. Their healthy development is seen
to be tributary of the "opening" of the family to the exterior,
that is of the variety of the relationships which the family has
with the socio-cultural environment; these relationships in fact
favor evolution at three levels: external fields, fluctuations,
and elements of judgement for the integration of transitions
into the epigenetic landscape.

2)   The family in crisis

From the paradigm point of view, a crisis arises when a
fluctuation cannot be dampened by the usual means, such as the
fluctuations originating from the biological development of the
offspring, and when there is no adequately structured state in the
chreod followed by the system. A first order transition is then
necessary in order to bring the system into another chreod, if it
exists, but a strong external field may be necessary: kinship
pressure or pressure from other social systems such as groups or
institutions.
The functional family is not sheltered from this situation;
a classical example is the family crisis arising from puberty.
Admittedly, the taboo of incest prevents the fluctuations generated
by this biological organiser from finding an adequately structured
state within the family system. Consequently, the rule according to
which the parents are responsible for the protection of their
children, particulary for sexual matters, should be replaced by
another rule defining a different hierarchic order, of the type
"the adolescent's relationships, including sexual relationships,
depend on socio-cultural regulations which are no longer relayed by
the parents". This change may necessitate long and trying negocia-
tions between subsystems; it will indeed be facilitated when several
hierarchically superior systems exert consistent pressures on the
family system, including the group of adolescents which imposes its
own norms.
But the family may also miss out on the opportunity to evolve

when the crisis occurs: the adolescent may be badly integrated in his group and may not notice the new directives, the family may have few exchanges with external systems and might lack the necessary field force, finally other hierarchically superior systems may actively strengthen the negative feedbacks which stabilized the old rule.

The following case is an example of "pure crisis" which shows the importance of an external field when two incompatible rules compete: Juanita P., 18 years old, is hospitalised after having had psychomotor fits which disappear at once. No psychopathological dysfunction is found either in her or in the family history, and she is normally adapted to her apprenticeship. Indeed, she dated a young man despite here father's prohibition who then chained her to her bed: whence cries, interventions of neighbors and of the police. The P. family, Spanish immigrants for 8 years, came from a village where the rule is strictly enforced that young girls do not go out in the evening. The external field including actions of neighbors, police and hospital, allowed the crisis to be solved in two days. This crisis, naturally, would not have happened in the Spanish village where the directives from the group of adolescents conform to local rules.

3.   The psychotic transaction family

The psychotic transaction family is a system both resilient and only slightly open to the exterior. Adaptation is poor because of a conjunction of several unfavorable conditions :

a)   hierarchically superior systems

Hierarchically superior systems cannot perform their function as an external field with respect to these families since communications are troubled: for instance, the rules governing the adult group do not actually bind the parents of such families, although they do know these rules perfectly; the environment does not understand the information given by the family on its functioning (20), and the family distorts, forgets or acknowledges the information input in an incomprehensible manner (21). These families are often socially isolated, because they are stuck in dysfunctional systems formed by their families of origin; the dysfunction is bound to anachronic and hidden rules such as the invisible loyalties (22).

Finally, the boundary with the exterior is not functional: it cedes to an unreal hierarchic structure where the family occupies a paranoid and/or megalomaniac position. For example, the term "hybris" assumed to be the basis of the schizophrenic game (23) signifies precisely that the boundary 'between gods and men" is not recognized. The "rubber fence" phenomenon (24) is also a well-known indication of dysfunctional boundaries. The extreme of lack of intra- and extra-systemic hierarchy is represented by amorphous families of hebephrenics, where words, feelings and acts seem to have lost all meaning (25).

In these conditions, relating with the family raises a number of problems for the therapist who obviously cannot reckon with incomprehensible communications. He has actually to rely on empathic responses to non-verbal messages, that is, affects or emotions, such as anguish, anger, depression. These components of symptomatic behavior often reveal rebellion against the system and are important for predictive assessment; during an acute psychotic break they have an exchange value and represent all that is not yet "schizophrenic" in the family. A correlation between the expressiveness and feeling tone of the family and the degree of the disturbance is mentioned by Beavers (12) and emphasized by Ferreira (26). Our own follow-up studies of families with psychotic transaction show that vivid affective tonality correlates with relatively favorable evolution after treatment (27).

In families with psychotic transaction hierarchic relationships between parents and children are incoherent. This incoherence has been abundantly described by the concepts of lack of boundaries between generations (28), of negative mutuality (29), of the "family ego mass" (30), and of parentification (22). All these notions refer to the fact that parents in these families are incapable of maintaining the superior hierarchic position which would enable them to function as external field with respect to their offspring. For these children, the various development stages cannot be negociated normally, particularly during "individuation-separation" processes (31).

b)   fluctuations

Fluctuations also occur in psychotic families: the biological organisers are the same as those in normal families, and interaction with the external environment does take place too. But direct observation of fluctuations appears to be difficult because of the strength of the negative feedbacks which are applied to them. In particular, all information which might risk to display, consolidate or change personal positions, is systematically smothered in order to avoid any conflict which might generate differentiation and autonomy. As the relational context is characterised by the incoherence of hierarchical positions, the fluctuations produced by analogous communications are not understood and their verbal formalisation is substituted for cultural clichés. As rules in these families are concealed, transgression of rules cannot be identified. As everything seems to be meaningless, it may be impossible to differentiate fluctuations and ruled behavior.

c)   negative feedbacks

In psychotic families, transactions are characterised by overpowerful couplings between subsystems, which prevent fluctuations from reaching the necessary dimension for nucleation. Repetitive negative feedbacks are readily observed and are probably the best clinical indication of a fluctuation taking place, they can even be used to test that an imposed fluctuation has actually reached the system.

Formal troubles of communication often represent negative feedback processes by coupling, such as the two following coupling modes :
1.   The "coupling by reflection" where the partner or partners of an interaction do not show the slightest reaction; the

communication is not acknowledged and is treated as though it didn't exist. This type of coupling comprises "silencing" (32), "perceptual defense" and other forms of unresponsiveness (33), described also by the term "underresponsiveness". Obviously indifference is only apparent, reciprocal attention is on the contrary extreme and divergences are hardly tolerated.

2. In "coupling by diffusion" the communication is acknowledged, but the acknowledgement bearing on the relationship is false: some pretend to know what others think, feel or imagine; personal affairs are treated as everybody's affairs. These communications comprise disconfirmations and other disqualifications which blur the meaning of the exchanged information. Another example is the phenomenon of "alignments and splits" (34), where any shaping of incipient coalition between two people of a triangle provokes a split and vice-versa any split provokes a coalition; here anything which is private to two people immediately spreads to three.

Systemic collusion between the members of a schizophrenic transaction system may go to great depths to dampen the fluctuations; for example, it is not risky for parents to speak of their hebephrenic child's need for autonomy, while this child hastens to undermine their statements by a stupid mimic, to signify his complicity with the persistence of the rule of family enmeshment.

d) evolutionary chreod

The evolutionary chreod in psychotic families is narrow and deep; it is characterised by a defensive "metarule" prohibiting the definition of relationships which generates conflicts tending to jeopardize the survival of the system. The fact that this metarule remains obscure guarantees the considerable resilience of the psychotic system which displays well known pseudo-adaptation variants such as the "façade-families" (35). The family not only does not learn from its experiences but it learns to deliberately ignore their meaning.

These manoeuvres to "stop time" do not avoid crises where symptoms come into being combining rebellion and complicity. If the environment (society, psychiatric hospital) only replies negatively, it reinforces the metarule by confirming that differentiation is dangerous (rebellion is illness). The system's resilience is thus increased, the chreod becomes narrower and deeper. Eventually the specifically psychotic symptoms are integrated as rules and as means of protection against the exterior; then the evolution towards chronicity is probable.

5. THERAPEUTIC STRATEGIES

To the extent that the therapists aim to make the family systems evolve rapidly towards behavior modes different from those which brought it to therapy, the paradigm assigns them with a certain number of definite functions. Apart from the obvious task of learning about the systems and about its detailed structure, these functions can be enumerated as follows :

1. External field function

In a crisis, a variable considered by the system to be essential to its survival, has reached the "alert stage" and cannot be corrected by the habitual means; this variable more often concerns the momentary assessment of the homeostasis' stability by the members of the family. As we have seen, verbal communication may be incomprehensible and the identification of the sensitive variable through non-verbal communications is the first function of the therapeutic system; through an adequate identification, it will establish a close interaction with the family system as a hierarchically superior system. From this position, the pressure necessary to destabilize the family system is applied as formalized in the therapeutic contract which enumerates the constraints to which the family is subjected. As soon as the interaction is achieved, signs of tension appear: anguish, agressivity, expressions of positive or negative feelings towards the therapeutic system, conflicts about the hierarchic positions; these signs should indicate that the family system is out of equilibrium near the limit of rupture, that is close to the walls of resilience of the chreod presently being followed: indeed, at this point the probabilities of change are maximal for a given fluctuation.

In the paradigm, achieved dissipative structures are stable only if the external field is maintained continuously, and the notion of hierarchy relies precisely on that continuity. In practice, if the therapeutic system has to vary, its variations should be <u>significantly less rapid</u> that those of the system being treated. In particular, the applied field remains invariable when the family system begins to move: fluctuations are recognized and transitions are acknowledged without implying any renegociation of the hierarchic relationship. There is a well-known rule that the therapists shall resist any attempt by the family to manipulate or contaminate them, and the deliberate or involontary transgression of this rule leads to the deadlocks described by the expressions "to be caught in the system", "to be triangulated" in Bowen's sense, or "to act out counter-transference" related to the therapist's personal problems.

2. Action on the system's parameters

This function, which is allied to the first, aims to place the system in conditions where the fluctuations may be large and numerous. Temporary interventions can be considered on certain parameters of the system, such as its dimension, its structure and the regulating loops which stabilize it. The application of the therapeutic field is already a change in external parameters of the system. Other possibilities include: the subdivision of the system in less coupled parts, as in the individual treatment, so as to diminish the dampening of fluctuations by negative feedbacks, or on the contrary to promote temporary alliances between certain members of the family, so as to amplify fluctuations to the point of nucleation. Negative feedback loops may be neutralized when the therapists assume control of the corresponding function; positive feedback loops may be consolidated by confirmations of perception in the appropriate language (speak in action (11)). Naturally, these actions will only be effective if the competence of the therapeutic system is recognized as well as its superior hierarchic position.

3.   Introduction of external fluctuations

When the system is thus sufficiently prepared, the therapists introduce external fluctuations so that the family may experience new structural variants. The privileged example is the experience of the continuity of the therapeutic relationship. The fluctuations should however be sufficiently close to the present structure so the family may perceive them clearly. Another possibility is to detect spontaneous internal fluctuations and to confirm them by an external fluctuation of identical structure.

4.   Control function

This function essentially consists in providing confirmations on the state of the system and of its relationship with the other systems of its environment. It is particularly called upon when transitions are completed and require an explicit redefinition of the relationship between therapist and family. By these confirmations the therapeutic system makes up for the limited resources available for the family to control the epigenetic landscape; the new rules which are established are thus stabilized.

6.   CLINICAL EXAMPLE

An example of treatment is described below: on the left are the clinical data whilst on the right the interpretations according to the paradigm are indicated.

During this limited therapeutic intervention, a unique fluctuation is imposed by working simultaneously on the system's parameters and two of its sensitive variables (F = father; M = mother; A.C. = patient; T, E and K = therapists).

Initial state

A.C., 21 years old, of a fairly wealthy family, had two schizophrenic fits of hebephrenic form at 17 and 20 years of age.

Readaptation at daily hospital is stagnant :	– void therapeutic contract
he stays at home, lying on his bed or on that of his	– symptom, allying two norms: obedience to the rule of cohesion and of autonomisation by provocation
sister. She protests vehemently, he replies by stupid smiles.	– opening of the crisis
The family alludes to hospital's incompetence.	– problem delegation to exterior institution

216

- ineffective external field
- established homeostasis under the form of pseudo-mutuality between hospital and family

Therapist T considers that the family colludes with symptom since it appears to fear that A.C. will have homosexual relations if he leaves home.

- metarule confusing cohesion with permanence

- negative feedback stabilizing the symptomatic path

1st session

The C's (F, M and AC) present themselves as an amorphous family with indifference

- system of high stability

T tells them that they have to come to a decision: "AC should stay in the family or should he leave it?" to which the family objects by disqualifications or silence.

- resistance to destabilization

T insists for half an hour and M finally asks "would there be an affective problem in his surroundings?"

- destabilization, unveiling of a sensitive variable

T decides to suspend the daily hospital treatment and suggests discussions with 2 experts on family problems.

- delimitation of the nuclear system

- coupling to the sensitive variable

2nd session

T is behind the mirror, and the therapists E and K speak with the entire family, 2 parents and 3 adolescents (2 sons, 1 daughter).

- installation of the external field and hierarchisation of the therapeutic system, T being at the head of the system

The session is very strained, but continues in an icy atmosphere.

- signs of destabilization

The problems of communication are relabeled as expressions of positive feelings, and all behaviors are defined as warrants of the union of the family.

- positive connotation of the homeostasis as helping the family cohesion: imposed fluctuation

E and K do a strong joining with parents.	– attempt to subdivise the system and hierarchisation within the system; encouragement of alliances between the parents and between the children: action on parameters.
Once the contract for therapy is proposed, F shows his financial preoccupation.	– parameter of the system, will be used later as a complementary sensitive variable

3rd session

Before the session, M. calls T to say that everything is fine, AC is studying and is staying in a neighboring town and that the other children would be busy at the time of the session.	– attempt to escape out of the therapeutic field by pseudo-adaptation – symptom: spontaneous fluctuation of AC towards autonomy (also indicative of his potential) while protecting the system from therapeutic interaction
The therapists do not move.	– continuity of external field
At the session, the whole family is present.	– functional external field
The parents inform of their decision to adhere to the contract.	– parental alliance confirmed: nucleation
At once, AC boasts that he stayed in bed during his stay in the other town.	– symptom: disqualification of the parents and complicity to the persistence of the metarule: negative feedback against nucleation
Multiple messages that the therapists are impotent.	– escape attempt out of the field
The therapists redefine the behavior of AC as a defiance to his father who seems to tolerate that AC squanders his money.	– imposed fluctuation of the same structure as the spontaneous fluctuation but relabeled as conflict – coupling to the complementary sensitive variable and fluctuation by relating it to conflict
The motherly overprotection is defined as love which AC abuses.	– neutralization of the negative feedback loop due to the guilt feelings of M.
The therapists concentrate on the problem of money. F is valorized by E and K, then supported by M who gives up the disqualifications.	– parental alliance: transition development

Prescription: "Either AC studies regularly and his father pays for his keep, or he earns his bread and pays board to his mother; otherwise he leaves the house".	- main imposed fluctuation, structured according to the spontaneous fluctuations (pseudo-adaptive symptom) and involving the complementary sensitive variable (F's economy worry)
Noisy rebellion by the adolescents who all feel their own personal situation threatened and counter-alliance of the parents.	- positive feedbacks reinforcing alliances and nucleation of the internal hierarchic order
F labels the prescription as realistic.	- nucleation of the prescription

following sessions

The prescription remains the center of the treatment.	- continuity of the therapeutic field
The alliance of the parents holds good despite trials (AC works sporadically, begs off acquaintances and his grandmother).	- slow second order transition, with fluctuations towards previous structures
M is cured of an obscure illness caught at the beginning of AC's psychosis. She attributes it to the therapists.	- experience of the adequacy of the new structure and positive feedback

8th and last session

The family decides to interrupt the treatment.	- negative feedback
The decision is acknowledged as expression of differentiation in the family.	- positive connotation : confirmation of the state of the system
Afterwards, AC has no more symptoms; he studies regularly and is in individual treatment with T.	- crisis over: stabilized transition

7.   SPECIFIC STRATEGIES

The evolutionary paradigm allows not only the description of the formal aspects of therapeutic treatment as mentioned above, but also of the acting mode of specific strategies used in practice, should they be or not inspired by systemic models. As an example, we analyse below two strategies of intervention in schizophrenic transaction systems in crisis. As described above from the paradigm point of view, these families represent systems caught in a narrow and deep chreod; the metarule in force prohibits the definition of relationships, definition which is considered to be the source of conflicts which are incompatible with the family cohesion (1). In these conditions, the immediate aim of the therapeutic intervention is to bring the family out of this chreod, in the hope that it may find another where the metarule differs sufficiently so that conflicts will open up and lead to a differentiation of people and of the rule network. In this perspective, the key strategies, positive connotations and paradoxal prescriptions, seem to act in the following way: the positive connotation consists in declaring the family cohesion achieved, which the members feel is threatened by the symptom at the origin of the crisis. This procedure has many simultaneous effects, the accumulation of which guarantees efficiency:

1)   It acknowledges the demand to restabilize the homeostasis. The therapists thus locate a sensitive variable and couple themselves to the family system (field function);

2)   It frustrates the family's attempts to focus on the threat. This has the effect of putting the system off equilibrium (field function);

3)   It confirms the existence of the nuclear system for itself, with its boundaries and its dominant·tendency, forced cohesion. This lasting and authoritative confirmation defines the therapists-family relationship in establishing a hierarchic order (field function). The non-definition of relationships with the exterior metarule is thus violated (fluctuation) but the system can accept it since the homeostasis has obviously been served;

4)   In addition, it transfers the charge of this homeostasis to the therapeutic system. Some of the negative feedback loops, which tend to stabilize the homeostasis, thus become superfluous: the system itself then becomes less stable, which corresponds to a shallower chreod (action on the parameters);

5)   It defines the relationships of all the members of the family as complementary to the system. This new internal hierarchic order constitutes the imposed external fluctuation which deviates from the rule of non-definition of internal relationships. The family may see in it a less expensive variant (positive feedback) since it is reassured about the cohesion, and it may opt for the new rule (transition) which is close enough to the previous one to be acceptable: the definition of the relationships is tolerated provided that family cohesion be reinforced by it.

The situation is then ready for the paradoxal prescription, which consists to explicitly prescribe his symptom to the identified patient in presenting it as being necessary to the family cohesion. There is paradox with respect to the part of the positive connotation which declared that this cohesion was already achieved, even taken care of, implying that the presence of a symptomatic patient is useless. One will recognize the paradoxal structure of a double bind including an explicit injunction (continue the symptomatic behavior to save cohesion), an implicit injunction which contradicts the previous one (the cohesion is achieved and between our hands, and needs thus not to be saved), and finally a prohibition to escape from the field noted in the therapeutic contract. However, contrary to the true <u>double bind</u>, there is no prohibition to metacommunicate on the situation: in fact, metacommunication is the only possible way out of the paradox, consisting precisely in recognizing that it is efficient and renders impracticable the development line comprising the symptomatic behavior.

Change thus comes about in two steps :
1. The fluctuation, imposed under the form of positive connotation, initiates the transition to an intermediary state where the metarule has undergone an acceptable change.
2. In this state, the paradox can be felt and destabilizes it imme- diately: it is necessary to abandon it, and everything happens as though the dysfunctional chreod had become narrower.

In general, the family will respond by transiting to another path in the same chreod, whilst loudly disqualifying the therapists. Sometimes, the new path will comprise a new symptom in the patient, or even in another member of the family. A new paradox should then be elaborated to prohibit this new path. The crucial point is that in a narrow chreod, the number of possible paths is <u>finite</u>, and when they are all blocked, the system has to abandon the dysfunctional chreod and must transit to another. This other chreod is, in principle, un- foreseeable, but the metarule will necessarily be different. The only alternative would be to cease to exist as a system (divorce, suicide, etc.). Selvini and her co-workers brilliantly showed how this operation proceeds step by step: in fact it modifies the system's epigenetic landscape by means of successive paradoxes with- drawing one by one all the dysfunctional chreod's states. The prac- tical result is that the higher metarule prohibiting the conflicts is eventually changed; it should then face up to the difficulty of living with a metarule which tolerates them; inexperience often justifies ulterior individual treatment.

7.   CONCLUSIONS

In order to demonstrate the explanatory power of the evolutio- nary paradigm offered by the dissipative structures, we have applied it to some forms of family therapy. For the normal development of a functional family, it explicitly shows up the crucial importance of environment relationships necessary for an adaptative evolution; it then appears that there is continuity between "healthy" and patho- logical development, and that this continuity corresponds to the pro- gressive impairment of the relationships which the less-adapted families have with their socio-cultural environment. Finally, the paradigm defines the specific functions which a therapeutic system should fill in order to compensate for the lack of exchanges with the socio-cultural environment and with the subsystems, in such a way as to reestablish the conditions in which the family may realize its evolution potential.

Thus the therapy consists in preparing various series of transi- tions between the temporarily stable stages of family structures. The strategies consist in the establishment of a strong therapeutic field, the introduction of moderate flucutations, the reinforcement of positive feedbacks, the attenuation of negative feedbacks and finally the respect and the confirmation of the original solutions which the family brings into play.

Naturally, these applications of the paradigm are still fragmentary and many problems remain to be examined. The most pressing are those posed by the dissipation of information and energy, and the most fundamental are those relating to the genesis of pathology, to the considerable resilience of this pathology and to the choice of the functional troubles which signal it. The paradigm suggests that theory of evolution in general and genetic epistemology in particular meet with problems of the same nature and that transdisciplinary studies will be useful. Finally, in the particular field of family therapy, the essential questions of finality and of the limits of the venture will perhaps find clear formulations.

REFERENCES

1. Haley, J. (1959) : Nervous and Mental Disease 129, pp. 357-374.
2. Jackson, D.D. (1957) : Psychiatric quarterly, Suppl. 31, p. 79.
3. Prigogine, I., Nicolis, G. and Babloyantz, A. (1972) : Phys. Today, nr. 11., 23; nr. 12, 38.
4. Prigogine, I. (1976) : In: Evolution and Consciousness, p. 93. Editor: E. Jantsch and C.H. Waddington. Addison-Wesley Publ. Co., Reading, Mass.
5. Haken, H. (1977) : Synergetics, Berlin, Springer-Verlag.
6. Weidlich, W. (1972) : Coll. Phenomena 1, 51.
7. Shumate Jr., P.W., Coleman, R.V. and Fivaz, R.C. (1970) : Phys. Rev. 1, 394
8. Piaget, J. (1975) : L'équilibration des structures cognitives, Presses universitaires de France, Paris.
9. Waddington, C.H. (1976) : In: Evolution and Consciousness, p. 243. Editor: E. Jantsch and C.H. Waddington. Addison-Wesley Publ. Co., Reading, Mass.
10. Jantsch, E. (1976) : In: Evolution and Consciousness, p. 1. Editor: E. Jantsch and C.H. Waddington. Addison-Wesley Publ. Co. Reading, Mass.
11. Minuchin, S. (1974) : Families and family therapy, Harvard University Press, Cambridge, Mass.
12. Beavers, B.W. (1977) : Psychotherapy and Growth. Brunner & Mazel, New York.
13. Wertheim, E.S. (1975) : Family Process 14, 285.
14. Bowen, M. (1978) : In: Family Therapy in Clinical Practice, p. 467. Jason Aronson, New York.
15. Watzlawick, P., Beavin, A.B. and Jackson, M.D. (1967) : Pragmatics of human communication. Norton & Co., New York.
16. Fivaz, E. (1978) : In: La crise de la famille. Hans Huber, Berne, Switzerland. To be published.
17. Bateson, G. and Jackson, D.D. (1964) : Association for research in nervous and mental disease, 42, chap. 19, 270.
18. Fivaz, E. : Autonomie et prévention dans le système à haut risque. To be published.
19. Kaufmann, L. (1978) : In: Umwelt und Mensch, Körperliche und seelische Auswirkungen, p. 145. Editor: A. Mercier. Peter Lang,

Berne, Switzerland.

20. Kaufmann, L. (1975) : Evolution psychiat. 40, 363.
21. Reiss, D. (1971) : J. Nerv. ment. dis. 152, 73.
22. Boszormenyi-Nagy, I. and Spark, G.M. (1973) : Invisible loyalties. Harper & Row, Hagerstown, Maryland.
23. Selvini-Palazzoli, M., Boscolo, L., Cecchin G. and Prata, G. (1975) : Paradosso e contro-paradosso. Editor: Feltrinelli, Milan, Italy.
24. Wynne, L.C., Rickoff, I.M., Day, J. and Hirsch, S.I. (1958) : Psychiatry 21, 205.
25. Wynne, L.C. and Singer, M.T. (1965) : Arch. gen. psychiat. 12, 201.
26. Ferreira A.J. and Winter, W.D. (1968) : Family Process 7, 251.
27. Kaufmann, L., Pancheri, E. and Ruiz, J. : Que devient la relation famille-thérapeute?, Etude catamnestique. To be published.
28. Lidz, Th., Cornelison, A., Fleck, S. and Terry D. (1958) : Arch. Neurol. & Psych., 79, 305.
29. Stierlin, H. (1969) : Conflict and reconciliation: A study in human relations and schizophrenia. Anchor Books, New York.
30. Bowen, M. (1960) : In: The etiology of schizophrenia, p. 346. Editor: D.D. Jackson. Basic Books, New York.
31. Mahler, M. (1969) : On human symbiosis and the vicissitudes of individuation, Vol. 1. Hogarth Press, London.
32. Zuk, G. (1965) : Family Process 4, 32.
33. Kaufmann, L. (1972) : Familie, Kommunikation, Psychose. Hans Huber, Berne, Switzerland.
34. Wynne, L.C. (1961) : In: Exploring the base for family therapy. Editors: N.W. Akerman, F.L. Beatman, S.N. Sherman. Family service association of America, New York.
35. Gastager, H. and Gastager, S. (1973) : Die Fassadenfamilie. Kindler, München.

223

SCHIZOPHRENICS´ OFFSPRING REARED IN ADOPTIVE HOMES x)
A FAMILY-DYNAMIC STUDY

Pekka Tienari, Ilpo Lahti, Mikko Naarala, Anneli Sorri
and Erkki Väisänen

Clinic of Psychiatry, Oulu University, 90210 Oulu 21,
Finland

Previous studies exploring the etiology of schizophrenia - both genetic and psychodynamic family studies -
have agreed on two points (Wender):
1. Schizophrenics have an increased prevalence of schizophrenia and other psychopathologies among their relatives;
2. Schizophrenic patients have often been exposed to a
variety of deviant psychological experiences during
childhood and later life.
In seeking to assess the effects of hereditary and family-dynamic factors separately, psychiatric research is
faced with the difficulty that disordered parents, who
have transmitted the genetic factors to their offspring,
have generally also brought them up. In a study of adoptive children given away for adoption early enough, discrimination between these two sets of factors is possible. Yet, the study of adoptive children has so far
been rather limited and based on small samples.
Heston´s (1966) index cases were adults who had been
born of hospitalized schizophrenic women and at birth
placed in foundling homes or in the care of paternal
relatives or adopted away. A matched control group
consisted of subjects who had been placed in the same
foundling homes. Of the 47 index cases, five were
schizophrenic as compared with none of the controls.
Rosenthal et al. (1971, 1975) and Haier et al.(1978)
selected their adult index cases in Denmark. They each
had a schizophrenic parent and had been adopted away in
their first four years of life. Their control group
consisted of matched adoptees whose biological parents
had never had a psychiatric admission for schizophrenia
spectrum disorder. Among the 69 index cases, three were
diagnosed as schizophrenic, but none of the controls.
Using the schizophrenia spectrum concept, the rate was
32 % in the index cases as compared with 18 % (Danish
psychiatrists who conducted the interviews) or 25 %
(Consensus diagnosis of American investigators) in the

x) This study is supported by Medical Research Council
   in Finland.

controls. They also interviewed 54 biological co-parents
of whom 19 were classified as having a diagnosis of
schizophrenia spectrum. The frequency of spectrum disorders in the offspring is about 3 to 5 times as high
when the co-parent has a spectrum diagnosis as when he
or she has not.

Kety et al. (1975) collected their 33 index cases
among adults who had been given up for nonfamily adoption in their first four years of life and who were
diagnosed as having a schizophrenic disorder. Their
control group consisted of matched adoptees who had had
no known psychiatric admission. The adoptive and biologic parents, sibs and half-sibs were evaluated with respect to schizophrenia and schizophrenia spectrum disorders on the basis of hospital records and personal
interviews. There were 11 cases of definite schizophrenia, 13 cases of uncertain schizophrenia and 37 cases
(21,4 %) of total schizophrenia spectrum among the 173
biological relatives of the schizophrenic adoptees as
compared with 3 cases of definite schizophrenia, 3 cases
of uncertain schizophrenia and 19 cases (10,9 %) of
total schizophrenia spectrum among the 174 biological
relatives of the control cases. The figures were smaller
among the adoptive relatives of both groups.

Wender's (1968) 10 index cases were adult schizophrenics who had been adopted by nonrelatives in their
first year of life. One control group consisted of
matched schizophrenics who were reared in the parental
homes, and the other of matched adult adoptees who were
psychiatrically normal. His results supported the
genetic theory: the adoptive parents of schizophrenic
patients had less severe psychopathology than the biological parents of the schizophrenic controls, but more
psychopathology than the adoptive parents of normals.
Wynne and Singer (1976) re-examined the results of
Wender with the Rorschach protocols of the parents at
their disposal. They found that with a narrower spectrum concept (including borderline schizophrenia and
schizophrenic psychosis) none of the three groups are
significantly differentiated as to parental psychopathology ratings. With a broader concept (which also
includes moderate to marked character neuroses) however,
the adoptive parents of schizophrenics are differentiated from the adoptive parents of normals. Margaret
Singer was able to give a correct blind diagnosis of the
offspring in each family on the basis of parental Ror-
schachs alone. All the 16 of the parental pairs who had
reared schizophrenic offspring were predicted by her to
have a schizophrenic offspring whether or not the relationship was adoptive or biological, while all of the 10
parental pairs with adoptive nonschizophrenic offspring
were predicted to have an essentially normal offspring.
Furthermore, the mean frequency of communication

deviances was equal in the adoptive schizophrenic and biologic schizophrenic parent groups, both being more than twice that found with the adoptive normal parents. The results of Wynne and Singer hence support both a genetic hypothesis and a psychosocial hypothesis.

OWN STUDY

In the present study, it has been possible to secure information on most of the women who were under treatment at the Finnish psychiatric hospitals on January 1, 1960, or were admitted in to those hospitals for treatment between January 1, 1960, and April 30, 1970, and were diagnosed as schizophrenics. When only those cases were taken into consideration in which the patients had been born in 1910-1954, a total of 9832 women meeting the criteria were found. The time and age limits were applied, because we believed the older case histories in hospitals to be unproperly filled and to have unsufficient information for diagnosis. We also wished to avoid diagnostic difficulties with people over 60 years. Regarding these women, continued efforts have been made for years to find out which of them, after giving birth to a child, have later given the child away for adoption. To this end, the population registers of each locality in which any one of the women concerned had resided during her life had to be consulted, for when a mother moves to another locality, the population register authorities of the new locality are not informed about any of her children possibly adopted away.

A total of 120 children given away for adaption have been identified. Judging by the information thus far secured by us, 93 of them have been placed in adoptive homes in their first four years of life and 10 later than that, while 12 have been adopted abroad and 5 by relatives. The number of these cases is likely to increase, however, because we are still in the process of covering all the psychiatric hospitals in Finland.

The subject series consists of the adoptive families into which children born of schizophrenic mothers had been adopted and placed during the child's first four years of life.

A control series consists of a double number of adoptive families in which neither the adopted child's biological mother nor his father has been under psychiatric treatment. This group will be matched with the subject group as regards the following parameters: the child's age and sex and the age at which he or she was placed in the family, the adoptive family's social class, its urban/rural background and its structure (father and mother vs. only mother or father). The families in the two series will be numbered at random in such a way that the psychiatrists who perform the personal examination

<u>will not know which of the two groups the adoptive fami-
ly belongs to.</u>

In the field study we must in practice investigate families living in various parts of Finland. The examination of each family will require at least two days, since the following will be necessary:

1. A careful individual interview of both parents and the "index child", including psychological tests (Rorschach test and an abridged version of the WAIS for all. MMPI only for children).

2. Examination of the parents´ interactional relationship and communication disturbances by means of conjoint interviews and the Spouse Rorschach.

3. Examination of the whole family, particularly the interactional relationships between the children and their parents, with conjoint interviews and application of experimental family-dynamic examination techniques, the Family Rorschach (Loveland 1963) and the interpersonal Perception Method (Laing 1966).

The interviews and the experimental parts of the study must be tape-recorded, in order that, in scoring them, use could be made of blind comparative classifications.

Every effort will be made to identify and locate the biological parents in both groups. All the possible registered information is being collected about the children and their adoptive and biological parents. This is not finished yet. By August 1978, we had discovered two index children having a registered diagnosis of schizophrenia, one border-line case and four neurosis cases. In the control group one had been found to have a registered diagnosis of psychosis and one neurosis.

By August 1978, we had investigated altogether 59 families. I shall now give some preliminary findings about them.

The schizophrenics´ offspring numbered 17, of whom 10 had been considered healthy and 7 disturbed by the interviewing psychiatrist. The mean score was 2.4. Of the 42 offspring of the controls, 31 had been classified as healthy and 11 as disturbed (mean 2.2).

The Mental health ratings of the children agree by and large with those of their adoptive families. Because of the small figures,the families have been here devided into two groups: Healthy (healthy, mild disturbances) and disturbed (neurotic, more seriously disturbed). The children brought up in healthy adoptive families were all classified as healthy, except one who had had alcohol problems. In disturbed families, the ratings of the adoptive children deviated considerably from each other. Most of the schizophrenics´ offspring had been classified as neurotic or mildly disturbed. The two classified as border-lines at the neurotic level

TABLE 1

THE MENTAL HEALTH RATINGS OF THE CHILDREN

	Schizophrenics' offspring	Offspring of controls
1. Healthy	3	10
2. Mild disturbances	7	21
3. Neurotic	4	6
4. Character disorders	3	2
5. Border-line	-	3
6. Psychotic	-	-
Altogether	17	42
Mean score	2.4	2.2

TABLE 2

CHILDRENS' MENTAL HEALTH RATINGS IN RELATION TO THEIR ADOPTIVE FAMILIES

	Healthy families		Disturbed families	
	Sch x)	controls xx)	Sch x)	controls xx)
1. Healthy	3	9	-	1
2. Mild disturbances	5	8	2	13
3. Neurotic	-	-	4	6
4. Character disorders	1	-	2	2
5. Border-line	-	-	-	3
Altogether	9	17	8	25
Mean score	1.9	1.5	3.0	2.7

x) schizophrenics' offspring
xx) offspring of controls

(4) had both been brought up in disturbed adoptive families: one in a schismatic family and the other in a family using character neurotic defences. The mean ratings were somewhat higher for the schizophrenics' offsprings in both groups as compared with the offspring of the controls.

As it can be seen from table 2, a total of 26 families had been rated healthy. Of their 26 adoptive children, 25 had been classified healthy and only one disordered (mean 1.6). Of the 33 disordered families, 16 had a healthy adoptive child and 17 a disturbed child (mean 2.8). The differences are surprisingly clear. The interviewing psychiatrist has made all the classifications (family, parents, children). These might have influenced each other. This will later be checked with blind comparative classifications from taped interviews and psychological test records.

TABLE 3

ASSESSMENT OF THE CHILDREN IN RELATION TO THEIR ADOPTIVE MOTHERS AND FATHERS

	Adoptive mother		Adoptive father	
	Healthy	Dis-turbed	Healthy	Dis-turbed
1. Healthy	11	2	10	1
2. Mild disturbances	14	14	13	14
3. Neurotic	5	5	3	6
4. Character disorders	3	2	1	4
5. Border-line	-	3	1	2
Altogether	33	26	28	27
Mean score	2.1	2.6	1.9	2.7

The mother was available for investigation in all the families. The father had died in three and was nonexistent in one. As it can be seen from table 3, the mental health ratings of the children agree slightly more closely with those of their adoptive fathers as compared with their adoptive mothers. Again, the healthy subjects and those with mild disturbances are classified as "healthy" and all the others as "disturbed".

The differences are more clear if we consider the ratings of both the adoptive parents together.

TABLE 4

THE ASSESSMENT OF THE CHILDREN IN RELATION TO THEIR
ADOPTIVE PARENTS COMBINED

	Both healthy	One disturbed, the other healthy	Both disturbed
1. Healthy	9	2	-
2. Mild disturbed	7	13	7
3. Neurotic	1	5	3
4. Character disorders	1	2	2
5. Border-line	-	1	2
Altogether	18	23	14
Mean score	1.7	2.4	2.9

In the families where both the adoptive parents were classified as healthy, the mean score for the children was 1.7. When both the adoptive parents were disturbed, the mean rate for the children was 2.9. All the children brought up by healthy adoptive parents were classified as healthy, except one who was neurotic and another who had alcohol problems. Seven of the 14 children with both the adoptive parents disturbed were classified neurotic or more severely disturbed.

REFERENCES

1. Haier, R.J., Rosenthal, D. and Wender, P.H. (1978): MMPI assessment of Psychopathology in the adopted-away offspring of schizophrenics. Arch. Gen. Psychiat. 35, 171.
2. Heston, L.L. (1966): Psychiatric disorders in foster home reared children of schizophrenic mothers. Brit. J. Psychiat., 112, 819.
3. Kety, S.S., Rosenthal, D., Wender, P.H., Schulsinger, F. and Jacobsen, B. (1975): Mental illness in the biological and adoptive families of adopted individuals who have become schizophrenic: A preliminary report based on psychiatric interviews. In: Fieve, R.R., Rosenthal, D. and Brill, H., eds. Genetic Research in Psychiatry. Baltimore: The Johns Hopkins University Press, p. 147.
4. Laing, R.D., Philipson, H. and Lee, A.R. (1966): Interpersonal perception. A theory and a method

of research. Tavistock publications. London.

5. Loveland, N., Wynne, L.C. and Singer, M.T. (1963):
   The Family Rorschach: a new method for studying
   family interaction. Fam. Process, 2, 187.

6. Rosenthal, D., Wender, P.H., Kety, S.S., Welner, J.
   and Schulsinger, F. (1971): The adopted-away offspring of schizophrenics. Am. J. Psychiat., 128,
   307.

7. Rosenthal, D. (1975): Discussion: The concept of
   subschizophrenic disorders. In: Fieve, R.R., Rosenthal, D. and Brill, H., eds. Genetic Research in
   Psychiatry. Baltimore: The Johns Hopkins University
   Press, p. 199.

8. Wender, P.H., Rosenthal, D. and Kety, S.S. (1968):
   A psychiatric assessment of the adoptive parents of
   schizophrenics. In: Rosenthal, D. and Kety, S.S.,
   eds. The Transmission of Schizophrenia. Oxford:
   Pergamon Press Ltd., p. 235.

9. Wynne, L.C., Singer, M.T. and Toohey, M. (1976):
   Communication of the adoptive parents of schizo-
   phrenics. In: Jorstad, J. and Ugelstad, E., eds.
   Schizophrenia 75. Psychotherapy, Family Studies,
   Research. Oslo: University of Oslo Press, p. 413.

PROTECTIVE CONSTRUCTIONS IN THE COURSE OF PSYCHOSIS: A FOLLOW-UP STUDY

Viljo Räkköläinen, Raimo Salokangas, and Päivi Lehtinen

Psychiatric Department, University of Turku, Finland

The essence of predisposition to psychosis has been described as a weakness of the ego (10), as an incoherence of the disproportionate archaic self structures (12, 13), as a failure in self-object differentation (e.g. 20), and also as a general fragility of the primary representative matrix (19), or as an insufficiency of the first cathectic processes (15, 16). Its timing and etiology are located within the mother-child dyad, to whose functional failure both the participants of the relationship give their share: for example a specific lack of empathy from the side of the mother, and, at least in some cases, also the genetic or otherwise "constitutional" unfitness in the developmental potentials of the child (1, 2, 3, 17, 22).

A phenomenological indicator of the proneness to psychotic fragmentation - and also its most striking pre-psychotic clinical sign - is the adaptive weakness and unfitness of the person to the requirements of ordinary life. In practice the adaptive unfitness leads to avoidance of, and, on the other hand, to peculiar intensive and formally regressive dependence on the interactions with the actual outer reality, in order to protect the defective psychic structures from the internal catastrophe of the disorganization panic.

In this representation these interactional arrangements of the potentially psychotic people with their immediate reality are called p r o t e c t i v e c o n s-t r u c t i o n s. We hope that our concept will convey the vitality of these interactions for the psychic integrity of the persons concerned, and also emphasize their typical concrete dependence on the environment, as compared with the more internalized and therefore functionally more autonomous intrapsychic structures characteristic of normal and neurotic people.

From the individual point of view the protective constructions can be understood as archaic omnipotent self structures (12, 13) held together by primitive defensive operations, e.g. projective identifications, gross denials and deep splitting processes (11, 26). These archaic forms of defence cannot, however, operate successfully without concrete support and contribution from the surrounding reality, for example without special efforts from the other people who form the most intimate interpersonal network of the persons concerned. That these other people often have their own vital investment in these transactionally constructed defensive operations for their own, quite similar reasons, has been shown by numerous family studies, for example by Stierlin (23, 24, 25). His transactional modes describe well the mutuality of these unions, whose participants form a primitively mirroring, caretaking and idealized "self-object world" (13) for each other.

The psycho-social and even the more depersonified and "nonhuman"environment can also serve for a matrix of these protective constructions via primitive symbolization processes (21). So there can be found cases where psychosocial institutions such as work, studying, social wellfare and in more symbolic forms even political and religious constituents of the culture are expected to perform as concrete infantile providers and participate in the fulfilment of the regressive needs of the poorly functioning archaic self.

On the other hand, the protective constructions also form a natural - and the only available - matrix for the person's potentials for his internally determined growth and participation in ordinary life. Its temptations, losses and frustrations, however, bring along another and different source of anxieties, whose mastering presupposes adaptive capacities which often are far beyond the persons internally defective adaptive apparatus that rigidly relies on the concrete support of the environment. In an unselected material of psychotic patients (27, 28) the onset of open psychosis was found to manifest itself at an adaptional impasse, where the needs to protect the personality from the Charybdis of the psychotic disorganization were in conflict with the coping tasks inherent in the Scylla of the average life process, and the peril could not be avoided.

It can be assumed that the dual functions of the protective constructions have their importance also as determinants of the fate of the psychotics after the initial outbreak. In the following we shall give some preliminary results of our seven year follow-up of the same material (27, 28) in order to clarify the later course of the shipwrecked. Accordingly, we shall focus here mainly on that part of our findings which indicates how far the patients have coped with the two primary and often conflicting tasks of their lives: to avoid open psychosis and, at the same time, to promote general growth and to maintain some adult meaning in their living.

FINDINGS OF THE FOLLOW-UP STUDY

The original unselected material of 68 borderline,

schizophreniform and nuclear schizophrenic patients, with open psychotic symptoms before or at the time of their first admission in the year 1969 into the Psychiatric Clinic of the University of Turku, was seven years later interviewed by the two other members of our team, Dr. Salokangas and Mrs. Lehtinen. The findings of each case were compared with the information obtained in the year 1969, in order to form a comprehensive picture of the development of the patient's psychotic symptoms and of the general course of his life during the years of the follow-up. For the purposes of this representation, sufficient information was obtained from every original case.

In table 1 are given some basic characteristics of the material when initially examined seven years earlier:

TABLE 1

	SEX	AGE	DIAGNOSIS
Total	68	16-19 years 12	Nuclear schizophrenia 43
Males	36	20-24 " 20	Schizophreniform 7
		25-29 " 12	
Females	32	30-34 " 10	Borderline 18
		35-39 " 9	
		40-45 " 5	

Table 2 indicates the variations in the outcome at the end of the follow-up period:

TABLE 2

SUICIDE		4	cases
GROUP I	chronically or recurrently open psychosis; developmental regression	21	"
GROUP II	no psychotic symptoms; developmental regression	5	"
GROUP III	long-term or recurrent psychosis; developmental progression	22	"
GROUP IV	no psychotic symptoms; developmental progression	16	"
	total	68	"

no psychosis (II+IV): 21 cases
psychosis   (I+III): 43   "

developmental progression (III+IV): 38 cases
developmental regression (I + II): 26   "

Four patients had commited suicide, two of them during the initial psychotic phase, and the other two a couple of years later.

The remaining 64 cases could be divided into four prognostic groups according to their ability to prevent subsequent open psychosis, and the other hand, to keep on a functionally progressive course in their lives.

The anamnestic and actual presence of open psychosis was determined according to the well-establishe clinical criteria. The concepts of "progression" and "regression" in life may need further elaboration. The general frames of reference for our estimations are formed by the current views of human growth given by psychoanalytic and interactional developmental psychology. To mention some examples, our views of human development were influenced by the findings of Anna Freud (6) and her coworkers (7) Erik H. Erikson (5), Kernberg (11), Mahler (17) and her co-workers (18), as well as by the observations of Stierlin (22, 24) and several other investigators of interactional normality and pathology (1, 2, 14). Thus, the numerous "hard","semi-hard" and "soft" facts from the different sectors of the patient's life were combined together and assessed to their implications for forward and backward trends in better self-realization and growing autonomy and coherence of the nuclear personality, and also according to their indications of growing or diminishing maturity and adult independence within the patient's human and psycho-social interactions.

Although based on thorough factual knowledge of individual cases, our impressions of progression or regression are not, however, estimations referring to any hypothetical statistical "normality". In the first place, they are assessments based on the e m p a t h y of the observer, which we consider the only available and reliable instrument we know to arrange meaningfully the idiosyncratic and complicated data from various sectors of the patient's life for such totalistic purposes as we did,especially in a material that contains perhaps more interindividual variability than any other unselected sample of human beings. Accordingly, regressive were considered the cases where the years of observation were characterized by diminishing coherence of the personality, increasing frustration of the possibilities for self-realization, as well as decrease in adult autonomy within the human and psycho-social interactions of the persons.Respectively, as progressive were seen the cases where, often with the great difficulties caused by the recurrent symptoms and gross obstacles due to malformations in their relationships with actual environment, the patients had been able to maintain some integrated adult meaning defined above,in their lives.

OUTCOME AND PSYCHO-SOCIAL INTERACTION

In the groups III and IV, 38 in all, the general course of life was deemed progressive, that is the patients had been able to maintain a trend to positive, age-adequate and growthpromoting grip with their psycho-social living, e.g. studies and working life. In the group III this had been possible despite of their recurrent or sometimes even chronically established psychotic symptoms. In most cases the growth was faltering, delayed, partial and also one-sidedly and selectively cultivated in some specific life sector. The typical dropping of standards and deferring of goals were also encountered frequently. It is to be noted, however, that the trend towards adult autonomy was maintained, and the regression-promoting, caretaking and protective means offered by society - e.g. long-term hospitalizations, pensions etc. were generally avoided, and if used temporarily, they were easily abandoned. In several cases, however, we were able to observe a skilful use of the "moratorium" inherent in the modern society within studies and part-time and other sheltered working conditions with tolerance to reduced achievement and working performance.

The regressive groups I and II, 26 cases in all, seemed to have lost their grip with autonomous psycho-social life after the onset of their psychotic symptoms, despite of the fact that only few had been openly psychotic for all the seven years of the follow-up. In the five regressive and stagnated cases of the group II no psychosis was seen after the inital outbreak. In general, the regressive patients had abandoned their studies and working, relying on the support of social well-fare and their relatives. Many of them were permanently pensioned or on long-term sick leaves. They stayed at home or had returned there, or used regularly and on long-term basis the care of mental hospital and other asylums provided by society. Sometimes they were able to use quite cleverly the supportive interactional possibilities offered to them, but only on a fragmented and regressive basis, obviously only to prevent further disorganization by remaining in a passive dependent position, not to promote their growth and autonomy.

OUTCOME AND THE INTERPERSONAL INTERACTION

The progressive groups III and IV were living in a more favourable and empathic interpersonal field than the groups I and II. Although they often lived in intensive symbiotic unions with their primary or secondary objects, these appeared as a rule more "holding" (19, 30), warm and also more empathic for the separative moves and other efforts of growth and individuation attempted by the patient. A successful severance of the symbiosis was also a relatively common finding, and sometimes even separation without actual breaking of the relationship was encountered.

In the regressive groups I and II the numerous symbiotic ties were of an extremely malignantly binding nature. Typically, these patients had remained in the grips of their stronger symbiotic partners, who were overtly inimical and showed a total lack of understanding towards the progressive needs of the patient. Gross and traumatic separations due to deaths, divorces and other abandonments were also more numerous than in the progressive groups. Some were living without any intimate natural human contacts at all, and many had none outside their all- consuming malignant symbiosis. Based on the retrospective scrutiny of their childhood and also other later pre-psychotic object relations, our impression was, that the patients in the progressive groups had also had, more often than in the regressive groups, in the otherwise generally unempathic early interpersonal atmosphere, experiences with a person who had shown genuine interest and love towards them.

THERAPEUTIC INTERVENTION IN DIFFERENT PROGNOSTIC GROUPS

The distribution of the different forms of therapy between each group of outcome is indicated in table 3.

TABLE 3

	I N=21	II N=5	III N=22	IV N=16	total N=64
Intensive individual therapy	5	-	4	4	13
Intensive individual therapy attempted	2	-	1	-	3
Family therapy	3	-	1	-	4
Family therapy attempted	4	-	-	-	4
Other therapeutic contacts	12	3	15	5	35
Temporarily hospitalized	14	2	17	3	36
Asylum	5	1	-	-	6
No ambulatory contacts	1	1	3	5	10

Because our analysis of the role of therapy in the outcome is at present in the beginning, only preliminary comments can be presented in this occasion.

The figures show surprisingly prominent clustering of all kinds of therapeutic efforts in the most unfavourable group of outcome. Besides almost every failed attempt of intensive family and individual psychotherapy, also some of the yearlong intensive therapies as well as long-term hospitalizations in psychotherapeutic communities are found in this group. These patients showed most striking general suffering and most severe and profuse signs of psychosis, which explains, of course, their being the targets of most frequent and massive therapeutic activities. Based solely on these pessimistic figures, the outcome of the therapeutic efforts can be understood as not very promising. In several cases of the longterm psychotherapies it was possible to see, however, that the classic end state of deteriorioation and dementia had not taken place; although their regression was severe and a chronic state of fragmentation prevailed, they had been able to maintain some living contact to the human world.

The five patients whose psychosis had been dormant but general development regressive have remained outside any serious psychotherapeutic efforts, perhaps due to the fact that their generally but "silently" frustrated state of living had been considered belonging to the realm of psychotherapeutic care,
either by themselves, their relatives, or by the professionals in the community mental health system.

The prognostically more favourable groups show two trends: The patients have the ability to gain from intensive individual therapy and other long-term forms of outpatient contacts, as well as brief hospitalizations. On the other hand, they also show in a few instances an ability to cope without therapeutic longterm contacts, after the initial or even between the recurrent brief hospitalizations in their later acute psychotic crises.

Although we consider our communal psychiatric system relatively advanced and also based on an adequate understanding of the nature of psychotic illness, some striking therapeutic neglects were seen retrospectively in our sample. One of them was the insufficient attention paid to the malignant symbiotic ties in which many of the poorly coping patients were living. This should imply in practice more efforts directed to them by some form of family therapy.

Some quantitative defects were encountered within the rehabilitative and other social measures aimed to improve the patients' living conditions. This observation was partly based on the rapid improvement of the general psychic and psycho-somatic state of some extremely neglected patients living with their inimical symbiotic partners, when taken to the understanding and warmly human atmosphere of the therapeutic community.

DISCUSSION

The psycho-social, interpersonal and therapeutic interactions referred to above are examples of the protective constructions encountered in an unselected sample of

potentially psychotic people. Of practical interest
would be, of course, a more detailed analysis of the different forms and their correlation with the various groups of outcome. It is our intention to find answers to
these questions later, and here we offer only some further theoretical comments about the nature of protective
constructions against psychosis.

Grotstein (8, 9) has recently spoken of the "infantile psychosis" as an early normal developmental phase,
preceding the "childhood neurosis". He also indicates
how its favourable solution via processes of internalization and structuralization is decisive to avoidance of
psychotic crisis, analogous to the succesful defensive
formations acquired in the vicissitudes of the Oedipal
struggle as a guarantee against neurotic regressions.
The same developmental sequence is stated explicitly in
Kohut's latest discussions on the pathogenetic precursors
of "tragic" (i.e. self-injured) and "guilty" (i.e.pained
by conflicting drives) aspects of existence (13). The
mastering of the residuals of maldevelopmen from these
two early, partly successive but partly also contemporate
although separate stages of growth is the cornerstone
of psychic health of every human being. However, because
of variations in innate potentials, as well as different
etiologial factors in the early interactional field, the
focus of the struggle is situated differently in individual cases.

A sample of patients with potential for psychosis
represents a specific subgroup of "Tragic Man": in their
strivings for a minimum of self-realization allowed by
their distorted and defective nuclear self, they also
have to keep constant watch against the continous threat
of the catastrophic panic which ensues in case of dissolution of the nuclear self. In order to comprehend better
the clinical manifestations and prognostic implications
of these two complementary but often conflicting tasks of
their lives the term "protective constructions" was introduced here mainly for the following reasons:

The protective operations against psychosis are
functionally akin to the defences against neurotic conflict. As clinical phenomena they exhibit, however, several differences which have important implications for
therapeutic understanding of these patients. For example,
a typical and also clinically important feature of the
psychotic and potentially psychotic patient is his transactional and intimate boundness to his immediate environment. This is explained by the genetic fact that protective constructions are residuals from the developmental
period where any defensive operation against anxiety must
rely on environment in a very concrete way because of the
insufficient state of psychic internalizations in general,
and especially due to the poor intrapsychic self-object
differentation of that stage (20, 26).

A special feature in a person predisposed to psychosis is the
peculiar concreteness of his living style, as exhibited
by his actions and interactions which are aimed to guarantee a minimum of safety and satisfaction in his life.
Even that can be understood as a consequence of the partly prestructural state of his defensive and other psychic
functioning. According to London (15, 16) that is due to
the cathectic insufficiency of his representational world
- which excludes the more flexible forms of relatedness
with the object world. A similar role of concrete acting
as a precursor and surrogate of internalized psychic
structures has also been indicated by Kohut (13) in the
healing processess of narcissistic defects, as a motiva-
ting force behind artistic activity by Bach and Schwartz
(4) and behind certain criminal deeds by Tuovinen (29).

From the viewpoint of the psychology of the self,
protective constructions are combinantions of the precursors of the archaic self and their respective world of
self-objects. That is why the protection as well as the
realization of the self are bound together, because of
their common functional matrix. Accordingly, the two
tasks are to be accomplished on this common field often
with tragic consequences due to the principal conflicts
in their preconditions: the task of protection presupposes regression in the transactions between the self and
the self-object, and, on the contrary, the realization of
the potentials imbedded in the nuclear self is based on
progressive development - above all a higher degree of
internalization, depersonification and deconcretization
of these constellations, as analyses of narcissistic
patients have indicated (12, 13).

Our findings, i.e. the proportionate number of patients in each group of outcome, give a hint of the possi-
bilites of potentially psychotic people to succeed in
these two primary tasks of their lives. The possible reasons for the different outcomes were also discussed,
mainly in terms of environmental determinants such as the
degree of maturity of the psycho-social interactions, and
also the malignan or benign nature of their symbiotic
ties with the interpersonal milieu. As was stated, the
protective constructions - of which these findings are
typical examples - have their individual as well as environmental counterparts, of whose combined potentials the
final outcome results. Besides correlations between the
the better outcome and the more favourable interactional
possibilities with the environment, we also observe in
some cases of poor outcome an individual inability to use
the matrix either to prevent psychosis or to achieve self-
realization. This was exemplified and documented clearly
in the cases of the intensive and skilfully conducted
longterm therapies of some of the patients in the poorest
group of outcome. In these cases it is difficult to blame
the current environment for the totally wasted life, or

for the progressive psychotic disorganization they simultaneously exhibited.

REFERENCES:

1. Alanen, Y.O. (1958): The Mothers of Schizophrenic
            Patients Acta psychiat. neurol. Scand.Vol.
            33. Suppl.124.
2. Alanen, Y.O., Rekola, J.K., Stewen, A., Takala, K.,
    and Tuovinen M. (1966):
            The Family in the Pathogenesis of Neurotic
            and Schizophrenic Disorders. Acta psychiat.
            Scand. Vol.42. Supp. 189.
3. Alanen, Y.O., Räkköläinen, V., Rasimus R., and
    Laakso, J. (1978):
            Indications for Different Forms of Psycho-
            therapy with New Schizophrenic Patients in
            in Community Psychiatry. Presented in this
            Symposium.
4. Bach, S., and Schwartz, L. (1972):
            A Dream of the Marquis de Sade: Psychoana-
            lytic Reflections on Narcissistic Trauma,
            Decompensation, and the Reconstitution of a
            Delusional Self. J. Amer. Psychoanal. Ass.
            20, 451.
5. Erikson, E.H. (1950):
            Childhood and Society. Norton, New York.
6. Freud, A. (1965):
            Normality and Pathology in Childhood. Int.
            Univ. Press, New York.
7. Freud, A., Nagera, H. and Freud, W.E. (1965):
            Metapsychological Assesment of the Adult
            Personality. Psychoanal.Study Child 20.
            Int. Univ. Press, New York.
8. Grotstein, J.S. (1977 a):
            The Psychoanalytic Concept of Schizophrenia:
            I. The Dilemma. Int. J. Psycho-Anal. 58;403.
9. Grotstein, J.S. (1977 b): The Psychoanalytic Concept
            of Schizophrenia: II. Reconcilation. Int.
            J.Psycho-Anal. 58;427.
10. Hartmann, H. (1953): Contribution to Metapaychology
            of Schizophrenia. In Essays on Ego Psycho-
            logy. Int. Univ. Press, New York 1964.
11. Kernberg, O. (1967): Borderline Personality Organi-
            zation. J. Amer. Psychoanal. Ass. 15, 641.
12. Kohut, H. (1971): The Analysis of the Self. Int.
            Univ. Press, New York.
13. Kohut, H. (1977): The Restoration of the Self. Int.
            Univ. Press, New York.
14. Lidz, T., Fleck, S. and Cornelison, A.R. (1965):
            Schizophrenia and the Family. Int.Univ.
            Press, New York.

15. London, N.J. (1973 a): An Essay on Psychoanalytic
                Theory: Two Theories on Schizophrenia. Part
                I: Review and Critical Assesment of the De-
                velopment of the Two Theories.Int.J. Psycho-
                Anal. 54, 169.
16. London, N.J. (1973 b): An Essay on Psychoanalytic
                Theory: Two Theories on Schizophrenia. Part
                II: Discussion and Restatement of the Speci-
                fic Theory of Schizophrenia. Int.J. Psycho-
                Anal. 54, 179.
17. Mahler, M.S. (1968): On Human Symbiosis and the
                Vicissitudes of Individuation. Int. Univ.
                Press, New York.
18. Mahler, M.S., Pine, F. and Bergman, A. (1975):
                The Psychological Birth of the Human Infant.
                Basic Books, New York.
19. Salonen, S. (1976): On the Metapaychology of
                Schizophrenia. Presented in the Finnish
                Psychoanalytical Society.
20. Schulz, C.C. (1975): An Individualized Psychothera-
                peutic Approach With the Schizophrenic Pati-
                ent. Schizophrenia Bull, 13, 46.
21. Searles, H.F. (1960): The Nonhuman Environment.
                Int. Univ. Press. New York.
22. Stierlin, H. (1969): Conflict and Reconcilation.
                Anchor Books, New York.
23. Stierlin, H. (1972): Family Dynamics and Patterns
                of Potential Schizophrenics. In Psychothera-
                py Schizophrenia, edid. by Rubinstein, D.
                and Alancn, Y.O. Excerpta Medica, Amsterdam.
24. Stierlin, H. (1974 a): Separating Parents and Ado-
                lescents. Quadrangle/ the New York Times
                Book Co, New York.
25. Stierlin, H. (1974 b): Shame and Guilt in Family
                Relations. Arch. Gen. Psychiat. 50, 381.
26. Stolorow, R.D. and Lachmann, F.M. (1978): The Deve-
                lopmental Prestages of Defences:Diagnostic
                and Therapeutic Implications. Psychoanal.
                Quart. Vol. XLVII No 1, 73.
27. Räkköläinen, V. (1976): Psychodynamic and Inter-
                personal Aspects of the Onset of Psychosis.
                In Schizophrenia 75 Psychotherapy, Family
                Studies, Research, edid. by Jørstad, J. and
                Ugelstad, E. Universitetsforlaget, Oslo.
28. Räkköläinen, V. (1977): Onset of Psychosis. A
                Clinical Study of 68 Cases. Ann. Univ. Turku-
                ensis Ser. D 7.
29. Tuovinen, M. (1973): Crime as an Attempt at Intra-
                psychic Adaptation. Acta Univ. Ouluensis Ser.
                D. 2.
30. Winnicott, D.W. (1965): The Maturational Processes
                and the Facilitating Environment. Hogarth
                Press, London.

TRANSPORT AND TRANSFORMATION OF MENTAL PAIN.
Svein Haugsgjerd
Gaustad Hospital, Oslo.

My own work is a continuation of the work done at Gaustad Hospital
by Dr. Ugelstad on psychotherapy with schizophrenic patients.
Currently, I am engaged in a project where a few patients are
offered a two year stay in a small ward where we try to apply an
object relations orientated psychoanalytic thinking to the group
processes, in a way I will describe later During the stay in the
ward - and probably afterwards in most cases- they receive
individual psychotherapy, with two sessions a week as standard
frequency. Simultaneously, we are doing diffferent kinds of
ratings, some weekly, some monthly, some less frequently. These
ratings will to some degree, mirror change in clinical condition,
but most emphasis is put on reflecting psychotherapeutically
interesting aspects of patient-therapist and patient-staffinter-
actions.
The Patients.
Until now, $1\frac{1}{2}$ years since we have started, 11 patients have been
treated in this ward, 5 males and 6 females. The age ranges are
from 20 to 48 years, average being about 28. Time since onset
of the illness ranges from 2 to 16 years, the average being
about 7 years. 3 patients are now treated as outpatients. we have
reduced medication on most of the patients, 2 of the outpatients
and 2 of the inpatients are currently without drugs.
The Ward
We have room for 8 patients. The staff consists of 6 persons,
three without any training. There is a very good atmosphere and
high enthousiasm in the staff group. I spend an average of $1\frac{1}{2}$
hours daily in the ward, including three group meetings per week.
A consulting psychologist spends 2 hours a week in the ward.
The psychotherapy.
Besides the consulting psychologist and I, we have four other
psychotherapists connected to the project and each has one
patient in therapy. For three of them, this is their first
experience with long-term psychotherapy with schizophrenic
patients. We have a case presenting meeting each week, and every
two weeks we have a staff-psychotherapist meeting.
The general orientation is psychoanalytic. Of the six therapists,
two of us have a formal psychoanalytic training, which is not yet
concluded. One of us has a Jungian analysis and considerable
experience with this kind of work. The psychotherapeutic
tradition in our hospital is initiated and very much influenced
by Dr. Ugelstad, who has conducted seminars and supervised
therapies for many years. Drs. Stierlin, Alanen, Freeman and
Meltzer have visited us during the last few years, giving seminars.
The last three years, I have been very much influenced by the
thinking of Drs. Bion, Meltzer and Grotstein. I have tried to
apply this in my own work, and these ideas have also been
favorably received by my fellow psychotherapists and the staff.

The Ratings.

We try to assess the change in clinical conditions through the Menninger Clinic Health-Sickness Scale in combination with the Quantified Mental Stats. These ratings are done every six months. At the same interval we do Schulz'Self-Object Differentiation Scale and the ego Profile Scale of Semrad and Greenspoon, and a Prediction Scale I have designed. Every month we do a clinical rating where I have tried to catch something of the development in the therapeutic process, especially the shift from schizoid-paranoid position to depressive position. Every month the same is done in a more detailed way.

In addition, the staff makes a weekly rating of their own emotions in connection to the interaction with each patient, while the therapists make a somewhat similar rating for each session.

Intentions of the Study

My intention is to be able to give a long-term description of typical growth processes in psychotherapy with patients like these, something that will increase the competence of myself and my collaborators, and probably also inspire more serious psychotherapeutic work in our own hospital and in other Norwegian hospitals where this neglected group of patients is concerned. Even if I try to assess the outcome, I do not expect that generalizations from this study about treatment outcome will be accepted in academic quarters. Something that I hope to be able to show, however, is that these 11 or more patients will benefit compared to matched controls that have not received psychotherapy. I also expect that we will be able to show that our special kind of application of psychoanalytic theories concerning schizophrenia can prove useful to the ward staff as well as to young therapists with still limited training and experience.

Even if the ward treatment period will finish next year, I hope that most of the patients, perhaps all, will have the opportunity to continue in therapy for several years. I intend to follow this group for another five years and possibly more.

Additional material.

Besides this study, I have a group of 5 female patients with similar conditions in psychotherapy. I have treated these for 2½ to 5 years now. Age at start of treatment was between 25 to 40 years, average 35, and time since onset of symptoms was from 3 to 23 years, average about 10 years. 4 of these are out-patients at present, 2 without any medication, the other 2 with a very small dosage. I also intend to follow this group for several years.

Principal focus in the psychotherapy.

In our way of conceptualizing, we consider the main problem of the patients to be their incapacity to tolerate separation.

No matter what the ultimate cause of this separation intolerance is. it is seen in what we call the uncontrolled, tyrannical rule of the processes of projective identification and the likewise unintegrated processes of splitting and idealization. A psychotic suborganization of the personality. originating from

the infantile paranoid-schizoid position, is dominating the
scene. There is an incomplete depressive integration, manifesting
itself in what Meltzer calls an incomplete dimensionality of
the mind: the mental space is not sufficiently developed to
allow for affects and anxieties to be contained, for thoughts
to be tranformed or symbolized or for life history to be integrated.
We consider the overall goal of therapy to be to help this
mental dimensionality, originating in the infantile depressive
position, to develop. To do so, we focus on the transference
relationship and the delusional content entering this
relationship. We focus especially on that part which is
located in the therapist's mind: the emotions and fantasies
induced by the patient's material and behaviour. The way we conceive
it, the patient is projecting the intolerable parts of his mind
into the therapist, in order to get rid of it, but also to
reintroject it. The good and gentle parts of the patient's mind
are also projected into the therapist, to safeguard them from
destruction. In this way, the patient is building up a therapeutic
alliance outside the borders of his own mind, placing emotional
"depots" inside the therapist. We also try to understand how the
patient is cooperating with our infantile symbiosis, part of our
libidinal motivation for becoming psychotherapists.
One main task, as we see it, is to receive what is projected from
the patient in the session, and let this be mentally "metabolized"
in our mind. This aspect, part of all therapy, is beautifully
described by Bion as "reverie". That means simply thinking about
and trying to understand what goes on in oneself under the
influence of the transference relationship and the material
the patient is bringing.
Through this process of containing what the patient is bringing,
defending the integrity of the therapeutic setting and one's
own capacity to think, the "geographical" confusion, that is
the self-object confusion, can gradually be sorted out. Even if
the therapist shows interest in learning more about the patient's
life, history and delusional world, one main theme where interpretations are concerned, has been the separation intolerance
as seen in the patient-therapist relation, including the
delusional part of the transference. This emphasis seems to
effectuate a diminishing of psychotic symptoms and a development
of some capacity to contain painful affects and memories and
express them. For several of them, this development has
included one or more crises, either dramatically with disturbed
behaviour, suicidal and homicidal threats, or silently with
accelerating projection of despair and resignation. These crises
which in some instances brought close the point of abandoning
the treatment program, have nevertheless proved to be potential
starting points for new growth, and are probably unavoidable in
some cases.
Even if some of these patients are now without medication and
without active symptoms, I still consider us to be in the
first part of the treatment. So far, in none of these patients
have we reached that point where the very tendency to mental
passivity, delusion formation and feeling persecuted and

influenced by one's own projected parts, is abandoned
once and for all.

Fundamental ideas in the work of the ward staff.

From the start we have tried to convey to the ward staff some
fundamental ideas from psycho-analytically orientated
psychotherapy. This sharing of ideas, which has taken place
quite informally through discussion of day-to-day situations
in the ward, has proven very fruitful. Here is a brief
acount of the main ideas in this exchange.

An immense amount of projective and introjective processes
(in a wide meaning of the terms) are going on continuously
for each and every one, both of the human and the non-human
environment. The very first day in the ward gave us an
opportunity to see the importance of this. F, a male patient
who had already been in the hospital for ten years,embarrassed
the other patients with his almost complete muteness and his
incessant tic-like face-making, grinding his teeth or
flapping his arms and shaking his fingers over his head when
anxious or excited. His name is a little uncommon in Norwegian,
and invited for a mocking nick-name that was soon adopted by
some of the patients. A staff discussion on one of the first
days, made us see that in the eyes of each of the other patients
the image of F was very closely linked to some very rejected,
despised and feared part of themselves. Every time lamentations
debasing remarks and questions concerning this patient and
his disturbing behaviour appeared in the group meetings, the
staff had in mind that these remarks were at the same time
questions about our opinions and attitude towards their own
most regressed, "crazy" and dependant parts. Precisely because
of this, we were especially happy when some months later, for the
first time, this patient could tell something coherent and
emotionally meaningful about his own life history in a group
meeting.

In the day-to-day staff discussions we focused very much on the
shifting sentiments of hope versus despair in each staff member
and emphasized the paramount projective origin of these
sentiments. Feelings of hopelessness, disappointment or anger
towards one particular patient was scrutinized mainly from the
vantage point of the patient's need to project these feelings
into us, to avoid feeling, hope and emotional attachment, which
in turn would imply experiencing separation, loneliness and
the misery of having been crazy for years. This way of thinking
helped us to tolerate the provocation of witnessing the
patient's hostility towards saneness and towards reality,their
stubborn decision to stay mad and even in some instances to grow
more mad when an emotional attachment to the ward and staff
developed and pieces of meaningful communication occurred.

The difficult situations arising from a patient's increased
agitation and uncontrolled emotionality, from a growing
sabotage of the ward's meetings and routines, or from disruptive
expressions of paranoid ideas, we have considered first of all
as an opportunity for expanding our capacity for understanding

248

and "reverie" in Bion's sense. In many instances we have also
been in need of action: enjoin the patient to control himself
or participate in meetings and so on, in some instances
increase medication and even to refer the patient temporarily
to a closed ward. But eventual administrative actions like
these have not been taken until we have discussed the counter-
projective part of our motivation to act.
Also where sentiments like hope, sympathy, tenderness and
closeness are concerned, we look upon it mainly as results of the
patients projecting upon us capacities they need to store
themselves, until they feel ready to make them their own.
This way of thinking in my opinion has the advantage that the
staff is less afraid to recognize and discuss the symbiotic
wishes and the depressive anxieties stirred up in us through
the interaction with the patients. This fosters a culture
of care in the staff group. When the partly projective origin
of the tender feelings evoked in staff working with rather
helpless, passive psychotic patients is not recognized,
guilt feelings very often occur, leading to defensive attitudes
like strictness and allowness, or intensified struggles with
sado-masochistic conflicts.
The staff very rapidly grasped the idea that the different
symptoms of the patients, be it mannerisms or delusional ideas
all served the purpose of clinging to the imagination of an
all-good symbiotic undifferentiated primal situation. denying
reality, knowledge, fear and sadness. In the group meetings
we experienced innumerable misrepresentation of our own
feeling states, disfigured through excessive projective
identification, splitting and idealization on the patients'
part. In general, the staff could tolerate this as defensive
vehicles, evacuating the intolerable painful parts of the
self   and safeguarding the good ones, necessary until
some capacity to contain both good and bad parts inside without
the bad parts devouring the good ones, is developed.
The idea that sadness is a valuable experience, a sign of maturation
and growth and a step towards sanity, was not only grasped by the
staff, but also gradually understood by the patients. We
witnessed this appreciation of sad feelings when A came to the
ward half a year ago. This woman, now 48, was hospitalized
because of a very stormy post partum psychosis 16 years ago.
She was abandoned by her husband and has spent all these years
in the hospital, mostly in a closed ward. In one of her first
group meetings one general remark on "parents" made her burst
into a quiet kind of sobbing, which continued until tne
meeting ended. Except for a couple of softly voiced suggestions
that she should tell us what made her sad, the whole group
sat attentively silent listening to her half an hour, without
any interruptions or disruptive outbreaks of restlessness
or mannerisms that are common in the group.

Transport and Transformation of Mental Pain
I use the term "transport" as a shorthand concept for all those
processes where externalizations of painful state in another

(be it similar or disimilar). By transformation I mean here every mental elaboration of a painful thought of any kind, through which it can be more fit for symbolization, communication and containment. These general terms are derived from psychoanalytic thinking, especially Bion's work. They are meant to be general conceptual devises that may be helpful for everybody working in social situations like a hospital ward. The nature of the staff's work can be described by taking this as a basic assumption: each one is continuously participating in the overall transportation system of mental pain, and through their own capacity for transformation ("reverie", "capacity to think") they contribute to the system's degree of maturity and contact with reality.

I will illustrate these processes briefly. B, a girl aged 20, suffered several losses in childhood, such as transfer to an orphanage when her mother committed suicide and so on. She has been ill since the age of 15. The day before her therapist's Christmas leave she suddenly screamed that she had swallowed a safety pin that stuck in the left side of her throat. The ward was in alarm, and she was brought to an emergency medical examination. No alien object was found. She then said that she had swallowed it last June, and that she would charge the hospital for not bringing her to X-ray examination and surgical treatment. She was very angry and upset, and the staff started to worry for what the situation would be in the Christmas holidays. During the staff's discussion we suddenly realized that the patient knew something she was not supposed to know: that her therapist was to have a minor surgical operation during his Christmas leave. Last June was the therapist's summer holiday. The double significance of a safety pin and the meaning of the left side was contemplated. Something sticking in the throat made us think of crying, and of a recent dream of hers where the earth was drowned by rising sea waves. We also thought about her frequently voiced worries that her therapist might loose his mind, and her pondering upon what was the worst alternative: that she would die before the therapist or that the therapist would die before her.

This discussion gave us all a feeling of having discovered something new about the depth of the longings for unity and the fear of separation both in this patient and in mankind in general, and also about the richness and subtlety in the capacity to symbolize conflicts like that, of the power of the passions involved in a psychotherapeutic process and of the beauty unveiled when a piece of psychological truth is uncovered. The patient K mentioned earlier, transported alot of pain onto the staff through his unceasing neglect of clothing and personal hygiene, frequent disappearances from group meetings, dropping out from all duties and so on. He very seldom uttered one word except yes and no and a few warding expressions. After several months he one day delivered some kind of self-justifying speech, emphasizing the fact that he had been in the hospital for 11 years and that no attempt to help him had been of any use.

250

This focus on the experience of time as endless and without hope, made us contemplate once more the fact we knew from his history: from age 3 to 4 he spent 11 months in an isolation ward in ageneral hospital because of a serious infectious disease, from which his brother died during the same period. Even if attempts to point out to him this connection was of no immediate significance, this situation bacame a starting point for a new and more profound understanding of the temporary necessity of his spreading an atmosphere of resignation and despair. After this first severe crisis in the relation between him and the ward staff, his mannerisms have gradually disappeared.

REFERENCES

Bion,Wilfred R. (1967): Second thoughts. Heinemann,London.
Bleger, José (1967): Estudio de la parte psicotica de la personalidad", in Simbiosis y ambigüedad.Editorial Paidos, Buenos Aires.
Grinberg, Leon, with Dario Sor and Elisabeth Tabak de Bianchedi (1975): Introduction to the work of Bion. Clunie Press, Strath Tay, Perthshire.
Grotslein, James S.(1977): "The psychoanalytic concept of schizophrenia" 11. Reconciliation in Int.J.Psycho-Anal.Vol.58 p. 427-452.
Meltzer, Donald (1967): The psychoanalytic process. Heinemann London.
Money-Kyrle,Ronald E.(1968): "Cognitive development" in: Int. J.Psycho-Anal.Vol.49, p.691-698.
Pao, Ping-Nie (1977): "On the formation of schizophrenic symptoms" in: IntJ.Psycho-Anal. Vol.58,p.389-402.
Searles, Harold F.(1975): "The patient as therapist to his analyst in: Peter L. Giovacchini: Tactics and techniques in psycho-analytic therapy.Vol.11. Jason Aranson, New York.
Stierlin, Helm (1974): Separating parents and adolescents. Quadrangle Books, New York.

POSSIBILITIES OF ORGANIZING PSYCHOTHERAPEUTICALLY ORIENTED TREATMENT PROGRAMS FOR SCHIZOPHRENIA WITHIN SECTORIZED PSYCHIATRIC SERVICE

Endre Ugelstad

Institute of Psychiatry, University of Trondheim, Norway

The main objective of this paper is to consider and discuss possibilities of organizing psychotherapeutic treatment programs for schizophrenia as part of the mental health service of a country, or rather of a county.

Through the Mental Health Act of 1961 the mental health service in Norway is in the first place the responsibility of each county, which on the average consists of a population of about 100 - 300 000 people. In each county there will be a further sectorization, in which the existing mental hospitals and psychiatric clinics will have catchment areas with from 50 000 to 120 000 inhabitants.

At the last symposium in Oslo, Strauss and Frader (9) discussed the justification of applying intensive psychotherapy for schizophrenia in community mental health centers in the States. One of their conclusions was that it seemed quite out of reach to offer schizophrenic patients in a catchment area even a modest amount of individual psychotherapy with the resources available in some of the best staffed centers. In one of their examples based upon a continuous case register, they found that approx. 550 schizophrenic patients pr. 100 000 inhabitant received psychiatric care over one year (1970). Out of this group well over 300 needed in-patient treatment. Approx. 40 were new admissions. Of the total patient cohort the schizophrenic patients represented only one-fifth. The solution hinted at is to develop methods by which it would be possible to select out schizophrenic patients for whom individual psychotherapy would make the greatest difference as to the further development of their lives, and their illnes.

Piotrowski (7) at the same symposium discussed plans for reorganizing the care of schizophrenic patients in a hospital-based community approach for a catchment area of approx. 100 000 inhabitants in Warsaw. He especially considers the usefulnes of psychosocial group treatment techniques. He advocates the use of these techniques in the hospital setting and for selected patients in the after-care clinic. In addition he for young schizophrenics stress the importance of a "continuous therapy

253

clinic" where for 3 h. once a week patients have individual contacts with therapists from a psychiatric team responsible for that age group.

OWN EXPERIENCES AND VIEWPOINTS

To organize the presentation of own experiences and viewpoints I will use some public health terms.

What would the terms <u>primary</u>, <u>secondary</u> and <u>tertiary prevention</u> signify in the case of mental health service for schizophrenic patients? It is evident that "what should be prevented against" have very different meanings in this connection, ranging from possible prophylactic intervention to hinder any outbreak of psychosis, to the task of preventing deterioration and profound regressions.

1. <u>Primary prevention</u> would cover interventions that are based on early recognition of children and adolescents belonging to certain high risk groups for developing schizophrenia at a later age.

2. <u>Secondary prevention</u> would aim at the identification of patients who are already in a prepsychotic stage and those falling ill for the first time with symptoms of schizophrenia. Up to now the overwhelming majority of this group has been hospitalized within one year of their illnes. For patients in remission most of the readmissions to hospital occur within 2 years, so the measures undertaken for secondary prevention should at least cover that time.

3. <u>Tertiary prevention</u> which aim at improvement, amelioration or upholding of deterioration in chronic schizophrenia may be connected with two different groups:
   a) treatment of chronic schizophrenic patients, living in the community or hospitalized for shorter periods during excerbarations and crisis,
   b) treatment of long-stay schizophrenics in hospitals.

Taking into account that this last-mentioned group (3b) still occupies over 50 % of the beds in our mental hospitals, I will start my discussion with some experiences with this group of patients, i.e. with <u>tertiary prevention</u>.

At Gaustad mental hospital, Oslo, which is our only remaining state hospital with University teaching functions, my collaboraters and I for the last 7 years have been treating long-stay schizophrenic patient either with intensive milieu treatment for $1\frac{1}{2}$ to 2 years on a small ward or with individual psychotherapy, or with a combination of these two approaches. During the 4 first projects it was possible to offer this kind of treatment to the great majority of our long-stay patients between 25 and 40 years old, having had a continuous stay on the average of 7 years, and to a substantial part of patients between 40 and 50 years old. In these cases earlier attempts at rehabilitation had failed.

A follow-up of 30 male patients from our first project after 4 years showed for the intensively treated group that over 50 % had succeded in establishing satisfactory lives of their own outside hospital. In the older age group nearly all patients had been able to leave the hospital, but then mostly to nursing homes and other protected dwelling places.

On the whole we had better results with our male than with our female patients. We thought this had to do with an over-hospitalization of young male schizophrenic patients.

In some cases it turned out that the individual psycho-therapy had a determining influence on the recovery of patients, earlier looked upon as deeply deteriorated and regressed.

The relative success encouraged our interest in carrying out the same treatment projects with more newly admittet patients(10),and on the other hand to find out more about the treatability of long-stay schizophrenic residents in other Norwegian mental hospitals. This was felt necessary as the patients at Gaustad hospital came from many counties in Southern Norway and could have been admitted to this hospital for many special reasons.

So I screened and interviewed long-stay schizophrenic patients in the mental hospitals covering two of the counties in Middle Norway and two in Northern Norway, having in their catchment areas in all about 600 000 inhabitants. Using a continuous stay of over 1 year as criterion for the long-stay schizophrenic population in the mental hospitals I found only 6 such patients pr. 100 000 inhabitants in the age group under 30 year, approx. 10 pr. 100 000 in the age group 30-40 year, 20 pr. 100 000 in the age group 40-50, then approx. 80 pr. 100 000 for those over 50 years old. The male/female ratio up to 40 year was found to be 2/1, between 40 and 50 like 1,5/1 and over 50 1/1.

In the 86 interviews carried out with long-stay patients in the 30-50 years old category, over 50 % of the men, compared with one-fourth of the women, stated positive interest to the aspects of rehabilitation, whereas the rest were evenly distributed between outspoken negative and ambivalent or hesitating attitudes.

Out of these findings it seems feasible within a county's psychiatric service to offer all younger long-stay schizophrenic patients intensive psychosocial treatment, e.g. by setting up small wards for combined group and individual treatment like in the Gaustad projects.

The other group to be considered under the heading
of tertiary prevention - those who come for ambulatory
treatment - we due to our present statistical methods
know the least about. It is supposed to consist of an
every increasing number of some hundred schizophrenic
patients pr. 100 000 inhabitants.

They exhibit many different needs for social and
psychological help. Many of them come to our after-care
out-patient clinics where they mostly are offered maintenance therapy with psychotropic drugs. They would also
in the future best be treated in special after-care clinics in each sector, in close collaboration with wards for
inter-mediate care, daycenters, social agencies and community doctors. In community mental health centers there
are evidence that they will receive less attention than
patients with acutely developed psychiatric problems.(3)

Where their problems are brought into focus by special efforts as in the Nacka project outside Stockholm,
their special psychotherapeutic needs in form of supportive psychotherapy seems to be met.

As to secondary prevention I will start with some
considerations based upon the Norwegian central register
of psychosis which give information on admissions of psychotic patients in Norwegian mental hospitals and psychiatric clinics back to 1916. According to the register
first admissions of schizophrenia pr. 100 000 inhabitants
have undergone considerable changes through the last 25
years, having before that time shown much constancy.

Whereas the yearly first admissions for schizophrenia
has decreased from approx. 14 pr. 100 000 to 7 pr.100 000
over these 25 years one striking finding emerges: When
the number of first admissions are distributed among age
groups the youngest group of patients - 15-29 years old,
with a peak between 20 and 25, show a decline of approx.
20 %, whereas the middle age group show a decline of
approx. 65 %. In this way first admissions of young
schizophrenics now counts for 50 % of all first admissions for schizophrenia.

If Astrup and Noreik's (2) findings as to the prognosis in schizophrenia still holds true, reckoning with
a risk of 23 % for developing severe defects for the
group under 30 years old at the onset, compared to only
3-4% for those older at onset, it would be likely to
conclude that the group of young schizophrenics,admitted
to hospital for the first time,are at a special risk for
severe forms of chronification,and should be looked upon
from the standpoint of the mental hospital as the most
important group for secondary prevention.

Another interesting finding for this group is that
the male/female ratio over these 25 years has been
2-2,5/1, whereas the ratio is 1/1 in the middle age
group.

This corresponds well with the finding reported above on the preponderance of male patients among the long-stay schizophrenic patients.

What may be the practical implications of this change in the pattern of first admissions of schizophrenia? It could be estimated in a catchment area of 200 000 people that each year there would appear only 7-8 schizophrenic patients under 30 years of age as first admission.

If each county had a psychiatric team of four professionals (a psychiatric nurse, a social worker, a clinical psychologist and a psychiatrist) whose main task was to evaluate, treat and follow up these patients for a five year period, their case load should not be unbearable, even if they at the same time directed attention to an equal number of young patients with diagnosis of reactive psychosis and borderline psychosis. The different psycho-therapeutic methods that would be applied has been delt with by Alanen and his coworkers (1).

For this group of young patients both individual and family psychotherapy could make a great difference as to their further development.

The problems of primary prevention has of late been subject to much interest especially in high risk groups. (11). The presentations and discussions on this topic at a WHO conference in Copenhagen 1975 dealt foremostly with preventive intervention with psychotic mothers and the possibilities of detecting some biological marker in children at special risk. Great caution were expressed as to the possible adverse effect of labelling an individual as belonging to a high risk group on the basis of yet very scanty evidence.

Another approach was reported by Goldstein (5) who in a clinic for disturbed adolescents have tried out measures - a.o. family TAT - for the identification of families at risk of contributing to the development of schizophrenic illnes in their off-springs. This would then lead to preventive family therapy along suggested lines. Similar ideas has been expressed by Bremer-Schulte (4) relying in the first place in identifying specific deviant styles of communication in families by collaboration with general practioners in an area. If it is possible to identify such families and help them before "closure" in the sense of Scott (8) occurs this probably would be the most promising approach at present for primary prevention.

CONCLUSIONS

The sectorization of psychiatric service opens up
for new possibilities of integrating hospital and community **psychiatry** in the treatment of schizophrenia.
An estimation based partly on statistics and patient
registration and partly on own treatment experiences (10)
seems to indicate that especially the following endeavours
could be practically realized and possibly contribute to
tertiary and secondary prevention.

1. To provide individualised psychosocial treatment
in hospital-based projects for younger long-stay
schizophrenic patients.

2. To establish psychotherapeutically working
psychiatric teams in each catchment area for long-
term treatment of identified young schizophrenic
patients and their families.

REFERENCES

1. Alanen, Y. et al. (1979): In this voulme.

2. Astrup, Chr. and Noreik, K. (1966): Functional psych-
    osis. Diagnostic and prognostic models. Thomas,
    Springfield, Ill.

3. Bockoven, J.S. and Solomon, H. C. (1975): Comparison
    of two five-years follow-up studies.Am.J.Psychiatry 8.

4. Bremer-Schulte, M. A. (1976): In: Schizophrenia 75,
    p. 187. Universitetsforlaget, Oslo.

5. Goldstein, M. J. (1977): In: Primary Prevention of
    Schizophrenia in High-Risk Groups, p.27. WHO Report
    on a Working Group, Copenhagen.

6. Haugsgjerd, S. (1979): In this volume.

7. Piotrowski, A. (1976): In: Proceedings II, Schizo-
    phrenia 75. Stencil. Gaustad Hospital, Oslo.

8. Scott, R. D. (1976): In: Schizophrenia 75, p. 265.
    Universitetsforlaget, Oslo.

9. Strauss, J. S. and Frader, M. A. (1976): In: Schizo-
    phrenia 75, p. 145. Universitetsforlaget, Oslo.

10. Ugelstad, E. (1978): Psykotiske langtidspasienter i
    psykiatriske sykehus. Universitetsforlaget, Oslo.

11. WHO.Regional office for Europe (1977): Primary
    Prevention of Schizophrenia. Report on a Working
    Group. Copenhagen.

COMMENTS ON THE CONFLUENCE OF PSYCHIATRIC PHENOMENOLOGY, INTER-PERSONAL THERAPIES, AND CLINICAL RESEARCH METHODS IN SCHIZOPHRENIA

William T. Carpenter, Jr.

Director, Maryland Psychiatric Research Center and Professor of
Psychiatry, University of Maryland School of Medicine, Baltimore, MD

Psychiatric phenomenology can be defined as the description, understanding and classification of experience and behavior relevant to mental disorders. The history of the philosophical basis for a phenomenologic appreciation of human experience is beyond the scope of this discussion, but Jaspers (1,2) provides a convenient point of departure relevant to clinical psychiatry. In his approach to psychopathology, Jaspers attempted to describe, classify and understand the mental phenomena experienced and expressed by patients. His discussion of the communication of experience is critical, since he taught that the clinician would develop an appreciation of another person's experience through two avenues of communication - language and empathy. To comprehend that which is subjective is difficult, and the communication of one's experience to another is a complicated task. Reliance on cognition and communication with language is inadequate to capture the essence of complex experience, a fact upon which psychoanalytic exploration is based. Much of what we "know" of another's experience is perceived through an empathic bond which allows us to develop a sense of the experience - feeling ourselves in the other person's shoes, as it were. Becoming experientially informed is an aspect of ordinary communication between persons, and the psychoanalyst makes explicit use of empathy in the consulting room.*

A discernible divergence between two important trends in psychiatry's attempt to understand the mentally ill has had an unfortunate impact on present practices relevant to schizophrenia. The emphasis of the psychoanalytic movement on understanding the individual patient greatly broadened and deepened the clinician's capacity to assess and describe subjective experiences. An emphasis on understanding of experience guided by psychoanalytic theory gave special emphasis to intrapsychic conflict and individual psychodynamics, but made a less important contribution to understanding the

---

* Jaspers is emphasized here because his writings made a signal contribution towards a psychiatric phenomenology. His background in philosophy influenced his conceptual approach to psychiatric patients, and it is his effort to transform philosophic phenomenology to psychiatric phenomenology that merits our attention. He is less important as a clinician exploring the subjective experience of schizophrenic patients. Better models for clinical exploration of intrapsychic experience can be found among contributors to this volume.

class of phenomena referred to as schizophrenia. Contrariwise, psychiatrists representing the diagnostic schools have emphasized the description of some aspects of the schizophrenic experience which are useful in identifying a class of patients, but give less attention to understanding the personal experience of schizophrenic patients. Hence, much importance has been ascribed to specifiable experiences useful to the diagnostic process (e.g., Schneider's first rank symptoms (3,4). Following Jasper's lead, some descriptive schools have placed particular emphasis on experiences about which the patient can give a verbal account, ignoring empathic communication on the assumption that schizophrenic patients cannot establish empathetic bonds. There is an explicit assumption that the schizophrenic's experience is not understandable within the framework of ordinary human experiences. This is consistent with Freud's dictum that the schizophrenic patient cannot establish a transference relationship and that schizophrenic psychopathology is not understandable through psychoanalysis.

American psychiatry has recently followed the lead of European colleagues in placing great emphasis on highly specifiable phenomena useful in the diagnosis of schizophrenia, with a de-emphasis on subtle, difficult to specify subjective experiences - phenomena which are critical in understanding the individual with schizophrenia (5).

The difference in emphasis between psychiatric schools described above is natural enough, and becomes important only when one recognizes a second, clearly untoward development in our field. The present situation, in most nations, is not of two influential schools of psychiatry which overlap, mutually enrich, and share in the shaping of psychiatric concepts and attitudes. Rather, one school has become dominant and eschews the contributions of the other. Any such conclusion does, of course, overstate the present situation, but I believe it fairly calls attention to a serious problem which already has caused extraordinary problems in our approach to schizophrenic patients.

This situation can be characterized as follows. The dominant set of attitudes relevant to schizophrenia can be described as the somatic-descriptive-psychopharmacologic axis.* Schizophrenia is assumed to be an illness - an assumption with which I agree. However, too often it is conceptualized within the narrow biomedical model (6). Investigations of pathogenesis are directed toward

_____

* Highly specifiable and difficult to specify are used descriptively to emphasize that we are dealing with human experiences in both instances, and that clinical observations are subjective. This is important since some diagnosticians assume that the use of clearly defined, special forms of hallucinations and delusions constitute a reliable and objective basis for diagnosis, while more vaguely defined or complex psychopathology creates an unreliable and subjective diagnostic process. In fact, both approaches are based on subjective judgments, and reliability in each case must be determined psychometrically rather than assumed. One approach has not yet been demonstrated to be more valid than the other. What remains as a fair distinction between the two approaches is the degree to which that psychopathology relevant to diagnosis can be crisply and clearly defined.

genetic and biochemical attributes and research into therapy is directed toward pharmacologic strategies. Descriptive psychiatry is pivotal and has taken the role of identifying highly specifiable phenomena which can be used to signal the presence of an illness, while giving little attention to more difficult to define phenomena which may be useful in understanding the individual with schizophrenia.

This oversimplification does not do justice to the best of the theoretical constructs or the most enlightened teachings about schizophrenia, but it reasonably characterizes the model which seems to shape the clinical experience of most schizophrenic patients. Evaluation is often brief and is experienced by the patient as non-personal. Diagnoses are rapidly made without a thorough exploration of the phenomena. Treatment decisions are predominantly pharmacologic and seem to be made automatically - often well in advance of an appropriate diagnostic evaluation. In most hospitals, patients presumed to have schizophrenia will be placed on medication immediately upon admission and drugs will continue as the major therapeutic modality, even when the patient proves unresponsive. Hospitals for chronic schizophrenia in the United States, for example, maintain large numbers of patients on medication for years despite conspicuous evidence of therapeutic failure. Emphasis on short hospital stay, prevention of admissions to hospitals, and influence of third-party financial arrangements all reinforce a seeming necessity to render a patient non-psychotic as rapidly as possible. In some places there is a serious threat to the clinician's capacity to treat a schizophrenic patient off medication during any phase of illness, since such an approach may be regarded as unethical by his colleagues, intolerable by ward staffs, and financially irresponsible by those supporting hospital treatment.

The narrowness of this conceptual approach to schizophrenia is also reflected in clinical research designs during the last two decades relevant to the cause and treatment of schizophrenia. Treatment evaluation is often unidimensional (e.g., discharge is the outcome criterion for inpatient studies, and readmission is the outcome criterion for aftercare studies) despite the fact that schizophrenia is a complicated, multidimensional illness. It is typical, for example, for studies comparing treatment methods for aftercare to accept readmission to a hospital as a sufficient indicator of course of illness, without making any effort to determine the degree of health in the readmitted patient or the degree of illness in the non-readmitted patient. Similarly, biologically based investigations of schizophrenia all-too-often have a narrow frame of reference from which one attempts to identify the critical neurophysiologic or neurochemical factor rather than conceptualizing the study as an attempt to identify one link in a chain or one piece of a puzzle. The simplicity of clinical concepts and clinical methods utilized in many investigations belies the knowledge afforded by the descriptive work of pioneers such as Kraepelin, Bleuler, Langfeldt, and others. The psychoanalytically-oriented clinician has a broader and deeper view of the schizophrenic patient, and it is here that the loss of influence of clinicians interested in psychoanalysis and interpersonal psychology is most keenly felt.

261

Enthrallment with the narrow biomedical model would not occur if vigorous conceptual input from those most interested in the sociology and psychology of illness was effectively integrated with biologic models of schizophrenia*.

The participants in this Conference and readers of this volume need not be reminded of the importance of interpersonal approaches to the schizophrenic patient. It may be necessary, however, to state clearly that the professional interest represented in this Congress has fallen on deaf ears in society and the mainstream of psychiatry. There are many reasons for this state of affairs, and I will list a few which reflect shortcomings in psychodynamic psychiatry:

1) Sigmund Freud's pronouncement that the schizophrenic patient is incapable of forming a transference relationship, hence schizophrenic phenomena cannot be explored psychoanalytically. Freud's dictum has gone without challenge in many psychoanalytic circles, and the limited experience upon which this observation was based has not been sufficiently criticized.

2) Many psychiatrists interested in psychoanalysis and interpersonal therapies avoid psychotic patients, emphasizing the treatment and study of neurotic and personality disorders. The implicit therapeutic nihilism and the reduction in the number of clinicians able to articulate the social and psychological aspects of schizophrenia have contributed to the narrow approach to schizophrenic patients now prevalent.

3) Whether by aptitude, attitude or arrogance, clinicians most interested in interpersonal therapeutic strategies in schizophrenia have abrogated the laws of clinical science, and have failed to establish methods for the assessment of the therapeutic efficacy of their techniques. Investigators interested in pharmacologic therapeutic strategies have not been so timid, and comparative treatment designs tend to reflect selection of patients, therapeutic maneuvers, and outcome assessments relevant to pharmacotherapy and irrelevant to psychotherapy. However, since these studies have gone

---

*This discussion is appropros to the current situation in research and clinical care in many parts of the world, but I believe that sensitivity to these problems is becoming evident. For example, in the process of formulating the Third Edition of the Diagnostic and Statistical Manual for The American Psychiatric Association, a multiaxial concept has been accepted. A new generation of clinical therapeutic trials are beginning to incorporate a broader range of human functioning into the evaluation process. Perhaps because of the prevalence of tardive dyskinesia and the lack of therapeutic results in many chronic patients, there is a renewed interest in non-pharmacologic approaches to the schizophrenic patient. Furthermore, there have been some advantages to the narrow biomedical focus in that clinical and laboratory methods suitable to the investigation of schizophrenic patients have been tested and refined. It is difficult in the initial stages of the development of a discipline to take into account the full range of considerations mandated by a full appreciation of schizophrenic phenomena, and the onus of integrating biologic, psychologic and sociologic data and concepts rests on all clinicians.

unchallenged, they have been received with conviction by the main-stream of psychiatry.

4) The important advances represented by decisive demonstration of a therapeutic effect on anti-psychotic drugs, and the demonstration beyond reasonable doubt of a genetic contribution to some forms of schizophrenia, have given a justified impetus to psychopharmacologic and biologically-based research efforts. However, the misinterpretation of this data as suggesting that interpersonal and intrapsychic factors are not involved in pathogenesis, and that interpersonal therapeutic strategies are irrelevant to treatment is indefensible. Yet, this assumption is often made, and psychodynamic workers have not pursued investigative work of the scope or methodologic sophistication required to maintain their sphere of influence. Notable exceptions (e.g., Wynne and Singer) can be cited, but this area of psychiatry has not been impressive in developing research strategies suitable for hypothesis testing and generation of new information and concepts.

What, then, is the relationship among psychiatric phenomenology, interpersonal therapy, and the current state of affairs in psychiatry? Opinions will be expressed on two aspects of this relationship. In another presentation (7), the theme of phenomenology guiding the initial evaluation of the psychotic patient was developed. The implications for diagnosis and therapeutic interventions based on an in-depth exploration and understanding of the patient's subjective experiences requires elaboration for some audiences, but not for the membership of this Congress. What is germane in this regard is that psychiatric phenomenology, rather than psychoanalytically-derived therapeutic goals, may provide a foundation for espousing the exploration of psychic phenomena as central to the psychiatrist's task. The long-term aims of interpersonal therapy are not likely to attract the mainstream of psychiatry into a careful and personal assessment of the psychotic patient's experience* The goals of psychiatric phenomenology (describing, understanding and classifying psychopathologic experiences) provides a more immediate rationale for establishing a therapeutic relationship. A comprehensive evaluation of the patient has implications for planning a broad therapeutic approach, for collecting information relevant to pharmacologic and psychosocial therapeutic strategies, and for ascertaining information relevant to diagnosis. It is also a rationale that is applicable to every patient, while the goals of exploratory psychotherapy are necessarily limited to the minority of patients with schizophrenia. The psychoanalytically-oriented psychiatric clinician is in the optimal position to assume leadership in teaching phenomenologic evaluation. The effort to establish a relationship, the assessment of strengths and weaknesses of the individual, the attempt to fully describe and understand the experiences of another individual, and the use of

---

* Emphasis on the mainstream of psychiatry does not imply that segments of the profession should not be devoted to work within narrow boundaries, be they psychoanalytic or neurobiologic. My concern is the extent to which isolation results in a reduction of clinical sophistication in the majority of professionals responsible for the care of schizophrenic patients.

the dyadic relationship are ordinary strengths of the psychotherapist. The detachment of evaluation from specific, long-range therapeutic goals, and the application of these techniques to a broader range of short-term goals, appears feasible and important. This approach has been detailed elsewhere (7).

A second area in which psychiatric phenomenology and interpersonal therapy should coalesce is in the formulation of clinical research methods. It should be obvious that there is a critical need for sensibly designed, carefully controlled studies of the therapeutic efficacy of interpersonal treatment strategies. The field is singularly deficient in this regard and, at present, it cannot be stated whether the failure to demonstrate a decisive therapeutic effect of interpersonal treatment is based on the inadequacies of the test or the lack of a strong therapeutic effect. Similarly, those clinicians working with schizophrenic patients in exploratory psychotherapy are in a position to observe those intrapsychic and interpersonal variables which best reflect the course of illness, and hence can be used to provide a valid assessment of change. Furthermore, the psychiatric phenomenologist will be sensitive to design requirements slighted in comparative treatment studies to date. Some examples will illustrate. Criteria for selection of appropriate patients must be clearly specified if treatment effects are to be studied. Too often patients with little potential for therapeutic benefit are selected, making negative results inevitable. In comparative treatment designs, patients appropriate for each therapy are required, otherwise the results are biased and hypotheses are not critically assessed.

Designs comparing interpersonal treatment strategies to no treatment can demonstrate an effect, but it is presently more important to tease apart the relative merits of pharmacologic and interpersonal strategies. The extent to which they reinforce each other in some phases of illness or in some aspects of psychopathology is not yet clarified. One approach may also interfere with the effect of the other. For example, some interpersonal therapies may mobilize patients into more demanding social situations, and the accompanying stress may undermine the stabilizing effect of medication. Contrariwise, the use of medication to eradicate psychotic experience prior to an attempt to establish a therapeutic relationship may seriously undermine the patient's confidence in the therapist's capacity to understand him as an individual with psychotic experiences. The long-term use of medication to prevent relapse may curb initiative and interact negatively with social rehabilitation programs. The psychiatric phenomenologist can designate those clinical criteria which will select patient populations suitable for testing the treatment hypotheses in comparative treatment designs, while simultaneously preventing unwitting patient selection which will bias prognosis in favor of one therapeutic approach. If most diagnosed schizophrenic patients were thought suitable for a drug trial, while only those with an active curiosity about their experiences are selected for psychotherapy, then a prognostic bias favoring the psychotherapy cohort may be hidden in the study design itself.

Careful attention to the pattern and course of illness will

help identify the phase of illness for which any particular treatment is expected to be effective. If, for example, a family therapy strategy is expected to reduce the likelihood of psychotic relapse, it would be inappropriate to test this proposition in patients who are continuously psychotic. A related error occurs when study duration is inappropriate. If one conceptualizes therapeutic benefit accruing after a year's treatment, a design emphasizing 6-month outcome is unsuitable. One can readily appreciate the difficulty in comparing a treatment which effects change in days or weeks with a treatment which effects change in months or years. Furthermore, it is critical that the clinical variables selected to reflect change be appropriate for the therapeutic strategies employed. Comparing pharmacotherapy and psychotherapy by determining short-term effects on hallucinations and delusions reveals that only drug treatment is effective in schizophrenia. However, if only object relationships following two years of treatment served as outcome criteria, the bias would be reversed. Both studies would disappoint the psychiatric phenomenologist who would expect change criteria and timing of assessment to reflect and test the basic tenets of each treatment. Clinical investigators should assess clinical variables central to the illness even though they may not be affected by the treatment under study. The demonstration of therapeutic limitations is almost as important as demonstration of treatment benefits. Finally, the follow-up of study patients is crucial, in order to determine the extent to which beneficial effects persevere after treatment is terminated. Work accomplishment in a therapeutic occupational program may not be reflected in future work ability in ordinary settings.

CONCLUSION

The above discussion is meant to illustrate the role of the psychotherapist and clinical phenomenologist in conceptualizing schizophrenia and implementing clinical methods suitable for the investigation of treatment strategies. Failure by those most interested in interpersonal strategies to become extensively engaged in designing clinical investigations has already had a profound impact on psychiatry. It is no longer acceptable to simply criticise the research clinician for failing to capture the richness of the clinical phenomena in his study design, or to note the inappropriate application of psychotherapeutic techniques. It is essential that we define the patients suitable for interpersonal interventions, that we designate clearly those aspects of functioning which may be enhanced and those aspects in which a therapeutic effect is not anticipated. We must become involved in establishing research investigations which will fairly test the tenets guiding the interpersonal treatment. In this regard, I have argued that psychiatric phenomenology may provide an intermediary role from which the psychotherapeutically-oriented clinician can conceptualize schizophrenia, can teach diagnosis, description and understanding of the schizophrenic patient, can more persuasively articulate the broad range of therapeutic considerations necessary to comprehensive treatment of the schizophrenic patient, and from which study designs can be promulgated relevant to testing the efficacy of interpersonal treatment. The field cannot afford a smug enthrallment

with intriguing theories. The clinical market place is a mess and
we must proceed with the mundane and frustrating business of establishing an empiric base for our work, adhering to the methods and
principles of scientific investigation. Failure to accept this
challenge will result in further deterioration of the psycho-
docial sphere of our profession, and schizophrenic patients will
be less likely to receive clinical care based on a full appreciation of their personal experience. The study of schizophrenic
illness(es) will be seriously compromised so long as a narrow
conceptual framework guides the investigator. In an illness(es)
which remains enigmatic, this latter effect will be tragic.

REFERENCES

1. Jaspers, K. (1968) : General Psychopathology. University of
   Chicago Press, Chicago, ILL.
2. Stierlin, H. (1974) J. Hist. Behav. Sci., 10. 213.
3. Schneider, K. (1939) : Clinical Psychopathology, Grune &
   Stratton, Inc., New York. NY.
4. Carpenter, W.T., Strauss, J.S., Mulch, S. (1973) Arch. Gen.
   Psychiatry, 28, 847.
5. Carpenter, W.T., Strauss, J.S., In. Disorders of the Schizophrenic Syndrome, Editor : L. Bellak, Grune & Stratton, New
   York. NY, in press.
6. Engel, G., (1977) : Science, 196, 129.
7. Carpenter, W.T. Treatment of the Schizophrenic Patient,
   presented at the Annual Meeting of the American Psychiatric
   Association, Atlanta, GA. 91978).

COLD WET SHEET PACK, TRANSITIONAL RELATEDNESS AND CONTAINMENT*

David B. Feinsilver, M.D.

Staff Psychiatrist, Chestnut Lodge, Rockville, Maryland

INTRODUCTION

Melinda is a 25-year-old girl who was admitted to our hospital, Chestnut Lodge, after she tried to kill her brother with a hatchet. She had been in and out of various treatment settings since age 11, shortly after her menarche, when her parents first noticed her strange behavior, which was diagnosed by the doctors as chronic undifferentiated schizophrenia.

In her first hour, Melinda presented to me as an obese, slovenly dressed, bland looking, chronically medicated schizophrenic patient. She spoke in fragmented, riddled, primary process "schizophrenese," but her eyes were bright and she seemed to be conveying quite clearly what she had been struggling with all her life. She spoke of yearning to be in the outside world and being prevented by vague and unclear forces that were victimizing her. She focused particularly on something she called "child abuse" and she described this as a mysterious identity switching phenomenon whereby her intelligence and capabilities were somehow taken from her. She added very pointedly that this tended to happen whenever she sought treatment and that she needed help to stop it.

Melinda's background history included the following information: She was described by her parents as an insatiable infant whom they could never placate, crying constantly despite the fact that the records of the pediatrician showed a normal weight gain and normal developmental landmarks. Each parent, for his own reasons, saw the developing child as insatiable, and this seemed to be the basis of a projective identification which then served to bring about a self-fulfilling prophecy for Melinda. Mother's own mother, the maternal grandmother, had become psychotic and was institutionalized for the remainder of her life shortly after mother's birth, necessitating mother's being placed in the care of a succession of relatives. Shortly after Melinda's birth, mother found it necessary to send Melinda away similarly to stay with various relatives and friends. Thus, mother recapitulated with Melinda her own early abandonment by her mother. Although father seems to have been the more nurturant parent, he has always felt a guilty need to restrain himself with

---

*Other versions of this paper were prepared for the River Oaks Symposium, New Orleans, March 11, 1978, and the Chestnut Lodge Symposium, October 6, 1978.

Melinda because of a sense of disloyalty to his family by a previous
marriage. He has kept this knowledge as a secret from Melinda to
this day.

Melinda and I began meeting 4 times a week, as is the custom at
Chestnut Lodge, while her medication was gradually being reduced
until she was completely off. Over the course of the next two months
Melinda began to experience a sense of regaining her intelligence and
capabilities. She spoke particularly of becoming intelligent, rich
and famous through some man whom she saw as possessing these qualities. Sometimes she was a famous daughter, sometimes a wife, and
sometimes the man himself. For example, her favorite identity was
Julie-Nixon-David-Eisenhower where she was both the famous daughter
of a famous man, a famous wife, and a famous man herself, which also
included a specific identification with her younger brother David as
well as myself, David. Melinda also made the point, however, that
whatever good she was experiencing was being diminished by a vague
feeling that she was being forced into a controlling, abusing,
sexually-tinged experience, but she would refuse to elaborate on
this.

One morning after a long weekend break towards the end of our
second month of work Melinda stormed into my office with fire in her
eyes, began spitting on me and screaming incoherently about child
abuse and rape. She did not respond to my attempts to stop her
verbally, and it seemed that if she had had her hatchet in her hand
she surely would have brought it down on my skull. She left the
office, but this assaultive threat escalated, both in the hours with
me and in her general behavior on the unit. I therefore decided
somewhat reluctantly, in the service of finding a way to continue our
being together, to have our hours with Melinda in a cold wet sheet
pack, or, as it is otherwise known at the Lodge, more simply "pack."

For those of you who may be unfamiliar with what a cold wet
sheet pack is, let me say briefly that it is a sedating, restraining
procedure which has been in use for many years, at least since the
mid-nineteenth century. As it is used in our hospital today, it
consists of placing disorganized, uncontrollably assaultive patients
for periods of up to 2 to 3 hours wrapped up on a bed in ice-cold
wet sheets totally immobilized, and covered with blankets. Without
going into much detail, for the purposes of this paper let me just
say that when patients first hear about the pack they usually think
of it as barbaric and torturing, as do most people who first hear
about it. Most patients when placed in it, however, usually very
quickly achieve a relatively tranquil state and speak of the pack as
a very comforting experience. In fact, most patients quickly reach
a point where they will ask on their own initiative for the pack when
they need it. Based on a few physiological studies done at the turn
of the century, the effectiveness of the pack is said to be due to a
reflex set off by the cold against the skin, triggering a generalized
rebound hyperthermic effect, which produces the net effect of a hot
bath. It is therefore found in psychiatric textbooks under hydrotherapy (7). In any event, I view the pack like many other aspects
of the "holding environment" (Winnicott's term) which have been found
empirically to be useful in physically controlling and containing

the disorganizing manifestations of schizophrenic illness and which
thereby make psychotherapy possible. Much of what is being presented
in this particular paper about the cold wet sheet pack might be shown
in other cases to hold true of other aspects of the "holding environment."

AIMS OF PAPER

In my work with Melinda while she was in pack, I began to notice
that the negative feelings that had been threatening our relationship
were now being projected onto the pack. In fact, it seemed that I
hardly existed any more for Melinda while the pack was being related
to with all the significance of a vital object. Gradually, however,
as Melinda began to relate to me more fully and my jealousy diminished, I was impressed with how she would seem to shift between first
addressing the pack and then me in the same manner. It occurred to
me that the pack was being used in much the same manner as a transitional object to maintain comforting contact with an object that was
otherwise being given up. Furthermore, I noticed how much I, in the
process, seemed to be acquiring for Melinda many of the characteristics of the pack, in many ways becoming synonymous with it and its
controlling, containing, and comforting aspects. I too had become a
transitional object and our relatedness was characterized by a mode
which I thought might best be termed "transitional relatedness."
Melinda's final coming out of the pack and being able to control herself could not occur, however, until a fuller, more assimilating
introjection and metabolization of these hostile projections in both
the transference and countertransference occurred, which is, as I
will explain below, what I think of as "containment." In this paper
I will attempt to show how case material demonstrating ambiguous
primitive processes can be elucidated by these concepts and the
relationship between them.

PRELIMINARY DEFINITIONS

1) My usage of the term "transitional relatedness" derives from
the concept of the transitional object first described by Donald
Winnicott in his classic paper, "Transitional Objects and Transitional Phenomena," (1953). Many have elaborated on this, but for the
purposes of this paper I should like to cite particularly two references: (a) Arnold Modell's book, "Object Love and Reality" (4) and
(b) Harold Searles' discussion of the relationship between symbiotic
phenomena and transitional phenomena in his recent paper, "Transitional Phenomena and Therapeutic Symbiosis" (5). I am using the term
"transitional relatedness" to mean the following:

> The type of relatedness established with a transi-
> tional object--relatedness that is (a) created by
> the self and under its control, but also includes
> presymbolic representation of the object (having
> simultaneous aspects of the self and object thereby
> brings it into the symbiotic realm as conceptualized

by Searles), (b) partly imaginary, partly real and
related to play, and (c) serving to comfort by
warding off separation anxiety.

2) My usage of the term "containment" follows from Bion (1) who
originated the concept, and Grinberg (2) and Langs (3), who have
elaborated on it. I am using the term "containment" to mean the
following:

The introjection, assimilation and metabolization of
a projective identification so that it becomes a more
integrated component of a developing whole-object
relatedness.

PHASE I: SPLITTING OF THE EMERGING UNCONTAINED NEGATIVE PART-OBJECT

In this first phase in the pack, lasting approximately 6 months,
Melinda attempted to maintain our relationship by exclusively identifying the pack as "the bad object" and our relationship as "the
good object." This was a classical situation of splitting and
countersplitting, where both Melinda and I were too quick to agree
that the pack was "the torturing, humiliating, child abusing rapist"
and that everything would be fine if I would just simply let her out
of the pack. We found, much to our dismay, that as soon as I would
let her out she would begin raging uncontrollably at me again as the
persecuting object.

PHASE II: INITIAL CONTAINMENT WITH ESTABLISHMENT OF TRANSITIONAL
RELATEDNESS TO THE PACK AND THERAPIST

During this phase, lasting approximately a year, there was a
process of shifting between Melinda's first involving the pack and
then me as the negative part-object, first as the relatedness became
totally destructive and then as it became more transitional, and
along with this came the beginnings of a more contained relatedness.

During this period Melinda would often speak of the pack as her
friend, her friend who tortured her, her friend who was making her
pay for vague, unspecified debts. Often she would lie in silence,
sometimes rather comfortably, and then suddenly start thrashing,
breaking out into a scream and accusing the pack of hurting her,
sticking knives into her chest, into her vagina; or accuse the pack
of paralyzing her arms and legs, giving her polio; but most of all,
she would speak of being forced by the pack into becoming somebody
else, some famous man, some famous woman and sometimes doctors.
Initially I was totally ignored, but gradually as I interpreted this
as various aspects of her needfulness there would be a noticeable
calming effect. She began to indicate very quickly, however, that I
was torturing her. After one apparently calming interpretation, for
example, she started up in a rather mournful tone, "Oh, why do you
have to wear those glasses; you see the baby, take them off, take
them off." My openly recognizing with her, however, her plight,

270

seemed to constitute an unbearable exposure of her infantile, dependent, symbiotic attachment to me, and therefore an intolerable humiliation. Soon the words themselves were experienced as intrusive symbiotic attacks. On another occasion she cut me off before I could even get the first word out, "Your words are cutting my throat like a razor, biting me, destroying me, killing me, making me into somebody else, making me into a beautiful blond and then cutting my hair, making me into a man." Often after such an attack she would emphasize her sense of fragmented, helpless, desperate longing by suddenly shouting out in a disconnected way, "I love you, Dr. Feinsilver."

The destructive nature of the object relatedness that was being dealt with is probably best conveyed with the very graphic example of Melinda's spitting. Typically, she would load up quite noisily, letting me know that a missile was about to come; then she would pucker up and just as she was about to let fly she would suck instead. Each time, however, my relief would be somewhat mitigated by a feeling that she was making a fool of me. There were also many times when she would spit, but would consistently either hit me or miss me, letting me know that I had to either quickly take cover behind her bed, or that I could rest assured that I was to be in the eye of the storm. But, of course, this too would always leave me feeling ridiculously at her mercy and under her control, which seemed to be precisely how she was experiencing what I was doing to her in the first place. This is, I think, a very concrete illustration of how projective identification operates and is indicative of how similar processes were probably operating in more subtle ways to create in me a sense of my being victimized by her as she felt she was by me.

It is difficult to convey the overwhelming sense of murderous rage that pervaded our relatedness from both sides during this time. A typical hour might begin with my walking down the path approaching her building and hearing her screaming 4 flights up, causing me to tense up with anxious anticipation, or to feel like turning back before I even started. Sometimes she would just surprise me with a blood-curdling scream when I would enter the room. "Murderer," she would scream in a way which made it quite difficult for me to be clear just who was doing the murdering and who was being murdered, she or I. This was such a vivid experience for me that I would often find myself backing out of the room, as if Melinda were not safely wrapped up in the pack.

I don't think I realized just how much I struggled with my own countermurderousness until I finally understood at some later time a curious experience I had repeatedly as I was leaving. Whenever I would approach one of the nursing staff to indicate that I was leaving, so that Melinda would not be left unattended, I did not know just how to say it, finding myself strangely paralyzed. I could only think of phrases that seemed to convey murderous intent, either by Melinda or myself: "Melinda is through—Melinda is through with her hour, through with her therapy, through with me"—meaning that Melinda was destroying me and our work. Or I might see myself as the perpetrator of destruction—"I'm through with Melinda, I'm finished with Melinda, I'm leaving," etc. It was only later on, after considerable struggle, when Melinda herself began to show signs of containing her murderousness, that I experienced a sense of freedom similar to hers and made the somewhat startling discovery that neutral phrases do exist, such as, "Melinda's hour is over now." And it suddenly didn't seem so bad after all to say, "Melinda is through now," or even, "I'm through with Melinda now."

After approximately one year of going on and on in this destructive way, Melinda gradually began to speak hopefully about getting well. One day, it seemed, she just started speaking of feeling that she was a baby being born, or a baby beginning to take steps. She compared herself to the heroine in "I Never Promised You A Rose Garden." She began to speak often of the pack as if it were a band-aid, or a splint, soon following this with more direct comments to me about my splinting her or bracing her and my providing her arms and legs. There seemed to be a sudden sense of freedom in the hours. At this point she began to spell out in words the precise nature of her problem and how she had come to experience her new-found sense of comfort and freedom. She spoke of being grateful for acquiring new arms and legs, but they were not hers. I was forcing her into becoming somebody else. I was making her into what she called an "identity murderer." It became clear that the comforting experience involved a sense of becoming a self-generating, active agent capable of standing on her own and holding her own, but this was achieved through a fusion experience of becoming identified with the other person, which she also experienced as destroying the other person. She summarized this predicament by stating specifically that she had the key now to the pack but that it was hurting her mother to use it. She called this her "identity strait jacket," which I think included a fusion with the pack as well as with myself. Melinda seemed to be experiencing a transitional sense of being a self-generating, creative, controlling agent, but still requiring external controls to adequately perform containing functions.

PHASE III: TRANSITIONAL PLAY

This ushered in a new phase, lasting about 6 months, in which transitional qualities in our relationship itself were elaborated into a type of playing which gradually evolved between us. The new relatedness which was emerging had qualities of freer, more interactive interchange, but also carried with it a striking curious ambiguity, which Melinda was apparently referring to with her term, "identity strait jacket." She might, for instance, address me as "the child molester--clothes stealer," apparently meaning that she was seeing me as the intrusive, controlling doctor who took away the identity elements she was adapting to sustain herself; but also at times this seemed to refer more to the negative image of herself which she was projecting onto me as a child who was taking from me identity she needed. It also wasn't clear whether she was addressing the pack or me, or ambiguously, all three of us at the same time. My attempts to interpret either from her point of view as a threatened child, or as a counterattacking child, or the ambiguous position itself, all seemed to generate little meaningful response, although it was clear that I was now being heard. Gradually I found myself intuitively wanting to play along with whichever projected role I seemed to be cast into. It is difficult to recall these exchanges because of their spontaneous improvisational nature, but they would go something like this:

"You have my clothes, you have my clothes, clothes stealer, you should be sued, punished, you should be punished."

I would respond, "Yes, I confess, I did it. Punish me. I deserve it. I did it because I was desperate. I couldn't help it, but I did it. Yes, I deserve it, punish me."

Often she would just repeat herself and we would go back and forth, getting increasingly playful. At some point though, Melinda would often pick up the role which I was playing, and then carry it further on her own:

"Yes, you made me take my mother's clothes; I took it, but you made me, forced me into it, you left me with nothing, you forced me to take mother's clothes, your clothes, father's clothes. Help me out of this strait jacket."

Often Melinda and I would play at this with such conviction that it was quite difficult to be certain where the reality was. For instance, when she would say something like, "Give me back my sweater," I would look down and wonder for a brief moment or two if it really were her sweater that I had on.

During this period, as Melinda and I played in this manner with these projective identifications, Melinda began to show increasing calmness and ability to control herself both during and after the hours.

PHASE IV: CONTAINED RELATEDNESS, SHARING OF RESPONSIBILITIES AND SELF-CONTROL

During this phase, lasting approximately one year, the final coming out of the pack was achieved, but not until there was a more complete working through, an introjection and "digestion" or "metabolization" of the transitional relatedness of the projected negative part-object, both in the countertransference and in the transference, until a more fully contained position, approaching whole-object relatedness, was achieved.

As Melinda and I began to feel more comfortable and there seemed to be no longer any obvious threat of assaultiveness, we decided to try having hours with Melinda out of the pack, but this initial attempt proved to be premature and failed, with Melinda very quickly resuming a position of attacking me as a persecutory object. She referred to coming out of the pack as making her feel guilty, "receiving a gold medal to steal--permission to commit identity murder--having to pay for weekend threads and patches." She also spoke of it as losing a stabilizing part of herself, "flying like a bird who suddenly loses his tail."

We then decided to restart Melinda on medication, Thorazine, 500 mgs. a day. Over the next several months there was an increased

calmness and clarity in her thinking. But just at this point I
suddenly and unexpectedly had to leave work for two and a half
months for emergency heart surgery. I was very surprised and gratified to hear reports throughout this time that Melinda was doing
very well, "holding her own," and she had no major outbursts and did
not require any packs.

When we resumed our hours, continuing with Melinda in pack as
before, she greeted me with the same kind of persecutory complaining
tone that she and I had been accustomed to, as if she were picking
up from where we left off in mid-sentence, as it were. This left me
with a very strange feeling that there had been no interruption and
no time had passed. The content of her complaints, however, gave
clear indication that she was well aware of my surgery and my return,
and that it had a very specific meaning to her. In fact, her first
words to me were, "Get the boy with the scar off my chest." She then
focused on complaints about the pack, it being too tight on her
chest, too heavy on her heart, choking her, keeping her from breathing
and then expressing the feeling that I should leave her and let her
out of the pack, as if the two were synonymous. If I did not, I
would die and she, a beggar, a baby, would also die.

Over the next several hours there was a gradual clarification,
through fairly coherent interchanges, that Melinda had established
a sense of stability while I was away by incorporating aspects of
me, particularly masculine qualities, and thus maintaining a sense
of my presence. She confessed this as her "June lie" (my sudden
departure occurring in June), and called this a part of her
philosophy of "can't have one, be one."

Furthermore, we clarified that her seeing me as the persecutor
related to how my return and actual presence caused her to feel
guiltily concerned that I would lay claim to my stolen parts. It
was at the end of one of these hours that I suddenly noticed that
I could now say to the staff with complete impunity, "I'm through
with Melinda now." Melinda's owning up to her role, containing her
projective identificatory processes, if you will, had a liberating
effect on me. But it remained for me to contain my projections onto
her before our relatedness could sustain the degree of sharing
responsibility necessary for Melinda to be seen out of pack.

Melinda would say, for example, that she had "eaten my peas and
spinach--was feeling strong and ready," but she would quickly add
uncertainly, "I still have the illness of needing switchable clothes."
I mistook this as a statement from her saying that we were still in
the same predicament, rather than part of her recognition of her
illness and the needs that go along with it. She became rather
explicit in how she saw her need of me in terms of separate entities,
"we have tea for thee, tea for me, oh how happy we will be." She
often spoke of requiring a separate entity outside herself to have
special claim absorbing power, such as "a special word, a magic word,
a magic key--a charge card." I continued to mistake all this demand
for a magical external solution as part of her disavowal, rather than
a rightful need to have a helping other who could help share the
containment of the negative aspects of the relatedness. To her
credit she would respond quite angrily to my interpretations of

persisting disavowal and let me know of her need for me to start picking up the ball, "No, the pack is your doing and I'm not going to have anything more to do with it." Several times she said, "You do not realize that I have graduated and you are sending me back to nursery school." One time she put the problem quite succinctly, "I have a small parking ticket to pay for and you are telling me that I have to pay for the whole goddamn parking meter."

I finally realized that I was placing an undue burden on her guilt-laden ego when I made a slip one day. I referred to her as I was speaking to an aide by the name of a much healthier borderline patient of mine. This was very striking to me. I was mistaking her identity just as Melinda was beginning to recognize herself as herself. I was being an identity murderer. Gradually I realized she had become too much of an idealized object for me, that I was unfairly expecting too much of her. I was indeed too involved in putting clothes onto her that were not hers, stealing her own clothes. The next hour went something like this:

Silence.

"Could you please loosen those damn restraints?"

"Well, you know, I've been thinking perhaps you don't need them anymore."

"Yes, I don't. I know I don't."

"Well, how should we go about it?" (trying to find a way to engage her in sharing this decision with me).

"Just reach down and see where it's anchored to the siderail of the bed and untie it" (impatiently).

"How do we know you're really ready?" (stubbornly pushing it).

She turns away in disgust and we sit 10 minutes in silence.

Suddenly she turns to me and says rather matter of factly, "I'm hot. Would you mind taking off this top blanket?"

"Sure."

"Oh boy. Whew. That's much better. Thanks."

Then followed another period of silence lasting about 5 minutes which was broken by her starting to wiggle about in the pack, moving one foot against the other. "What's the matter?" I asked.

"My feet are hot. Would you mind taking off my socks?"

"Okay." As I removed her socks I experienced a strange global, intensely sensuous but entirely asexual feeling, which made me think to myself that there probably was a dirty old rapist being contained somewhere in this therapeutic striptease.

"Whew. Thanks. That's much better."

Then followed 3 minutes of silence interrupted by Melinda starting to thrash in the pack again from side to side.

"What's the matter?"

"You know, I'm still pretty hot in here. Would you mind taking off the top sheet?"

"Well, what if I just go ahead and take off the whole damn thing"

"Yeah, oh yeah. Good idea. You do that" (respectfully allowing me credit for the idea). "I'll just lie here."

I do, and she does; we then continue in silence for another 10 minutes, the end of our allotted time. Just as I was about to call time, Melinda said, "Now you've given me a ring on my toe and I guess I passed my physical examination, so maybe I won't need it anymore."

275

"Yes, it's a lousy thing to keep going through. How about if we try next time sitting up in chairs and talking for the hour?"
"Yes. Good idea."

SUMMARY

I have presented the transference-countertransference evolution in the early stages of the work with a severely regressed chronically schizophrenic patient, emphasizing how the work progressed through a regression in which primitive part-object, symbiotic processes evolved from a primitive, totally split-off, uncontrollably destructive process to a more mature relatedness, which then contains the destructive forces. Achievement of the more contained relatedness has been shown to be intimately related to the development in both the therapist and the patient of the "contained" metabolized introjection of the projected, destructive, primitive part-object relatedness. And this has been shown to pass through a "transitional" stage where first the cold wet sheet pack and then the therapist himself serves as a transitional object, a creation of the self, which has elements of the destructive part-object, but also comforts.

I should like to conclude with Melinda's own words in our first hour after coming out of pack, which I think sums up very well in her own new-found level of conceptualization what was, and would continue to be for some time, the essence of her problem: "Every time you come around I seem to get pneumonia" (she had a cold at the time). "But you cure me with warmth."

ACKNOWLEDGEMENTS

1. I am deeply indebted to Dr. Harold Searles, who has supervised the work with this patient, for providing an atmosphere of very stimulating and illuminating discussion.

2. I am also very grateful to my friends and colleagues associated with Chestnut Lodge who have commented on earlier drafts of this paper.

REFERENCES

1. Bion, W.R. (1962): Learning from Experience. Basic Books, New York.
2. Grinberg, L. (1968): Symposium on Acting Out and Its Role in the Psychoanalytical Process. Int. J. Psycho-Anal., 49, 171-178.
3. Langs, R.J. (1976): Bipersonal Field. Aronson, New York.
4. Modell, A.H. (1968): Object Love and Reality. International Universities Press, New York.
5. Searles, H. (1976): Transitional Phenomena and Therapeutic Symbiosis. Int. J. Psycho-Anal. Psychotherapy, 5, 145-204.
6. Winnicott, D.W. (1953): Transitional Objects and Transitional Phenomena. Int. J. Psycho-Anal., 34, 89-97.
7. Wright, R. (1940): Hydrotherapy in Psychiatric Hospitals. Tudor Press, Boston.

ON BEING EARNEST AND BEING RIDICULOUS

A.R. Bodenheimer.

Postgraduate Medical School and Department of Clinical Psychology, University of Tel-Aviv, Ramat-Aviv, Israel

1. SOME TYPICAL SITUATIONS TO BEGIN WITH

Sarah is fourty years old and no one knows, for how long she's been psychotic. Her elder brother had died many years ago in a mental institution, since then her family regard psychiatry as an instrument of death - and it is their right to do so. She would never had met a psychiatrist, had the parents not been old and helpless and had the family not been about to dissolve.

Sarah has been living at home, mostly withdrawn and fitfully aggressive against her frightened parents. Here she sits now, dressed like a clown, smelling unwashed, playing with her fingers and talking to them.

Sarah's family comes from the Middle East and therefore the entire family clan is present in the reception room: father, mother, brothers, sisters, brothers-and-sisters-in-law and their children as well as myself and two coworkers.

Here she sits, addressing her fingertips - nothing and no one else.

What next ?- You may speak to her and ask her some questions. Needless to say, she will not answer but will intensify her smiling attention to her fingertips. You could, of course, speak to one of her relatives. This is what usually happens and convinces Sarah of her nonexistence. You might try throwing an interpretation at her. Most likely nothing will happen again, although I do not want to exclude the possibility of her acting insulted and insulting at the same time. Perhaps something will come of this, but the risk is too great that this might shock her even more brutally than an electric convulsion and thus bring about her further encapsulation. Another alternative would be to gently touch her shoulder. Most likely she will pull back or else check your advance by spitting at you; spitting is to be preferred. At this stage, however, the risk of insulting her bodily integrity is too great. Finally, you might just sit and wait. Most likely you will wait until tomorrow, next year or next decade.

Let us try this possibility at last: Sit and speak to your own fingertips and then to Sarah's. Approach her in the language of her own choosing - and find out what will happen.

Another situation: David strides along the ward with his hair combed low over the left side of his forehead and a tight moustache and a fanatic glance. There is no question of whom he is impersonating.

Are you really expected to raise your arm and shout "Heil Hitler" ?- Already in his days Eugen Bleuler pointed out that the paranoic patient lives in what Bleuler called double bookkeeping. David knows he is not Adolf Hitler. Why ridicule him and yourself by playing along ?

Let me tell you what helped me to cope with this situation: I first told him that he makes me afraid - I did <u>not</u> tell him that this surely had been his intention (because I wanted to avoid to appear as the person who knows everything and is always right).- Later on David and I were able to weigh the question why he needed to be feared in order to be taken seriously.   to

What is the factor common the two situations, catatonic child-like Sarah and frightening paranoic David ? I would like to elaborate on the thesis that both of them, as far as their behavior indicates, try to find a way of coping with their anxiety, more accurately: their specific anxiety towards appearing laughable.

We now leave the two scenes and concentrate on the problem which they pose.

2. THE PROBLEM

The problem of earnestness and ridiculousness confronts us in general with the incompatibility between pairs of opposites. Delusion is not to be considered as the counterpart of reality, to mention one single example. Lie is not the counterpart of truth, or at least not the only one.

As to what concerns being earnest versus being ridiculous, let us study these two concepts: What are the possible relationships between being earnest and being ridiculous ? Let us first examine the question according to principles of arithmetic:

I can be earnest and be taken earnest by you.
I can be earnest and be ridiculed by you.
I can laugh and you can laugh with me.
I can laugh and you can laugh at me.
I can laugh and be taken in earnest by you.
I can be ridiculous and be ridiculed by you.
I can be ridiculous and be taken in earnest by you.

This is the place where an arithmetic problem is replaced by a human one:

To laugh is not the same as to ridicule.
To laugh is not the same as to be ridiculed.

But: Whe I laugh and you laugh, it is not yet clear whether you laugh with me on the subject which made me laugh — whether or not it makes you laugh — or whether you laugh because I am ridiculous. Your reaction leaves that open. When I am earnest and you laugh, who is ridiculous ? What is ridiculous ?- If I feel ridiculous, I can make you laugh by telling a joke. So you laugh. I have succeeded in mani-pulating the situation by means of anticipation, i.e. by preventing you from laughing at me and diverting your laughter to the joke and away from myself.- Does this ring a bell in the ears of psychothera-pists ?

Let us now leave aside the situation of the clown who has been made all too familiar by Karl Valentin, Picasso, Miller and Boell, all of whom have been moved by the discord between the attainable goal — of making people laugh — and his own deprivation, after the laughter has died down. Sarah speaking to her fingers and David acting as Hitler are both inverting the scene of clowning by making clowns of others, doctors included. In order not to be laughed at, they put us into the position of ridicule: Sarah by leaving us alone without an answer, David by causing us to shout "Heil Hitler". The difference is not all too big. What concerns the purpose, it remains the same.

Looked at from this point of view the problem is threefold:

a: You can leave the patient ridiculous and spare yourself. So you are out of things and your patient remains lost and lonely.

b: You can accept the offer by falling into the trap of being ridiculed by your patient — the gap will remain.

c: You take your patient earnestly, even if he is accustomed to ridiculing himself.

This third possibility brings you close to your patient, but you risk to be ridiculed by the outside world. This however is the gateway to Sarah and David: being earnest in the face of a behavior, that tempts to shut yourself off from the patient by laughing and taking the risk of appearing ridiculous in the eyes of the outside world.

Being earnest in spite of the laughter from outside on condition that the patient feels taken in earnest — this is the simple and very unheroic path of the psychotherapist with his psychotic patient.

I maintain that this concept is one approach, perhaps among others, towards an understanding of the loneliness in psychosis and a way to overcome it.

3. ON BEING WRONG AND BEING RIGHT

What has been claimed until now, needs to be specified in a more meaningful direction:

Being earnest refers to the person, not to the thing he represents.

Being ridiculous refers to the person, not to the situation.—

I would like to explain this in David's behavior: It would neither make sense nor be of any help if I would make his convictions my own. Participation and partisanship are not identical. What is required here is participation. Partisanship will not contribute.

Let us leave Sarah and David for a short moment and mention another example of a psychotic patient: Vincent van Gogh was lucky enough to have two persons close to him, his brother Théo as well as a doctor called Gachet. Théo entered a state which is at least near to what we call Folie-à-deux and ended up by following his elder brother in death only one year after Vincent's suicide. As for Dr. Gachet, he was the first to appreciate his patient's art. In many ways he proved himself as a partisan of van Gogh. Partisanship goes as far as that:

> "Today I saw Dr. Gachet again and I am going to paint at his house on Tuesday morning, then I shall dine with him and afterwards he will come to look at my painting. He seems very sensible, but he is discouraged about his job as a country doctor as I am about my painting. Then I said to him that I would gladly exchange job for job..."
> (letter, written by Vincent van Gogh to his brother and sister-in-law from Auvers-sur-Oise, May 1890).

Dr. Gachet shows partisanship in many ways. This is what prevented him from participating in his patient's life. Telling his patient about his own dicouragement leads towards an inversion of rôles. On the other hand Dr. Gachet's highest appreciation — and even admiration — of van Gogh which finally rose to a state of idolatry, was unfavorable to a mutual participation. He received Vincent's unique expression but failed to notice in it a personal address (more than a superpersonal testimony) which demanded <u>reply</u>*. Therefore neither of these two persons, both of whom have been so close to van Gogh, were able to prevent the fatal end.

We now return to David: His convictions are not my concern for the time being. I am not yet competent to decide whether he is right and he is not the least bit interested in my opinion. It is for me to bring him back to himself and to the question of whether ha can afford to think and act as he does and of what use his behavior is to him. Neither more nor less than that.

The question of methodology is only how this is best to be achieved and where the problems and dangers lie. It would be of no help, if I would claim that David from his point-of-view is right; he does not want to know what my opinion is in that respect. If, on the other hand, I would let him know that I feel he is wrong – what would come out of that ?

Every kind of interpretation confronts us with this problem, whatever be the interpretation. Therefore we avoid any kind of interpretation and restrict ourselves to answering, as described before.

4: DANGERS TO BE AVOIDED IN THE ANSWERING ATTITUDE

Were I not certain of addressing an audience of experienced psychotherapists, I would hesitate to develop this topic.

When I sit facing Sarah playing with my fingers and then with hers, all that in the presence of her family and my coworkers, taking the risk of being ridiculous, I have to be convinced that I am to some extent in control of:

a: <u>the play drive</u>. Once more: behaving as Sarah does is not to play but to mirror her, even in a distorting mirror, in order to enable her to answer me after she discovers I speak her nonverbal language;

b: <u>the power drive</u>: David behaved like Hitler in order to avoid being manipulated. If we assume that I am to find a common language with him, the intention cannot be for me to convince him of my convictions, but to overcome this confrontative situation at its whole;

c: <u>the aggression drive</u>: there are other situations not described here such as spitting back after having been spat upon. Here the danger exists that answering on equal terms will turn to aggressive behavior. It may be that my patient's spitting was meant to be aggressive – my spitting back, however, must be free from aggression. In this way my patient's spitting can lose its aggressivity and eventually turn into words;

d: <u>the sexual drive</u> which, in a way, results out of the aforementioned drives.– Enough has been written about the problem of getting on with the sexual drive in psychotherapy. So we need not to describe it in full account.

*Further details regarding the differentiation between address and reply on the one hand and expression and interprtation on the other as well as the problem of being right or wrong in psychotherapy may be found in the author's book "Verstehen heisst Antworten" which is presently in print at Schwabe & Co., Publishers, Basle, Switzerland.

5. WHAT IS LAUGHABLE WHEN YOU LAUGH ?- WHO IS RIDICULOUS WHEN YOU LAUGH ?

Is Sarah ridiculous ? Or is Sarah's behavior laughable ?- I do not
know. I am earnest in her presence. Therefore I play with my fingers
and thereupon with hers and I do so for two reasons:
a: I want Sarah to perceive that she is not alone in her way of
behaving. I would like her to feel that playing with one's fingers
can be regarded as a way of speaking, even if it does not conform to
everyday behavior;
b: I want to come to an understanding of what a person feels about
when he plays with his fingers and speaks to them. How else could I
experience such a feeling than doing the same thing and behaving the
same way as Sarah does ?
     But I never laugh, or even smile, in presence of Sarah, follow-
ing Bergson's contemplation of laughter: "We laugh every time when a
person appears as if he were an object". All our intentions concerning Sarah may be expressed in one single sentence: to make a subject
out of an object.-
     Is David ridiculous ? As diabolic as it appears, the importance
to conceive what is going on, justifies to cite David's sinister model
who once admitted: "For a long time they all laughed at me — now the
laughter got stuck in their throats". I am sure every kind of explanation or interpretation would produce the same effect upon David. It
has not been possible but at a much later date that David confessed :
"I wanted to make people afraid — so I felt you were the person who
was in earnest with me". Let us remember the Roman Emperor Caligula's
saying: "Sicut oderint" — Be it that they hate me as long as they are
afraid of me !

     The basic problem is: Laughter does not make a difference
between laughing with... and laughing at...
     Jokes, in general, tend to overcome the gap between these two
possible intentions of laughing by very brutal means in that they are
told only about people who are absent — dead or alive but actually
placed somewhere else. So the persons in question are not able to
laugh with you anyhow and as a result get automatically laughed at.
That is the perfidy of cracking jokes.
     Should you, however, make a joke in presence of the person to
whom it refers, that person is being dealt with as if he were absent
— the result being, that person is absent.
     But the technique of joking is capable to achieve even more:
When you joke and laugh together on whatever subject or person with
the very exception of one single person who remains earnest for whatever reason (may be he did not understand the point or he is deaf or
things appear to be too serious to be laughed at), that one is totally
falling out of the group — he is absent, even dead, as much as he may
still be present materially.-
     That is the situation felt by a psychotic patient — and even
felt much better than by healthy people in their unsensitive rudeness.
     So the behavior of a psychotic patient appears somewhat differ-
ent, that is to say it appears very adequate to some unconscious intentions of joking that have been fundamentally elucidated by Freud.
     If we take that technique and intention of joking into consider-
ation, it will help us to accept the fact that he is neither ready nor

willing to differentiate between your laughing with him and laughing at him.

On this occasion we ought to remember that a schizophrenic person does not laugh at a joke, as upsetting good as it might be, and not even when he told the joke by himself. A schizophrenic person can tell you a story full of jokes, he will get angry with you when you laugh.

The laughter of a schizophrenic person, on the other hand, has two meanings that differ fundamentally from the laughter which follows joking. A schizophrenic person laughs:

a: to make you laughable at a situation when any opportunity to contact you is eliminated. So the excluded one excludes you from his mind by ridiculing you;

b: to bring a situation towards the state of explosion when there are no words left to verbalize what is to be said.

Both those reasons for laughter include one mutual meaning which is this:

Better not to be than to appear ridiculous.

6. "ALL YOU NEED IS LOVE"

Society, including psychotherapists, seems to be in need of a person who, like a Shakespearian clown, plays the rôle of the ridiculous.

For a long time psychotic patients have been ridiculed by the public. During the last three decades the needle of the balance has continuously switched from schizophrenic patients towards their parents. I think, there is no need to point out that ridiculing does not exclude a cryptic anxiety.

It is quite obvious what is the motivation behind that tendency to ridicule the parents of schizophrenic patients:

a: partisanship instead of participation leads to identification with the person as a representative of our convictions;

b: "the weak one has to be protected against strength or even violence". The insecurity – or even anxiety – of parents is regarded as primordial aggressivity;

c: the desire of the therapist to be loved by his patient forms the image of a common enemy. Who could be regarded as more dangerous an enemy than parents ?

I refer only to my coworkers' experience as well as my own by saying that we never succeeded in a lasting recovery of psychotic patients when we were not able to build up a good and very close relationship with the parents of our patients. We are aware that this is not always possible to achieve, but I would like to leave the question open who is to be blamed for that failure.

Moreover it seems more important to me that the psychotherapist take his patient in earnest (in the way described beforehand) than to pretend that he loves him.

Taking our patients in earnest is at times more difficult, because the situation may require from us that we follow him towards a constellation in which both of us appear laughable or even ridiculous. It is more difficult, because it requires more of a commitment from our side.–

Thy shalt love Thy Neighbor as Thyself – this single and simple sentence necessitated an Old as well as a New Testament for its

282

explanation and we still do not know what it means and how to realize it. Will the psychotherapist succeed in what Moses and Jesus could only try to achieve ?

One last remark to end with: So much has been said about the isolation of the psychotic personality and how to overcome it. One of the most gruesome forms of isolation, if not the most gruesome, is that of being ridiculed. It is therefore worthy of our special attention.

SUMMARY

The problem of the ridiculous and the earnest is discussed, especially in the aspect of confronting the ridiculous. The therapist who undertakes to be earnest together with his patient, as ridiculous as the therapist's behavior might appear, will have found a way to overcome the isolation in which the psychotic person lives.

The meaning of earnestness and a kind of a "methodology" — the Answering Behavior — are described.

REFERENCES

1. Benedetti, G. (1976): Der Geisteskranke als Mitmensch. Vandenhoeck & Ruprecht, Göttingen.
2. Bergson, H. (1900, trad. 1914): Das Lachen. Diederichs, Jena.
3. Bleuler, E. (1911): Dementia Praecox oder Gruppe der Schizophrenien. Deuticke, Leipzig und Wien.
4. Bodenheimer, A.R. (1978, in print): Die drei Phasen der schizophrenen Psychose und ihre phasenspezifische Psychotherapie. Schweiz. Arch. Neurol., Neurochir., Psychiatrie.
5. Darwin, Ch. (1872): The Expression of Emotions in Man and Animal. London.
6. Freud, S. (1905): Der Witz und seine Beziehung zum Unbewussten. Imago, Vol. VI, London.
7. van Gogh, V. (1890, ed. 1963): Letters. Ed. M. Roskill. Fontana/Collins, Glasgow.

OUR KNOWLEDGE OF SCHIZOPHRENIC THINKING.
A CHALLENGE AND A RESPONSIBILITY

Torsten Herner, M.D.

Stockholm, Sweden

My attempts, both oral and written, to present two
fundamental psychological phenomena, revealed during
psychotherapy with a chronic schizophrenic, have been
submitted in the course of over 20 years to an overwhelmingly sceptical audience. In the first of these
phenomena the patient perceives his body as a mirror i-
mage of the union of his parents. This signifies a split
body image. It is then feasible to interpret the body's
sagittal plane as the bond of union between these two
halves, which correspond per se to the parental figures.
The second phenomenon implies that the patient's "I" can
be reflected in a "Thou" solely in a "face to face" or
"eye to eye" situation. The two phenomena have certain
attributes in common; they represent concepts of the patient's own body, which thereby appears with both its
twin and its reflection. The importance of these two
phenomena, however, does not consist solely in their potential for interpretation as characteristic of schizophrenic thought, and confirmation thereby of the percep-
tiveness of Eugen Bleuler's designation of the disease.
For if we recall that the phenomena described in schizophrenic patients as symptoms can also be interpreted as
regressive experiences and modes of behaviour down to
levels of the time immemorial of the individual, we
shall perhaps realise that we here discern an attribute
common to all mankind - although wholly beyond the grasp
of human memory and reasoning. Under such circumstances,
this must be the object of completely different interest.

Indeed it is possible to conceive of the two phenomena as fundamental for our mental functions, perhaps
primarily for orientation and reasoning. The first basic
phenomenon is attributed to the neonatal period, and the
second to the moment early in suckling when the infant,
in his very first "I-Thou" situation, suddenly perceives
himself as a being separate from its mother.

Another circumstance which must be adjudged a challenge is that these two con epts, and all the ideas associated with them through th years, derive from my
work with a single individual; furthermore, from the only chronic schizophrenic patient who underwent an at-

285

tempt at really serious psychotherapy. Therefore it
would be hardly surprising that this theory were rejected as sheer speculation.

'Nevertheless there were reasons why I persisted in
these cogitations. One was the irresistible quality of
these ideas. For they simply could not be refuted, despite my own scepticism on their emergence.

Another reason is the bond between these ideas and
the circumstances in which they appeared. For the therapy with the said patient was begun at a very active stage in my own development. This took the form of, _inter
alia_, unbeliavle brief psychotherapeutic sessions with
neurotic patients, where the results, which unfortunately could seldom be followed up, nevertheless proved to
be astoundingly good.

My theory was buttressed by a third bulwark, namely
extensive literary studies throughout many years. These
could not, however, be confined to psychiatry and psychology, since there proved to be limited scope for such
a study. Here it was necessary to transcend the limitations, and search out other fields of research into human nature and the human situation - problems which were
observed and treated long before the emergence of psychiatry or psychology as we know them today. Within these bounds, however, examples have accumulated of parallel observations and theories. It is appropriate to mention some of the major authors; the two philosophers,
Hegel and Cassirer, Bachofen, Buber and Eliade, who studied mythology and religion, the cultural anthropolo-
gists Hertz, Baumann and Lévi-Strauss, the linguists von
Humboldt and Roman Jakobson, but also the psychiatrist
Rothschild and the psychologist Seymour Fisher. The
most interesting material is derived from Baumann, Lévi-
Strauss and Cassirer, and from many of the works quoted
by the latter in his _Philosophy of Symbolic Forms_.

The purpose of my lecture is not to present schizophrenic thinking as such, but merely a fraction of an
wholly unknown quantity. The two basic phenomena, comprising this fraction, provide a distillate of schizophrenic reasoning. This distillate represents the basis
of a completely new mode of thought. The word "new" must
be applied with caution, for our interest lies not in
new theories but in the rediscovery of a forgotten knowledge, which has never yet been recognized in psychiatry. Only during the last three years could the value of
this new reasoning be appreciated. This work produced
excellent results with surprising speed, during the
plumbing of the personality which is an integral part of
all insight therapy. I therefore intend to devote a
forthcoming book to my approach in such therapy. This
will involve detailed reports on the course of a neurosis, a borderline state, and a sexually abnormal patient. This lecture does not allow of so explicit an account.

The lecturer's status as an outsider, with no affinities to any school, also represents a challenge. My personality evolved within the framework of Nicolai Berdyaev's Christian freedom philosophy, which overwhelmed me at the age of 46; its onset resembled an avalanche, which had immediate repercussions on my work as a psychiatrist. Perhaps my very alien status incited me to attempt the administration of a corpus of knowledge which, despite its seeming implausibility, yet could be perceived as the infrastructure of human phenomena, both normal and abnormal. But these ideas long withheld their fruit.

During this period I had no little difficulty in handling the internal and external disruptions, which must be manifest for the advocate in spe of a theory which in our best interests should be rejected out of hand. For if it is indeed true that - for reasons which will not be discussed here - schizophrenics by bizarre and bewildering means present concepts which are characteristic of the very first stages of human development, then it must be humilating in the extreme for an adult to revert to levels of immaturity which he has left far behind, consigned to the dark abyss of oblivion. Thus it goes without saying that our defence mechanisms are mobilized against such a reactionary theory.

My approach to therapy has been likened to a reflection encompassing all levels of development for both parties. This process can only gather impetus, however, if the therapist can penetrate the very deepest layers of his own unconscious. At the start of this mutual reflection the patient wishes to remain on the surface but gradually - at first punctually - touches the once unconscious levels of his mind. The attributes which the patient there discovers would be terrifying unless already recognized by the therapist.

Furthermore, such an approach involves a mutuality also in the dialogue which prompts the therapist's active participation in interpretation, and also allows him openly to report his own experiences and values at the moments when he considers them to promote the therapy. The therapy embraces critical scrutiny of the patient in his/her relationship with both parents. Thus it concentrates on the patient's imagination as articulated in dreams, day dreams and delusions. There the patient is enabled to face his parents once more in all the levels in which he was the focus of their interest and protection in his childhood. Thus his perception is concentrated throughout on the patient's bodily reality, and the bond with the bodies of the two individuals who were, and still are, essential for his physical existence. The work on these confrontations promotes the articulation of the very relationship which, in the indivual's earlier development, led not to liberation but to entrapment by guilt or compulsion. Here the oedipal problem is reiterated, in both its heterosexual and its inverted (homosexual) form, but also much earlier relationships, such as suckling, face to face and eye to eye encounters, and occationally birth.

An attempt as abstract description of the interaction between the various processes triggered by such therapy could start from the similarities and differences already inherent in the very phenomenon of reflection. In this phenomenon, and in the duality thereby implied, are contained the prerequisites for a dialectic approach. The similarities which emerge during the reflection are simultaneously apparent and real. The same is true of the differences which condition the reflection. For the differences signify the imminence of a conflict, in other words a thesis/antithesis constellation, which may become accessible to dialectic processing in a mode of constructive value for the patient. The patient who is in no wise prepared therefor is astonished, but fascinated by the unusual features of the situation. In the therapist's interpretations of the material proffered by the patient the demonstration of contrary phenomena carries great weight. Many of the tenets which the patient previously regarded as self-evident are placed in question, first by the therapist but later by the patient himself. In the final phase of therapy the patient may see himself as being in a previously wholly alien situation of inner lability - although constantly in its dialectic opposite, namely a sense of security based on the unreserved trust in the therapist. This trust is essential if the patient is to be prepared to surrender so much of all he once perceived as a support - but also to enable him with a feeling of freedom to hearken to the synthetic processes which appear within himself as expressions of rearrangement of the depths of his personality, and thus the beginning of a true emancipation.

It is important especially in this closing phase to pay attention to fleeting bodily sensations, which are reported by the patient. Such experiences are apt to provoke the patient's disquiet, while the therapist's reaction is the direct opposite. The therapist interprets stomach ache, nausea, vertigo, headache etc. as reactions from the patient's body image indicative of shifts toward increasing integration. The security, not to say joy, at such comments which the therapist displays, and the allegorical explanations he can offer have a calming influence on the patient.

The patient may derive considerable benefit if the therapist is capable not only of describing specific situations in the abstract, but also of explaining the material offered by the patient in concrete terms. When articulating the patient's own comments the therapist can indict the patient for his choise of words, in order to demonstrate the more profound, purely etymological significance - unbeknown to the patient - of an expression, and sometimes even associate this with the patient's own body image. Nevertheless the capacity thus to alternate between abstract and concrete in the treatment of the patient's material would seem dependent on the therapist's awareness that the human body may be regarded, although not solely, as a symbol. He must also perceive that the concepts associated with the body image provide the condition for human orientation in time and space, and for the achievement of allegorical and dialectic reasoning.

This approach to another human being imposes a heavy burden on the therapist. The total concentration - as here - on the body involves serious risks. A maximal contact must therefore be balanced by absolute detachment. Neither party's physical integrity may be violated in any respect. On the psychic level, however, the therapist is mercilessly exposed, a fact which presumably accelerated our mutual communication. The patient's work on his own and his parent's body images also modifies his demands on the therapist; consequently the problem of transfer receded so far as the therapist is concerned. Nevertheless, in these cases it was surprising to witness the vital significance of the patient's idea of his parent's body images. Thus the foot fetishism of a male patient vanished once his former conception of his mother as a neuter creature was replaced by an awareness of her femininity.

Yet the heaviest load of responsibility for the therapist is the following truth. He manipulates the spiritual depths of another human being, using his knowledge of schizophrenia. This presumably involves grave risks, although I found no evidence thereof. Yet in the actual breakthrough a 35-year-old woman treated for three days (10 hours altogether) in August 1978 expostulated: "But this is duality of personality!" The reply was: "Yes, but in the service of health". Nevertheless, the treatment with this duality of personality is a very serious matter. It may be likened to the tampering with atomic fission which has petrified mankind since autumn 1945.

At first it was by no means self-evident that this approach could be repeted. To my astonishment, however, not only did it prove possible, but the approach could be applied to different forms of mental distress. This model has won a foothold in Sweden. Various colleagues have reported favourable results from emulating my approach with their own patients.

This lecture makes no claim to explain schizophrenia. On the other hand, it implies consent to those who perceive a prophetic aspect in schizophrenics. For the sufferer can not only teach us the approach outlined above. The disease also involves a concept of the society which contravenes many current prejudices. The putative discernment of a long-forgotten truth imposes a heavy responsibility. My theories accentuate both the central significance of sexual identity for the development of personality, and the concomitant, incontrovertible value of <u>both</u> parents for the individual's normal growth. New light is shed on the importance of the family in an age in which its value is questioned. The battle <u>between</u> the sexes, which is now fought on so many fronts, loses all meaning when reduced to the natural tension prevailing between the parental figures <u>within</u> the individual. At the same time, both parents are assigned absolute equality by virtue of their shared likeness and difference.

Thus we may apply to the schizophrenic the words of Psalm 117/118:

> "The stone which the builders rejected
> has become the head of the corner.
> This is the LORD's doing;
> it is marvellous in our eyes."

TOWARDS COMPREHENSIVE TREATMENT OF CHRONIC SCHIZOPHRENIC PATIENTS

John S. Strauss, John P. Docherty, William H. Sledge, and
T. Wayne Downey

Yale Psychiatric Institute, Department of Psychiatry, Yale
University School of Medicine, New Haven, CT

Psychiatry lacks a theoretical foundation for organizing the comprehensive treatment of chronic schizophrenic patients. The need for developing such a foundation derives from several sources: the diversity of current theories about schizophrenia; the multiplicity of treatment interventions available; the many institutions or settings within which treatment can be carried out; and the wide range of mental health and related disciplines working with such patients. Clearly some approach is required for choosing among or even combining the various treatment orientations available. To this end, a sound conceptual basis can help ensure that the individual patient receives optimal care. This report will develop three ideas to help construct such a foundation.

The multiplicity of theories for understanding schizophrenia is striking. These include biological, behavioral, cognitive-developmental, social and psychodynamic orientations. Each of these represents a particular approach to the use of evidence and its interpretation, and a particular way of thinking about psychopathology generally and schizophrenia in particular.

There is also a large number of methods for treating schizophrenia. Within the psychosocial sphere, individual psychotherapy, family psychotherapy, occupational therapy, and a variety of other treatment approaches including graded living programs and social skills training are available (1). Additionally, there are powerful biological modes for treating schizophrenic patients. The increase in the number of available treatment modalities, while providing valuable additions to the therapeutic armamentarium, may also confuse the treatment picture and, on inspection, demonstrate how limited our information is regarding the particular effectiveness of various treatments and how to select and integrate them.

Our basic assumption in developing a strategy for organizing a comprehensive approach to understanding, evaluating, and treating chronic schizophrenic patients is that often no single current theory or treatment method is sufficient. Rather, we assume that several approaches may have specific but overlapping usefulness in dealing with the conflicts, skill deficits, and apparent problems with perceptual and cognitive functioning that these patients often have.

But what concepts or constructs can be employed to facilitate recognition of the specific usefulness of each of the multiple theories and treatments? One approach is to retreat somewhat from theory to more of an observational perspective. A "neodescriptive"

291

approach can be defined to provide an improved structure for thinking about the complex issues involved. Such an approach is descriptive in that it involves attending to a wide range of observable phenomena. It is "neodescriptive" in its focus on reliability of observation to ensure that various observers are observing and noting the same events, and its use of statistical procedures for grouping and analyzing the information collected. By combining these elements, a neodescriptive approach can use observation to suggest patterns of pathology and treatment response. It is important that such an approach not end only in counting and classifying as with some descriptive orientations, but that it imply underlying psychobiological structures and suggest optimal types of intervention.

Beyond the neodescriptive orientation, a second concept in this proposed structure is the hypothesis that treatment interventions, such as group, family, and individual psychotherapy and psychotropic medications, as well as the various activities therapies and vocational training, seem to involve three distinguishable components: a motivational-value-conflict orientation dealing with affect, subjective experience, and internal psychological issues, a stimulus management component, and a skills orientation focusing more on competence factors.

The third aspect of the proposed structure involves the careful articulation of the causal model employed to understand illness and develop a treatment plan.

THREE COMPONENTS FOR A THEORETICAL STRUCTURE

I. NEODESCRIPTIVE APPROACH

Two recent developments in descriptive psychiatry, data suggesting the multidimensional nature of manifest behavior and findings suggesting the existence of several discrete and hierarchically-related states of consciousness in schizophrenic patients, are important for organizing understanding and treatment of these patients. The common element of both these developments is the recognition of a differentiation in the patient which may relate to the multiplicity of theory and treatment.

A. Manifest Behavior: Multiple Dimensions of Function

The importance of a multidimensional orientation for assessment, formulation, and treatment has been demonstrated from many sources. In a series of studies carried out as a part of the International Pilot Study of Schizophrenia (IPSS), for example, data strongly supported the multidimensional nature of course of disorder. In that study, performed under the auspices of the World Health Organization, the National Institute of Mental Health, and the nine participating centers, a sub-study was undertaken in the Washington Center involving a detailed analysis of certain diagnostic and prognostic characteristics in schizophrenia (2).

Findings from this sub-study showed: 1) That cross-sectional symptom diagnosis, no matter what system was used, was relatively limited in predicting outcome. This suggested that a concept of a symptom-defined disorder predicting the totality of outcome function was of limited validity. 2) Rather than outcome having a single entity, it was found actually to be constituted of several semi-independent functions. These included duration of hospitalization during the follow-up period, social relations functioning, severity of symptoms, and occupational functioning. Although these various measures correlated with each other to a limited extent, they were largely independent. Thus, for example, many patients with severe symptoms had adequate work functioning. Of all of the outcome measures, duration of hospitalization in the year prior to follow-up interview was the least related to the other measures. 3) That there were several predictors of the various outcome measures. These predictors included previous level of social relations function, previous duration of hospitalization, and previous level of occupational function. 4) That there was a striking correspondence between predictor and outcome measures. Each of the predictors (e.g., occupational function) had its closest relationship to the corresponding outcome function (e.g., occupational function). There was also some cross-over, however, in that, for example, level of occupational function also predicted follow-up level of symptom severity to some degree.

Based on these findings, it was suggested that there are four basic predictor-outcome dimensions or axes: symptoms, course, social relations, and occupational function. It was hypothesized that each of these axes represents a system, a certain area of function with some specific etiologies and factors that relate to its course and treatment. At the same time, these various "systems" are open and linked in that they have significant interactions.

The existence of the four systems was demonstrated even more impressively at the five-year follow-up in which it was found that the two-year follow-up results were highly significant predictors of their corresponding five-year functions. Since then, these findings which are compatible with other studies which have looked at one or another of the characteristics have also been found to exist in non-schizophrenic patients with psychiatric disorder severe enough to require hospitalization (3). They have also been found in schizophrenics and non-schizophrenics in other cultures, for example, in a separate study carried out in Taiwan (4).

Based on these findings, it has been suggested that in a wide range of severe psychopathology, semi-independent systems of function exist that must be considered as basic components in pathological, recovery, and treatment processes. It is assumed that these systems probably are bio-psycho-social in nature, having etiologies at a genetic level and from early environmental experience, as well as from more recent precipitating situations. For example, social relations functioning may relate to genetic tendencies that involve perceptual sensitivity to stimuli associated with early relationships to parents, and to more recent relationships with family and peers. Social relations are also probably strongly affected by social class and subcultural membership. Although in this sense social relations probably represents a system in itself, it is also open in relation to the other systems, being influenced by occupational functioning, symptoms, and those characteristics determining hospitalization.

B. States of Consciousness: Stages of Decompensation and Recompensation

Besides the multidimensional approach to viewing schizophrenia, a longitudinal approach noting the evolution of disorder is also essential. The work of Manfred Bleuler (5), for example, has shown in detail how varied the vicissitudes of schizophrenia are over an extended period of time. More recently, Docherty, et al. (6), have reviewed studies of short-term evolution of schizophrenia and conducted further studies on this topic. From this work, it was suggested that the process of decompensation and recovery from psychosis is marked by the following stages: 1) Equilibrium, a phase during which the individual is in relatively free and untroubled functioning within himself and in relation to his environment; 2) Overextension, in which the person often feels overwhelmed, irritable, and unable to keep up with environmental happenings; 3) Restricted consciousness, a stage during which withdrawal and depression are particularly marked; 4) Disinhibition, a phase in which beginning loss of connection with reality is noted, including such phenomena as depersonalization and derealization, and in which impulsive behavior, sometimes of a hypomanic nature, occurs; 5) Psychotic disorganization, a stage in which there is gross loss of touch with reality, including such symptoms as hallucinations, delusions, and bizarre disorganized behavior. 6) A sixth stage has also been identified, psychotic resolution, in which disorganization diminishes, but systematic delusions and hallucinations are established. Docherty, et al., described several instances of the progression of these phases, for example, one case in which a 31-year-old patient with a ten-year history of schizophrenic disorder decompensated during a period of hospitalization. Nurses' notes described the evolution of her disorder in a way that showed a striking adherence to these sequential phases (6).

It has been suggested that each of these stages represents a distinct state of consciousness which has a specific and unique organization. For example, if these states are viewed in terms of their adaptive significance in Restricted Consciousness there is an effort to narrow the range of consciousness and restrict the scope of experienced mental content. Thus, depression with its slowing of thought and preoccupation with nagging doubts or worries is a paradigmatic form of restricted consciousness. In Psychotic Disorganization there is an effort to cope with an insoluble problem by dissolving the organization of consciousness which permits recognition of that problem.

Taken together, the multidimensional and longitudinal studies of behavior and states of consciousness in the area of descriptive psychiatry bring into relief a third aspect of function: underlying psychological processes and structures, such as level of object relations and self-object differentiation, which are not directly observed or reported but inferred from data such as projective test responses. Some instruments for comprehensive assessment of this level of psychological function exist, and it will be interesting to interpret their results in terms of manifest behaviors and states of organization described above.

294

II. PSYCHOEDUCATIONAL TREATMENT

Treatment approaches to schizophrenic disorders can be characterized by the relative emphasis given to three components. One component involves impact on problems of meaning, another involves dealing with behavior, and the third involves stimulus management.

The importance of several components to treatment highlights the crucial role of the nature of evidence admitted by different orientations and the importance of not systematically excluding an entire perspective. Some schools of thinking about schizophrenia tend to focus almost entirely on behaviors and skills, others focus equally exclusively on subjective experience, inferred internal structures, or psychodynamics, while still others focus almost exclusively on stimulus overload or deprivation. It seems to us that any of these orientations in itself is incomplete, and that the whole range of available data is important. This includes behaviors and competence, as for example noted in general observations or specialized assessment of skills, information on underlying processes that may be available from psychotherapeutic and projective test sources, and data on abnormal stimulus receptivity or response. A psychoeducational approach to treatment can incorporate all three components, focusing on behavior, meaning, and stimulus management. Although there is no strict one-to-one correspondence between specific treatment modalities and problem areas, treatments can be prescribed to cover the major areas. Thus, for example, antipsychotic medication might be used to help reduce stimulus and response sensitivity. Social skills training might be provided to teach basic modes of interpersonal behavior around dating or employment that severely disturbed patients may never have acquired. And individual psychotherapy might be provided both to serve as a medium for acquiring close interpersonal ties and to help the patient develop a cognitive-affective structure for integrating past and present conflicts, demands, and goals.

III. MODELS OF CAUSALITY

The third aspect of the comprehensive approach to treatment is a complex view of causality (7). One common orientation to thinking causally regarding schizophrenia and its course is a linear view, as in "the patient was admitted to the hospital and improved on chlorpromazine." The implication of this view is the assumption that chlorpromazine caused the improvement in the patient's condition. It ignores such factors as the patient's perhaps having left a difficult environmental situation, or the possible therapeutic value of the hospital milieu.

A somewhat more complex causal model is the interactive one, in which several factors, operating at different levels (e g., biological, psychological, and socio-cultural) act together to influence the course of disorder. The third and most complex causal model is the transactional model. This orientation suggests that there are feedback loops by which various aspects of a system influence each other. For example, the safe environment of the hospital may lead to diminished fear and interpersonal defensiveness which might then enhance the ability to relate to others, leading to a reduction of symptoms. This symptom reduction may in turn further facilitate the ability to relate to others. Although by far the most difficult orientation to study systematically, it is our belief that the transactional model is probably the most accurate causal view of processes in schizophrenia and other functional psychiatric disorders. Of course, if a single cause for schizophrenia that was both necessary and sufficient were discovered, or a single treatment that was sufficient were found, our hypothesis would be demonstrated as incorrect or at least of not much practical value.

The importance of assumptions - often implicit - about causal models arises frequently in clinical practice and research. For example, in one case conference about a schizophrenic adolescent, it began to appear that a choice needed to be made between the views of developmental contributions emphasized by the psychoanalyst discussant and the biologic emphasis of a staff member. Clearly such a choice would be necessary only if one assumed a simple linear causal model rather than an interactive or transactional orientation. To fit our assumption about the complex nature of causality in schizophrenia, two questions, not one, regarding causality are crucial: 1) What factors affect a disorder, and 2) How do they interact.

IMPLICATIONS OF THE THREE CONCEPTS FOR COMPREHENSIVE TREATMENT OF SCHIZOPHRENIA

The following guidelines for facilitating optimal comprehensive treatment of the individual schizophrenic patient are suggested by the three concepts we have discussed:

1. Evaluation must be systematic and extensive. The multidimensional perspective of manifest behavior clearly reveals that assessment of one area - such as symptoms - can not be generalized to other areas, such as social function or need for hospitalization. Each dimension must be individually assessed.

2. Evaluation must be an on-going process. The studies of decompensation and recompensation highlight the often profound and fluid shifts in level of organization which characterizes schizophrenic patients.

3. Current disturbance in manifest behavior or state should be cross-hatched with the multiaxial framework for understanding schizophrenia in order to generate a truly comprehensive dynamic formulation.

4. Thought should be given to the range of impact of a selected therapy on each of the major dimensions of manifest behavior. Some therapies have a narrow focus - for example, the behavior therapy of phobia is almost entirely limited to the symptom axis. Individual psychotherapy may directly address both symptoms and social function.

5. In terms of the phasic aspect of psychiatric disorder, treatments would need to be evaluated in relation to their likely impact on the specific phase of psychological organization currently characterizing the patient. Thus, for example, psychotropic medications might be useful during a phase of psychotic disorganization, but not during a phase of restricted consciousness. Interpersonal closeness occurring in psychotherapy might have to be studied and adjusted for one phase in contrast to another.

One useful concept in considering phase-specific differences in treatment is a stabilizing/destabilizing parameter. In some phases of disorder, a destabilizing influence might be necessary to encourage patients to leave fixed but maladaptive types of organization such as in a phase of psychotic resolution. In other phases, such as disinhibition, a stabilizing orientation to treatment might be optimal to prevent more disorganization. Various treatment modalities or their variations would need to be classified in terms of their stabilizing and destabilizing roles.

6. In any treatment plan involving several forms of intervention, the interaction between the therapies and their impact on behavior, meaning, and stimulus management must be considered. Such consideration may permit greater integration of the treatment modalities and greater treatment effectiveness. For example, the interaction of psychotropic medications and skills training may suggest the need for determining the optimal balance of tranquilizing and stimulation the two provide.

7. Finally, in the formulation of an overall treatment plan, care must be given to the causal model which is considered most likely. For example. prediction should be made regarding the expected interactive sequences if antipsychotic medications for a disorganized patient may generate a tranquilizing effect that will influence the patient and his family to become destructively re-engaged.

The following case presentation illustrates several of these points:

A patient, whom we shall call Tom, was hospitalized for the first time in his life in a psychiatric hospital at the age of 18 when, three days after starting college, he became acutely psychotic. His symptoms included severe agitation, delusions of reference, and the belief that a malevolent force was causing him to think and act against his will. He heard voices, but would not report their content, although he would often appear to respond to them.

Tom's earlier life experience had been, from a superficial point of view at least, unremarkable. He was the third child of a middle-class family, with a brother three years older and a sister six years older. He had always been an outstanding student at school and had friends, apparently, but on a relatively superficial basis. On several occasions when he had attempted to stay with them overnight or had visited relatives in other cities, something always somewhat obscure happened so that he returned home prematurely.

At the time of the hospitalization, Tom received intensive psychotherapy, family psychotherapy, and on occasion, chlorpromazine. Within two months the symptoms receded, he was able to concentrate, and was discharged home receiving continuing individual psychotherapy and family psychotherapy. Following three more months without recurrences of symptoms or dysfunction, he started college in the city where his family lived, and became acutely psychotic once again. He was rehospitalized, treated again with the same treatments, this time for a period of four months on a full-time inpatient basis, following which he worked part-time in the community and then again returned home, still on a regime of individual and family psychotherapy. For a while, there was no recurrence of symptoms or dysfunction, and after another four months Tom once again returned to college. Within a few weeks, he was again rehospitalized with an acute psychotic episode.

It would be easy to say that Tom should have remained on maintenance medications, not returned home to his family, or to provide some other "solution." However, in the following discussion, we shall pursue the hypothesis that mistakes were made. and are commonly made, in the assessment, formulation, and treatment of Tom and other similar or even more chronic patients. These errors do not require a new single solution, but rather a conceptual and treatment approach which can benefit from incorporating the three concepts discussed above.

In reconsidering the patient Tom, utilizing the three concepts will help in developing a broader context of understanding and treatment. The neodescriptive model involves the macro-descriptive assessment of symptoms, social, familial, and occupational functioning, and previous duration of hospitalization interdigitated with the microdescriptive assessment of stages of decompensation and recovery. Using this model provides a broad base of knowledge for introducing various kinds of clinical interventions. Data for a multiaxlal description were present in the initial case description. More attention to the various axes might have alerted Tom's clinicians to the fact that with the superficial social relations and the rigidly-defined work/school adaptation, Tom would be unlikely to recover from his psychosis in a short time without subsequent decompensations. Although the use of individual and family psychotherapy together with medications may have helped to build stronger cognitive-affective abilities and assist with stimulus management, in the absence of social skills and school/work assessment experience the treatments given were not provided intensively enough in situ in a way that might have generalized their impact. Nor were deficiencies in the areas of interpersonal and school functioning noted or dealt with in depth so that Tom was sent to face problems of finding new friends and studying in a non-family environment without having experienced the graded learning in these areas that might have made such a transition less stressful.

In terms of the phases of recovery, it would seem likely that in the phases of psychotic disorganization the schizophrenic patient has limited capacities to abstract information from his environment. In principle, this would make more discrimination in the use of treatment approaches critical. Considering this, assessment of the various components of interpersonal (including family) function and what we would assume to be the conflicted nature of educational function in this boy might have led the treatment to downplay complex interpersonal areas and enter into a skills assessment and implementation program in the phase of disinhibition. In this phase, attempts might have been focused to establish work function and in the process circumvent rather than directly address the more complicated interpersonal issues. In ways such as this, the neodescriptive approach to axes and phases of functioning could be integrated with the psychoeducational approach to the use of treatment modalities.

Further, in relation to the microdescriptive approach to the states of consciousness, noting shifts in restricted consciousness or disinhibition in the process of recovery might make it possible for the alert clinician to titrate the use of medication more precisely, to plan shifts and changes in treatment based on entry into or exit from a particular phase.

298

Attention to descriptive dimensions and phases, using a psycho-educational orientation to dealing with problems of behavior, meaning, and stimulus management, and considering complex causal chains can help to provide a more systematic approach to comprehensive patient assessment and treatment.

The implication of these concepts for Tom's treatment are that he would need to be involved with his clinical team in an on-going and continuing process of data collection, diagnosis, and re-assessment. Information would have to be gathered in a systematic manner in an on-going way to clarify and deal with apparent causal processes as they unfolded. We feel in retrospect that the absence of such an orientation was a serious shortcoming for the evaluation system in use at the time. It placed grave limitations on the scope of clinical understanding from which treatment could be carried out. In reviewing the treatment that Tom received, we suggest that it could be based on serial re-assessments and gauging the likely impact of specific treatment modalities used and available. A view of treatment as being for a disorder, ignoring specific functions and phases, we believe is common, but not optimal. Hopefully with a more articulated orientation, the graded treatment needed for ensuring skills in relating and school work would have kept up with the primarily psychotherapeutic approaches to conflict around separation to help assure that Tom would have an optimal chance (perhaps with some extra assistance from psychotropic medications to help with stimulus management) to overcome the separation problems that he had on re-entering college.

In many other fields of knowledge, increasing emphasis is put on understanding complex combinations of variables. In physics, political science, sociology, economics, and biology, for example, systems approaches have been found increasingly useful. Although such approaches have been tried in psychiatry, they have often been too generally defined to provide more than a hypothetical ideal. By using the three concepts described above, we hope to suggest a more specific basis as a foundation for clinical practice and research.

REFERENCES

1. Strauss, J.S., Downey, T.W., and Sledge, W.H. (1978): Presented at the Annual Meeting of the American Psychiatric Association, Atlanta, GA.
2. Strauss, J.S. and Carpenter, W.T. (1978): Schiz. Bull., 4, 56.
3. Strauss, J.S., Kokes, R.F., Harder, D.W., Gift, T.E. (1979): Submitted for the Annual Meeting of the American Psychiatric Association.
4. Strauss, J.S. and Chen, C.C. (1977): Presented at the VI World Congress of Psychiatry, Honolulu, HA
5. Bleuler, M. (1978): In: Nature of Schizophrenia: New Findings and Future Strategies. Editors: L.C. Wynne, R.L. Cromwell, and S. Matthysse. Wiley, New York.
6. Docherty, J.P., VanKammen, D.P., Siris, S.G., and Marder, S.R. (1978): Am. J. Psychiatry, 135, 420.
7. Sameroff, A. (1973): Am. J. Orthopsychiat., 43, 744.

INDEX OF AUTHORS

pack
124
pairing
74
panic
240
paradoxal prescription
220
paradoxical intervention
183
parental group
39
parentification
141, 213
participation
279
passivity
28
pathogenesis
260
perceptual act
127
perceptual defence
127
perception
5
phenomenology
259, 263
parmacotherapy
265
phobia
145, 296
physical sensation
5
positive connotation
142, 145, 220
prevention
254, 257
primal fantasy
151, 152, 153, 155, 156,
159
primary process
101, 102, 126
private practice
200
prognosis
49, 53, 56
projection
27, 269
projective identification
233, 246, 249, 270. 271
protective construction
233, 234, 240, 241

pseudo-hostility
179
pseudo-mutuality
179
psychodrama
133
psychosocial hypothesis
227
psychotic inclusion
162
psychotropic medication
297, 299

readmission
261
reality
8, 12, 49, 51, 79, 154, 172,
233, 234, 294
reality construction
127
recovery
294
regression
28. 79, 80. 101, 111, 124,
236, 239, 276
rehabilitation
47, 56
rejection
41, 141
relational reality
173
relaxation
134
resilience
207
rivalry
49
role-playing
133

schizo-affective psychose
188
sectorization
258
self
10, 25, 26, 138, 189, 233,
234, 240, 241, 276
self-control
273
self-representation
89

self-therapy
  40
separation
  246, 250
sexe
  156
sexual identity
  28
sexuality
  154, 168
social ability
  50
spectrum disorder
  226
splitting
  175, 246, 249, 270
spontaneity
  133
stimulus
  295
structural triad
  61
staff
  111, 115
suicide
  91, 236
supervision
  185
symbiotic relation
  50
symbiotic union
  237
symbolization
  250
symptom
  34, 293
synergetic
  206
synesthesia
  125
system theory
  143

therapeutic community
  113, 193, 194
therapist
  5, 11
thought disorder
  8
time experience
  127

token economies
  112
tolerance
  122
transference
  15, 27, 31, 33, 36, 53, 123,
  131, 162, 163, 260, 269, 273
transition
  206, 208, 209, 215
transitional object
  269, 276
transitivism
  34, 35
triangular relationship
  61
trust
  288

unconscious
  32

vectorial perception
  137

ward
  20
Ward Atmosphere Scale (WAS)
  114
withdrawal
  21, 27